THE NEW FACES OF CHRISTIANITY

Also by Philip Jenkins

Decade of Nightmares: The End of the Sixties and the Making of Eighties America

Dream Catchers: How Mainstream America Discovered Native Spirituality

The New Anti-Catholicism: The Last Acceptable Prejudice

Images of Terror: What We Can and Can't Know about Terrorism

The Next Christendom: The Coming of Global Christianity

Beyond Tolerance: Child Pornography on the Internet

Hidden Gospels: How the Search for Jesus Lost Its Way

Mystics and Messiahs: Cults and New Religions in American History

The Cold War at Home: The Red Scare in Pennsylvania 1945–1960

Synthetic Panics: The Politics of Designer Drugs

Moral Panic: Changing Concepts of the Child Molester in Modern America

A History of the United States

Hoods and Shirts: The Extreme Right in Pennsylvania 1925–1950

Pedophiles and Priests: Anatomy of a Contemporary Crisis

Using Murder: The Social Construction of Serial Homicide

Intimate Enemies: Moral Panics in Contemporary Great Britain

A History of Modern Wales 1536–1990

Crime and Justice: Issues and Ideas

The Making of a Ruling Class: The Glamorgan Gentry 1640–1790

THE

NEW FACES

OF

CHRISTIANITY

Believing the Bible in the Global South

✝ ✝ ✝ ✝ ✝ ✝ ✝ ✝ ✝ ✝ ✝ ✝

Philip Jenkins

OXFORD
UNIVERSITY PRESS

2006

OXFORD
UNIVERSITY PRESS

Oxford University Press, Inc., publishes works that further
Oxford University's objective of excellence
in research, scholarship, and education.

Oxford New York
Auckland Cape Town Dar es Salaam Hong Kong Karachi
Kuala Lumpur Madrid Melbourne Mexico City Nairobi
New Delhi Shanghai Taipei Toronto

With offices in
Argentina Austria Brazil Chile Czech Republic France Greece
Guatemala Hungary Italy Japan Poland Portugal Singapore
South Korea Switzerland Thailand Turkey Ukraine Vietnam

Published by Oxford University Press, Inc.
198 Madison Avenue, New York, NY 10016
www.oup.com

Oxford is a registered trademark of Oxford University Press

Library of Congress Cataloging-in-Publication Data
Jenkins, Philip, 1952–
The new faces of Christianity : believing the Bible
in the global south / Philip Jenkins.
p.   cm.   Includes bibliographical references and index.
ISBN-13: 978-0-19-530065-9 (cloth)
ISBN-10: 0-19-530065-3 (cloth)
1. Christianity—Forecasting.
2. Christianity and culture.
I. Title.
BR121.3.J45 2006
270.8′3—dc22
2006015490

9 8 7 6 5 4 3 2 1

Printed in the United States of America
on acid-free paper

Contents

Acknowledgments

I want to thank a number of friends and colleagues for their help and counsel through the years, by no means confined to the process of writing this book. From the State College community, these include Tuvia Abramson, of the Penn State Hillel; Fr. Fred Byrne, O.S.B., now of St. Vincent's Abbey, Latrobe; Paul Grabill, of the State College Assembly of God; and Fr. Larry Hofer, of St. Andrew's Episcopal Church. I would also thank Jonathan Bonk, of the Overseas Ministries Study Center, New Haven; Elyse Cheney, my agent; Peter Gomes, of the Memorial Church, Harvard University; Randee I-Morphé of JETS, Jos Evangelical Theological Seminary, Nigeria; Cynthia Read, of Oxford University Press; and my colleagues Roger Finke, Gregg Roeber, and Iyunolu and Sylvester Osagie. I also want to acknowledge my debt over the years to the work of two scholars, Lamin Sanneh and Andrew Walls.

As always, my greatest debt is to my wife, Liz Jenkins.

Preface

In my 2002 book *The Next Christendom*, I remarked on the different approaches to the Bible that prevailed in the churches of the global South, of Africa, Asia, and Latin America. I observed that "Southern churches are quite at home with Biblical notions of the supernatural, with ideas like dreams and prophecy. Just as relevant in their eyes are that book's core social and political themes, like martyrdom, oppression, and exile. In the present day, it may be that it is only in the newer churches that the Bible can be read with any authenticity and immediacy, and that the Old Christendom must give priority to Southern voices. . . . Looking at Christianity as a planetary phenomenon, not merely a Western one, makes it impossible to read the New Testament in quite the same way ever again." I also wrote of the new Christianity's undergoing a "return to scriptural roots." My thoughts on this theme developed further when I had the opportunity in 2004 to deliver the William Belden Noble lectures at Harvard's Memorial Church, and this book grows directly from those presentations.

I will address a number of specific issues here. Though the term "global South" conventionally refers to Africa, Asia, and Latin America, in the present book I will touch on Latin American matters only in passing. This is because in matters of Bible reading and interpretation, many African and Asian societies have a good deal in common, especially in the relative novelty of the faith and its recent emergence from non-Christian backgrounds. In terms of approaches to the Bible, similarities with Latin America certainly exist, but the differences are too marked to make possible any kind of meaningful generalizations.

Also, with all respect to the magisterial work of Lamin Sanneh, I will continue to use the term "global Christianity" in ways that I fear he will find unsatisfactory. Professor Sanneh draws a distinction between "global" Christianity, which has been introduced into Africa or Asia as an extraneous presence, and "world" Christianity, which is more spontaneous and rooted in the lives of the (mainly poor) inhabitants.[1] While his underlying point is well taken, I feel that the distinction is difficult to draw in practice.

On another matter of terminology, scholars of African Christianity are long accustomed to speaking of AICs, African independent churches. That usage made sense in colonial times when small churches founded and led by black Africans were being compared with global white-led denominations such as Catholics, Methodists, and Anglicans. Once the colonial empires ended, though, these colonial churches became just as autonomous and African, and their leadership was no less local in origin and orientation than the so-called independents. Hence, while the term AIC remains in use, the description for which the letters stood has changed. Some speak of African-instituted churches, some of African-initiated, or African-indigenous. The only defense for such a floating term is that the label AIC does define an important reality that demands some kind of common descriptor, and whether they are speaking of initiated, instituted, or independent, scholars are referring to the same range of groups. More recently, writers note the fluid boundaries that separate the AICs from the newer charismatic congregations conveniently labeled PCCs, Pentecostal and charismatic churches, and perhaps the two types might usefully be brought together under a common heading.[2] In this book, though, I will be using the term AIC, with whatever qualms about exactly what the acronym should stand for.

THE NEW FACES OF CHRISTIANITY

SHALL THE FUNDAMENTALISTS WIN?

Our understanding of the Bible is different from them. We are two different churches.

Archbishop Benjamin Nzimbi (Kenya)

In recent years, gatherings of the worldwide Anglican Communion have been contentious events. On one occasion, two bishops were participating in a Bible study, one an African Anglican, the other a U.S. Episcopalian. As the hours went by, tempers frayed as the African expressed his confidence in the clear words of scripture, while the American stressed the need to interpret the Bible in the light of modern scholarship and contemporary mores. Eventually, the African bishop asked in exasperation, "If you don't *believe* the scripture, why did you bring it to us in the first place?"

Christian denominations worldwide have been deeply divided over issues of gender, sexual morality, and homosexuality. These debates illustrate a sharp global division, with many North American and European churches willing to accommodate liberalizing trends in the wider society, while their African and Asian counterparts prove much more conservative. These controversies are grounded in attitudes to authority and, above all, to the position of the Bible as an inspired text. Fifty years ago, Americans might have dismissed global South conservatism as arising from a lack of theological sophistication, and in any case, these views were strictly marginal to the concerns of the Christian heartlands of North America and Western Europe. Put crudely, why should the "Christian world" care what Africans think? Only as recently as 1960 did the Roman Catholic Church choose its first black African cardinal. Yet today, as the center of gravity of the Christian world moves ever southward, the conservative traditions prevailing in the global South matter ever more.[1]

Of course, Christian doctrine has never been decided by majority vote, and neither has the prevailing interpretation of the Bible. Numbers are not everything; but at the same time, overwhelming numerical majorities surely carry some weight. Let us imagine a (probable) near-future world in which Christian numbers are strongly concentrated in the global South, where the clergy and scholars of the world's most populous churches accept interpretations of the Bible more conservative than those normally prevailing in American mainline denominations. In such a world, then surely, Southern traditions of Bible reading must be seen as the Christian norm. We will no longer treat the culture-specific interpretations of North Americans and Europeans as "theology"—that is, as the real thing—while the rest of the world produces its curious provincial variants, of "African theology," "Asian theology," and so on. We will know that the transition is under way when publishers start offering studies of "North American theologies." As Joel Carpenter observes, "Christian theology eventually reflects the most compelling issues from the front lines of mission, so we can expect that Christian theology will be dominated by these issues rising from the global South."[2]

If in fact the numerical strength of Christianity is increasingly in the South, that might suggest a decisive move toward literal and even fundamentalist readings of the Bible, to the horror of American or European liberals, and the delight of conservatives. Having said that, intellectual traditions change and develop over time, and there is no assurance whatever that approaches popular today will still prevail in twenty or fifty years time. But current controversies do raise questions about the future of Christian thought, and they challenge popular assumptions about the seemingly inevitable directions it will take. In an earlier age of conflict in American Protestantism, in 1922, Harry Emerson Fosdick asked, "Shall the fundamentalists win?"[3] In North America, they clearly did not. On a global scale, though, matters might develop differently.

Anglicans

Over the past decade, the worldwide Anglican Communion has provided the most visible front in North-South struggles over biblical authority. Though current divisions have a long prehistory, the immediate detonator was the 2003 decision by the U.S. Episcopal Church to ordain Gene Robinson—a noncelibate homosexual—as bishop of New Hampshire. Meanwhile, the U.S. church was considering forms of blessing for gay unions or marriages, and similar gay-friendly moves were at least under discussion in other global North churches, including ones in Canada and the United Kingdom.

At first sight, such reforms seem to run contrary to repeated and explicit biblical condemnations of homosexual acts. Still, Northern liberals could overcome biblically based objections by placing scriptural injunctions in a contemporary social and cultural context. Old Testament texts could be assigned to an older ritual and criminal code made obsolete by the Christian revelation. One satirical item widely circulated on the Internet noted that while the book of Leviticus indeed prohibited homosexuality, it did so in the context of other archaic and bizarre regulations. "Touching the skin of a dead pig makes me unclean. May I still play football if I wear gloves? . . . Lev. 25:44 states that I may indeed possess slaves, both male and female, provided they are purchased from neighboring nations. . . . Can you clarify? Why can't I own Canadians?"[4]

More difficult to challenge are the New Testament prohibitions on homosexuality. In his first letter to the Corinthians, St. Paul places homosexual behavior on a moral par with adultery, theft, and idolatry. Yet, as liberals argued, the New Testament too was written in a society that accepted slavery and condemned homosexuality, and since the regulations provided in the text about both matters are thoroughly culture specific, they need not bind modern believers. Few Christian denominations today enforce the detailed rules that Paul pronounced about how men and women should wear their hair during services, though the passage occupies a larger share of I Corinthians than do his remarks on homosexuality. While the basic spiritual and moral truths of the Bible remain, societies change over time, and so do detailed rules of conduct. Putting the argument in admittedly extreme terms, Bishop Robinson himself asserted that "Just simply to say that it goes against tradition and the teaching of the church and Scripture does not necessarily make it wrong."[5]

Such a liberal interpretation appalled many church leaders in the global South, who reasserted a strict obedience to scriptural authority. According to Nigerian primate Peter Akinola, the most visible critic of Northern liberals, "I didn't write the Bible. It's part of our Christian heritage. It tells us what to do. If the word of God says homosexuality is an abomination, then so be it." The Nigerian hierarchy explains further, "The primary presupposition is a high view of Scripture as inerrant and a sufficient guide in all matters of faith and conduct, such that its ethics and injunctions are of timeless relevance, notwithstanding man's constant tendency to hop from one ethical paradigm to another." Instead of relativism, his church would accept the "revealed position of Scripture, which we believe to be the mind of God."[6]

Not all Southern Anglican leaders were so inflexible. The important South African church was prepared to allow individual provinces to make their own decisions in matters of sexual morality. Yet overwhelmingly, African and Asian leaders denounced the U.S. church for abandoning the clear principles of the Bible. Kenyan archbishop David Gitari called gay unions "immoral and contrary to the Bible." Given the vast moral capital he had earned during years of heroic struggle against that nation's dictatorship, his statement carried special weight.[7]

In the growing North-South confrontation, Southern conservatives find ample justification in the language of scripture, noting the hostility between the worldly-wise and the (godly) foolish, those who remain unseduced by secular learning. Using the Pauline epistles, Nigerian church leaders identify modern liberal Westerners with the pagan Greeks of old: "[In] spite of their pride in their wisdom (the Greek love of *sophia*) they had become utterly foolish. The last stage had been reached."[8] To adapt the famous image offered by Tertullian, that great African thinker, Christians of the global South are citizens of Jerusalem, and they follow the Bible; Americans and Europeans, residents of Athens, obey secular texts. And what has Athens to do with Jerusalem? Or as that other African thinker, Augustine, framed the contrast, one must be a citizen either of Jerusalem or of Babylon.

Reading in the Global South

Though Anglicanism is an important tradition, claiming some eighty million adherents, that only represents around 4 percent of Christians worldwide. Still, the kind of split that we have seen in the Robinson affair has emerged across denominations, especially in matters of gender and sexuality. Other churches have watched Anglican conflicts with some alarm, fearing that perhaps they might be getting a foretaste of future debates among Lutherans, Methodists, Presbyterians, and perhaps, someday, even Roman Catholics. When Sweden's liberal Lutheran Church tried to enforce its views on traditionalist diehards, conservatives placed themselves under the authority of Kenyan bishop Walter Obare Omwanza, who denounced the official church for practicing "a secular, intolerant, bureaucratic fundamentalism inimical to the word of God and familiar from various church struggles against totalitarian ideologies during the 20th century." He attacked the Swedish ordination of women as "a Gnostic novelty," which "cannot tolerate even minimal coexistence with classical Christianity." Similar disputes surface not just in international meetings, but also within North American religious communities with large immigrant populations.[9]

We often encounter the same range of conservative themes in the religious thought of African and Asian Christians. These include a much greater respect for the authority of scripture, especially in matters of morality; a willingness to accept the Bible as an inspired text and a tendency to literalism; a special interest in supernatural elements of scripture, such as miracles, visions, and healings; a belief in the continuing power of prophecy; and a veneration for the Old Testament, which is considered as authoritative as the New. Biblical traditionalism and literalism are still more marked in the independent churches and in denominations rooted in the Pentecostal tradition, but similar currents are also found among Roman Catholics. Any acquaintance with African or Asian Christianity soon indicates the pervasive importance of the Bible and of biblical stories.[10]

Several factors contribute to a more literal interpretation of scripture. For one thing, the Bible has found a congenial home among communities who identify with the social and economic realities it portrays, no less than the political environments in which Christians find themselves. For the growing churches of the global South, the Bible speaks to everyday, real-world issues of poverty and debt, famine and urban crisis, racial and gender oppression, state brutality and persecution. The omnipresence of poverty promotes awareness of the transience of life, the dependence of individuals and nations on God, and the distrust of the secular order.

Furthermore, Christianity—like any dynamic ideological or religious system—adapts to respond to its rivals or neighbors. In European history, Roman Catholics placed such heavy emphasis on "high" Eucharistic theology because they experienced such vigorous controversies with Protestants who challenged their ideas at every point. Lacking such competition, Orthodox Christians never felt the need to define their views on these matters as precisely. Today, similarly, Christians of the global North and South differ because of the main threats they perceive in their respective cultures. Joel Carpenter notes how, facing the challenges of secularism, postmodernity, and changing concepts of gender, Euro-American academic theology still focuses "on European thinkers and post-Enlightenment intellectual issues. Western theologians, liberal and conservative, have been addressing the faith to an age of doubt and secularity, and to the competing salvific claims of secular ideologies." Global South Christians, in contrast, do not live in an age of doubt, but must instead deal with competing claims to faith. Their views are shaped by interaction with their different neighbors and the very different issues they raise: Muslims and traditional religionists in Africa and Asia, not to mention members of the great Asian religions. Accordingly, "the new Christianity will push theologians to address the faith to poverty and social injustice; to political violence, corruption, and the meltdown of law and order; and to Christianity's witness amidst religious plurality. They will be dealing with the need of Christian communities to make sense of God's self-revelation to their pre-Christian ancestors." And in all these matters, they find abundant material in the scriptures, often in passages that resonate little with Northern theologians.[11]

In consequence, the "Southern" Bible carries a freshness and authenticity that adds vastly to its credibility as an authoritative source and a guide for daily living. In this context, it is difficult to make the familiar Euro-American argument that the Bible was clearly written for a totally alien society with which moderns could scarcely identify, so that its detailed moral laws cannot be applied in the contemporary world. Cultures that readily identify with biblical worldviews find it easier to read the Bible not just as historical fact, but as relevant instruction for daily conduct; and that even applies to such unfashionable books as Leviticus.

I am not, of course, proposing a simple kind of geographical determinism shaping religious belief. We can hardly speak of how "Africans" approach a given topic, any more than how Europeans do: Scots think one thing, Sicilians quite another. Nor are those societies in any sense uniform: Scots laborers presumably read one way, Scots professors another. Attitudes toward biblical interpretation and authority follow no neat North-South pattern, still less a rigid chasm between liberal North and conservative South. We find "Southern" expressions in the North, in the form of charismatic, fundamentalist, and deeply traditionalist belief; and those currents exist, however unhappily, in most liberal-dominated churches. If global South clergy express their faith that God will intervene to reward or punish contemporary states and societies, so do such high-profile American Christians as Pat Robertson and Jerry Falwell. Nor is it difficult to find North Americans who accept pristine New Testament views of exorcism and spiritual healing. For Pentecostal believers in North America and Europe, spiritual warfare is a strictly current reality, while the modern Vatican accepts a clear, if limited, role for exorcists—to the embarrassment of most Northern Catholic faithful, and many clergy. *The Screwtape Letters* by C. S. Lewis continues to have a sizable readership among conservative Christians of all shades, at least some of whom take seriously its accounts of demonic temptations.[12]

At the same time, liberals and Northern-style feminists are by no means unknown even in the most fervently traditional-minded African and Asian churches. Despite all the financial difficulties faced particularly by African universities, global South scholars form a distinguished part of the global community of biblical learning, reading and publishing in the mainstream journals of Europe and North America; and international ties are reinforced by visiting appointments, by conferences and seminars. Naturally enough, given the colonial and postcolonial histories of their nations, many such scholars have been shaped by radical theological perspectives, by liberationist and feminist thought.[13]

As in the United States and Europe, global South churches produce a spectrum of theologies and interpretations. The North-South difference is rather one of emphasis. Conservative and literalist approaches are widely known in the global North, but in most mainstream churches, such views are regarded as controversial and reactionary, and they are treated with great hostility in political discourse and the media. Even more suspect are explicitly supernatural or charismatic themes, such as exorcism and spiritual healing. In contrast, biblical and theological conservatism clearly represent the Christian mainstream across Africa and Asia, while ideas of supernatural warfare and healing need not the slightest explanation, and certainly no apology. They are rather at the heart of lived Christianity.

Reading the Readers

This conservative emphasis might sound counterintuitive in light of the sheer volume of radical or liberationist work stemming from Africa, Asia, and particularly Latin America. Since the 1970s, many scholars have been fascinated not just by the distinctive interpretations emanating from the global South, but by their enormous potential for reshaping Christianity worldwide. In 1995, R. S. Sugirtharajah—one of the most impressive and wide-ranging of these scholars—wrote that "there is at present an explosion of interest in Third World biblical interpretation" and that surge of interest has continued unchecked. Often, though, it can be difficult to tell which of these voices accurately represent the thought of the wider Christian community in those societies. Generally, attention focuses on academic or educated opinions, on the voices of professors, bishops, and church leaders, the sort of people who write books that get published in Europe or North America; but this emphasis can give a distorted view of global South traditions.[14]

Sugirtharajah, himself a distinguished postcolonial scholar, writes scathingly of the appropriation of "third world theologies" by Western academics, who overemphasize those currents they find attractive, while ignoring others they find less palatable or sensational. Liberation theology in particular has been thoroughly "colonized." Citing some of the celebrity writers in this genre, he comments, "While espousing and retaining grass roots interest, the theologies of [Gustavo] Gutiérrez, [Leonardo] Boff and [Jon] Sobrino largely fall within the Western academic syntax, which makes them easy to incorporate." He quotes a dismissive comment that the Kairos document, a legendary product of South African liberation theology, "is better known in Germany than to Zulus."[15]

In terms of the amount of work readily available in the West, one might easily assume that African or Asian churches are obsessed with liberation theologies, with black theology, feminism, and womanism, when in fact, we could easily assemble a substantial volume of texts devoted to highly conservative social and political stances. Among all the hundreds of titles by global South Christian writers and theologians published in the United States, only a handful give any inkling of the vast popular interest in themes of healing, spiritual warfare, and exorcism, of mission and evangelism, topics that occupy much of the daily attention of African and Asian believers. This liberal or radical tilt does not represent any kind of ecclesiastical conspiracy to silence authentic popular voices. Rather, publishers produce books that interest them and reflect their particular outlook, books that will moreover find a North American audience, and the most active firms in this area of religious publishing overwhelmingly favor progressive and feminist theologies. They do not pretend that their offerings represent any kind of sample of Christian opinion in global South nations, nor should they be taken as such.[16]

Issues of unconscious bias even surface in what seems to be the most populist method of finding what ordinary Christians think, namely the exercises in which scholars "read with," that is, engage in directed Bible studies with groups of uneducated and often illiterate believers. These encounters can be very fruitful, and the readings that emerge are often creative and illuminating. Even so, it is the academics who determine the texts to be read and who formulate the questions, often with the goal of leading their groups to address issues of gender or progressive politics that interest the researchers.[17]

These comments are not meant to understate the significance of radical approaches in the rising churches, especially in some countries—South Africa comes to mind. But the texts and interpretations favored by scholars and, often, prelates differ substantially from those that emerge from studies of ordinary believers: the woman in the Sunday congregation or the man at the revival meeting. For this demotic thought world, we must look to more commonplace sources, such as sermon texts, writings by local clergy and seminary educators, testimonies, best-selling memoirs and devotional works, or the kind of popular Christian writing that appears so often in popular media. Often, the attitudes we find might indeed be socially progressive in some ways, but they are deeply supernatural and (seemingly) superstitious in others.[18]

Moving South

In many ways, then, Christian communities in global South nations share certain approaches to the Bible and to biblical authority, and these are sufficient to mark real differences with the outlook common in Europe and North America. Divisions over the nature of biblical authority matter because the weight of numbers within Christianity is shifting so decisively to the churches of the global South. Partly, this is a matter of demographic change and the rapid growth of the relative share of the world's population living in Africa, Asia, and Latin America. Since the 1960s, populations have fallen or stagnated in Europe and North America, while global South birth rates have remained far higher—spectacularly so in Africa. Today, there are about two billion Christians, of whom 530 million live in Europe, 510 million in Latin America, 390 million in Africa, and perhaps 300 million in Asia, but those numbers will change substantially in coming decades. By 2025, Africa and Latin America will vie for the title of the most Christian continent. A map of the "statistical center of gravity of global Christianity" shows that center moving steadily southward, from a point in northern Italy in 1800, to central Spain in 1900, to Morocco by 1970, and to a point near Timbuktu today. And the southward trajectory will continue unchecked through the coming century. As Todd Johnson points out, Spanish has since 1980 been the leading language of church membership in the world, and Chinese, Hindi, and Swahili will soon play a much greater role. In our lifetimes, the centuries-long North Atlantic captivity of the church is drawing to an end.[19]

The figures are startling. Between 1900 and 2000, the number of Christians in Africa grew from 10 million to over 360 million, from 10 percent of the population to 46 percent. If that is not, quantitatively, the largest religious change in human history in such a short period, I am at a loss to think of a rival. Today, the most vibrant centers of Christian growth are still in Africa itself, but also around the Pacific Rim, the Christian Arc. Already today, Africans and Asians represent some 30 percent of all Christians, and the proportion will rise steadily. Conceivably, the richest Christian harvest of all might yet be found in China, a nation of inestimable importance to the politics of the coming decades. Some projections suggest that by 2050, China might contain the second-largest population of Christians on the planet, exceeded only by the United States. More confidently, we can predict that by that date, there should be around three billion Christians in the world, of whom only around one-fifth or fewer will be non-Hispanic whites.[20]

The effects of these changes can be witnessed across denominations. The Roman Catholic Church, the world's largest, was the first to feel the impact. Today, two-thirds of its adherents live in Africa, Asia, and Latin America, and that total does not include people of the global South residing in the North. By 2025, that proportion should rise to 75 percent, a fact that will undoubtedly be reflected in future papal elections. The Anglican Communion —historically, the "English" church—is becoming ever more African dominated, so that the Nigerian branch will soon be its largest representative. The Seventh Day Adventist Church also epitomizes these trends. In the 1950s, the church had around a million members, mainly concentrated in the United States. Today, the church claims some fourteen million members, of whom only one million are located in the United States; and among even that American million, a sizable share are of immigrant stock. Of the churches with Euro-American roots, those that are expanding do so by becoming rapidly more Southern in composition. Those that fail to expand retain their Euro-American identity, but they are shrinking perilously in terms of market share. The Orthodox Communion, still firmly rooted in Eastern Europe, offers a worrying model of apparently irreversible demographic decline. Christianity worldwide is booming, but at least in relative terms, "Western" Christianity is stagnating, while the old Eastern Christianity may be facing terminal crisis.[21]

Seeing Christianity "going South" in our lifetimes, we think of John Updike's wry comment "I don't think God plays well in Sweden. . . . God sticks pretty close to the Equator." That remark seems true today, and it will be ever more so in years to come.

The End of Fundamentalism

At least in the short term, the growth of Southern churches portends a conservative shift in theology and in attitudes toward biblical authority. By North American standards at least, the ideas expressed by African churches in the sexuality debates certainly seem fundamentalist. Liberals might indeed discern all the elements of that unholy trinity identified by Peter Gomes—bibliolatry, culturism, and literalism—a religion of the letter rather than the Spirit, one that worships the text rather than God.[22]

Yet in discussing the use of the Bible by contemporary theologians in Africa, Asia, and Latin America, we see the limitations of the whole concept of fundamentalism. In the United States and Europe, the term usually suggests a bull-headed obstinacy in the face of scientific facts, a tendency toward repression, especially directed against women or the sexually unorthodox. If that is in fact the future of Christianity, then it is not just theological liberals who have cause for concern, since the new face of Christianity would look disturbingly like the worst stereotypes of radical Islam. But as in the case of Islam, sincere or passionate religious involvement need have no negative connotations, and might easily be reconciled with social and political progress.[23]

Definitions are critical. Media coverage of any topic, religious or secular, is shaped by the need to summarize complex movements and ideologies in selected code words, labels that acquire significance far beyond their precise meaning. Though designed as guideposts for the perplexed, such words all too often tend to stop intellectual processes. One such demon word is fundamentalism, which was originally a description of a particular approach to reading Christian scriptures, but has now become a catch-all description for ultraconservative intolerance. Used thus, the term becomes purely pejorative and, often, subjective. The term "fundamentalism" expands to cover anyone who treats a religion as something that should shape one's daily life, provided that leads to conclusions that the speaker does not like. If your reading of the Bible inspires you to help the poor, that is passionate religious commitment. If it leads you to denounce homosexuality, you are a fundamentalist. In the modern U.S. context, the term "evangelical" is well on the way to acquiring such connotations, as a label for intolerant (white) social conservatives.

But "fundamentalist" need not have such dreadful connotations, especially when applied across religious boundaries. In its origins, the word implies a strict belief in the divine inspiration and inerrancy of the entire Bible text. Growing as it does out of debates within Christianity, the term can only with difficulty be applied to other faiths. It represents an American-Christian response to an American modernism. Muslims have their own form of reactionary fundamentalism—*usuliya*—though its implications are rather different from the Christian sense of the word. In a sense, all Muslims are fundamentalists by virtue of their approach to scripture, in that they view the Quran as a text inspired or dictated by the divine. No vaguely orthodox Muslim would accept that Muhammad had anything to do with the composition of the Quran, as his role would rather be seen as receiving dictation. In Christian terms, such a view of scripture would by definition be fundamentalist, but that kind of interpretation has no necessary implications for social or political stances. A Muslim who believes faithfully in the inspired Quran can, in theory, be a feminist, a daring scientific pioneer, or a progressive social reformer.[24]

Among Christians likewise, attitudes to Bible interpretation can be a poor guide to belief or conduct. It can in fact be difficult to determine who is a Christian fundamentalist, since the whole debate simply matters less outside North America. One African independent church, for instance, scorns the term: "We read the Bible as a book that comes from God and we take every word in the Bible seriously. Some people will say that we are therefore fundamentalists. We do not know whether this word applies to us or not but we are not interested in any interpretation of the Bible that softens or waters down the message. We do not have the same problems about the Bible as white people have with their scientific mentality."[25]

Other global South evangelicals distinguish their beliefs from fundamentalism in the American sense. In the Philippines, an evangelical umbrella organization asserts, "If fundamentalist is understood to mean a person who believes that the Bible is the only authority, then we are not fundamentalist, for we have a place for traditions, creeds and councils, but they are all subject to the supreme and final authority of Scripture. If fundamentalist means one who always interprets the Scripture literally without regard to the context, we are not fundamentalists for we believe in grammatical and historical exegesis."[26] Even Creationism, which in North America represents an acid test for religious loyalties, has different implications for global South churches, since evolution plays little role in debates over education. While Creationist beliefs are widely held, members of many large and influential churches, including Catholics and Anglicans, are quite at liberty to believe in the principle of evolution, however literalist they might be on other biblical matters.

Even harder to fit into fundamentalist ranks are Pentecostals, who constitute a large proportion of the world's newer Christian population. Since its origins in the early twentieth century, the Pentecostal movement now claims at least 350 million adherents worldwide. Though Pentecostals vociferously proclaim the power of the Bible and biblical authority, they reject the fundamentalist tenet that God's revelation ended with the scriptures. Instead, they give high regard to prophetic, inspired, and mystical teachings, and apply a prophetic exegesis to the scriptural text. In terms of Friedrich Schleiermacher's classic distinction of styles of Bible reading, their approach is feminine, based on "creative intuition and immediacy with the text. . . . Pentecostal hermeneutic is feminine, eschatological, organic, and helps the audience to recognize the signs of the times and to discern what God is doing in today's world."[27] To adapt Harry Fosdick's question, Bible-believing Pentecostals and charismatics stand a much better chance of winning than do fundamentalists, if we define the latter with any degree of precision.

Conservatives and Liberals

If the word "fundamentalist" needs to be used cautiously, so do those familiar ecclesiastical labels "liberal" and "conservative." Though most African and Asian churches have a high view of biblical origins and authority, this does not prevent a creative and even radical exegesis, as texts are applied to contemporary debates and dilemmas.

I have written here of religious and scriptural conservatism, but that term need not carry its customary political implications. Euro-American believers are used to drawing a sharp distinction between the political consequences of different styles of Bible reading. According to popular assumptions, liberal approaches to the Bible emphasize messages of social action and downplay supernatural intervention, while conservative or traditionalist views accept the miraculous and advocate quietist or reactionary politics. The two mindsets thus place their main emphases in different realms, human or supernatural.

Now, even in the United States, that distinction is by no means reliable. There are plenty of left-wing evangelicals, deeply committed to social and environmental justice. But in churches of the global South, the division makes even less sense. Many churches take very seriously the supernatural worldview that pervades the Christian scriptures, with the recurrent themes of demons, possession, exorcism, and spiritual healing. Yet readings that appear intellectually reactionary do not prevent the same believers from engaging in social activism. In many instances, biblical texts provide not only a justification for such activism, but a command. *Deliverance* in the charismatic sense can easily be linked to political or social *liberation*, and the two words are of course close cognates. The biblical enthusiasm we so often encounter in the global South is often embraced by exactly those groups ordinarily portrayed as the victims of reactionary religion, particularly women. Instead of fundamentalism denying or defying modernity, the Bible supplies a tool to cope with modernity, to allow the move from traditional societies, and to assist the most marginalized members of society.[28]

When Northern-world observers discuss the churches of the Two-Thirds World, labels such as fundamentalist and literalist, liberal and conservative can distract from the real issues that Christians face in their own very different societies. Only when we see global South Christianity on its own terms—as opposed to asking how it can contribute to our own debates—can we see how the emerging churches are formulating their own responses to social or religious questions, and how these issues are often viewed through a biblical lens. And often, these responses do not fit well into our conventional ideological packages.

The socially liberating effects of evangelical religion should come as no surprise to anyone who has traced the enormous influence of biblically based religion throughout African-American history. Writers such as James Baldwin suggest how utterly saturated black American culture was, and remains, in the thought and language of the Bible, and of biblically derived hymns and prayers. Black American politics are still largely inspired by religion and often led by clergy, usually of charismatic and evangelical bent; black political rhetoric cannot be understood except in the context of biblical thought and imagery. Yet having said this, African-American religious leaders are generally well to the left on economic issues, as are many evangelicals in Latin America, and also independent and Protestant denominations across Africa. All find scriptural warrant for progressive views, most commonly in prophetic and apocalyptic texts. When viewed on a global scale, African-American religious styles, long regarded as marginal to mainstream American Christianity, now seem absolutely standard. Conversely, the worship of mainline white American denominations looks increasingly exceptional, as do these groups' customary approaches to biblical authority. Looking at this reversal, one is reminded of a familiar text: the stone that was rejected has become the cornerstone.[29]

Rich and Poor

Looking at some recent North-South clashes, some might despair at the cultural gulf that seems to yawn between the older and newer churches, which are divided by their common scripture. In a worst-case scenario, the dominant forms of Christianity in North and South might become mutually incomprehensible. To adapt slightly the words of Benjamin Disraeli, old and new worlds would constitute in fact "Two Christianities between whom there is no intercourse and no sympathy; who are as ignorant of each other's habits, thoughts, and feelings, as if they were dwellers in different zones, or inhabitants of different planets. The rich and the poor."[30] The prospect of such a religious division is intriguing for Northern-world ecclesiastical politics, as both liberals and conservatives have seen the growing numbers of global South Christians as confirming the validity of their own particular views. During the 1970s and 1980s, liberals and radicals rejoiced to hear liberationist and feminist voices emerging from the churches of the Two-Thirds World. More recently, U.S. and European conservatives have come to see, in the moral and sexual traditionalism advocated by the growing churches of the global South, an enticing vision of the theological future. In their different ways, both sides assume that the global South represents the future of Christianity, and that that future is ideologically congenial.

Though particular denominations might split along North-South lines, for many reasons, we are not likely to see a clear break of the epochal kind that separated Western Catholics from Eastern Orthodox, a repeat performance of the great Schism of 1054. Straightforward North-South clashes are not likely. Most obviously, as we have seen, neither Northern nor Southern Christianities represent any kind of solid front. "Northern" approaches and beliefs are found in the South, and vice versa.[31]

Also, of course, views will change over time. North-South crossovers will only increase with globalization, with the influence of Northern media and academe across the world, while swelling populations of global South migrants in the North will give a more Southern quality to many North American and European congregations. Furthermore, African and Asian Christianity will develop and diversify as these faiths develop deeper roots, build more elaborate institutional structures, and engage in new theological debates. Only recently has Christianity become a mass faith in many of the nations that today constitute such obvious bastions—such as Nigeria, Uganda, Korea, and China. As the religion develops, churches will develop a greater range of theological and biblical attitudes, and probably spawn a new liberalism. In some churches, that liberalism will in turn drive new generations of conservative and fundamentalist protesters against what they see as a betrayal of the authentic faith. The consequence will be an ever-widening diversity of churches and sects, making any concept of unified "Southern" Christianity ever more problematic.

Hypothetically, we might even imagine more extreme moves away from orthodoxy in coming decades. Cultures or societies that are literalist or even fundamentalist in one generation can in later years become liberal, if not highly skeptical of all forms of faith; and that pattern occurs frequently—though not inevitably—across faith traditions. In European history, seventeenth-century Calvinism was a rigorous and often intolerant faith, with a tradition of militant political activism that we can legitimately compare to today's puritanical varieties of Islamic revivalism. By 1680, the most visible Calvinist territories were the Netherlands, Scotland, Switzerland, and New England; which were also the heartlands of Enlightenment thought and religious liberalism a century later. We can argue about why such a transition should have occurred: perhaps Biblicism and fundamentalism build determined self-reliance. If you believe your understanding of the scripture gives you direct access to the divine, you are unlikely to accept the authority of flawed human authorities in this or any other matter. In the 1770s, the British government thought it was dealing not with an American War of Independence, but a "Presbyterian Revolt." But for whatever reason, historical experience suggests that fundamentalists often have good grounds to worry about their liberal grandchildren. We can speak with fair confidence about the ethnic composition of the world's Christians in fifty or a hundred years, but we must be on shakier grounds when it comes to predicting attitudes to authority or orthodoxy.

Whose Readings?

For the foreseeable future, though, the fastest-growing segments of Christianity worldwide will share certain approaches to biblical authority and interpretation, and understanding these approaches is essential for anyone interested in secular affairs. In fact, seeing how the Bible is often used today to create a vocabulary and intellectual framework for contemporary debates and problems, we recall similar developments in other societies undergoing revolutionary religious change. Throughout, current events recall the impact of the Bible on the making of Europe during its age of Christendom, the Middle Ages and Early Modern period, when biblical texts and themes influenced social thought, art, cultural perceptions, narrative traditions, and the very concepts of history and nationhood. Europeans came to see the tales of the Bible as their own stories, as biblical passages and stories shaped the perceptions of all different sorts of people, tyrants and rebels, reformers and conservatives. In modern Africa and Asia too, whether we are interested in politics strictly defined or in wider social concerns—attitudes to gender and family, wealth and poverty, debt and development—the Bible provides a critical guide to worldly matters, much as it did in Europe in 1600 and the United States in 1850.[32]

We can also appreciate how far social and cultural circumstances help determine religious outlook. However much believers might cite the obvious meaning of the "plain text of scripture," that Christian scripture is a very large and complex set of documents, and different portions and emphases seem relevant in some settings but not others. It is fascinating, and sometimes shocking, to see how Christians in very different parts of the world emphasize such radically different portions of the scripture, to the point that it sometimes seems that they are not just offering differing interpretations, but actually reading different books.

In trying to understand such variations, we must begin by asking what we regard as normal, and that can in itself be a surprising exercise. From a North American point of view, we might seek to know how and why African or Asian Christians came to have such strikingly conservative beliefs, and we can certainly find explanations for that. Sometimes the explanations are not too complimentary. In the Anglican sexuality debates, some liberal activists have blamed the conservative opposition on the personal ambitions of Archbishop Akinola, who is portrayed as seeking almost papal powers to interpret doctrine and scripture. Other liberals accuse African leaders of ignorance, of bigotry, even of becoming the paid tools of ultraright American tycoons. At an Episcopalian gathering in 2002, one gay activist condemned African conservatives for "monkeying around" in the church: "All I have to say to these bishops is: Go back to the jungle where you came from!"[33] Sober academics seek other reasons for the charismatic nature of much global South religion. Why, for instance, do these churches so emphasize healing, visions, and prophecy? Perhaps, one might suggest, they are rather too much in contact with their pre-Christian roots, with traditional worlds of healing or magic or shamanism. For Northern liberals, contemplating a belief in demons and exorcisms based on a fundamentalist reading of scripture, this seems to be the realm of cults, not Christianity.

Yet many Africans and Asians respond that their views are grounded in the abundant evidence of scripture; they ask how any reasonable reader could exclude healings and miracles from the Christian message. Have liberal Americans and Germans never read the gospels or the book of Acts, in which miracles and exorcisms so proliferate? If Southern Christians have compromised with animism, have not Northerners sold out to scientism, materialism, and determinism?

On both sides, the same kinds of question might be asked about other points of obvious North-South difference. To adapt a phrase from Lamin Sanneh: whose reading, whose Christianity is normal now? And whose will be in fifty years time?[34]

In short, the growing significance of Christianity in global South nations demands to be understood by anyone interested in the future development of those regions. But considering such different forms of the faith raises questions about the "Western" forms of Christianity that have so long been regarded as normative. Looking at the impact of the Bible in the Two-Thirds World—the choice of texts and the manner in which they are read—should remind Northern churches of aspects of the scriptural tradition that might have seemed lost or—as in the case of apocalyptic or healing—tainted beyond recovery. Fresh Southern readings help restore these traditions to their ancient centrality within Christian thought, but without the ultraconservative implications that "fundamentalism" has acquired in our own culture. The more exposure we North Americans and Europeans have to such readings, the harder it might be for us to approach that scripture in the same way again.

POWER IN THE BOOK

The Bible is alive—it has hands and grabs hold of me, it has feet and runs after me.

Martin Luther

Why are global South churches so conservative in their approach to biblical authority? African and Asian leaders dismiss any charge that they remain ignorant of American or European textual scholarship, or critical approaches to the Bible. Archbishop Akinola himself stresses that "Our position is not simply representative of the opinion of an insignificant minority who are blinded by cultural biases and uninformed sentiments in a world of well-read and 'broad-minded' scholars."[1] The statements of conservative Southern clergy, such as the Nigerian Anglicans, make clear that they know the rival arguments and interpretations arising from historical criticism, but they choose to reject them.

Certainly, readers are often struck by the direct relevance of the Bible to the lived realities of contemporary society; but we must also take account of the means by which the Bible has arrived in these Christian cultures. The Bible is still a relatively new book in most of Africa and Asia, where Christian communities are still in the initial phases of a love affair with the scripture, before the texts and stories become familiar or hackneyed.

In speaking of novelty, I am not ignoring the far older Christian origins in such nations, especially China, but thinking rather of the modern phase of growth. In this sense, Christianity in its present forms represents a new force even in Latin American lands such as Brazil, a land with Christian roots dating back five centuries. Yet the more biblically centered versions of the faith, whether Catholic or evangelical, represent a much newer arrival, as does the whole attendant culture of Bible study and popular Bible reading. The Bible did not occupy anything like its central role in the belief or worship of the vast majority of Christians until the second half of the twentieth century. Only in the 1960s did Bible reading acquire its exalted status among Latin America's lay Catholics, while the massive growth of Protestant and Pentecostal communities begins in the same era. Today, though, Latin American nations—above all, Brazil—are among the world's greatest producers and consumers of Bibles.[2]

Also, in most settings, the Bible did not arrive as one book among many, but came together with certain revolutionary assumptions about the nature of reading and the means of communicating information. Understanding the means by which the Bible is understood and communicated allows us to appreciate the special weight of authority that the text bears in global South churches.

Missionary Memories

In most of Africa and Asia, Christianity traces its origins to Euro-American missionaries, and that inheritance might have contributed to the particular emphases that the religion acquired in those cultures. The very negative image of missionaries in contemporary Euro-American popular culture allows critics of global South churches a powerful rhetorical weapon. Of course (it is claimed), African clergy are so conservative, they are just parroting what the missionaries told them. In this view, conservatism arises not from any characteristics peculiar to Africa or "the South," but rather from the nature of the mission process. During the Anglican debates over homosexuality in the 1990s, U.S. Episcopal leader Barbara Harris complained that "the vitriolic, fundamentalist rhetoric of some African, Asian and other bishops of color, who were in the majority, was in my opinion reflective of the European and North American missionary influence propounded in the Southern Hemisphere nations during the eighteenth, nineteenth and early twentieth centuries." Feminist scholar Hyun Kyung Chung complains that Korean Protestantism is "literally frozen from the nineteenth-century American missionary theology, based on biblical fundamentalism."[3]

We would expect the missionary legacy to be conservative in tone. Indeed, we can see a kind of Darwinian process of cultural selection, by which conservative ideas were more likely to reproduce and sustain themselves. Through the nineteenth and early twentieth centuries, Western Christians who ventured into the mission fields were more commonly drawn from conservative churches, or from conservative and traditional-minded branches of mixed denominations. Less fervent believers, or the more broad-minded, tended to stay at home. Missionaries were also likely to pay attention to prophetic and apocalyptic beliefs: one incentive for the missionary movement was the apocalyptic belief that the gospel must be preached to all the world before the second coming of Christ could occur. Evangelicals took seriously notions of spiritual warfare, and they saw the pagan realms through which they traveled as being in thrall to forces of darkness. And after the factional feuds over biblical authority at the end of the nineteenth century, evangelical missionaries became ever more explicit about the claims and the reliability of the Bible.

It is hardly surprising, then, that churches built on these foundations should lean toward evangelical, literalist, and apocalyptic ideas. In recent years, the Anglican churches most fervently opposed to gay ordination and gay unions—Nigeria, Kenya, Uganda—were founded by the evangelical Church Mission Society, while the more liberal South African province reflects the influence of its Anglo-Catholic founders, who were more open to critical biblical scholarship. Also, though Christianity has long since gained deep roots in most of Africa, a constant influx of American and European preachers and revivalists brings regular new calls to biblical orthodoxy. Across the continent, ideas of spiritual warfare owe much to the work of British Pentecostal evangelist Derek Prince, while Germany's Reinhard Bonnke has led some of the largest and most spectacular revivals in the history of Christianity.[4]

Of course, this foreign influence is only part of the story. We must be cautious of perpetuating stereotypical notions of the white missionary drilling his ideas into the heads of his obsequious native listeners, almost literally at gunpoint. While missionaries began the process of Christianization, they had little control over how or where that path might lead. As we trace the spread of Christianity across Africa and Asia from the nineteenth century onward, we see the role of grassroots means of diffusing beliefs, through migrants and travelers, across social and family networks. As it passed from community to community, the message was subtly transformed. Missionaries might introduce ideas, but these would only succeed and gain adherents if they appealed to a local audience, if they made sense in local terms. Sometimes missionaries themselves were appalled at the radically different and radical forms that the Christian message took as it was absorbed into local societies. African and Asian believers created their own apocalyptic, messianic, or healing movements, which restated Christian teachings in forms appropriate to local traditions.[5] At the same time, ideas that clashed with local sensibilities failed to develop local roots, most obviously the injunctions to be faithful subjects of the respective colonial empires. Missionaries could successfully introduce the Christian framework and the texts that supported it, but once they had done so, these beliefs acquired lives of their own.

The same observations apply when scholars discuss newer waves of evangelism, which spread what appears to be a close facsimile of U.S.-style fundamentalism. To use the title of one important study, the growth of such churches around the world seems at first sight to constitute *Exporting the American Gospel*. Undoubtedly, U.S. money and influence help to shape worship styles, and in religious matters as in secular, Western media exercise a potent influence worldwide. But as in earlier eras, the ideas presented by the would-be "exporters" of American-style evangelicalism must compete with many other strands of Christian belief and practice, often with deep roots in a particular culture; and we cannot automatically assume that the ideas backed by the richest resources will triumph. Similar points, incidentally, apply to the forms of radical Islam exported from the Arab Gulf and backed so enthusiastically by oil money. The communities to whom such ideas are targeted might be poor, but they do not constitute a cultural blank slate on which foreign notions can be inscribed at will.[6]

The question is not so much how particular ideas are presented, but why these rather than others should dominate the marketplace, why they should achieve so large and enthusiastic a following. No Nigerian is dragooned into going to hear Reinhard Bonnke, though millions attend his revivals voluntarily. In discussing the impact of Derek Prince on West African ideas of exorcism and deliverance, Paul Gifford suggests that Euro-Americans were not introducing these themes, but rather offering them attractively in a modern-looking Western package. The content was accepted because it meshed so perfectly with deeply rooted African themes. As Gerald West observes, "Africans have not negotiated with the Bible empty-handed, nor have they been passive receptors."[7]

Reading the Word

To understand the very high respect accorded to biblical authority in the global South, we must look beyond the missionary inheritance and take account of the means by which the Bible arrived in particular societies. In some cases, the Christian scripture arrived in nations in which the idea of sacred writing was already familiar, and so was an exalted view of the power of text, so that the Bible effectively took the place of older holy writ. Not every alleged case of continuity must be accepted uncritically, since writers sometimes make such accusations for polemical purposes, but some of the carryovers are suggestive. David Kwang-sun Suh remarks that "Christianity in Korea has been and is thoroughly indigenized into the Korean religious cultures. The hierarchical structure of the Korean churches is more Confucian than Christian. . . . The literary Biblical fundamentalism of many Korean Christians is in fact deeply rooted in the old ethos of neo-Confucian literalism rather than in influences from outside sources."[8]

More commonly, though, Christianity grew in societies in which literacy was restricted to only a tiny elite. In modern India, Christianity has enjoyed its greatest success among people of the lowest and most despised castes, the Dalits or Oppressed; these people were specifically forbidden to learn the Sanskrit that would give them access to the Hindu scriptures, and typically they were illiterate in any language. In much of Africa, the Word arrived in the same package as the revolutionary idea of the written word, and it takes a real act of imagination to recall the power and the authority of the written text. In some areas, the word "reader" might be synonymous with Christian.[9]

In the beginning was the book, and a strange idea it was. Yvonne Vera's novel *Nehanda* presents a fictionalized but credible account of an African's first encounter with a white Christian cleric, in the opening years of the twentieth century, in what is today Zimbabwe. Seeing the missionary reading, the African, Kaguvi, asks him, "What will happen when these leaves turn to dust?" The European explains, "There are many copies of this book, and more can be produced. This book can never die." Kaguvi is puzzled, all the more so when the clergyman asserts that he only worships one God: but is not the immortal book a god? "Kaguvi is fascinated. The priest's god can break into many pieces. But he also feels pity for a god who has to manifest himself in this humble manner. He does not understand why a god would hide behind the marks on a page. 'He is inside your book, but he is also in many books. . . . Your god is strange indeed.'" In some mysterious way, the book is associated with the power of divinity.[10]

The new Christianity advanced alongside literacy, in societies in which orality had been the traditional form of communication and knowledge transmission. As in the first Christendom of medieval Europe, the shift from orality to literacy gives an enormous symbolic power to the written text, to the Book, which in many cases might be the only actual book in a given household. In much of modern Africa, even many pastors might not own any books except a Bible, and even that not an elaborate study edition.[11]

Even when people began to read, they were not immediately at ease with books or texts. Not for generations would books and magazines be something that one picks up casually in an idle moment. To understand the attitudes of the newly literate, we can look at the global impact of John Bunyan's seventeenth-century text *The Pilgrim's Progress,* which enjoyed phenomenal success in Christian Africa. According to South African scholar Isabel Hofmeyr, part of Bunyan's appeal was that he himself grew out of a plebeian culture that, in terms of the status of literacy, resembled much of twentieth-century Africa: in this sense, like was speaking to like. Bunyan himself was literate, but he came from a society still rooted in oral culture, with an ambiguous attitude toward the written text. Though documents carry immense weight, they are mysterious things, glimpsed in visions or bestowed by angelic visitors. In *The Pilgrim's Progress*, documents appear as flying scrolls or cryptic engravings on a throne. Texts "are held in awe, but not entirely trusted," so that their authenticity must be confirmed by a mystical visitation, by a dream or vision. The status of texts and writing is further complicated by the oppressive ways in which documents are used by the elite forces of government and law. "Documents are paradoxes. On the one hand, they are props in the theater of ruling, policing and dragooning. On the other, they betoken spiritual authority." Documents can be passes—papers that the police demand to see before they allow one to travel—or they can be passports to heaven.[12]

In such a semi- or neoliterate world, the power to read can itself be seen as a miraculous phenomenon. Some modern African prophets report receiving the gift of literacy through heavenly intervention, or transmit their revelations through special scripts revealed to them through divine inspiration. The Xhosa prophet Ntsikana "discovered hymns fully formed on the hem of his cloak." Reading such stories, Americans might recall the career of prophet Joseph Smith, with his secret writings, angelic interventions, and mystical decoding stones, and his scorn for accredited religious experts. Another South African prophet, Isaiah Shembe, reported, "No, I have not been taught to read and write, but I am able to read the Bible a little, and that came to me by revelation and not by learning. It came to me by miracle. . . . God sent Shembe, a child, so that he may speak like the wise and educated." Supporting his revelation, Shembe quoted Matthew 11:25, in which Jesus praised God for revealing his wisdom to infants while concealing them from the wise. This verse has a special appeal for radicals and prophetic figures challenging the religious establishment, particularly when the conflict is framed in North-South terms, as nonwhite "infants" confront complacent white scholars.[13]

The special value attached to the written text does not mean that new Christians were credulous or believed every word of the new story to which they were exposed—often, they asked acute questions—but the emerging churches were generally built on a profound veneration for the written text. In a traditional society, the ability to read the Bible becomes an act of self-assertion, confidence, and potentially resistance.

Speak in Our Tongues

Also recalling the older European experience, the Word arrives in familiar speech. While Hebrew or Greek has its own arcane power, the translated text presents the inspired word of God in vernacular speech, at once domesticating the divine and elevating the language that becomes its vessel. This point is difficult to convey to an American or British audience that has always known an English Bible, which knows that St. Paul—like Shakespeare—had the irritating habit of writing in obscure Elizabethan speech, with all its *thou*s and *thee*s. Yet some accounts of the European Reformation help us to reconstruct the original impact of the vernacular. Martin Luther himself knew the seductive power of the Bible, and countless readers of his German translations reported similarly unnerving encounters with the text. After the early English protestant John Rogers was captured by church authorities, a bishop lectured him about the foolishness of putting vernacular texts into unlearned hands. After all, he said, this Bible is just dead words, unless and until it is interpreted by qualified experts. *No!*, cried Rogers, *the Scripture is alive! It burns.*[14]

For over four centuries, European and North American Christians have recognized the paramount need to translate the scriptures into local vernaculars, as the foundation for Christian growth in those societies. As Kwame Bediako observes, the history of African missionary Christianity is the history of Bible translation. Today, at least one book of the Bible is available for approximately 650 of Africa's 2,000 languages, and 150 languages have complete Bibles. And a translated Bible defies conventional images of missionary imperialism. Once the Bible is in a vernacular, it becomes the property of that people. It becomes a Yoruba Bible, a Chinese Bible, a Zulu Bible; and the people in question have as much claim to it as does the nation that first brought it. It is no longer English or French.[15]

The sheer scale on which these translations are circulated is mind-boggling. In 2004 alone, the United Bible Societies distributed 25 million Bibles. If we consider only the largest nations involved, the figure included 3.8 million in Brazil, 3.3 million in China, 2 million each in Malaysia and South Korea, 1.2 million in India, almost a million in Nigeria, and 900,000 in Indonesia and Japan. And those figures refer only to complete Bibles, not counting New Testaments, portions of scripture, or selected readings. In India, some 30 million selections and "portions" were circulated, over and above the complete scriptures. All told, in just one year, the Societies distributed 390 million versions of the scriptures, complete or partial. Once the Bible is made available in cheap editions and circulated widely, it has the potential to initiate social revolution. Reportedly, Mao Zedong was so impressed by the collections of pocket-sized scriptures circulating in the China of his youth that he imitated the device in his legendary Little Red Book, which in the 1960s was one of the best-selling books on the planet.

To understand the impact of vernacular scriptures, we might draw parallels with the spread of Christianity through Dark Age Europe, during the creation of the first Christendom. Though people accepted religious ideas and objects from the "civilized world" of that time, this did not mean that they were join-ing the Roman Empire, any more than modern Southern-world Christians become American or French, or that receiving an exported gospel means they are joining the West. As Peter Brown writes, "The arrival of objects or per-sons charged with the charisma of distant places did not carry with it the modern sense of dependence on a distant and 'superior' center. Rather such objects and persons could be seen as coming in a sense from heaven. They were welcomed because they were thought of as helping the local society to establish a 'vertical' link with an overarching cosmos, which was shared by center and periphery alike."[16] For modern believers too, the Bible—especially in the vernacular—offers a direct link between the community and the kingdom of heaven. Cardinal Newman once remarked that all ages are equidistant from eternity; but so are all places, Rome and the distant cliffs of Ireland in the Middle Ages; Los Angeles and Lagos today. The use of vernacular scrip-tures means that all Christendoms are equidistant from Jerusalem.

We can contrast Muslim and Christian attitudes to the question of trans-lation. Reading the Arabic Quran, Muslim converts worldwide are offered the opportunity to share equal participation in the glorious history and cul-ture of Islam, which becomes just such a "superior center." Christians, mean-while, with the Bible in their own tongue, can claim not just the biblical story, but their own culture and lore in addition. In different times and places, each missionary message can have a stirring appeal. But for Christians in contem-porary Africa and Asia, it is this newly discovered Bible that fascinates, and that burns within. Reading this book opens the door to real inner power.

Reading Together

For modern Northerners, reading the Bible is usually a personal, individual experience, and even for the most pious, the experience of reading scripture does not differ utterly from the act of reading nonsacred texts. However holy the book, reading is reading. Yet private, silent reading on an individual basis is not the only means of taking in the scripture, and perhaps not the most effective. The way in which the Bible is publicly read in modern church ser-vices commemorates a time when this was the customary way that the faith-ful would hear the word. Throughout the New Testament, we find references to hearing and listening. People hear the word, hear the call; they respond to the voice of Jesus, the voice of one crying in the wilderness. The Gospel of John, particularly, is strongly auditory, while references to voice and voices pervade Revelation, a work directed to "him that heareth." In the North African church of Augustine's time, Bible study was a matter of collective listening to reading and explication. Augustine himself stressed the physical stamina required of those who wished, for instance, to understand the psalms. He asked, "If [those in the theater] had to stand so long, would they still be at their show?"[17]

The ancient custom of hearing the Word is very much a living tradition in contemporary churches of the global South, giving a quite different quality to the reception and the impact of the text. Passages are shared, aurally and communally, with an audience with old-established expectations about the nature of oral tradition and communication. Also, communal reading occurs in a sacred setting, whether in reading and study groups or in the context of worship. The words might be flanked by familiar prayers or hymns that evoke the traditions of the community. This pattern is suggested by an account of an all-night vigil service held by a Zimbabwean independent church: "Preachers punctuated their sermons with frequent repetitions of the phrases 'Peace be with you apostles!' or 'Peace be with you, children of God!' . . . to which the people responded 'Alleluia! Amen!' Also in AIC style, preachers expounded the designated passage (Colossians 3) verse by verse, the scripture being read by an evangelist who stood with each preacher at all times. The reader's visual prominence emphasizes the authority of the written word and the preacher's accountability to it." Drawing on such practices, Jean-Marc Éla describes what he believes would be the best mode of presenting the Bible to Africans. Instead of merely reading, churches should present "a festival of language shared by the whole community, which includes grasping the Word, searching for its meaning, questions and answers, prayers and chants." Readings should have an incantatory quality, with presenters making full use of body language and vocal tones.[18]

The results can be impressive. Itumeleng Mosala comments that Africans —especially members of the AICs—"have an oral knowledge of the Bible. . . . [M]ost of their information about the Bible comes from socialization in the churches themselves as they listen to prayers and sermons." Studies of such sermons note how much attention they devote to expounding the biblical text, and this is as true of mainline churches as independents. Roman Catholic churches, meanwhile, have wholeheartedly adopted the lessons of the second Vatican Council in placing scriptural reading and interpretation at the forefront of liturgical life.[19]

Experiencing scripture communally promotes exalted concepts of the nature of the group that hears the sacred words, a sense that the religious community becomes the vehicle for the divine message. Interpreted by ordinary believers, validated by the common experience of the Christian congregation, the Bible becomes the word of Christ's church, which cannot be gainsaid. A story told by Musimbi Kanyoro suggests just what a text can mean in a communal setting. She reports reading a Pauline text in a northern Kenyan community, concluding with the good wishes that Paul sent two thousand years ago to the Corinthian church, "My love be with all of you in Christ Jesus." "The community, which had been listening silently, responded in unison, 'Thank you, Paul.' They were thanking Paul for sending them greetings, not the reader for reading the text to them."[20] Paul might not have been physically present, but he had been kind enough to send his best wishes. In such a setting, we can easily imagine the willingness to accept the explicit moral or doctrinal rules presented in such a text.

In other ways too, the demographic makeup of Southern Christian churches promotes ideas of religious authority and reliance on inspired texts. Today, half the inhabitants of this planet are under twenty-four, and of those, almost 90 percent live in the global South. What else marks the landscape and soundscape of a Third World society so definitively as the abundance of its children? Young adults predominate in Southern churches—and mosques—and that profile shapes attitudes to faith. We think of the kind of idealism we will find in such a congregation of the young: the fire, the openness to changing the world and overthrowing natural hierarchies, the openness to ecstasy. We think also of the desire for certainty, for absolute standards; the denial of subtleties and compromises, of shades of gray; the rejection of hierarchy and experience, the quest for immediate experience and direct access to the divine; and the need for absolute conviction. In the Euro-American tradition, this demographic profile sounds like the Methodist revival of eighteenth-century England, the American revivals of 1740 or 1798; and that age structure will continue to be the central fact in global religion for at least the next half-century. Such congregations respond avidly to messages grounded in the assured certainty of revealed scripture.

The word "community" may mark the single most striking difference between older and newer churches, with all that implies for the understanding of authority. Much as it might discomfort members of both faiths, the Christianity of Africa and much of Asia has a great deal in common with the Islam of those regions, not the violent extremist Islam of popular nightmare, but the ordinary lived religion of hundreds of millions of people. In Muslim cultures, the Quran, too, is less a book for private study or devotion than a work of art to be recited, preferably communally. As the Hadith declares, "He who does not recite the Quran melodiously is not one of us." In both cases, Muslim and Christian, one commonly hears the scripture, as well as reading it, and looks to the text not just for theology, but for detailed instructions about the organization of everyday life. Though their attitudes to translating the text differ, many Christians treat the Bible with the same sense of perfect inspiration with which a Muslim views the Quran. Ernest Ezeogu draws an apt analogy: "The popular view of the Bible in Africa approaches the Islamic view of the Koran—'composed by God in eternity for all eternity, then revealed to mortals in time, through divine inspiration understood as dictation.'"[21] The presence of neighboring Muslim communities, with their reverential attitude toward scripture, may have influenced Christian attitudes toward the Bible. For practical reasons of recruiting and retaining church members, Christians do not wish to be seen paying any less regard to their own scriptures than Muslims devote to the Quran.

Other resemblances between the faiths include the sense of the collective or communal, and a radical notion of social justice rooted in the prophetic tradition. Both Christians and Muslims share a powerful apocalyptic sense of a final confrontation in which nations and peoples will be judged. Both understand that states and kingdoms exist at the pleasure of God, and that God's laws take precedence over human. In Africa particularly, the Christian-Islamic or Abrahamic parallels and linkages make much more sense than the familiar North American notion of the merely Judaeo-Christian.

Telling Stories

Reading the Christian scriptures is thus an awe-inspiring experience, but even for those who cannot read, the Bible acquires immense potency. To speak of scripture and Bible—writing and book—is to imply literacy, yet often biblical ideas and texts spread by the methods appropriate to oral cultures. In such a setting, memory is a critical skill, the kind of memory that usually deteriorates with literacy. One account of a Trinidadian Baptist community reports, "Several older informants, including one with over fifty Bibles in his collection, are unable to read. Illiterate Baptists attempt to disguise their inability to read by committing long passages of the Bible to memory." In East African AICs, illiterate believers learn key verses by heart. They also make a habit of carrying their Bibles with them so that, when needed, they can ask a literate friend to read the text for them.[22]

Attracted to the faith, new believers avidly seek access to the Bible, by whatever means are open to them. Bible societies try to cater to all levels of readers, offering illustrated versions and cartoons where possible, but any kind of text proves beyond the skills of many. As in the European Middle Ages, those who find reading difficult receive instruction through storytelling or through drama. When a modern American congregation witnesses its children performing a Christmas play or Epiphany pageant, the event's appeal is largely based on the cuteness factor, on seeing the children mastering their lines and relishing their improbable costumes: it is difficult to recall a time when such performances represented a powerful form of Christian education for young and old. The medieval tradition of ritual drama and the public reenactment of biblical scenes still flourishes in the Philippines, especially, and in Catholic Latin America—the Mexican *posada* recreates the events surrounding the Nativity. And while Protestants disdain such performances as prone to superstitious excesses, they too use alternative means of learning. Writing of peasant communities in northeastern Brazil, Carlos Mesters reported how "They are using song and story, pictures and little plays. They are thus making up their own version of the 'Bible of the Poor'. Thanks to songs . . . many people who have never read the Bible know almost every story in it." (I respectfully doubt this last statement.)[23] Such alternative means of teaching fit wonderfully well into some Asian cultures: Chinese Confucian scholars had for centuries encouraged popular music, drama, and ritual, in order to instill correct values into an illiterate populace.

Similar methods have resurfaced in the modern Christian context. As Kwok Pui-Lan writes, "Asian women do not write commentaries on the Bible; instead they talk about it and devise skits for discussion, dramatizing and performing the Bible." In Indonesia, one missionary reports the use of the Bible in a poor migrant community that maintained a subsistence life in a refugee camp. In the mid-1990s, the text chosen was the book of Ruth, read at the rate of a chapter a week. "The widows formed their own group. 'I am Naomi' said one relating her personal Naomi biography. 'You are Orpah.' 'I am Ruth.' The biblical novelette of failure in economic migration brought out stories of the dead-end life that the women were leading in the Patisomba transit station. The strategy which the resilient Naomi and Ruth drew up and carried out successfully fired their imaginations. On the final Sunday, they presented their findings to the whole congregation in a series of dramatic declamations. Meanwhile, youth had studied the same texts on the beach. They presented a dramatized version of the story from the point of view of the young women."[24]

When presenting the Bible to what was until recently a nonliterate public, one finds that certain parts of the text work better than others. Throughout the history of Christianity, Bible translators have had to make judgment calls about the order in which particular books will be presented in a new language, and in a few cases, whether certain books should be attempted at all. The ancient translator of the Bible into the Gothic tongues passed over the books of Kings, because his potential readers already knew far too much about battles and assassinations. More modern Indian translators have confronted the issue of translating books concerning the sacrifice of oxen and cattle, texts with the potential to appall a Hindu public. Must the church really admit that the prodigal son was treated to a fatted calf? But even avoiding such pitfalls, the decision to present books in a certain order must have consequences for the kind of Christianity that will be built on those foundations. As Gerald West asks, what kind of faith could emerge in the coastal East Africa of the mid-nineteenth century, when for a while the only two available biblical books were Genesis and Luke? Most challenging are closely argued literary tracts such as the Epistles of Paul, which force translators to find local words for the very technical concepts familiar to Hellenistic Judaism. Philippine scholar Daniel Arichea remarks, "Having worked with the United Bible Society for 16 years, I know that translators don't want to touch Romans until and unless they have to, and often that means never!" At the other extreme of accessibility are the parables and straightforward historical narratives.[25]

On the positive side, the stories that do succeed in such communities work very well indeed, largely because they are received by an audience well accustomed to oral tradition. Such listeners can appreciate story twists that can be lost on readers in long-established Christian societies to whom the general outline of the story is too familiar, for whom the punch line is not a surprise. Hearing a passage well told, an audience accustomed to storytelling can be really affected by narrative features that emerge less strongly in reading, such as the devious irony at which the author of the Fourth Gospel was so adept. To take one example from many, Matthew and Luke state that Jesus was born in Bethlehem; John only mentions the fact obliquely, by having it denied by a hostile mob.

This sense of affinity with the Bible's ways of presenting its message is not surprising, given the oral form in which those sayings and stories originally circulated before being canonized in writing. Appropriately, the passages that work best today are those that most closely recall their origins in oral transmission, the stories and parables, hymns and wisdom literature, psalms and proverbs. The Kenyan audience that cordially thanked Paul was responding to the most conversational portion of his epistle. One reason for the popularity of Revelation in the global South is that the book so often betrays its oral or neoliterate sources, and represents an anthology of hymns, oracles, and visions. The work's attitude to written texts—those awesome but cryptic things—is very much that of *The Pilgrim's Progress*. Nor, of course, are oral cultures troubled by what seem to be the laborious and repetitive style of storytelling that sometimes characterizes biblical accounts—see, for instance, the double account of Peter's vision in Acts 10 and 11. That is just what storytellers do.

John Lonsdale remarks on the seductive impact of the Bible's stories to ordinary converts in orally based cultures: listeners may find them much more attractive than the stark moral exhortations that Muslim preachers drew from the Quran. "Christian scholars among Kenya's up-country peoples found a book in which national and personal destinies were often gloriously intertwined and in their own language, . . . and whose images and proverbial formulae found their way into Testaments old and new, making the Bible very much their own tribal story." And within a few decades, those biblical stories permeate oral culture, as the narratives through which people interpret their own lives, their own societies. At this stage the Bible becomes "a national store house of folktales." When we approach the Bible in this way, learning to read the text is a later, and not inevitable, phase of Christian development, a new way of learning the stories of faith that give the book its appeal—but the stories come first. In the words of one Malawian pastor, "Listen to me my brother. You must have time to ponder upon this book. You must read it when you wake up in the morning, when you go to bed in the evening. You must read this book. There are good stories in this book. There are stories of salvation."[26]

Sacred Music

Music also becomes a critical weapon of mass instruction. Again, this recalls the circumstances of Europe's Reformation era, when literacy rates were low and some languages possessed little in the way of written or printed vernacular literature. Creative reformers solved this problem by teaching scripture and Protestant doctrine through easily memorized verses or songs. This was a successful technique, for instance, in Gaelic Scotland. Protestantism came slowly to Wales because my ancestors were unable to read the splendid Bible translated into their own language in the 1580s. The turning point came half a century afterward, when a country parson took Protestant doctrines and biblical lessons, and transformed them into verses, songs, and jingles that soon echoed round every country fair and market. Not till the end of the seventeenth century did a network of schools teach the mass literacy that the general public needed actually to read the text. In England, the metrical settings of the psalms were a powerful evangelistic weapon in the Puritan arsenal.

Later evangelical revivals made enormous use of hymns, which often based themselves on biblical passages or closely paraphrased them. One favorite source was the book of Psalms, itself an ancient collection of hymns and prayers, and psalms provide the basis for such popular English hymns as "O God, Our Help in Ages Past" and "All Creatures That on Earth Do Dwell." Through frequent singing of hymns, through the association of texts with emotionally powerful music, Christians internalize biblical passages, stories, and doctrines. However much Protestantism may claim to be a religion of the Bible, it would be truer to describe it as a faith of the Bible and hymnbook.[27]

This history finds many parallels outside the realms of Western Christianity. A Chinese tradition of Christian poetry and hymn writing dates back at least to the seventeenth century, when Jesuit Wu Li presented Christian teachings in the canonical forms of Chinese literature.[28] One song includes the lines

> Late in Han
> God's Son came down from heaven
> To save us people
> And turn us towards the good.
> His Grace goes wide!
> Taking flesh through the virginity
> Of a Holy Mother
> In a stable he was born.

The phrase "Late in Han" performs the same function as the well-known credal statement that Jesus "suffered under Pontius Pilate." By giving a specific historical date to the event, it ensures that the incarnation is located in an actual time and place, rather than becoming (for instance) a recurring moment in the human consciousness.

In Africa, the hymnody of the Coptic Church preserves traditions dating back to ancient Christian times. Appropriately, given the long history of persecution suffered by that church, themes of suffering and martyrdom are much in evidence. One hymn telling of the suffering of Daniel's friends in the fiery furnace remains "the most beloved hymn in their hymn book (that all are supposed to know by heart)."[29]

Modern African churches have made great use of music, both imported and autonomous; and at least since the beginning of the twentieth century, believers across the continent have deployed local musical traditions to the service of praise and worship. So central, in fact, is music to African cultures that institutions of all kinds are commonly riven between the official head and the music leader, whether the musician is a church worship leader or a school choirmaster: music matters. Of Isaiah Shembe, it has been said that his "greatest traits as a churchman and leader of people were his faith-healing powers, coupled with his musical gifts"—two closely related manifestations of charisma. Shembe, like many founders of independent churches, was a prolific composer of hymns, and like them, he drew heavily on vernacular styles. Commonly, African hymns adapt popular musical genres such as wedding songs and praise songs.[30]

In modern East Africa, the hymns of the historic revival movements have a power at least comparable to what "Amazing Grace" conveys to Americans. The East African equivalent would be the astonishing "Tukutendereza Yesu," the anthem of the great revivals of the 1930s and a song that can still reduce a secular-seeming crowd to tears.[31]

Tukutendereza Yesu
Yesu Omwana gw'endiga
Omusaigwo gunaziza
Nkwebaza, Omulokozi.

We praise you Jesus
Jesus Lamb of God
Your blood cleanses me
I praise you, Savior.

Over time, such hymns acquire ever-richer narrative associations, stories of how martyrs went to their deaths singing it, of how hearing the hymn softened the hearts of persecutors; and these stories add still more to the impact of the work.

Many hymns stick close to the biblical text. One popular Nigerian hymn is a paraphrase of the famous Christological text in Philippians, which is itself believed to be an ancient hymn or liturgical chant:

He is Lord, He is Lord, amen
He has risen from the dead, he is Lord
Every knee shall bow
Every tongue confess that
Jesus Christ is Lord.[32]

Ghanaian composer Ephraim Amu adapted biblical texts in his songs in the Akan language, with great effect. One work is a meditation on Paul's declaration of Christ's victory over death, in 1 Corinthians 15:55–57:[33]

What joyful news is this?
The Lord's Power has defeated death
And the place of the dead for us
. . .
A day is coming when tears shall turn
Into songs of jubilation
The Lord's power will give abundant hope
Shout the battle cry of victory
Oseyee! Oseyee! Ose aye!

The Dinka people of the Sudan—long victims of that nation's bloody wars and persecutions—have a rich tradition of such hymns, unsurprisingly focused on the cross. One calls on God to accept his people,

For we are your children
And let us carry your cross and follow after you
Let us be like Simon, the man of Cyrene, who went with you to
The place of the skull.[34]

Simon of Cyrene is one of the few New Testament figures of indisputably African origin.

In Tanzania, contemporary Anglican hymns use vernacular settings of Bible texts, using a dialogue between soloist and choir. One hymn, "Kisha Nikaona" (Then I Saw), freely quotes the verses from Revelation 20:1–2, about the angel descending from heaven to lock up the ancient dragon.[35] The chorus then sings,

> It was the time when they locked him up for a thousand years
> That real devil and Satan who so tricks people on earth today
> Now, my brother/sister, frustrate his tricks today
> Truly that snake has no power over us again

The Bible makes its impact on a community through hymns and prayers as well as through the text itself, and a hymnbook can be an object almost as cherished as the Bible itself.

Zimbabwean scholar Ezra Chitando also points out that the practice of giving highly charged biblical names "constitutes oral theology of the first order." Just as Muslims express their faith from day to day by their personal names—"servant of the merciful," "servant of the mighty"—so do African Christians. Zimbabweans bear Shona names such as Tinashe, "We have a savior," or Anesu, "God with us," while a family that has patiently borne many burdens may name a son Kudakwashe, "His Will." Such names have no more theological content than the familiar American John or Michael, but the fact that they are given in contemporary language means that their implications are more likely to strike the listener.[36]

More recently, newer technologies bring the Bible to a mass public, regardless of people's reading ability. Radio has long served such a purpose, while evangelism has been transformed by television broadcasting, cable, and particularly video. One effective tool has been the *Jesus* video, the 1979 film version of the gospel story that has been circulated in tens of millions of copies worldwide, and that is often used to introduce potential converts to the faith: controversially, it is said to be particularly effective among Muslims. The video has been translated into nine hundred languages to date, and all these versions can be accessed via the Internet, as well as through videocassettes and filmstrips. Its sponsors claim that the film has been responsible for two hundred million "decisions for Christ." But other organizations and churches have also ventured into contemporary technologies. One writer claims that "indigenously produced video films in Nigeria constitute a cultural and social revolution," by making biblical and particularly charismatic messages available to all. Films such as *Living in Bondage* and *Captives* teach doctrines of deliverance and sanctification while constantly reminding believers of the dangers of the occult. Seventy such films were produced annually in the mid-1990s, over a thousand by 2001, and the growth continues to accelerate.[37]

My Bible and I

Whether in global North or South, belief in the absolute authority of scripture shapes the ways in which biblical texts are used. Ghanaian Catholic bishop Peter Sarpong has said, "To talk to the African of the centrality of the Word of God is to carry coals to Newcastle. Africans believe the power of the word." If every word is true, then the whole is contained in each part, and indeed in each verse. This encourages the use of popular proof texts, which are cited very much as aphorisms and proverbs were used in traditional African and Asian societies. To quote a recent study of the AICs, "For the African Christians, the Bible has come to take the place of the traditional ancestor whose authority cannot be disputed."[38]

At its worst—whether in Africa or North America—this literalist approach can lead to a selective reading of the scripture, a stress on passages that confirm familiar ideas or prejudices, and a neglect of context. Texts thus become little more than bumper sticker slogans. This vice does exist, though in practice, believers draw on themes and passages that appear especially relevant to their life circumstances, and that can be used to challenge the status quo. Kenya's Victor Zinkuratire notes how the AICs try to "read the Bible contextually so that it might address their daily needs, problems and concerns, the way their traditional religion did before the arrival of Christianity and the Bible." Grant LeMarquand cites an analogy taken from one of the most discussed miracles of Jesus: "African exegesis does not seek to understand the text merely for its own sake or out of an intellectual curiosity. African exegesis is need-driven and faith-oriented. . . . The faith of the woman with the issue of blood is often seen as a model for the exegete. Her faith was not detached and merely cerebral but engaged and committed to life."[39] Also modifying the strict reliance on scriptural verses is the strong tradition of prophecy and charismatic experience prevailing in many churches, in which texts are adapted to the needs of the church's situation.

Yet the sense of inherent authority—and authority framed in terms thoroughly familiar to the culture in question—helps explain the deeply proprietorial attitude to the Bible, and the reluctance to challenge an explicit command or prohibition. In one African chorus, the believer sings,

My Bible and I
My Bible and I
Oh what a wonderful treasure
The gift of God without measure

We will travel together
My Bible and I

As a Zulu song teaches, *Aka na mandla uSathane / S'omshaya nge vhesi*:
"Satan has no power / we will clobber him with a [biblical] verse."[40]

So great is the power of the text that for some Christians, the physical
object of the Bible itself becomes a locus of spiritual power, which in some circumstances can become superstitious or near-magical. In medieval Europe,
the word "grammar" was the source of grimoire, that is, a magical text for
evoking demons. Some Western countries still require witnesses in court to
swear on the book.

Sathianathan Clarke tells a story that indicates the aura surrounding the
book in the Indian context. He reports teaching sessions in southern India for
Dalit activists. To make a point, he writes, "I delicately tossed the Bible on the
ground in front of me saying that there was nothing intrinsic to the material-
ity of the Christian Scripture that made it holy and venerable. Two reactions
ensued. First, the activist closest to me picked it up and moved it away from
me. He later confessed that he was afraid that I might kick the Bible with my
foot by mistake which would have been a big insult to the whole Christian
religion. [Many] also shared their fear that I was going to do something
dreadful with the Bible. They asserted that for them the principles for universal human rights came from the Bible."[41]

The Bible is also assumed to be effective in combating evil and sickness. A
century ago, the great West African evangelist William Wadé Harris explicitly used the Bible as the mighty symbol that overwhelmed all fetishes and
pagan amulets, almost a superfetish in its own right. More recently too, in one
Kenyan congregation, "Some prophets and prophetesses will not only pray
for the patient but will also place the Bible on the patient." In India, Clarke
tells how, while visiting a Christian Dalit community, he was asked to help a
poor Hindu woman who was sick, and to grant her the healing powers of the
Bible. He prepares to read an appropriate text, but those assembled tell him
not to bother, because the woman is illiterate, and anyway knows nothing of
the Christian scriptures. Instead, he should place the Bible on her head as he
prays for her. "I could not resist slightly opening my eyes at some point of the
prayer to catch a glimpse of the intense and expectant posture of trust that
was expressed by all those in the room, Christian and Hindu Dalit alike.
Truly, it was a picture of reverence, awe, and mystery. . . . In this instance,
the Bible was not read but there was a distinct view of what it was and what
it could perform." For a modern Christian in West Papua, "The Bible is very
authoritative. From my first to my fifth child, I have always put the Bible next
to their heads when they sleep so that God will protect them."[42]

The Bible can be a tool for divination, replacing the arsenal of traditional oracles.[43] This idea is familiar to Westerners from the *Confessions* of St. Augustine, who famously heard the instruction to "take and read," and whose life was changed by the passage that first struck his eyes. In vernacular African usage today, a Bible is commonly used as a sacred object with inherent power to defeat evil forces and spirits. A study of ordinary Nigerian Christians found that "[t]he Bible is used to ward off evil spirits, witchcraft and sorcery, it is placed under the pillow at night to ensure God's protection against the devil, it is put in handbags and cars when traveling to ensure a safe journey, it is used in swearing to bring God's wrath upon culprits. . . . [The Bible] is regarded entirely as a book of devotion, a rule of life and a norm for morality." Ezeogu recalls that for a first-generation Igbo Christian, "[w]henever you saw my father open the cabinet and bring out the Bible, you know that there is big palaver in the village. There must certainly be a dispute which has defied the ingenuity of the village elders and the only way to settle it would be for one of the contending parties to swear an oath. And for this my father's Bible was the most reliable means. . . . [M]y father's Bible had replaced the sacred staff (*ofo*) of the traditional religion as an object of oath taking, thanks to the example of the colonial court-room formality." Also in West Africa, some AICs teach what is almost a cabalistic approach to the text, with an interest in angelic names and secret interpretations of the Bible text, taught only to initiates. At the other extreme of sophistication (or of sophistry) is the Wordless Bible, a teaching device that Euro-American evangelicals have employed since the nineteenth century. The teacher holds up a book containing only colored pages and uses the colors as visual aids from which to preach on basic Christian truths—black for sin, red for blood, white for redemption, gold for heaven. In illiterate communities in modern Asia and Africa, the message gains its power because the audience has such awe for the notion of the Book and the lessons that it potentially contains.[44]

The mystical awe inspired by the Bible text sometimes encourages suspicions about the existence of other lost or secret portions of scripture. After all, the whole history of colonized peoples teaches them that the winners write and rewrite history, often excluding the narratives of the defeated. Some West African peoples claim that secret and more extensive Bible texts that once existed provided not just additional spiritual insights, but also practical information about how Jesus carried out his miracles, and possibly how the West achieved its technological superiority. Giving credence to the idea of a Western conspiracy to suppress biblical texts, Africans note that some books are found in Catholic but not Protestant Bibles, and they pay attention to the rediscovery of lost gospels such as Thomas. Asian Christians know that Thomas was reputedly the Apostle of Asia, and some scholars speculate whether that rediscovered text has any special relevance for them.[45] Now, Africans or Asians have nothing like the Western fascination with lost or hidden gospels that has become such a popular fad in recent decades, but their deep immersion in the canonical text inevitably arouses a thirst to find more of the same.

Reading Outside

Whether or not they can read, then, Christians around the world show their enthusiasm for the scriptures, in whatever form they can find them. At the same time, the Bible and the attendant Christian culture can exercise a real attraction for non-Christians, who are fascinated by its ideas and its literary qualities, even if they might ultimately be repelled by the claims of the religion as a whole. This appeal might seem surprising to a Euro-American audience for whom biblical stories and images are part of the air they breathe, almost the ambient noise of Western culture. Many English speakers, for instance, readily use phrases from the great Bible translations (a thorn in the flesh, sour grapes, through a glass darkly, skin of my teeth, pour out my heart) without any sense of their religious origins.

Yet many contemporary stories suggest the amazing impact of these familiar themes outside the old Christendom. Christianity exercises an intellectual and emotional fascination, often partly due to the means by which it has been absorbed into a particular culture—how, for instance, biblical stories are transformed into vernacular hymns or poems, sutras, or sagas. People immersed in a given tradition, with its well-established philosophies and narrative forms, suddenly find those adapted to express this strange and radical new doctrine, which appears at once deeply alien and strangely familiar. In the novel *Things Fall Apart*, Chinua Achebe describes the impact of the missionary presence on one young Igbo man, in what would become Nigeria: "It was not the mad logic of the Trinity that captivated him. He did not understand it. It was the poetry of the new religion, something felt in the marrow. . . . He felt a relief within as the hymn poured into his parched soul. The words of the hymn were like the drops of frozen rain melting on the dry palate of the panting earth. Nwoye's callow mind was greatly puzzled."[46]

The fictional Nwoye became a convert, but that was not the inevitable outcome of such an encounter. In modern Chinese literature, Christianity remains a divisive topic because of its historical association with Western imperialism, and one of the most vigorous critics of the faith is essayist and journalist Xiao Qian. Yet in the 1980s even he professed himself "a devout lover of church music, Xmas carols, the Messiah, and the hymns. . . . I'm fond of religious architecture too. I love to sit in an empty cathedral, smell the incense and gaze at the painted glass. I love many passages from the Bible, especially 1 Corinthians, chapter 13." (This is the passage in which Paul declares, "If I speak in the tongues of men and of angels, but have not love, I am only a resounding gong or a clanging cymbal.")[47]

Other intellectuals find in Christianity more than merely an aesthetic appeal. One of China's leading avant-garde writers is novelist and screenwriter Bei Cun, who startled his admirers by suddenly converting to Christianity in 1992. In his Kafkaesque story "The Marriage of Zhang Sheng," he suggests the impact that even a casual encounter with the Christian scripture might have on a receptive mind. Glancing at a Chinese-language Bible, the troubled scholar hero finds the passage from Romans 1, beginning "For the wrath of God is revealed from heaven against all ungodliness and unrighteousness of men." Now, this is a critical passage in the Christian encounter with the non-Christian world, long a foundational text for Western missionaries. It asserts that those deluded human beings who forget God fall into paganism or false philosophy, and thence into systematic immorality.[48] Without acknowledging God, what standard can the world offer to judge truth or virtue? In a modern context, the Pauline chapter suggests the failure of relying upon mere human ideologies that neglect God—an explosive statement in modern China, with its Communist values sinking into ever-deeper crisis. With his intellectual assumptions in ruins, all from this single reading, Zhang Sheng is soon driven to accept Christianity, much like what had occurred to his real-life creator, Bei Cun.

Social scientists warn against too-ready use of the word "conversion," with its implications of sudden road-to-Damascus enlightenment. They prefer to speak of recruitment, the act of joining a faith, while one's degree of active commitment to the group can be measured in various objective ways. While such caution about terms is praiseworthy, we also need to remember that rapid and emotional conversions to Christianity do occur, and that biblical texts and stories can play a critical role in this process, whether they are read or heard. As F. F. Bruce remarked, "There is no telling what may happen when people begin to read the Epistle to the Romans." Arguably, the less familiar Christian ideas are in a given society, the more novel and unexpected, the more likely such texts are to have this kind of revolutionary effect. In such settings, the Bible's hands and feet can indeed grab the unsuspecting reader or listener.[49]

Confirming the Word

For many reasons, then, we can expect religious and particularly biblical texts to carry great weight in Southern churches. And before seeing this "Biblicism" as a sign of youth and immaturity, we might well ask whether liberal Northern or conservative Southern readings are more dated in their own ways, or cling too specifically to particular cultures. Each in its ways is rooted in particular assumptions about modes of interpretation, and historical or literary criticism.

By what standards, for instance, do churches decide whether particular biblical verses or passages carry special weight, or might be less authoritative than others? Except for the hardest of hardcore fundamentalists, American Christians rarely believe that each and every verse of scripture carries the same degree of inspiration, and hence the same value. Instead, many assume an implicit hierarchy of texts, based on what is commonly viewed as the best scholarly opinion. So, for example, the assumption that St. Paul did not really write the Pastoral Epistles attributed to him—the letters to Timothy and Titus—means that these can be treated as less serious, less authoritative, than the apostle's undoubted words in Romans or the Corinthian correspondence. To claim that "Paul didn't really write this" consigns the Pastorals to a semi-apocryphal status. At one synod of the Church of England, a clerical presenter made the remarkable argument that since no scriptural texts prohibited the ordination of women, modern conservatives should not "set up artificial and inept lines that no one can defend." Apparently, in such a view, the explicit prohibition on women's leadership or teaching authority found in 1 Timothy 2:11–12 no longer even counts as part of the New Testament. Opinions can differ about the authority that such a passage should command, but for many believers, it literally has been read out of scripture.[50]

This selective approach is based on a great many rarely examined assumptions about the nature of reading and authorship, and about how texts are read and received. To take an example, one very popular passage in African Christianity is the closing section of the Gospel of Mark, 16:14–20, which concludes, "And they went forth, and preached everywhere, the Lord working with them, and confirming the word with signs following." This is the charter or foundation text of African missionary practice. (The equivalent passage in Matthew 28:18–20 is also much cited.) Since it occurs at the end of Mark's Gospel, the reader might assume that the passage represents the real point of the book, and that impression emerges even more strongly for those who hear the gospel read or told: these are the parting words that remain with you. The passage is widely quoted. Jean-Marc Ela, one of the continent's leading Christian writers, asks, "In the African environment, shouldn't the church take Jesus at his word in the gospels in making use of the power granted to it to lay hands on and heal the sick? (Mark 16.18)." The scripture gives the authority to heal and exorcize, to triumph over the powers of evil, and the visible signs of that triumph, especially in healing, prove the truth of the word. As a Korean Pentecostal theologian remarks, "Even the promise of the Lord for supernatural power as recorded in Mark 16:15–18 is understood in the context of mission."[51] Texts and deeds go forward together, in a way that recalls the earliest Christian ages.

For such readers, then, the conclusion to Mark thus carries a weighty theological agenda, which it lacks for mainline churches in the global North. For most liberal churches, not only does this section have negligible authority, it literally is not found in many Bibles, since a solid historical consensus has concluded that it was not part of the original text of Mark, but was rather the work of a second-century editor. Further discrediting the passage, the text is popular with extremist Holiness believers in some rural sections of the United States, who prove their faith by handling serpents and drinking poisons. Far from confirming the word, such disreputable "signs following" actively favor the scholarly consensus that the Marcan passage has no place in the Bible.

The liberal view thus claims the right to assess the value of particular texts based on historical criticism. The African view effectively follows more contemporary theories of reading and interpretation, stressing the role of the communities that receive and use the texts in question. From this perspective, it makes little difference to argue that a given text is clearly not from the hand of its supposed author, if it is received as authoritative by the churches that read it. Nor, unsurprisingly, do Northern churches make headway when they try to place the Pauline condemnations of homosexuality in a social or historical setting. If the text says it and the church believes it, that authority is decisive enough. The nature of the reading community is critical. In this sense, literalism has much in common with postmodern theories of reading.

Looking at this history, we can understand the shocked disbelief of global South Christians, Anglicans and others, over recent liberal reforms in North America and Europe. As everyone knows in practice, many biblical passages can be sidestepped or politely ignored. It would take a stubborn pastor to enforce the rules that St. Paul laid down about hair care for the women in his congregations. Yet there is a difference between flexibility and openly flouting a lengthy series of explicit biblical injunctions. Given the history of global South Christianity, especially in Africa, it would have been foolish to expect any other response. Whatever their disagreements over particular issues, the newer churches see the Bible as a dependable and comprehensive source of authority; and this respect extends to the whole biblical text, to both Testaments.

✝ 3 ✝

OLD AND NEW

If present day Africans still find it difficult to be at home with the Old Testament, they might need to watch out to see if they have not lost their Africanness in one way or the other.

Madipoane Masenya

When Uganda was receiving Christianity in the late nineteenth century, converts coped well enough with the seemingly arbitrary rules laid down by the white missionaries, but only until some younger people began the subversive task of reading the Bible for themselves. They were first shocked, and then elated, to discover the tale of King Solomon, who fitted so well the ideal of African royalty, while flouting missionary prohibitions against polygamy. "Everywhere in the chief's villages, they were talking of the man who had one thousand wives. Every time two people met, they discussed the situation." Ultimately, they decided that the missionary must have lied about the principles of Christianity, presumably because he himself was too poor to afford additional wives. The new faithful were unimpressed by the missionary's explanation that Solomon's situation predated the coming of Christianity, so that the Old Testament must be taken as only a shadow of the New. As the chief demanded, "How is it that King Solomon had all those wives? And he loved them too, the book says." "But Solomon was not a Christian. . . . He lived before the coming of the Lord." "But didn't you tell me everything in the Bible was true?" The missionary must then embark on the intellectually perilous exercise of explaining that words in the Bible, while all true and divinely inspired, are true to varying degrees.[1]

The missionary encounter with Uganda highlights a fact that is at the same time one of the great strengths of the Bible in African Christianity and one of its dangers, namely that the Old Testament seems to speak so directly and familiarly to local conditions. While making the book popular, this congeniality also raises questions about the relationship between Old and New

Covenants that Western Christians thought they had settled long since. To a lesser degree also, newer Christian communities in Asia must reconcile the claims to truth of the two Testaments. Not only does the Bible carry special authority as a divinely inspired text, but this respect must be paid to larger portions of the text than would be customary for many Northern-world Christians. If not quite a different book, the Bible of the South is perhaps a good deal larger than its Northern counterpart.[2]

The Hebrew Bible and the Christian Bible

Changing attitudes toward the Old Testament represent a fundamental shift in the modern history of Christianity. Through most of that history, the Old Testament represented the foundation on which Christianity was built, with Abraham, Moses, and the prophets acting as precursors and often symbols of the Christ that was to come. The two unequal halves of the Bible spoke to each other, so that Jesus was multiply foretold by the Hebrew prophets, to the extent that the book of Isaiah became something like a fifth gospel in the early church. For Catholics, the Virgin Mary was prefigured by the tale in Exodus of the bush that burned without being consumed. Abraham's preparing to sacrifice his son foreshadowed the crucifixion. In some early Christian texts, the search for Old Testament prototypes becomes so avid that virtually every reference to "wood" prefigures the crucifixion, while "water" signals the blood of Christ. Such types and parallels run through the cycle of readings in the liturgically oriented churches, and have influenced art and architecture. Many churches with elaborate stained glass offer a two-storey pattern, with the lower frames containing Old Testament themes; and the upper parts, the New Testament tales that represent their fulfillment. Christian readers drew on Old Testament history as their own, and the church was the new Israel.[3]

The term "Old Testament" itself indicated this sense of historical development: there were two testaments or covenants, one of which gave way to the other. All but forgotten, except by academic historians, was the ancient heresy of Marcion, who denied this continuity, and rejected the flawed God of the Old Testament and the scriptures that told of his deeds. For Marcion, selected portions of the New Testament constituted the only true scripture, the entire and sufficient Bible, which proclaimed the good God of Jesus. Orthodox Christians scorned this rejection of the Hebrew scriptures, which were wholly adopted into the faith.

In modern times, and for a variety of reasons, the Old Testament has enjoyed decreasing prestige within Christianity, and this decline represents a complex and underrated social phenomenon. Partly, Western Christians follow a well-established heritage in subordinating the Old Testament to the New, since the ritual and political rules of the Old Testament have been superseded by the new dispensation of Christianity. But other factors have come into play in relatively modern times. In popular thought, many believers associate the Old Testament with those aspects of Christianity that they find uncongenial, including the stories of Creation and the Fall, the vision of God as angry judge rather than loving parent, the justification of war and ethnic cleansing, and the pervasive legalism. (I am of course presenting popular stereotypes here, rather than my own view of the text.) These tendencies are most acutely obvious in a ritualistic, clerical, and legally oriented book like Leviticus. The Old Testament sets in sharper contrast the radically new, antihierarchical, and supposedly antilegalistic message of Jesus. Marcion's influence flourishes today among those who have never heard his name. It is almost as if Western Bibles today should be printed with a consumer's warning at the beginning of the Old Testament declaring, "This part should not be taken seriously."

But other calls for reevaluation were better grounded, morally and intellectually. For liberals, the main difficulty was, of course, the continuing religion of Judaism, which laid claim to the same scriptures. For most of Christian history, Judaism was frankly regarded in terms of supersessionism, the idea that the Old Covenant had lost its validity and that Jews were to be blamed for willfully resisting the true Messiah. Some New Testament passages, especially in Revelation, contrast the new church with the old synagogue, the suggestion being that Judaism has failed to see the light of truth. Even Benjamin Disraeli, that great Hebrew Anglican, wrote that "Christianity is completed Judaism, or it is nothing. Christianity is incomprehensible without Judaism, as Judaism is incomplete without Christianity." Other Christians took a more sinister view of Jews as impostors, as enemies, as conspirators against the true faith. But at best, if Christians were the inheritors of the Old Testament as well as of the New, if in a sense they were the new Hebrews, then old Hebrews were redundant.[4]

The proper relationship between the sister religions was thoroughly reevaluated following the growth of visible Jewish communities in the leading advanced states, and the revelation of Nazi atrocities provoked a cultural and intellectual crisis. From the 1950s, Americans in particular were deeply sensitive about Christian assertions that excluded or demeaned Jews or Judaism. The term "Judaeo-Christian" now entered general speech as the description for Western religious roots. At the same time, religious writers sought a neutral term for the Old Testament that lacked the suggestion of supersession: they commonly used "Hebrew Bible," while the New Testament became the "Greek Bible." (The terms First and Second Testaments are also used.) Though the goals underlying such a change are laudable, the implications are far-reaching. The New Testament thus becomes the Christian scripture, while the Old Testament is conceded to Judaism. Christians still make abundant use of Old Testament passages—social activists commonly cite the prophetic books—but while the Hebrew Bible is a rich spiritual source, it is in a sense used only with permission.[5]

We can debate the perils of trying to cut Christianity loose from its Jewish roots, but such issues scarcely arise in most of the new Christian world. With the significant exceptions of South Africa and Argentina, substantial Jewish communities do not exist in most Southern Christian countries. African and Asian churches feel little need to accommodate Jewish sensitivities about the ownership of the "Hebrew Bible."[6] That statement is not intended to indicate callousness or historical blindness, and global South leaders freely cite the Holocaust as an instance of gross human sinfulness. A crucial leader such as South Africa's Anglican Archbishop Ndungane might begin a sermon with a quote from Elie Wiesel, and he asks whether "the annihilation of six million Jews presents a seemingly insurmountable obstacle to further theological thought—how is it possible to believe in God after what happened?" But the horrors of anti-Semitism are seen as European problems, a close parallel to the racism and imperialism inflicted on the Third World, rather than a structural sin of the Christian religion. In terms of the scale of bloodshed, the catastrophe of the Holocaust was no greater than events outside Europe. To quote one Taiwanese scholar, "Starting from the period of colonization of Asia by the West, during the two world wars, during struggles for independence and during the so-called revolutions, many holocausts have happened and millions of people have lost their lives. . . . The countless victims in Asia have been crying out from the hell, but they are rarely heard on earth."[7]

Our Testament

Cultural affinities with the biblical world lead African and Asian Christians to a deep affection for the Old Testament as their story, their book. In Africa particularly, Christians have long been excited by the obvious cultural parallels that exist between their own societies and those of the Hebrew Old Testament, especially the world of the patriarchs. While the vast majority of modern Africans have no direct experience of nomadism or polygamy, at least they can relate to the kind of society in which such practices were commonplace.[8]

Equally familiar is the prominent element of sacrifice in Hebrew ritual. Still, in much of Africa, social events frequently involve some kind of sacrifice or libation, as do celebrations of key events in the ceremonial year. In a much-quoted study, Fr. Justin Ukpong drew many parallels between the Hebrew practice of sacrifice described in Leviticus and the modern institution as known among the Ibibio people. In what sounds like an account of an Old Testament mindset, another observer notes, "In a Nigerian traditional setting, salvation is seen as a group affair and it is in the present. For a community to be saved from some kind of epidemic, afflictions, abominations, bad death and even wars, a price is paid. There is an atonement to please the gods. The medium of atonement is the shedding of the blood of animals."[9]

Even in relatively small things, African and Asian readers need no gloss to understand Hebrew customs and forms that strike North Americans as archaic and incomprehensible. Was God angry with David for taking a census of the people of Israel? Gikuyu readers instantly appreciate the taboos associated with counting and enumeration. Unlike their Western counterparts, moreover, many African and Asian Christians think it only reasonable that the Bible should include lengthy genealogies for key figures, most obviously Jesus himself: how else does one situate a figure and assert the basis on which he claims authority? Without roots and family, a political or religious leader has no plausible claim to one's loyalty or even attention. Chinese scholar Fook-Kong Wong notes that "the genealogical lists in Chronicles bear witness to God's intimate knowledge and remembrance of his people." Reading a text like Lamentations, meanwhile, a Chinese scholar imbued in traditional culture will automatically turn to the millennia-old tradition of Chinese lamentation literature, which suggests still other dimensions for the Hebrew form.[10]

For African believers, the pleasant shock of recognition is especially strong in the first twelve or so chapters of Genesis. In the calling of Abram, readers with any sense of African roots will encounter many well-known ideas. The story tells of the origin of a tribe or clan with particular claims to a precious tract of land, a promise sealed by the construction of an altar and an act of sacrifice, and an emphasis on the rights of a community rather than an individual or a nuclear family. The story even takes place near a sacred tree. And the movements of the patriarchal clans are often driven by the endemic threat of famine. In his analysis of the first eleven chapters of Genesis, a study that has had a profound influence on African Bible scholarship, Yoruba scholar Modupe Oduyoye comments that "one might call [these chapters] the Scriptures to all human beings, since there is little specifically Jewish in the material, and yet a lot that is Afro-Asiatic."[11]

Andrew Walls once commented, "You do not have to interpret Old Testament Christianity to Africans; they live in an Old Testament world." The seeming Africanness of the patriarchal world helps explain the power of a stunning film like the Malian *Genesis* (1999), a retelling of the biblical tale of Jacob and Esau, the hunters and the shepherds, in thoroughly West African guise. And as, today, nomadism becomes an ever more marginal part of African life, the concept still provides a valuable rhetorical tool in discussions of social and economic conflict. The conflict between nomads and agriculturalists, Cain and Abel, can also symbolize the tensions between country dwellers and city dwellers, colonized and settlers, blacks and whites.[12]

Nor is this affinity confined to Genesis. Commenting on 1 Samuel, Gerald West lists some thirty "African resonances," ways in which the text rings true to southern African readers today. Among these, he includes the dynamics of polygamous families, "endemic conflict with neighboring tribes . . . the need to visit a seer on occasions . . . possession by spirits . . . [and] women dancing and singing in recognition of the exploits of their men." That too was a world in which men aspired to be "buried with their fathers." South African theologian Madipoane Masenya goes so far as to suggest that there must be something culturally amiss with an African who does not recognize a kinship with the Old Testament.[13] Could an equivalent remark conceivably be made of European or North American Christians today?

It is precisely the "primitive" features of ancient Hebrew religion, which distress many modern Westerners, that have long endeared it to Africans. In the nineteenth century, rationalists and liberal reformers in Europe and the United States sought to rescue Christianity from its roots in the regional mythologies of primitive communities. Society had moved on, they felt, and so should notions of religious authority. At the height of the Modernist Crisis in the United States in the 1890s, anthropologist James Mooney declared that the patriarchal ancestors of the biblical Hebrews were no better than modern-day American Indians. They "had reached about the plane of our own Navaho, but were below that of the Pueblo. Their mythologic and religious system was closely parallel." If much of the Bible was the record of the barbarous tribes of ancient Israel, how could it be presented as superior to Indian legends and tales? Myths are myths. But such contextualization has a very different effect on contemporary peoples who share much of the economic structure and social commonplaces of those "primitive" societies. Mooney was writing in 1892, the same year as the foundation of an "Ethiopian" church in South Africa, a native church that boasted of its links to Hebrew religion.[14] While one society was stressing primitivism to demean or minimize scriptural authority, another was proclaiming its linkage with that very same archaic tradition.

Our Story

In claiming a direct connection with the ancient Hebrew world, African Christians are following a potent Euro-American tradition. For Christians throughout history, the Holy Land was no mere piece of Levantine real estate, but a spiritual terrain as real as the profane soil under one's feet. Seventeenth-century Scots Presbyterians spoke of their nation as stretching from Dan to Beersheba. In his prophetic visions, William Blake saw in London a whole imagined Hebrew geography:

> The fields from Islington to Marybone,
> To Primrose Hill and Saint John's Wood:
> Were builded over with pillars of gold,
> And there Jerusalem's pillars stood.

A few years later, Joseph Smith gazed over the hills of upstate New York and saw the clashing kingdoms and armies of displaced Hebrew populations.

Modern Christians, too, seek ancient parallels to their situation. In south and east Asia, theologians correctly note that the gospel originated in an admittedly distant corner of the same continent, and they seek distinctively Asian elements in the faith. Using an unfashionable ethnic classification, Korean Wonsuk Ma writes that "Asians should remember that the revealed words were given to Orientals (Hebrews for the Old Testament, and primarily Jews for the New Testament). Since God uses human thought mechanisms, His revelation assumes a close affinity to Oriental worldviews." The task for modern theologians is to strip away the Western accretions, to recover a gospel that, in the modern world, is returning to its natural social setting.[15]

But few moderns try to plant their own roots in Hebrew soil as enthusiastically as do Africans. By placing biblical religion and thought in an African context, some Christians suggest that the Hebrews drew extensively on preexisting African cultures. As one Cameroonian pastor remarked, "We recognize our own history in the Pentateuch. We feel that we possibly stem from this history of the Hebrews, because our customs and those of the Hebrews are so similar." Some independent churches speculate about their possible descent from the Lost Tribes.[16] But to varying degrees, Afrocentric ideas have exercised a powerful appeal on mainstream Bible scholars, who reject the popular American division of Arab North Africa from "Black Africa": the continent is one. Modupe Oduyoye's book *The Sons of the Gods and the Daughters of Men* was "[an] Afro-Asiatic Interpretation of Genesis 1–11," using linguistic evidence to claim a direct connection between the ancient Semites and the peoples of West Africa. The theory still exercises a real appeal for West African Christians.

Later scholars have mined the possible biblical references to African territories, to Egypt and Ethiopia of course, but also to Cush, a term that on some but not all occasions has an African context. Other names too, such as Midian, acquire African dimensions, so that Jethro becomes not just a black African but the brains behind the career of his son-in-law Moses. Drawing on such passages, Joseph Enuwosa terms Africa "a continent that bred men used to save Israel and humanity. It gave shelter and refuge to men with a divine task." The most popular single passage in Africanizing the Bible is from Psalm 68, "Princes shall come out of Egypt; Ethiopia shall soon stretch out her hands unto God," a foundation text of the "Ethiopian" churches that emerged in the 1890s (Psalm 68:31). An Ethiopian eunuch was the first (probably) Gentile convert identified in the book of Acts.[17]

And although such discussions normally focus on the Old Testament, Jesus has also been subject to Africanization. One recent Kenyan newspaper article on Jesus' missing years asked, "Could he have taken a long trip through Africa, perhaps, like Ibn Battuta, spending a few weeks in Mombasa? Could some Western biblical editor have removed those parts of the original Bible that described Jesus' stay in East Africa? We cannot be sure. What we can be sure about is that the Bible as a whole has been doctored to fit and serve the interests of those who wrote and re-wrote it." Modern Christians are on much firmer ground when they assert the African roots of the early church. Defending the authentically African character of the faith, a modern minister of South Africa's United Congregational Church declares that "Christianity originated from the Middle East, then spread to parts of Africa such as Egypt, Ethiopia and parts of what is presently Mali. The church is older in Africa than in Europe."[18]

Africa's Old Testament

Modern African Christians readily claim direct continuities from Judaism. Preaching on the book of Esther, one Zimbabwean pastor assures his congregation, "God is on the side of the Jews. As long as you are of Jewish origin, ie, of a Christian background, no one will touch you. Witches will come but they won't touch you." During the Rwandan massacres, imprisoned Tutsis awaiting death hoped—vainly—that they would be rescued, "the same way as the Jews were saved by Esther."[19]

Reinforcing this perception of the "new Jews" is Musa Dube's account of her experiences "reading with" a group of women from a South African AIC. The text was Matthew's account of the Canaanite woman who begs Jesus to heal her daughter. Jesus agrees, but only after declaring that he has been sent to the lost sheep of Israel, with the implication that the Gentile world is not his concern. The passage raises obvious questions about the nature of Jesus' mission. Indeed, some readers have even asked whether the universal message proclaimed by Christianity was a distortion of an original Jewish-centered message. Despite prodding, though, the African readers resolutely refused to confront these questions, because most could see no problem. As Christians, they were clearly part of the House of Israel, while the Gentile "dogs" referred to those without faith. Where was the problem?[20]

Some AICs believe that Old Testament rules and customs do in fact bind modern Christians, to the extent that many Ethiopian and Zionist congregations have a distinctly Judeo-Christian character. As Bengt Sundkler remarked of the independent churches, "In some quarters, the differences between the Old and New Testament standards are felt as a problem, and where this is so, the Old Testament standard is generally accepted."[21] Such churches adopt Old Testament codes about dietary laws and taboos, prohibit pork, practice circumcision, and allow polygamy. Some follow a Saturday Sabbath, with the explicit Old Testament texts reasserted by prophetic visions.

One such Hebraic-oriented movement is the Nazaretha Church, the followers of Isaiah Shembe, which flourishes among the Zulu people of South Africa. In the words of Zulu leader Mangosuthu Buthelezi, church members "place great spiritual emphasis on a specific diet which identifies certain foods which they believed should not be eaten by those who seek the spiritual enlightenment promised by our Saviour. . . . [The] Shembe Church has re-established the Sabbath as the holy day and has made a long-standing tradition of emphasizing personal hygiene and washing, the same way it was emphasized in Galilee two thousand years ago." The Shembes claim to follow the ancient laws of the Nasoreans, or Nazarenes.[22] The worship of one West African group, the Mosama Disco Christo Church, is centered upon its Temple. In strict accordance with the Old Covenant, on only one day in the year may the high priest enter its Holy of Holies.

We might be tempted to consign these practices to the religious fringe —though such churches attract large numbers and exercise real political influence. The Nazaretha Church claims a million members. But for many mainstream thinkers too, Christianity's relationship to the Old Covenant raises challenging questions about the role of traditional religion. Around the globe, Christians recognize that their faith grows from the religion of the Old Testament, and they draw freely on the thought and ritual of Judaism, though omitting the ritual requirements. But if in fact African traditional religion can so plausibly be linked to the faith of Abraham, Isaac, and Jacob, might not that be seen as a worthy predecessor of modern African Christianity? Can traditional religion properly be seen as Africa's Old Testament, with all that implies about its relevance for modern practice?

No Other Gods

In some ways, the presence of living pagan traditions, in the present or recent past, reinforces the relevance of the Old Testament for African and Asian

Christianity. This reality gives such churches a very different emphasis to what we might expect in Europe or America, where "paganism" suggests an artificial modern construction. The pagan presence in Africa and Asia gives a powerful reality to biblical accounts of the evils threatening God's chosen people, whether the Old Israel or the New. Texts about idolatry and the overthrow of hostile gods read relevantly here, whereas they serve as embarrassments or worse to a tolerant and inclusive North. An American preacher who invokes the first commandment—you shall have no other gods before me—is speaking metaphorically, warning his or her congregation about the idolatrous pursuit of wealth or material influence. An African, in contrast, may well be offering a strict and quite literal order about avoiding pagan rites. The verse means what it says, avoiding other gods.[23]

Throughout the Old Testament, a pervasive rhetoric denounces all forms of idolatry and condemns rulers who so much as tolerate the existence of pagan or primal religion, who allow the cult shrines to survive on the hillsides. Other popular texts still cited and preached literally include the story of the golden calf, which is presented in its original context as a pagan idol, rather than a symbol of materialism. The model text for noncooperation and non-toleration is Elijah's victory over the prophets of Baal in 1 Kings 18, which culminates in the defeat and massacre of Israel's foes. In the New Testament too, Paul in Athens issued a classic warning against the foolish belief in images and idols. Some contemporary African preachers draw on such texts in order to denounce the pagan traditions that might still attract Christian believers. The martyred Ugandan leader Janani Luwum praised foreign missionaries who had "no option" in suppressing the "evil practices" of traditional pagan religions.[24]

Given this background, it may sound strange to find so many modern writers and theologians speaking of traditional religion as Africa's Old Testament. Yet parallels are often drawn, particularly by Roman Catholic scholars who in recent decades have become deeply committed to inculturating the Christian message. Writing on changes in ancient Hebrew society, Fr. Victor Zinkuratire notes the shift from ancient communitarian Yahwism to the more sinister worship of the foreign god Baal. "Similarly in Africa the transition from the egalitarian way of life to the modern state system has weakened the positive values found in African traditional religions and cultural practices—a kind of African Yahwism—and strengthened the present process of secularization, analogous to the influence of Baalism in Israel."[25] In this reading, the sinister religion of Baal is associated not with Africa's Old Religion, but rather with its foreign modernizing enemies.

For some thinkers, traditional religion had features that should not be given up too lightly. In 2000, the Catholic archbishop of Bloemfontein, South

Africa, proposed that the churches might follow secular society in adopting some form of blood sacrifice. "Sacrifice to the ancestors continues to be a very common practice among Africans. The slaughtering of an animal—cow or sheep—takes place wherever there is a funeral or a marriage feast, or in times of illness, unemployment, family feuds or the birth of a child. Is there a way to integrate this custom with their Christian belief as a step towards meaningful inculturation? . . . [E]ven sophisticated black Christians slaughter animals as part of their tradition of communing with their ancestors at important occasions in their lives."[26]

To take another issue, primal religions are usually located in a specific landscape, with a veneration for a particular set of landmarks, for rivers or mountains. In a colonial context, such reverence for the land carries special weight, so that native communities who might accept being displaced from some areas of their territory will fight indomitably to preserve sacred land. In theory, Christianity rejects this localized sacredness, encouraging believers to fix their attention on sites and landscapes existing far away, on the soil of Palestine. But if traditional religion does have a kind of quasi-canonical status, that might legitimize the notion of sacred land.

John Mbiti, one of the most distinguished African theologians, remarks admiringly how readily the independent churches decided to incorporate the old notion of sacred land into their Christian practice. He writes, "The churches have sacred places (mountains, beaches and villages), where members go for pilgrimage and special worship. Some are given biblical names. The land is very significant for them." For Mbiti, this lesson needs to be learned by the mainstream churches as well: "African Christianity needs a theology of the land. . . . Christianity in Africa has no theology of the land. This is probably the most urgent theological issue facing the church in our continent today." Meanwhile, Korean Pentecostals have enthusiastically absorbed older notions of landscape, in the form of their popular "prayer mountains." Allan Anderson comments, "Beliefs in the mountain as the place to which God descends, are not only part of Korean tradition but are also ideas fully at home in the Old Testament. . . . Traditionally, the many mountains of Korea were believed to be places where good spirits lived, and both shamans and ordinary pilgrims would receive power from the particular spirit on each mountain." The prayer mountain movement is "a culturally relevant form of Christian practice that reflects the ancient spirituality of Korean people."[27]

Such a comprehensive approach ideally draws traditional believers to Christianity, allowing the faith to make free use of traditional symbols and rituals, albeit in converted and Christianized form. Yet critics also urge that such borrowings raise the danger of compromise or pollution, creating in effect not a stronger indigenous Christianity, but a syncretistic religion that has more in common with pagan animism than with anything authentically Christian. In the 1970s, Nigerian thinker Byang Kato protested against any "African theology" that compromised itself with older taboos and rituals. Any such theology that failed to take account of critical doctrines of original sin and a fallen humanity would signal "a funeral march of Biblical Christianity and a heralding of syncretism and universalism." To varying degrees, this controversy has surfaced sporadically since that point, though it has diminished as African Christianity has become stronger and more self-confident. But the debate indicates once more a sense of perilous proximity to the Old Testament, with all its dangers and advantages.[28]

Reading from the Old

But even if one rejects Afrocentrism, or is skeptical about alleged links to Hebrew cultures, the fact remains that global South Christians—and Africans above all—retain much greater veneration for the Old Testament as a living source of authority than do Euro-American churches. This is one reason why, in recent debates, global South Anglicans insisted that Christians were indeed bound by the moral laws of the Old Covenant. Western objections that such laws are found only in books such as Leviticus rang hollow, given their implication that such a book must not be part of the "real Bible," which alone deserved obedience.

In other ways too, attitudes to the Old Testament give a very different emphasis to the Bible reading of modern African Christians. Some surveys of popular sermon texts give some idea of the most favored Bible passages, and these observations can be amply confirmed from many different genres of writing. Among Old Testament books, Genesis is probably the most cited, with Exodus and Isaiah also much used. Ecclesiastes and Proverbs are also beloved across the continent, for reasons we will explore shortly.[29]

Among New Testament books, Africans show a strong preference for Matthew among the gospels, though John is much used for evangelism and educating new converts. The taste for Matthew is not hard to understand. We need not follow generations of Sunday school classes that characterized the book as the "most Jewish" gospel, since in various ways, every component of the New Testament stems from Jewish culture. For half a century, scholars have emphasized that the Gospel of John is no less purely Jewish than Matthew. But Matthew most explicitly engages with Old Testament ideas and is most anxious in every particular to portray Jesus as the fulfillment of Old Testament prophecy, the new Moses. African readers are far more comfortable drawing connections between the testaments than are their Northern-world counterparts. As Grant LeMarquand rightly says, "[P]erhaps Marcion has cast such a shadow over the West that it is easier for westerners to see the *discontinuities* between Testaments."[30]

The issue of the relationship between the covenants helps explain the popularity of the book of Acts, a favorite in African biblical exegesis. Once readers draw parallels between the Old Covenant of Judaism and their own traditional religion, they see how Acts fits directly into contemporary debates. Generally, the text suggests that Christians do not have to renounce most of their older culture. Just as Greeks and Romans did not have to be Judaized to receive salvation, "so also should the Igbo not be Europeanized or Americanized by the missionary message in order to be saved." Among the passages most often cited from the book are the day of Pentecost and the pouring out of spiritual gifts; the story of Cornelius and the extension of the gospel to the Gentiles; and the account of the Council of Jerusalem, which laid down the relationship between Gentile and Jewish Christians. Also discussed are Paul's statements that the old customs, the old law, contained a foundation on which the new religion could build. At Lystra, he declares, "In the past, He let all nations go their own way. Yet He has not left himself without testimony." In his famous Athenian sermon, he introduces himself as the envoy of the unknown God for whom the Greeks had previously been seeking. Across Africa and Asia, this kind of approach rings true for modern missionary practice. As Dickson Kazuo Yagi observes, today's Asian churches live "in the times of Paul, planting a convert church in virgin soil," and they identify with his methods of presenting the Christian message.[31]

The Blood of the Lamb

The relationship between Old and New Covenants makes sense in Africa in a way that it cannot in a society that does not, for example, have any recent acquaintance with sacrifice. Reading the New Testament, and particularly the Pauline epistles, Northern readers observe sympathetically how the gospel is made available to the Gentiles—to their predecessors, in fact. In reading thus, they pay less attention to the many texts that deal with the more agonizing question, of how the old Elect, the people of Israel, can be fitted into the New Covenant.

One contribution to this debate was the Epistle of the Hebrews, an anonymous tract long attributed to Paul, which includes some of the shrewdest argument (and some of the best Greek writing) in the whole New Testament. Though many modern readers know passages from Hebrews—the cloud of witnesses, or the definition of faith as the evidence of things not seen—they see little relevance in much of the argument. The epistle assumes deep knowledge of the Jewish Temple ritual, and it describes how this has been superseded by the once-and-for-all sacrifice of Christ, who is now the ultimate high priest.[32] The author knows a great deal about sacrifice, not just its religious significance, but also the practical minutiae: he knows that the sacrificial blood is not just shed, it is sprinkled.

However rich the argument, the complex discussion of sacrifice and thus priesthood seems like a matter for historians curious about how early Christians defined themselves against Judaism. Euro-American readers might turn with surprise to the account of Hebrews in the work of Kwame Bediako, one of the most influential of African theologians, who uses the intriguing heading "The Epistle to the Hebrews as OUR Epistle." For Bediako, "the value for us of the presentation of Jesus in Hebrews stems from its relevance to a society like ours with its deep tradition of sacrifice, priestly mediation and ancestral function." In Ghana, where sacrifice marks the turning points of the year, "the traditional purificatory rituals of Odwira, repeated year after year, have in fact been fulfilled and transcended by the one, perfect Odwira that Jesus Christ has performed once for all. . . . The Odwira to end all Odwiras has taken place through the death of Jesus Christ."[33] Hebrews thus becomes a powerful argument in current controversies. It is a decisive weapon for those African Christians appalled at the idea that adopting blood sacrifice would represent a form of "meaningful inculturation."

The same Old Testament elements that give Hebrews an African feel are also present in other New Testament books, and above all, Revelation. Fidon Mwombeki, a Tanzanian Lutheran leader, writes of the many ways in which that book speaks clearly to Africans. For modern Africans, as for the original audience of Revelation, "The dead are still living in the other world, and they influence the life of those in this world." He discusses the exalted picture of God and the common belief that the future can be seen through visions, dreams, and revelations. Moreover, he writes, "the dominant symbols of the lamb, the throne, the blood, and the animals are common in African religious symbolism. The sacrificial blood, as well as innocent human blood crying from the ground (Rev 6:10), correspond to present-day African beliefs. No one in Africa can expect to get away with shedding innocent blood. At the same time, the lamb as the animal of sacrifice slaughtered for the sins of humanity is a dominant symbol both in Revelation and in African beliefs."[34]

Only readers in a culture familiar with sacrificial tradition are in a position to appreciate fully the numerous allusions to this practice throughout the New Testament. A quick search of the New Testament produces over ninety uses of the word "blood," not counting cognates or related concepts such as *altar* and *lamb*, so it is scarcely an exaggeration to describe the text as soaked with images of sacrifice and redemptive blood.[35] The goriest texts of all are Hebrews and Revelation, which between them account for 40 percent of these references. The same two books account for nine of the New Testament's twenty-one uses of the word "altar."

Appropriately, evangelical religion, with its central notion of being saved in the blood, has exercised immense appeal in modern Africa. Recall the impact of hymns like the "Tukutendereza Yesu," the song of the blood of the lamb. When observers complain that revivals and healing crusades make little explicit reference to evangelical theology, that is partly because pastors can reasonably assume their hearers will already know so many of these doctrines. A sacrificial society is uniquely well equipped to understand theories of atonement, which can never have more than metaphorical power in a culture such as our own. It is one thing to sing of sacrifice, to hymn the power in the blood; it is quite another to have seen and smelled the event take place.

And sacrifice assumes priesthood. As in the European Middle Ages, Christian clergy in contemporary Africa look to Old Testament passages concerning the priests and Levites, tending to enhance the already high status of religious professionals familiar from traditional society. This theme emerges strongly in Hilary Mijoga's valuable study of Malawian sermons. The pastor of one independent church reminds his flock, "The Bible tells us that when offering our harvest thanksgiving we should not forget the Levite and the sojourner. In our case the Levite is our evangelist and the sojourners are his followers, ie the elders and deacons." In other churches, the Levites are presented as the band and church musicians, with the priests as guardians of sanctuaries. Describing the persecution inflicted upon the church by the unconverted Saul, another preacher tells how "[h]e killed pastors, elders, members of the choir, children who followed Jesus."[36] This elision of historical time recalls medieval European images of Old Testament figures as European kings and priests; or paintings of the Virgin Mary receiving the news of the Annunciation, as she reads the Hours of the Blessed Virgin.

Just as influential are Old Testament ideas of prophecy, which have done so much to shape modern African Christianity, especially among the AICs. At least since the 1880s, prophets have proliferated in Africa. Old Testament imagery has contributed mightily to the self-concept of the prophets themselves, to their understanding of their mission, and to the extensive literature that has grown up around the more successful figures. Recalling Jonah, we hear how Simon Kimbangu fled from his prophetic calling, before finally accepting it; while William Wadé Harris became the Black Elijah. Modern prophets claim to have received material symbols of the prophetic gift, recalling the live coal from the altar placed on the mouth of Isaiah (Isaiah 6). The aptly named Zulu prophet Isaiah Shembe received the gift of prophecy when lightning burned him, leaving a scar on his thigh. To his followers, he was at once both the biblical Isaiah and a modern manifestation:

Praise Jehovah . . .
Because he is benevolent for ever more
He remembered his people
He sent them Isaiah his servant
Because he is righteous.[37]

The fascination with prophetic utterances leads readers to treat visionary texts with immense respect. One Zambian Anglican convert besieged his clergy, seeking enlightenment: "When I asked them about the Bible they would not give me true answers. I was very much puzzled about Daniel and Revelation. But they said, 'these are only dreams. You need not read those books. They are very hard and nobody can understand those books. It is better to read the Gospels.' But there was a great demand in my mind to understand these." As we have seen, the dismissive phrase "only dreams" is peculiarly unconvincing in an African context, as is any attempt to minimize the power of the book of Revelation. Prophecy is presumed to be a normal element in the life of the church, and something must be wrong with any Christian communities that do not evince this kind of prophetic activity.[38]

Ways to Live

The Old Testament deals at great length with matters of sacrifice, with prophecy—and with wisdom. In different ways, churches in Africa, Asia, and Latin America show their enthusiasm for those books that are generally known as wisdom literature, books that offer practical means for living in the world. The best known of these in the generally accepted Old Testament are the books of Proverbs and Ecclesiastes—both traditionally regarded as the work of King Solomon—as well as Deuterocanonical works such as the Wisdom of Solomon, and Sirach (Ecclesiasticus). In the New Testament, the wisdom tradition is represented by the Epistle of James.[39]

Wisdom texts are very widely cited by church leaders and scholars of a startlingly wide variety of political and cultural perspectives, and they often provide sermon texts. In Africa, the book of Proverbs enjoys a popularity and authority that would surprise many Americans, who have little patience for sentiments they might regard as either outdated or trite. In the newer Christian world, the Bible's practical rules for living supplanted the traditional proverbs and popular wisdom that were so central to oral cultures. Judaeo-Christian wisdom literature exercises such a fascination because it so closely reflects genres very familiar to pre-Christian and preliterate societies around the world, societies that commonly had wisdom traditions of their own. Even in Nordic Europe, the wisdom tradition was found in the *Hávamál*, reputedly the teachings of the god Odin.

Attitudes to proverbial wisdom sharply divide traditional and modern cultures. Many African societies treat proverbs and wise sayings as the collective wisdom of the ancestors, handed down to instruct the living, and citing such texts ("the elders say") represents a knock-down argument from which there is no effective appeal. Modern societies, in contrast, with vastly more access to written texts, prize novelty of expression and condemn works that imitate or reproduce the thoughts of others. This would have been a strange concept for the many past societies that regarded imitation as a token of respect to superior wisdom and authority and that would scarcely have understood the concept of plagiarism. In the post-Enlightenment West, though, much biblical scholarship has been devoted to detecting the real authorship of particular texts: Did Paul really say this or not? Is this passage part of the authentic text?

In the West at least, most readers regard proverbs as tired clichés, probably indicating a lack of culture or imagination on the part of the speaker. The word "sententious" derives from exactly this sort of *sententia*, or would-be weighty epigrams. In popular culture, this pathetic image is well represented by Forrest Gump ("Stupid is as stupid does"). And having been created for a traditional society, agricultural and patriarchal, proverbial wisdom seems irrelevant or worse today. The book of Proverbs contains the notorious advice to parents about sparing the rod and spoiling the child, which today looks like a scriptural warrant for child abuse.[40]

Yet Proverbs and other wisdom texts enjoyed much greater significance in earlier stages of Christianity. Some scholars hold that the biblical figure of Wisdom, presented as an emanation from God, influenced the New Testament notion of the Logos who became incarnate in Jesus Christ. Some early believers probably saw Christ as wisdom incarnate, and Jesus himself proclaimed that "Wisdom is justified in her children." Such a Christology is intriguing, since Sophia, Wisdom, is a feminine figure. Some reconstructions of the celebrated lost Gospel Q stress its resemblance to wisdom literature, to those popular manuals that used proverbs and sayings to advise ordinary people how to survive in their society, how to behave in the presence of the rich and powerful. The famous Gospel of Thomas uses exactly this format to present the message of faith. It begins, "These are the secret sayings which the living Jesus spoke," and it presents the teachings through a linked series of wisdom sayings. Whatever the truth of this theory of Christian origins, wisdom literature does have a glorious past.[41]

Contemporary African or Asian Christians might or might not be comfortable with every detail of the moral or social advice in Proverbs, but their knowledge of traditional culture and religion permits them to recognize the genre as an old friend. "For the African the proverb, according to [Chinua] Achebe, is 'the spice by which Africans chew kola.'" Madipoane Masenya writes, "If the [Old Testament] Wisdom appears like a thick forest to those from the West, to Africans, it is more like a plain." Theologian Mercy Oduyoye recalls her childhood growing up at a Methodist girls' boarding school in Ghana. Every day began with a religious-oriented school assembly, at which every girl had to recite a biblical text. "It was our tradition to quote from the book of Proverbs, Ecclesiastes or the Sermon on the Mount; Proverbs was our favorite. Proverbs were already a part of our culture and we schoolgirls could easily get away with converting Akan proverbs into King James language and then simply inventing chapter and verse numbers."[42] Elsa Támez has shown how most of the insights of the book of Ecclesiastes find direct parallels in the familiar proverbs of modern Latin America.[43]

If indeed traditional religion is Africa's Old Testament, then its proverbs are a core component of its scriptures. Catholic sister Anne Nasimiyu-Wasike argues, "The oral literature of the African people is their unwritten Bible. This religious wisdom is found in African idioms, wise sayings, legends, myths, stories, proverbs and oral history." A modern Catholic Bible commentary finds "no contradiction between biblical wisdom and African wisdom since both are based on human experience and inspired by God himself."[44] Sermon texts often draw on proverbs, both traditional and biblical. In a Malawian independent church, a preacher describing the book of Jonah remarks, "There is a saying which goes *choipa chitsata mwini* [an evil thing follows its perpetrator]. Desertion of Jonah was a sin before God."[45] Using a proverb in this way tends to localize and Africanize the story, reinforcing its direct relevance for the community.

When African churches cite biblical texts with such enormous respect, they are treating them with the authority that they would earlier have accorded to the "words of the elders." This does not necessarily imply a slavish literalism. As most listeners realize, proverbs and wise sayings use metaphor and analogy, which demand a certain amount of decoding, and such a common-sense approach must be applied to scripture. Indeed, the skills used in assessing proverbs can usefully be deployed when reading a controversial text like Revelation. "Many African languages are full of symbols; people used to speak in symbols, proverbs, riddles and so on. Through these forms of language the transmission of ethical and religious values is intended. Revelation can be a challenge to revitalize African traditions."[46] A background in traditional oral cultures can be an excellent foundation for Bible interpretation.

An Epistle of Straw

Besides Proverbs, African Christians relish the practical day-to-day advice offered in the Letter of James. Arguably, James may be the single biblical book that best encapsulates the issues facing global South churches today, and its influence is as evident in Asia and Latin America as in Africa. James is much cited in the context of spiritual healing, of persecution and resistance, of activism and social justice, even of interfaith relations.

Although James forms part of the New Testament, it very much bears the imprint of the Old, and it uses and comments on traditional wisdom texts, including Proverbs and Ecclesiastes. However much wisdom themes surface elsewhere in the New Testament, James is its only entire work of wisdom literature. Moreover, the authorities and examples cited in the epistle itself are Old Testament figures particularly beloved in these churches: Job as an ideal of innocent suffering, Elijah as a model miracle worker, Abraham as the type of unquestioning faith. In Euro-American tradition, the epistle has a long record of disturbing conventional Christian assumptions, sometimes—not always—by arousing social activism. The spiritual odyssey that culminated in the foundation of Mormonism began when Joseph Smith meditated on James' advice to pray to God for wisdom.[47]

As I will often have occasion to mention James's letter, it might be useful here to describe what is not a well-known component of the New Testament (the text can be found in full in Appendix 1). James, firstly, is not a letter in the sense of Paul's letters: it lacks any personal details, greetings, and so on. It is rather a sermon or exhortation. It is also unusual in its relationship to the early Christian tradition. James quotes the words of Jesus more extensively than any other epistle, and does so in very ancient forms. He cites such familiar sentiments as loving your neighbor as yourself and not judging others. In feel as much as substance, the epistle often recalls the Gospel of Matthew, and particularly the Sermon on the Mount. James never directly mentions such doctrines as the incarnation or resurrection, or even the crucifixion, though the "coming of the Lord" presumably refers to Christ. James's work is strongly practical in nature, defining pure religion as care for the poor and powerless. He flatly rejects the theory of justification by faith, and sections of the letter sound like a direct rebuttal of Paul's letter to the Romans, though scholars debate this.

The Epistle of James has enjoyed a mixed reputation in Western Christianity, and many early Christians were dubious about placing it in the New Testament canon. Early Protestants disliked the writer's affirmation of the value of works over faith. As Martin Luther commented, "St. James's Epistle is really an epistle of straw compared to [St. Paul's letters], for it lacks this evangelical character." Though he valued the text, Luther also doubted its apostolic authorship. (The other texts that he would have reduced to a semicanonical status were Hebrews and Revelation, both of which enjoy widespread popularity in the global South.) Yet whatever its origins, the sense that the letter was conveying the original spirit of Jesus' followers gave it special impact. Even better for modern readers, and buttressing its authority, these sayings purportedly stem from Jesus' own brother.[48]

Especially in the AICs, James is a great source for sermon texts. Studying West African churches in the 1960s, Harold W. Turner noted that James was the most-cited work in sermons, perhaps because in both form and content, it so much resembled familiar wisdom literature, with all its "aphorisms, epigrams and similes." Although Turner was describing conditions in one region some decades ago, the influence of James is still obvious across the spectrum of African churches. A recent commentary remarks that "James addresses things that concern African cities. . . . In a continent that experiences much suffering, the concerns in James' letter are very much ours also."[49]

In its combination of literary styles, no less than the themes it addresses, the epistle offers much to global South churches. James was written for emerging churches still trying to define the distinctions between Christian and non-Christian worlds, and it offers a set of rules for life as an unpopular Christian minority in a hostile non-Christian culture. One African commentary notes that "James uses a particularly friendly way of addressing his Christians on the day to day problems they (and we too) are likely to meet."[50] To take a pressing example, how far should worldly distinctions of wealth and power be reproduced within the Christian community? Undoubtedly, James speaks directly to class issues, though the revolutionary activist interpretation is by no means the only possible reading. The text is directed at poor believers who must face constant stress and temptation, without facing despair and without envying the rich, whose fate is in God's hands. In passages with an apocalyptic tone, James reminds his listeners that the lot of the rich deserved little of their attention, since God will sweep away the wealthy at the coming judgment. Yet poor global South Christians need not be actively leftist or revolutionary in their politics to find solace in such words, as they are deluged with the images of wealth and success presented by Western media and advertising.

Above all, the letter demands that the Christian life be manifested in practical deeds rather than affirmations of faith. For Ugandan church leader Kefa Sempangi, reading James 5:16 constantly forces the Christian to ask him- or herself, "Are you repenting? Are you walking in the light? Are you being broken?"[51] The emphasis on deeds rather than words does not mean that these churches fail to appreciate ideas of salvation by faith alone. Rather, they identify with James' assumption that Christians are joining the church from a mainstream community with radically different values, pagan or secular, into which Judeo-Christian ideas have not yet begun to penetrate, so that church members need practical lessons in living in an alternative society. This view of the cultural gap separating believers from the cultural mainstream is one that Euro-American churches might have to rediscover sooner than they might think.

The Rule of God

In Asia as well as Africa, an Old Testament orientation has strong political implications. Mainline churches—Anglican, Lutheran, Methodist—share a Hebrew-inspired worldview in which rulers and priests are judged as to how faithfully they enact and enforce God's laws. States, no less than individuals, need to be open to receiving the word of God. Even in a matter as weighty as deciding the leadership of a great nation such as Nigeria, prophets and prophecies played a decisive role in persuading the Christian Olusegun Obasanjo to run for the presidency in 1999, in order to fulfill what was seen as a divine plan.[52]

Old Testament models can support ideas of the godly nation and national chosenness, ideas quite familiar through European history, and especially in the U.S. political tradition. Religion is communal rather than individual, and nations are punished for their collective sins. In debates over morality and sexuality, Southern church leaders reject the notion that societies should tolerate the sexual misdeeds of individuals, because personal immorality becomes part of a national burden, a collective offense against divine law, which invites retribution. This vision of a godly society would have made excellent sense to American colonists of the seventeenth and eighteenth centuries, who proclaimed days of fasting and penitence to atone for the sins of the land. The fusion of the moral and political potentially contributes to a harsh view of individual deviance. At the same time, though, the strongly collective sense of belonging to God's people is reflected in a desire for social justice, and opposition to dictatorship and exploitation.

Preachers search the Old Testament history for examples of God's rewarding the faith of his people and punishing backsliding. One popular text is found in 2 Chronicles: "If my people, which are called by my name, shall humble themselves, and pray, and seek my face, and turn from their wicked ways; then will I hear from heaven, and will forgive their sin, and will heal their land." The healing is a matter for both land and community, rather than of individuals. Conversely, a country that refuses to bow its head will be punished, not only through the obvious means of divine retribution—plague, war, and famine; challenges that exist today as far more than literary devices —but by curses that could blight a nation for generations to come. West African preachers today blame the region's underdevelopment on its long enslavement to particularly bloody and obstinate forms of heathenism.[53]

In their selection of Bible readings and sermon texts, African and Asian churches show an acute awareness of the necessity for community righteousness, for the maintenance of the godly nation. Popular preaching texts stress correct conduct, urging believers to show their faith by obedience. Besides the inevitable James, other popular passages for African preachers include 1 Samuel 15:22, "to obey is better than sacrifice, and to hearken than the fat of rams." Matthew's gospel offers rich pickings for preachers, with practically oriented texts such as "bear fruit worthy of repentance"(3:8). The need for deeds as well as words is reinforced by this text from Matthew (7:21): "Not everyone who says to me, 'Lord, Lord,' will enter the kingdom of heaven, but only he who does the will of my Father who is in heaven." Such a theology is even illustrated, perhaps, by the enunciation of the Lord's Prayer. An English bishop visiting Kenya noted how, "without a pause at the end of the line after 'be done,' the people prayed 'Thy will be done on earth—as it is in Heaven.'" He "speculated that that was because Kenyans lived closer to the soil than did Britons, who, not seeing the connection between God and the environment, leave an uncomprehending pause between God's will and the earth on which it should be seen to be done."[54]

In his study of sermon texts in South Korean Protestant churches, Andrew Kim notes the popularity of related texts. These include verses such as "Righteousness exalts a nation" (Proverbs 14:34); "Now if you obey me fully and keep my covenant, then out of all nations you will be my treasured possession" (Exodus 19:5); and "Blessed is the nation whose God is the Lord, the people he chose for his inheritance" (Psalms 34:12). In the South Korean case, we can see many reasons why such texts would have special force, beyond the common tendency to respect the continuing validity of the Old Testament. A society with a strong Confucian foundation regards a religion as more than a set of beliefs, but rather a package of authoritative prescriptions for the correct way to live. At the same time, the presence of living non-Christian traditions is a constant reminder of the temptation of straying from God's ways, of worshipping foreign gods. And Korean Christians are agonizingly aware of the fate that awaits them should God remove his protection. Very few miles separate them from the nation of North Korea, a potential threat to which they can plausibly apply all the biblical warnings originally presented in terms of Assyrians or Babylonians.[55]

Old and New Jews

The enthusiastic use of both Testaments in Southern Christian churches can lead to readings that seem troubling in terms of their attitude toward the living tradition of Judaism. In the absence of the reality check provided by the continuing presence of Jewish communities, Christians freely contrast the old and discredited world of the synagogue or Temple, the old Law, with the new law of Christ. Just as Euro-American Christians long felt no need to accommodate Muslim religious sensibilities, so many African or Asian Christians can imagine Jewish realities without applying their conclusions to living individuals.

Particularly in the independent churches, anti-Judaic readings are quite common, though anti-Semitic doctrines are largely absent. Look, for instance, at the words of a modern follower of the Shona prophet Johane Masowe: "When we were in these synagogues [the European churches] we used to read about the works of Jesus Christ. . . . cripples were made to walk and the dead were brought to life . . . evil spirits driven out. . . . That was what was being done in Jerusalem. We Africans, however, who were being instructed by white people, never did anything like that. . . . We were taught to read the Bible, but we ourselves never did what the people of the Bible used to do."[56] The synagogue reference is not directed against modern Jews, and the speaker would have little sense of what distinguished Jews from the larger category of white people. Still, few Euro-American Christians would refer to synagogues so dismissively, because so many of them have actually seen such a building, or know friends who attend such an institution.

The relationship between old and new laws was in the headlines in 2004 when Mel Gibson's film *The Passion of the Christ* aroused controversy in many nations around the world, Christian and Muslim. Some African and Asian societies experienced debates reminiscent of those in the United States about the film's alleged anti-Semitism, with liberal church leaders in South Africa condemning the film. More commonly, though, where objections did surface, they concerned the work's excessive violence, rather than its religious sensibilities. Generally, church leaders praised the film far more uniformly and enthusiastically than did their counterparts in North America and Europe. Manila's Catholic archbishop urged, simply, "All Christians should try to see this film." Leaders of smaller independent churches not only praised the film, but spoke frankly of the Jewish misdeeds it exposed. In South Africa, one of the film's advocates was a leader of the Shembe church, which, as we have already seen, has adopted many Hebraic practices. Nevertheless, a spokesman in 2004 declared, "They [the Jews] were responsible for the death of Jesus Christ. Why do we have to hide what is recorded in the Bible?"[57]

Quite different from such raw sentiments are the attitudes expressed by Southern Christian thinkers influenced by liberation theology. At first glance, few Northern-world readers would fail to celebrate the socially liberalizing and progressive impact of new forms of Christianity. Surely, we can agree, the kind of reforms being undertaken in the name of Christianity today echo trends in Western societies in bygone years? In some ways, though, the more radical the readings, the more determined believers are to shape a new humanity free of traditional distinctions and prejudices, the more easily their views define themselves in opposition to the old order presented in the Bible, namely the Temple, the priesthood, and the ancestors of what would become Judaism. Though liberal and progressive thinkers are quick to repudiate any anti-Semitic current, we sometimes encounter phrases that would be unlikely to appear in mainstream North American Christianity, because of the stark distinction they draw between Jesus and the Jewish society from which he came.

This is especially true when the rivalry between Jesus and the priestly elite is framed in terms of race. Some Latin American theologians portray Jesus as a characteristic product of the Galilee's mixed and marginalized society, a mestizo, who enters the great city of Jerusalem in order to confront the arrogance of the wealthy pure-blooded elite, to challenge their prejudices of race and class. The message is clearly directed to the societies of North and Central America, and the racial challenge is directed against Anglos, or against Latino elites who pride themselves on their pure Spanish descent. Not for a second do such accounts intend any slighting of Jews or Judaism, but the portrait of Jerusalem and the Temple elite can read uncomfortably.[58]

Unintentionally, Brazilian-based theologian Alessandro Gallazzi also offers what can be read as a dim view of Judaism. In an essay on Ezekiel's august vision of the restoration of the Temple, he condemns the text's underlying tendency toward oppression and violence. Indeed, he says, "Our base communities read Ezekiel 40–48, critically because its teachings are totally unacceptable in our context." The text assumes a vision of priests and priesthood that is in sharp distinction to the liberating vision of Jesus. It is not difficult to understand why he (and they) read in such a way, given their social setting in a Latin America marked by a struggle between "the church of the Temple —official, despotic, structured, static and eternal" and the democratic base communities.[59] But in its implications, the argument gives little credit to the Jewish tradition. In India, too, Christians from the lowest untouchable castes —the Dalits—sympathize enthusiastically with Jesus' attack on the Temple establishment, precisely because of their own bitter experience with oppressive Hindu elites in the modern world. Though their rhetoric is really directed against contemporary elites, without reference to actual modern Jews or

Jewish communities, it takes the form of bitter denunciations of ancient Judaism.

Precisely because modern African churches identify with the Old Testament thought world, radical-minded Christians have a special incentive to denounce Jewish customs. In both independent and mainstream Christianity, church authorities regularly cite Old Testament passages to justify the social order, especially in gender matters; and many Christians accept Hebraic customs relating to blood taboos or gender roles. Inevitably, liberation theologians, and especially feminists, stress the hidebound prejudices of the society that Jesus denounces, in order to confront the modern church leaderships of the global South. The goal is to stress the idea of a new creation, both individual and social.

In order to maximize the rhetorical effect, modern reformers portray Jesus as the ultimate smasher of taboos, and in doing so, they exaggerate the restrictions of Second Temple Judaism, the restraints it places on women and its obsession with ritual purity. Discussing circumcision, a Taiwanese scholar writes, "Marked by this sacred sign, the Jews attain a special sense of Judeocentrism and look down on the uncircumcised pagans and even more on women, who lack anything to be circumcised. As for pagan women it hardly bears mentioning what double degree of discrimination is in store for them. . . . Patriarchal consciousness in biblical Judaism uses age, gender, blood and race to treat others as foreign or of inferior status." "Judeo-centrism and patriarchal bias" are inextricably linked.[60]

When discussing Luke chapter 8—a passage central to African feminist theology—writers emphasize the systematic oppression inflicted upon women and the marginalized. In stressing Jesus' spectacular rejection of taboos and impurities—concerning blood, the presence of corpses, and touching women —modern African writers are explicitly confronting the older assumptions of their own societies, but they phrase their ideas in terms of Jesus' confrontation with Judaism. Teresa Okure writes how the woman with the issue of blood overcame the "crippling cultural taboos imposed on her" by contemporary Jewish society. "To continue to exclude women from certain Christian ministries on the basis of outmoded Jewish taboos is to render null and void the liberation that Jesus won for us."[61]

In some instances, the break between Old and New Covenants becomes so sharp as almost to make Jesus—and even the Christian God—a rebel against Judaism. Jesus thus rejects the "patriarchy of Judaism." Kwok Pui-Lan writes of "a suffering God: a God who cried out on the Cross, who suffered under the long Jewish tradition, the God who was put to death by the military and political forces, who was stripped naked, insulted and spat upon." Taiwanese theologian C. S. Song contrasts Jesus' loving Father, Abba, with "the God of retribution . . . the God of legalism, the God of religious absolutism, the God of theological dogmatism." A publication by the World Council of Churches claims that "Jesus died as a result of the clash between his God and the god of Pharisaic Judaism. . . . Jesus' crucifixion marked the temporal triumph of the patriarchal god of Judaism. . . . Christianity has fallen back to the patriarchal god of Judaism with even greater zeal. . . . The god of the clan will sanctify anything including militarism, war, sexism, apartheid, as long as it serves the interest of the clan."[62] The shade of Marcion walks in such passages.

Jewish observers charge some Southern writers with caricaturing Judaism to the point of active anti-Semitism. Amy-Jill Levine complains, "In delineating the evils of colonialism . . . some feminist critics identify Jesus with their own self-articulated abject situations, and they identify those biblical peoples who do not follow Jesus—that is, 'the Jews' (rarely the Romans)—with their oppressors." In response, African and Asian writers flatly disavow any anti-Semitic intent, but are still reluctant to forego their attacks on Old Testament traditions, precisely because they are so relevant to their immediate social and political concerns. Kwok, for instance, writes that Okure and other African women theologians "are encouraging African women to rise up and seek wholeness in their lives; they are not primarily concerned with putting down the Jewish tradition."[63] The very immediacy of Old Testament concerns and realities gives a contemporary relevance to anti-Judaic elements in Christianity that have long been thought obsolete in the North Atlantic world.

✝ 4 ✝

POOR AND RICH

Those cultures which are far removed from biblical culture risk reading the Bible as fiction.

Musimbi Kanyoro

The Southward movement of Christianity implies not just a change in the ethnic composition of the world's believers, but also a fundamental shift in their social and economic background. The average Christian in the world today is a poor person, very poor indeed by the standards of the white worlds of North America and Western Europe. Also different is the social and political status of African and Asian Christians, who are often minorities in countries dominated by other religions or secular ideologies. This historic social change cannot fail to affect attitudes toward the Bible. For many Americans and Europeans, not only are the societies in the Bible—in both Testaments—distant in terms of time and place, but their everyday assumptions are all but incomprehensible. It is easy, then, to argue that the religious and moral ideas that grew up in such an alien setting can have little application for a modern community. Yet exactly the issues that make the Bible a distant historical record for many Americans and Europeans keep it a living text in the churches of the global South.

For many such readers, the Bible is congenial because the world it describes is marked by such currently pressing social problems as famine and plague, poverty and exile, clientelism and corruption. A largely poor readership can readily identify with the New Testament society of peasants and small craftsmen dominated by powerful landlords and imperial forces, by networks of debt and credit. In such a context, the excruciating poverty of a Lazarus eating the crumbs beneath the rich man's table is not just an archaeological curiosity. This sense of recognition is quite clear for modern dwellers in villages or small towns, but it also extends to urban populations, who are often close to their rural roots. And while some resemblances might be superficial, their accumulated weight adds greatly to the credibility of the text. The Bible provides immediate and often material answers to life's problems. It teaches ways to cope and survive in such a hostile environment, and at the same time holds out the hope of prosperity.[1]

This sense of familiarity offers great potential for evangelism, since African and Asian readers can be shown that the biblical message is in its origins anything but a Western import. As Wonsuk Ma argues, presenting the Bible in a way suitable for American Christians means forfeiting its potential relevance for those peoples who today constitute the vast majority of believers. "If we put much emphasis on Israel's history, but neglect issues surrounding us, such as poverty, corruption, street children, the sex industry, oppressive rules, human rights issues, devastating environmental concerns, rising prices, etc., are we doing our job right?"[2] The Bible lends itself startlingly well to contemporary purposes.

Blessed Are the Poor

Particularly appealing are the parables, in which Jesus incorporated so many observations of contemporary conditions. Writing of contemporary Central America, novelist Francisco Goldman remarks that "Guatemala certainly feels biblical. Sheep, swine, donkeys, serpents—these are everywhere, as are centurions, all manner of wandering false prophets, pharisees, lepers and whores. The poor, rural, mainly Mayan landscape has an aura of the miraculous. . . . [It] is the perfect backdrop for religious parables about fields both barren and fertile, fruits and harvests, hunger and plenty." Across Africa and Asia, millions of modern readers know roads where a traveler is likely to be robbed and left for dead, without much hope of intervention by official agencies. They relate to accounts of streets teeming with the sick. They understand that a poor woman who loses a tiny sum of money would search frantically for coins that could allow her children to eat that night. In many countries, readers appreciate the picture of the capricious rich man, who offers hospitality on one occasion, but on another day demands payment of exorbitant debts and obligations, and who must not on any account be offended. Today, though, the person would not be a generic magnate or Hellenistic princeling, but a corrupt official of a ruling party.[3]

The geographic world of the parables is a familiar terrain of small cities and straggling villages, making it easy to draw local analogies. A Malawian preacher relates easily to the notion of a city on a hill: "Before someone sees a person here at Chinamwali, that person will first see the houses which are on top of that hill because they are visible. Are our works as Christians visible to people outside?" Very little adjustment is needed to make such stories ring even more true. Wonsuk Ma advises preachers to incorporate discreet infusions of "Asian symbolism and equivalence. David can be a boy watching carabaos (Asian water buffaloes) in a muddy rice field, or Jesus rebukes a mango tree. It takes creative imagination."[4]

These local interpretations emerge visually in the vernacular artistic traditions that have flourished in recent decades, and that are well represented in the décor of churches and seminaries. To quote an admiring U.S. journalist, "Not since Europe's Renaissance has such a large and varied body of living Christian art been produced" as in contemporary Africa, and this art is firmly based on local imagery. A Malawian painting of the Annunciation shows "an African woman kneeling in front of a hut and winnowing maize." Portraits of Mary with her child naturally show her carrying the baby on her back, in African style. And some of the local touches are well observed: "The main actors in the parable of the lost [prodigal] son are portrayed in an urban setting as well-dressed city folk with suits and ties."[5] Like the residents of ancient Galilee, modern African villagers understand the temptations of migrating to the city, and the hazards. What they do find mind-boggling is the father's willingness to take back a son who had so abominably ignored his family obligations, the same kind of amazement that Jesus presumably intended to stir among his original listeners.

Another parable tells of the day laborers, hired at different stages of the day in order to work in the vineyard. At the end of the day, the landlord pays each man the same wages, to the chagrin of those who worked the longest. In its original context, the parable presumably refers to the resentment felt by faithful and observant believers against newer adherents to God's law, either the lost sheep of Israel or the Gentile converts. But in all the discussions of the text, only recently did a scholar think to ask the opinion of those perhaps best qualified to comment, namely day laborers themselves.[6]

Casual day laborers are a familiar enough phenomenon in the United States, especially in the South and West, in areas of high Latino immigration. Around the world, casual labor is often the unpleasant fate awaiting young men: "For accommodation, they squat with friends and relatives in the slums. One meal a day is a blessing for them." When biblical scholar Fr. Justin Ukpong asked a group of Christian Nigerian workers about the parable, they responded at length to a story that touched so exactly on their situation.[7] Initially, they read the story as an allegory rather than a parable and tried to identify each figure with a real-world original. Based on their experience, they were reluctant to accept that the landlord represented God, because his behavior was so arbitrary and clearly unjust, though absolutely typical of the sort of employers they themselves knew. As in the case of the prodigal son, this point was presumably intended to trouble hearers of the original story. Hearing the story today, the modern laborers thought that Jesus was condemning oppression and selfishness, while pointing out how reluctant the rich were to acknowledge pervasive injustice or to change the system.

In another study, Ukpong sought the reactions of poor farmers to the parable of the dishonest steward, of what he calls the shrewd manager. A rich man dismisses his steward, who promptly engages in some financial sleight of hand designed to ingratiate him with the neighboring farmers, discounting their debts to his master. The master, though, praises him for his ingenuity, a twist that has called forth lengthy discussion from diligent commentators. Ukpong's readers instantly applied the tale to their own circumstances. In a society in transition from traditional peasant agriculture to a money economy, managers and middlemen played a pivotal role, lending farmers the money they needed to survive, but at exorbitant interest, of 50 or 100 percent annually. Instead of reading the story from the point of view of the rich man (who presumably symbolizes God) or of the steward, they read from the stance of their own peasant counterparts, who desperately needed debt reduction, by whatever means it came. However despicable his motives, then, "[t]he manager's action is restitutive and is an action of self-criticism," tending to promote social justice.[8]

In both cases, the modern readers formulated readings that worked for them, and these were not necessarily the meanings heard by Jesus' original audience. But however close these may or may not be to the meaning of the passages in the early church, the experiment indicates once more the ability to comprehend the society of Jesus' time, to read across the centuries.

A Grain of Wheat

Jesus lived in an agricultural society intimately familiar with planting and harvest, a world of grain, grape, and olive; and metaphors from this life pervade his teaching. Much of this language is difficult for modern readers in the West—without a commentary, or at least a lively interest in gardening, how many American Christians can make much sense of the critical vine and branch metaphor in John 15? And for all the enthusiastic language of "harvest" preached by Euro-American evangelicals, few have much idea when the actual physical harvest occurs in their part of the world, and few could say whether last year's harvest season was particularly rich or poor. Metaphor apart, how many have actually labored in a real vineyard?

Most Southern Christians are only a generation or two away from an agriculturally based society, in which traditional rituals were believed to maintain prosperity. In such a world, the notion that death is required to produce life has an intuitive plausibility largely lost in urban societies. One Tamil hymn announces,

> We are the wilted kanai plant,
> O divine one, gracious Lord
> You are the farmer who makes it sprout
> O divine one, gracious Lord
> We are the cotton fields that do not yield,
> O divine one, gracious Lord
> You are the farmer who makes them grow
> O divine one, gracious Lord.

Christians in Africa and Asia pay close attention to Bible passages that assume an agricultural world, or that promise growth and a rich harvest. The parable of the sower is one obvious example. In liturgically oriented churches in Africa, services for blessing fields or seeds draw on older ideas from traditional religion, but they firmly emphasize the role of the one God in granting prosperity. Passages used in this context include God's original blessing of the Creation—the instruction to be fruitful and multiply—but also more specifically Christian texts, such as Jesus' words in the Gospel of John about a grain of wheat dying in order to produce much fruit. The popularity of this passage in African churches helps explain the resonance of the title of Ngugi wa Thiongo's *A Grain of Wheat*, one of the greatest of modern African novels—and written by a severe critic of Christianity. The book uses the death-and-rebirth theme preached by white missionaries—one must die to sin and convert to Christ—but builds on this a more complex debate over exactly what must die. Through the resurrection of his African identity and culture, the hero becomes a Christ figure.[9]

On occasion, the social background of global South readers allows them to see dimensions of the text that have been largely lost in a postindustrial world. I was once talking with some West Africans about the Bible passages that made particularly good sense in an agricultural society. Not surprisingly, they mentioned the parable of the sower and the grain of wheat, but they were evidently moved by the verse about sowing in sorrow and reaping in joy. The passage comes from the short Psalm 126, which in the King James version reads as follows: "They that sow in tears shall reap in joy. He that goeth forth and weepeth, bearing precious seed, shall doubtless come again with rejoicing, bringing his sheaves with him."[10] For modern Christians anywhere around the world, these verses relate naturally to the Resurrection, and to Paul's discussion of the body sown in corruption, in 1 Corinthians 15. But why are the sowers weeping in the first place? If the question occurs at all to someone from a Western and nonagrarian background, that person might imagine some kind of *Golden Bough*–style ritual for the spirit of the corn that was to die and be reborn.

My friends, though, understood the reality of the situation. When the psalm was composed, they realized, times must have been very hard, and food short, a situation with which they could identify. People would have been desperately tempted to eat their seed corn but resisted the temptation because they knew, if they did that, they would have nothing to eat the following year. Commenting on the Near East in the 1850s, traveler W. M. Thomson remarked, "In seasons of great scarcity, the poor peasants part in sorrow with every measure of precious seed cast into the ground. It is like taking bread out of the mouths of their children; and in such times many bitter tears are actually shed over it."[11] Not only does this setting explain the verse, but the association of sowing and sorrow helps explain the very widespread mourning rituals that in the Middle East and elsewhere accompany sowing, commonly invoking some dying deity.

Forgive Us Our Debts

Another biblical theme cited far more in Southern than Northern churches is that of debt and debt forgiveness, the subject of prolific texts in both Testaments. For U.S. Christians, debt is rarely raised as a pressing religious issue, however intense the problem might be for particular households. If neither efficient nor fair, mechanisms of credit are impersonal and well regulated. But in Africa and Asia, coping with debt and credit is a vital everyday issue, for communities and for individuals. Unlike the situation in the United States, property ownership is not sufficiently widespread to make institutions such as mortgage lending commonplace or reliable.[12] People find what security they can offer—including themselves and their bodies—and at whatever interest they can obtain. In some societies, forms of debt slavery still function, while moneylenders and usurers threaten terrible physical sanctions against nonpayers. Sometimes, repayment can be made by providing young relatives as sex workers in neighboring cities. Such injustices have their parallels at the national level, as many global South nations find hopes of development thwarted by unthinkably vast debts, often incurred by larcenous past dictatorships. Debt of various kinds is, in short, a fundamental fact of life, and a basic obstacle preventing the advancement of self or society.

In this context, New Testament parables about debtors and moneylenders come to life, and we can appreciate just how much Jesus spoke about debt. Recall the parable of the unjust creditor, which Jesus tells to illustrate the need to forgive time and again. In the story, a king forgave a man who owed him the unimaginably vast sum of ten thousand talents. The forgiven man then refused to be merciful to another person who owed him a tiny sum. Hearing about this, the king repented of his generosity and threw the original debtor into jail.[13] Debt thus became a central symbol of sin, with God as the ultimate creditor. Any first-century listener knew that debt and credit were matters of everyday survival, and that the decision to grant mercy and thus to save a livelihood was a real test of generosity and virtue. That aptly describes the situation of debtors and creditors in many of the emerging Christian nations, where the creditor is still seen as a human being with a face, a person with whom one can plead or reason, as opposed to a bureaucratic institution with inflexible rules.

Not only is the debt issue prominently discussed in the Bible, but it figures centrally in the best-known Christian prayer. Most Romance languages preserve versions of the Lord's Prayer in which the "trespasses" for which we seek forgiveness are debts, a relic of the Vulgate Latin ("Et dimitte nobis *debita* nostra, sicut et nos dimittimus *debitoribus* nostris"). Spanish versions of Matthew translate the terms as *deudas* and *deudores*, the same words used in a regular commercial transaction. Even English-speaking Christians who use the King James Bible read a Lord's Prayer in which disciples ask, "And forgive us our debts, as we forgive our debtors."

For nations, too, biblical concepts such as Jubilee provide the textual foundation for the global debt forgiveness movement that mobilizes theologically conservative leaders almost as much as liberationists. In chapter 25 of Leviticus, activists find a sweeping vision of social and economic liberation, a year of unshackling in which all debts are to be forgiven, and captives freed. In turn, the concept echoes through the New Testament, especially in the Lord's Prayer. The text was once famous enough to be inscribed upon America's own Liberty Bell: "Proclaim liberty throughout all the land unto all the inhabitants thereof: it shall be a jubilee unto you; and ye shall return every man unto his possession, and ye shall return every man unto his family." Of course, the idea of Jubilee also has a central role in the African-American tradition.[14]

Liberation theologians uncover a treasure trove of such references advocating debt reduction as a fundamental component of social justice. In 1990, the flagship journal *Revista de Interpretación Bíblica Latinoamericana* devoted a special number to the theme of "Perdónanos nuestras deudas," "Forgive us our debts," seeing debt elimination as at once a practical policy and an apocalyptic sign. Apart from the Jubilee, activists turned to the debt cancellation outlined in the book of Nehemiah, in which all would have their property restored.[15] This vision of a fresh start is all the more powerful for churches that place the Old Testament on par with New. For them, the passage offers an actual policy to be pursued, rather than just a vision of apocalyptic times. If a state established in God's name was intended to liberate itself thus from time to time, why should not Christian societies today pursue the same practice? The appeal of Leviticus also raises other incidental questions. If this book and other Old Testament texts so obviously teach relevant truths in these matters—and liberating truths—why should they be rejected in matters of sexual morality?

Four Horsemen

In other ways too, global South societies are familiar with dangers and disasters that seem all but irrelevant in North America, but that would have resonated with the biblical world. To take just one nation, "the Philippines is among the many Third World countries that has seen too many funerals, too many deaths of various causes. None of our days pass without some news of massacre somewhere, death toll at a landslide accident, huge earthquakes claiming hundreds of lives, volcanic eruption tearing down houses and burying entire communities."[16] In 2004, the Western media devoted much attention to the cataclysmic tsunami that killed some two hundred thousand around the Indian Ocean, but most natural disasters in Asia and Africa receive scant notice.

The Bible's wisdom literature is so popular, in part, because of its profound sense of the transience of life. From many beloved passages in the Epistle of James, one of the most used African sermon texts is James 4:14, which seems uncannily relevant to the conditions of everyday life: "Ye know not what shall be on the morrow. For what is your life? It is even a vapor, that appeareth for a little time, and then vanisheth away." In the New International Version, the NIV, life is a mist. Echoes of this text often resurface in paraphrased form. In the Sudan, which for some forty years has suffered repeated civil wars and the vicious persecution of non-Muslims, one Christian chorus teaches the grim truth that "You are here today but tomorrow you'll be here no more / Our only hope is Jesus Christ, so receive him now."[17] In the aftermath of the 2004 tsunami, sermons in south and east Asian churches made great use of James.

Another text that speaks to a world of poverty is Job, that ultimate meditation on innocent suffering, though modern readers might ask why whole societies are allowed to suffer, rather than just individuals. South African theologian Tinyiko Sam Maluleke wrote a "Letter to Job—From Africa," in which he described the fate of Lady Africa. "Having lost everything she once had, Africa now sits on a rubbish dump outside the city gates. Africa had been victimized and raped by explorers, slave traders, colonialists and dictators born out of her own womb" and had suffered all these agonies despite her vast piety. Teresa Okure aptly calls Africa "a martyred continent."[18]

Observing the contours of poverty in recent years, African and Asian scholars turn to biblical passages that not only complain of misery and the suffering of the innocent, but specifically point to the disasters facing children. Reading in a world of child soldiers, child prostitutes, and obscene infant mortality rates, church leaders from all traditions note just how much of the Bible addresses the plight of the very young, from the despairing cry of the young Ishmael on the verge of death, to the massacre of the innocents, to the healing miracles that Elijah and Jesus performed on children. Child theology makes great sense to a church increasingly dominated by the young and poor.[19]

This sense of transience and frailty extends not just to individuals and families, but to whole nations. While global North nations certainly experience disasters, very rarely do these events threaten the existence of a society or large numbers of its people. In 2001, catastrophic terrorism in the United States killed three thousand on a single day, while the AIDS epidemic has caused hundreds of thousands of deaths since the early 1980s. At no point, though, did such calamities threaten the functioning of society, and the AIDS disaster was largely confined to particular groups and subcultures. Elsewhere in the world, though, epidemic diseases and natural disasters remain a common part of life, giving a special relevance to the biblical language of plague, drought, and famine. Even secular development workers use the language of "plague" to characterize the swarms of locusts that devastate large sections of Africa.[20]

Under such cumulative challenges, nations can literally collapse, a truly frightening idea in a world in which nationhood does so much to determine our identity. Nations disintegrate as poverty, hunger, and natural resource issues drive ethnic and political tensions, resulting in the failed states that are the nightmares of international policymakers, in Afghanistan and Somalia, Liberia and Sierra Leone. In the immense lands of the Congo, war alone has killed some four million over the past decade. Even in Latin America, we think of a country like Colombia. Since the 1940s, the country's history has been bathed in blood, marked by massacres and ethnic cleansing, by rape and kidnapping, crime and mutilation. The guerrilla wars in Peru in the 1980s and 1990s killed some sixty thousand. In turn, such situations spark refugee crises and famine emergencies.[21]

A postcolonial world appreciates the provisional character of nationhood. Realistically or not, the British and French tend to believe that their nations have always existed and will continue to do so, whatever disasters they might experience at particular times. Nor do Americans seriously contemplate the end of their national experiment. In contrast, many African and Asian countries have only existed in anything like their present form for a few decades, often emerging from long periods of colonization or foreign dominance. Against this background, it is easy to understand the Old Testament idea that a nation's existence depends upon God's favor. Southern-world Christians identify with Old Testament warnings that righteousness must prevail at the national and communal levels; that the survival of nations is in the hands of a closely observing God, who uses worldly instruments to reward or punish his peoples.

Where no earthly authority has a plausible claim on our faith, how natural it seems to assert only the absolute truth of the divine, as the standard beside which all earthly powers so conspicuously fall short. This approach gives a contemporary feel to the Hebrew prophets, who warned the people of Israel of the doom that awaited them if they forsook the God who had made them a people. In the Sudan, Marc Nikkel comments, "No OT passage is better known than Isaiah 18. . . . Survivors recall how they've seen the corpses of their kinsfolk 'left to the mountain birds of prey and to the wild animals' (v.6). Isaiah's prophecies of annihilation and hope are fulfilled today."[22] The chapter in question has such contemporary force because its geographical setting is precisely the land "beyond the rivers of Ethiopia," also giving it an application to such war-torn lands as Congo and Rwanda. Literally, the prophet seems to be writing about Africa's Christians today.

Not only particular books but whole genres come alive in the circumstances of the global South. Writing against the background of political and religious repression in China, Archie Chi Chung Lee has protested "the loss of lament." Lamentation was in antiquity a well-known genre, a literature of mourning and grief, bemoaning the fall of a state or society; it was also a mainstay of traditional Chinese culture. In the Bible, this model is represented by the Lamentations of Jeremiah. Lee, however, notes that for the West at least, lament no longer has anything like its ancient centrality, and that contemporary ignorance needs to be reversed. "The voice of the exiled and desperate community must be released in this current time of sorrow and loss so that grief-stricken and wretched people can make their own voices heard with all their power. . . . For them, the book of Lamentations has survived and, in its role as literature of survival, will continue to provide the means of survival for suffering humanity." According to a Catholic Bible commentary, "Lamentations can be considered as a prayer book for Africans"—a grim statement, but undeniably true.[23]

Being Filled

Much like Europeans in bygone centuries, many modern Africans and Asians read biblical tales of plague and famine as powerfully contemporary. Perhaps only hungry eyes can appreciate just how thoroughly images of food and feasting, eating and starving, pervade both Testaments, inevitably since the ancient Near East thoroughly understood the real danger of famine. Through-out the Bible, being filled with food is for most people an unusual prospect, as was true for most societies before the eighteenth century, including those of Western Europe. In Luke's Magnificat, Mary celebrates a radical vision of a society in which God will fill the hungry, while sending the rich away empty. When the prodigal son comes home, driven by famine, he is given a very material banquet, complete with fatted calf. In Second Temple Judaism, the messianic age was symbolized by the splendor of a great banquet, an inconceivably glorious time in which everyone would actually have enough to eat, and this banquet theme underlies the ancient Christian symbolism of the Lord's Supper, the Eucharist.

Encountering such visions of plenty has an immeasurably greater impact in a society that knows hunger than in a Western community where the most prominent food-related story of the last year or two was an alleged obesity epidemic. John Lonsdale remarks how, in much of Africa, "political power is often expressed in the imagery of the belly, of eating and being eaten, or of being famished by political failure. The Bible and the belly are each as homely as the other." A bribe, meanwhile, is commonly called a "bite," as in the Mexican *mordida*. The fascination with food shapes readings of scripture. Jean-Marc Ela writes, "Christians are celebrating the Eucharist while entire populations are vulnerable to the weapon of grain, and condemned to live on imported food products. Is the question of food essential to our faith? Of course!" The spirit of the biblical world is movingly summarized by the con-temporary grace said by rural Chinese Christians: "Today's food is not easy to come by. God gives it to us. After we eat it, we will not be sick. God pro-tects us so that we can have the next meal. He protects us so everything is prosperous and we have peace. All our family members, from young to old, need the protection from God."[24]

Nor can most African or Asian readers be complacent about the easy availability of water. The numerous biblical passages about ready supplies of water mean a great deal in modern nations that can only dream of such a luxury. Such readers share the amazed expectation of the Samaritan woman at the well, when Jesus promises her a reliable source of living water. Within a few years, perhaps half the world's people will live in countries that are water stressed.[25]

While most nations have avoided outright famine, disasters have struck particular regions over the past thirty or forty years, repeatedly in northeast-ern Africa and parts of India. In the late 1950s, China was hit by one of the worst famines in history, a manmade disaster that might have killed twenty million; two million more perished in North Korea as recently as the mid-1990s. Against this background, modern Christians can appreciate just how often famine drives the stories of the Bible, from the tale of Joseph's brothers through the late-first-century world depicted in Revelation. Some of the tales most popular in modern Africa and Asia concern Elijah and Elisha, prophets of the ninth century B.C.E., whose careers are firmly set in a time of drought and famine. Elijah miraculously prevents the rain from falling for three years, while providing unlimited food and oil for faithful followers. Still in New Testament times, it was Elijah's ability to control the rain that the Letter of James cited as the most notable sign of his power.[26]

One of the most harrowing stories of the whole Bible occurs in Elisha's time, when a woman begs the king to enforce the agreement she had made with her neighbor in response to the raging famine. First they would eat the son of one woman, then the son of another, but the other woman was reneging on the deal. Would the king not grant her justice, by ordering the second act of cannibalism? However grotesque the story, millions of modern readers can understand the desperation that lies at its center. They know that, while men can sometimes flee a famine-stricken area, women remain behind with the children.[27]

Food shortages form the subject of modern Christian hymns and writings. Ghanaian writer Afua Kuma declares:

> The famine has become severe.
> Let us go and tell Jesus!
> He is the one who
> When he raises his hands
> Gives even our enemies their share
> And our brothers bring head pans
> To carry the food away.

The radicalism of one statement can hardly be appreciated in societies that do not know famine: not only does God grant food in time of hunger, but He even pours blessings on our enemies.[28]

The prevalence of hunger and natural disaster helps explain the enormous popularity in Christian Africa and Asia of the book of Ruth, a tale of a society devastated by famine, in which women survive by depending on each other and on trusted kin. In the American context, the book attracts some interest from feminist scholars, while Ruth's plea to Naomi, "entreat me not to leave thee," is included in blessing rites for same-sex couples. In the global South, the book's interest lies in how the various characters faithfully fulfill their obligations to each other and their relatives. The book becomes a model, even a manual, for a situation that could arise all too easily. Musimbi Kanyoro writes, "The book of Ruth is loved because it has something for everyone in Africa. Africans read this book in a context in which famine, refugee status, tribal or ethnic loyalties, levirate marriages and polygamy are not ancient biblical practices but the normal realities of today." For Chinese theologian Wai Ching Angela Wong, the book fundamentally concerns the ethical treatment of strangers, exiles, and outsiders, "the problem of conflicts emerging between rival communities. . . . I always regard Ruth 1:14–17 as one of the most moving passages in the Bible. It is not only in the bonding of women that most feminists have found comfort, but also the difficult political message it entails."[29] What the North reads in moral or individualistic terms remains for the South social and communal.

Plague

The language of plague naturally thrives today, given the persistence of epidemic disease in tropical regions. Even today, scarcely noticed by the advanced world, malaria still kills some two million each year, mainly in Africa, and mainly small children. Recently, poor nations of Africa and Asia have been the chief victims of AIDS, which threatens to annihilate communities and wreak untold damage on the survivors. Some thirty million Africans are now HIV-positive, and the infection rate in nations such as Zimbabwe and Botswana is probably around 35 percent. In any given year, the disease kills around 2½ million in sub-Saharan Africa. The continent has millions of AIDS orphans, a number far beyond the capacity of traditional communities to absorb. The epidemic transforms every aspect of life. One cannot even greet a friend with the familiar "How are you?" since the person might well be laboring under a literal death sentence: you really don't want to hear the answer.[30] Since the areas worst hit by the disease are often the centers of the growing Christian churches, we can say, quite literally, that the church has AIDS.

Knowing the facts of death cannot fail to affect religious sensibilities. A sense of the transience of life is hard to convey to a Northern society in which most people confidently expect that they will die at an advanced age in a hospital or nursing home, and in which one knows that children will very probably reach maturity. But the numbers suggest a very different picture for the rest of the world. In the advanced nations of North America and Europe, life expectancy is normally in the upper seventies. In most of sub-Saharan Africa, the comparable figure is in the forties, with Malawi, Botswana, Zimbabwe, Zambia, Angola, and Mozambique in the thirties—that is, roughly half the U.S. age at death. In much of Africa, AIDS means that life expectancy figures are worse today than they were in the 1960s. Matters are still more frightful if we use the DALE system—Disability Adjusted Life Expectancy—the measure devised by the World Health Organization (WHO) to assess the years that an average person can expect to live in full health. By this standard, Euro-Americans can expect more than twice as many years of healthy life as most sub-Saharan Africans, and three times as many as the very poorest. To quote one WHO official, "Healthy life expectancy in some African countries is dropping back to levels we haven't seen in advanced countries since medieval times." Of course, Africans respond to urgent calls that they convert before they have to face death and judgment. All rational people know that life is a vapor, a mist.[31]

African Christians can scarcely imagine the horror of AIDS except in terms of a biblical plague, sometimes—as in the Old Testament—a punishment for the people's sins. In Malawi, where one-seventh of the people are HIV-positive, a typical sermon notes, "Today we have embraced AIDS. God has been sending different kinds of diseases but because people were thinking that these were little, they did not listen to preachers. Just as God did with the Egyptians, he has sent us the last plague, AIDS. People know that some of them are dying but they don't change their bad behavior. God is fed up with our sins and sending us different warnings." This sermon was delivered at the Last Hope Adventist Church, a name that acquires dreadful relevance in the circumstances. Another sermon used as its text Numbers 14:11–13, "how long will this people despise me?" in which a furious God threatens to disinherit his rebellious people, to eliminate them through pestilence, and choose a new nation as his own. The preacher warns, "Brethren, see AIDS, a disease without a cure, everywhere AIDS. That plague, that plague has come about because we despise God."[32]

Rivers of Babylon

Also recognizable from the biblical world are ethnic and tribal rivalries that can lead to deadly violence. While Americans and Europeans are no strangers to racism and religious bigotry—witness the carnage in the Balkans during the 1990s—most Northern-world churches at least preach tolerance, while ethnic divisions rarely have the deep ritual qualities that mark tribal distinctions in Africa. Reading the tale of the Good Samaritan, many Westerners have a vague impression that, then as now, a Samaritan was a kindly person with a penchant for good deeds, rather than a deeply suspect foreigner, so that the subversive element of the original parable is quite lost. In an African setting, though, tribalism can be a lethally sensitive topic, and modern analogies allow readers to understand perfectly well the gulf separating Jews and Samaritans. Instead of the first-century setting, they can imagine the story set amidst the contemporary tension between Hutu and Tutsi, between Arabs and black Africans in Sudan or Chad, between Muslims and Christians. Even in such a situation, a member of the hated enemy group behaved so wonderfully to one of your own: was he then your neighbor? Some modern African Christians find in the New Testament accounts of Samaritans practical advice for how they might learn to live with and communicate with their Muslim neighbors.[33]

In other ways too, the life conditions of global South Christians are very different from those of the Old Christendom. Exile and displacement are constant realities, in the case of forced exile, but also of mass migration, from villages to cities, from poor Southern nations to wealthy Northern lands. Though most such movement is voluntary—or at least, not an immediate response to violence or starvation—people afflicted by social and cultural disruption naturally turn to their Christian faith for assistance and protection. Among Latino Catholics, the hazardous illegal migration to the United States has given rise to a whole subculture of devotions to saints and heavenly protectors, to the Virgin of Guadalupe, to the martyred priest Toribio Romo. Many, also, turn to their New Testaments.[34]

Willingly or not, many modern Christians belong to the Church of the Uprooted. The modern prevalence of exile gives special appeal to those large sections of the Bible that concern the threat of exile, the experience of deportation and its traumatic aftermath, and the enduring racial tensions that resulted from these experiences. When evangelical leader Kefa Sempangi fled Idi Amin's regime in the late 1970s, he wrote, "Since our escape from Uganda we had felt a deep kinship with David, the fugitive king"; and with the psalms commonly attributed to him. Namibian writer Zephania Kameeta updates one familiar text—Psalm 137—thus:

> By the rivers of foreign countries we sat down as refugees
> there we wept when we remembered the land of our birth
> We stopped singing our beloved songs of liberation. . . .
> Remember Lord what the oppressors did
> The day they turned us into refugees
> Remember how they kept saying "Let us destroy them completely."

Just as gripping are the sections of the New Testament in which readers learn that all human beings are exiles, that here they have no abiding city. Reading the Letter to the Hebrews, exiled or displaced Africans learn that "without abandoning their struggle to regain home and property, they should nevertheless look ahead to 'a better and lasting possession'. . . . [W]e too should consider ourselves 'strangers and foreigners' in this world."[35]

Themes of exile fascinate Christian academics of global South origin, often themselves migrants, who have moved to Europe or North America in search of better lives and opportunities; and Psalm 137 often provides a vehicle for nostalgic longing. Writers note the paradox that, in contrast to the peoples of the Old Testament, their own exile is strictly voluntary, and the Northern Babylon at which they have arrived is a destination they have sought after for many years. Their attitudes to the shift are thus ambiguous. While the move from the Philippines or El Salvador to America might be symbolized as a journey from Canaan to Egypt, and mourned in the bitter language of psalms, the speaker rarely wants to fulfill the passionate promises of return.[36]

More directly relevant to contemporary readers, though, are the problems of ethnic and cultural identity involved in exile and migration, and in the process of globalization. Such issues have less impact on North Americans and Europeans, since it is their values that are to varying degrees spreading throughout the world, but matters are very different for the recipients of new ways of thinking and living. In trying to interpret these changes, Christians turn to those sections of the Bible that portray Jews and, later, Christians trying to exist and survive in the shadow of dominant empires and cultures, often far from their homelands. Old Testament prophets and priestly leaders struggled violently against the religious contaminations that the children of Israel brought back with them from Mesopotamian exile, and they denounced interracial marriage in terms that today are quite unnerving. Other passages are more benevolent. But materials are available for shaping contemporary discussions of identity and assimilation.

Issues of cultural survival and assimilation arose in many societies emerging from colonial rule. Writing of the Hong Kong residents who fell under Chinese rule in the 1990s, Fook-Kong Wong observes, "Like the Jewish Diaspora who returned to Jerusalem, they find that their values are not quite the same as those who never left their homeland." Were they British or Chinese? In such debates, readers turn to biblical accounts of exile, adjustment, and resistance. One such account is the book of Esther, the tale of a beautiful exile at the Persian court who conceals her Jewish identity and ultimately saves the Jewish people. As a study of multiple identities, Esther has attracted the attention of Chinese diaspora scholars.[37]

Other scholars search the book of Acts, and the cosmopolitan Mediterranean world depicted there, to understand such popular contemporary themes as migration, integration, and the limits of assimilation. In Acts, we read about the critical importance of possessing the correct credentials for citizenship, of integration problems even within religious communities, of mixed marriages, and of people needing to be skilled in multiple languages.

Such passages sound wonderfully modern when read in the modern Chinese Diaspora, no less than for Korean, Filipino, or Vietnamese Christians.[38]

A Minority Faith

Issues of identity and coexistence become critical as Christians are ever more likely to live alongside members of other major religions, whether Hindus, Buddhists, or Muslims. Of necessity, this fact forces Christians to think differently about their faith than communities that for centuries have seen themselves as part of a "Christian world." For one thing, the demands of coexistence help explain the deep conservatism of global South churches on moral issues. African and Asian Christians have plenty of reasons not to yield to Northern-world attitudes on homosexuality, but their views are constantly reinforced by their neighbors of other faiths. In Africa, more sympathetic Christian attitudes in these matters would cause a destructive rift with Islam, which remains implacably opposed on gay issues. Ironically, the quest for tolerance and coexistence between faiths contributes to what liberal Americans regard as intolerant attitudes on matters of morality.

Not only do Christians increasingly live in the global South, but they are more likely to live in countries in which they experience marginal status. In much of Africa, it is plausible to envisage a Christian nation, or at least to think of Christians living in clearly defined communities, strictly demarcated from other religious groups. The situation is very different in south and east Asia, where the absolute number of Christians is not far short of the total in Africa, but spread among a much larger population. Some three billion people live in this region, roughly half the human race, and the Christian proportion of the population is at most 10 percent, even if we accept the most optimistic estimates. Christians make up between 5 and 10 percent of China's population, 3 to 5 percent of India's. In Indonesia, Vietnam, Malaysia, and Taiwan, likewise, Christians are very much in the minority, with between 6 and 10 percent of the national totals. Only the Philippines has an overwhelming Christian majority, with South Korea perhaps moving in that direction.[39]

In contrast to older Western assumptions, contemporary Christians often constitute minority populations—in most of Asia, very small minorities— and in many cases, Christianity appeals to socially marginal groups; to the poor, to tribal populations, to those of low caste or of no caste. Even when Christians draw from established middle-class or elite groups, their history and culture clearly mark them off from the ancient roots of those societies. To be a Christian in much of Asia is to experience the status of aliens, of social exiles within their own lands.

In seeking to understand this minority status, Christians find in the Bible several possible strategies for survival and growth. For some Christians, minority status and discrimination promote a siege mentality and encourage separatism. As we have seen, biblical texts can be used to portray other religions as utterly damnable and forbidding any kind of cooperation. Persecution and religious conflict can inspire deep interreligious hostility, which finds expression in apocalyptic texts, while Christians of low-caste origins see in Jesus' message a welcome condemnation of the hierarchies and rituals of contemporary Asian religions. But other modern Christians explore the Bible in order to justify coexistence and cooperation between faiths and cultures. This last current of thought deserves stressing in light of the common Western assumption that literalist or fundamentalist religion must be automatically intolerant and that the upsurge of Christianity must inevitably lead to interreligious conflict.

Of necessity, attitudes change as religions learn more about each other's beliefs. Traditional ideas of Christian mission sought to liberate non-Christians from their error, and for many believers, it scarcely mattered whether the infidels were Hindus or Buddhists, pagans or idol worshipers. But should condemnations of paganism extend to the major world religions, with their ancient scriptures? Hinduism and Buddhism are great world religions, which have, to varying degrees, shaped the consciousness of entire cultures and nations. If Asian Christians reject those religions as diabolical, they are opting for an absolute secession from society. When modern Christian thinkers consider these faiths, they find it difficult to believe that God was not in Asia before the missionaries brought the gospel. In various ways, it seems, perhaps the Spirit was working in the other religions. As Joel Carpenter observes, "Questions about Christian identity in plural settings and queries about the presence of God in the pre-Christian past . . . pervade Southern and Eastern Christian thought."[40]

Interactions with other religions have consequences when we read Bible passages that consign non-Christians to perdition. As Dickson Kazuo Yagi points out, "The Japanese Christian cannot blind himself to the fate of the 99.2 percent of his people who die without Christ. Can the good fortune of the Christian 0.8 percent of the population occupy 100 percent of the concerns of Yellow Theology?" Based on his experience of southeast Asia, Daniel Arichea warns against "consigning to hell two thirds of the world's population."[41] Should all rival faiths be seen in terms of the prophets of Baal? Should any?

Practical issues of survival apart, it is tempting for Christians to see their own religion as one voice among many, to stress commonalities with the mainstream Asian religions. This approach has sparked controversy in the

Roman Catholic Church, which has bitter memories of mishandling interfaith relations in bygone years. If church authorities had responded more
generously in the seventeenth and eighteenth centuries, perhaps China and
Japan would have become bastions of global Christianity, instead of perse-
cuting the religion to the verge of extinction. In modern times, liberal theologians have engaged so wholeheartedly in interreligious dialogue that they face
charges of syncretism and of abandoning the specifically Christian claims
to truth. The Vatican has criticized some Asian-Catholic thinkers for their
overdaring explorations in these matters. In one long-running conflict in the
1990s, Sri Lankan Fr. Tissa Balasuriya earned excommunication for (among
other things) protesting against doctrines of original sin, denying that bap-
tism is essential for salvation, and claiming that other religions offer valid
paths to God. All these ideas grew out of his interactions with other faiths,
especially Buddhism.[42]

But even when they remain within the fold, many mainstream Catholic
leaders in Asia hold views about other religions that are considerably more
liberal than those of the Vatican. Asian theologians commonly hold that
Christianity needs to engage in a triple dialogue—with other religions, with
other cultures, and (throughout the process) with the poor. And such views
are echoed by bishops' conferences and by regional church synods. One
Japanese bishop has said that "Mother Teresa did not impose Christianity
but respected other religions, and Asian churches are influenced by her principle. We share that philosophy with her. An absolute theory of Christianity
doesn't work in Asia, and we won't be able to work to save people with that
idea." We should be cautious in assuming that such inclusive liberalism necessarily characterizes the ranks of the ordinary faithful: the Latin American
experience in the 1970s and 1980s reminds us just how far out of step prelates
and theologians can be with the laity. But for many Catholics at least, the fact
of minority status has inspired a fundamental rethinking of Christian claims
to unique status.[43]

Such liberal approaches transform attitudes to mission. Newer Protestant
and Pentecostal churches in Africa and Asia are still deeply committed to
making disciples of all nations; and their missionaries can be found in all parts
of the world. Some Christians—especially Chinese and Koreans—believe
that the missionary imperative extends to converting the Muslim lands of
the Middle East, at whatever risk to their lives. Optimistically, they hope to
appeal to a common Asian identity, spreading a gospel originally designed
for "Orientals." Yet troubling memories of imperialism raise doubts about
the idea of any people's going to convert others to its own superior point of
view, and of trying to discredit older religions. For Catholics—at least for
church leaders and academics—mission should take the form of confessing or

proclaiming one's own Christian faith, of persuading outsiders by example, and of showing how Christianity meshes with the established faiths of a region.[44]

Coexistence and dialogue are justified from biblical texts. Chen Nan Jou, for instance, praises the universalist message of the book of Jonah, in which non-Jews are repeatedly treated as decent and sympathetic, and in which the Gentile city of Nineveh accepts God's judgment. Also tempting are the prophetic passages that envisage all nations coming to Jerusalem at the triumphant end of history, not necessarily accepting Christianity in its fullness, any more than early Christians felt the need to accept Judaism. Conversion need not mean abandoning one's old faith as false. Even Paul's speech on the Areopagus, with its condemnation of idolatry, provides a foundation for Christians trying to speak to other religions, to show that ideas in foreign cultures form a foundation for the Christian revelation. Such modern Christians are engaged in very much the same tasks that faced their ancient predecessors, who had to incorporate the upstart Christian literature into the dominant cultures of ancient Greece and Rome.[45]

Over the past half-century, global South scholars have stressed the parallels between the Christian scriptures and those of other faiths. Sometimes, this can be done with great plausibility, as when the Gospel of John is read in the context of Indian mysticism or set aside the almost contemporary *Bhagavad Gita*. Some modern Asian Christians see the Jesus portrayed in the Gospel of Thomas as a mystical instructor in the Asian mode, a guru, and find this idea more appealing than the imperialist-tainted image of the cosmic Lord. Other theologians attempt the same comparative task for Confucianism and other spiritualities rooted in China. In a book entitled *What Has Jerusalem to Do with Beijing?*, K. K. Yeo offers chapter titles such as "*Li* and *Jen* (Torah and Spirit) in Romans" and "The *Ming* of *T'ien* (Will of God) in Amos and Confucius."[46]

Wisdom Speaks to Wisdom

But it is the wisdom texts that offer the most alluring linkages between religious traditions. Biblical wisdom literature grew out of social settings that are immediately recognizable today, in their intense social stratification, in the omnipresence of poverty, and, above all, in the transience of life. Because they speak so exactly to real-world conditions, texts like James appeal not only to millions of global South Christians, but also to members of other faiths who share the same social and economic circumstances. In trying to formulate an Asian-Christian theology, Jesuit thinker Aloysius Pieris argues that any "Asian context" must first take account of two inseparable realities, namely "overwhelming poverty [and] multifaceted religiosity," and wisdom literature speaks to both aspects. Its breadth of appeal gives a special meaning to the familiar classification of James as a catholic or universal epistle.[47]

James has very little that would offend the strictest Muslim, while much of the content echoes the Quran. Particularly appealing is the letter's attitude toward the future and its assumption that all worldly conditions are transient. So uncertain is life that James specifically warns against even saying that you are planning to do something or to travel somewhere, because you do not know if you will live to do it. Any such plans should be accompanied by the provisional phrase "If God wills," an exact parallel to the Arab-Muslim custom of inserting "Inshallah" when expressing any plan or intention. In Latin America, the equivalent phrase, and a sentiment much heard, is "Si Dios quiere." James portrays God as "compassionate and merciful," a familiar Muslim characterization (5:11). Not surprisingly, the epistle has been proposed as a basis for missionary inroads—for Christians seeking to convert Muslims and vice versa. Just as plausibly, it offers common ground for interreligious dialogue.[48]

James acquires its greatest value as a bridge between faiths in a Buddhist context. In 1974, Kosuke Koyama saw the letter as an invaluable tool in his quest for a distinctively Asian manifestation of Christianity. Drawing upon his experiences as a missionary to Thailand, Koyama advocated a popular-oriented water-buffalo theology that could speak to the overwhelmingly poor masses who were unacquainted with Christian tradition. He imagines welcoming the apostle James to Thailand, where his epistle fits so well into traditional concerns, so much so that it reads like a translation of a traditional Buddhist sutra.[49]

In so many ways, James speaks appealingly to an Asian audience. As Koyama says, "[Y]ou are very good in the use of picture language. . . . These images remain with us." Just as important, James speaks to familiar religious concepts, particularly transience: "All decays! All is transient!" He also praises detachment and self-control. James makes it clear that evil stems from within the individual, from misdirected desires and passions that must be combated, and that anger and intemperate speech give rise to much conflict. "'Bridle your tongue,' your letter says to us. Right indeed!" As in many premodern cultures, James knows the very high value that attaches to speech, and the vital necessity of judging one's words. As one recent African commentary on James notes, "From the African point of view the words of 3:1–12, 4:11–12 call for special reflection. Here we are reminded of the importance of words in African communities. The word can be a medicine but it can also be a poison." Also reflecting the values of traditional societies, the apostle praises the virtues of slowness—"listeners should be slow to speak, and slow to become angry." As a Thai audience might remark, "We like this word 'slow'," all the more so as society modernizes and accelerates. And finally, religion must be judged by how far it encourages good works, by its active commitment to the needs of others.[50]

Supporting the notion of James's appeal to Buddhists, the current Dalai Lama provided an admiring introduction for a recent reprinting of the text. He finds strong linkages between James and the Tibetan Buddhist genre of *lojong* or mind training—a term that could serve as an excellent alternative name for the wisdom genre. Like Koyama, the Dalai Lama dwells on James's praise of the virtues of slowness, "be swift to hear, slow to speak, slow to wrath." This was "the most poignant verse of the entire letter," he writes. The declaration that "your life is a vapor" "beautifully captured" the basic and seemingly universal doctrine of transience.[51]

Of course, Koyama was suggesting not that James was a crypto-Buddhist, but rather that the epistle rings true for Asian societies marked by extreme disparities of poor and rich, and by rapid social change. These commonalities have if anything become even more obvious since Koyama first published his book in the 1970s. Modern southeast Asians have witnessed their societies being transformed by globalization and modernization, and for some years, many felt that their nations were destined for inexorable growth. Yet, as Pacific Rim nations found in the late 1990s, such growth can halt suddenly, causing untold social wreckage. At such times, wisdom literature is very appealing.

Its awareness of transience, deception, and self-deception explains the contemporary appeal of Ecclesiastes (Qoheleth), another book with what seems like a highly modern social setting. Like James, it too was written in circumstances of rapid social change and wildly uneven economic development, when modernity and social progress meant relaxing older cultural norms to accommodate a foreign-based global order. One modern commentator remarks, "The situation in Jerusalem presupposed by Ecclesiastes is strikingly similar to many aspects of the situation in Indonesia today, where a culture of resignation prevails both for the discarded poor and the vulnerable middle class." Yet then as now, public protest was futile and dangerous: "Curse not the king, no not in thy thought; and curse not the rich in thy bedchamber: for a bird of the air shall carry the voice, and that which hath wings shall tell the matter." Living in such a society demands special skills, forcing the wise person to understand its pervasive deceptions. Accordingly, "the quietly accommodating, passionless sage lived in awe of a silent, distant, perplexing, unpredictable and thus totally free deity."[52]

In a world of constant change and decay, the wise person maintains detachment, and modern Asian-Christian thinkers see this basic insight as a lost element of Jesus' message. Indian Jesuit Michael Amaldoss argues, "In

Asia, Jesus would have been seen as a Sage, who had realized in his own life the readiness for total self-gift, even unto death. . . . He was a wanderer, a *sannyasi*, who had no roots because he belonged to everyone everywhere, a pilgrim always on the move taking one more step, in the company of many others, on the way to the kingdom." Perhaps, Amaldoss suggests, such wisdom-rooted images of Jesus offer the best chance of spreading the Christian mission in Asia.[53]

Its apparent worldliness can make Ecclesiastes an embarrassment to some Western Christians. In Thailand, for instance, it was one of the last books of the Bible to be translated. Yet as Thai Christian leader Seree Longunpai points out, this reluctance was ill-placed, as the book acquired a significant following among those with a Theravada Buddhist background. For such an audience, the portrait that the author gives of himself, the world-weary aristocrat, often recalls the image of Prince Gautama; and the book's teachings suggest Buddhist doctrines. In a world of social deprivation and the decay of traditional standards, such an image is attractive.[54]

The global enthusiasm for wisdom literature offers an ironic commentary on older missionary expectations about the kinds of Christian teaching that could expect to be received most warmly outside the bounds of traditional Christendom. Surely, they felt, people would respond most warmly to the ethical splendor of the Sermon on the Mount, or the exalted mysticism of the Gospel of John; and both texts have their appeal. Few, though, could have predicted the warm reception accorded to such seemingly prosaic volumes as Proverbs, Ecclesiastes, and James.

Health and Wealth

Most inhabitants of the "next Christendom" truly are, at present, the wretched of the earth, often poor and persecuted. Yet withdrawal and passivity are by no means the only solutions that churches offer in the face of deprivation. Around the world, many highly successful churches teach some variant of the gospel of prosperity, the controversial belief that Christians have the right and duty to seek prosperity in this world, to obtain health and wealth here and now. Now, this idea is certainly found in some American churches. The successful Atlanta-based evangelist Creflo A. Dollar argues, "The Bible makes it so very clear: Preach the Gospel to the poor. What's the Gospel to the poor? You don't have to be poor anymore! . . . Poverty is a curse. We have tried to equate humility and poverty, but it's just not sound. It's a curse. Jesus came to set us free from the curse of the law. Sin, death, sickness, and poverty are parts of that curse."[55] The Christian quest for personal success and prosperity was exalted in Bruce Wilkinson's 2001 blockbuster

The Prayer of Jabez, which sold some eight million copies in its first two years in print. Yet few sizable denominations preach this message, which many regard with great suspicion. For critics, the prosperity gospel suggests something like a superstitious cargo cult from an anthropology text: if we follow these rituals, divine forces will bring us rich gifts. Yet as people have recognized at least since the time of the book of Job, virtue and faith often go unrewarded in this world, and the ungodly do, regularly, flourish.

But promises of prosperity underlie the success of major African and Asian churches, those congregations for which even the term "megachurch" seems like understatement. The world's largest church is reputedly the Central Full Gospel Church in Seoul, South Korea, which claimed a half-million members during the 1990s. The church teaches "the threefold blessings of Christ, i.e., health, prosperity, and salvation," as promised in 3 John 2 ("Beloved, I wish above all things that thou mayest prosper and be in health, even as thy soul prospereth"). Prosperity-oriented South Korean pastors read the Beatitudes in the Gospel of Matthew (5:3–10) as literal promises, with definite this—worldly relevance: " 'Blessed are the meek, for they will inherit the earth' (literally interpreted as gaining land ownership); and 'Blessed are those who hunger and thirst for righteousness, for they will be filled.' They also maintained that illness, poverty, business failure, or any other misfortune is simply due to sin and spiritual impurity."[56] Such readings represent almost a reversal of conventional readings of the Beatitudes, in which the blessings of the meek and hungry suggest that these states of life epitomize Christian virtues.

For prosperity teachers, such conditions are instead curses to be ended by faith, and ended soon. Nigeria's successful evangelist David Oyedepo claims a divine mandate to "make My people rich." So enthusiastic has been the response to this message that since the late 1990s, he has built the amazing Faith Chapel, which seats fifty thousand. Prosperity preachers find promises of wealth throughout the Bible. Paul Gifford argues that, for Ghana's churches, "The Bible functions primarily as a repository of narratives, overwhelmingly of the miraculous, about (in what appears to be their order of importance) Abraham, Joseph, Elijah and/or Elisha, David, Daniel, Joshua, Moses and Job." The perceived Africanness of his story may account for the preeminence of Abraham, especially since the Pauline letters so often make him a pivotal figure in emerging Christian theology. As understood in the prosperity churches, the story of Abraham tells how rich material rewards followed faithful observance of a covenant and the fulfillment of a divine promise. Joseph lived a classic rags-to-riches, or rather prison-to-palace, story while David rose from shepherd boy to king.[57]

Across Africa, the same texts bolster the gospel of prosperity, the promise of rewards to come in this life. Of course, 3 John 2 is employed, as is Psalm 91, which, as we will see, is a very popular text in healing, exorcism, and spiritual warfare. But prosperity doctrines also ground themselves in other passages. The third chapter of Galatians promises the "blessing of Abraham," which prosperity churches interpret in strictly material terms. In Mark, Jesus promises, "There is no man that hath left house, or brethren, or sisters, or father, or mother, or wife, or children, or lands, for my sake, and the gospel's, But he shall receive an hundredfold now in this time."[58] In 2 Corinthians 9, Paul explicitly says that giving generously will bring rich rewards.

From the gospels, perhaps the most widely quoted verse is John 10:10, "I am come that they might have life, and that they might have it more abundantly," which is a mainstay for churches across the theological spectrum. Largely drawing on this verse, the image of Jesus as life giver and source of life is a dominant aspect in African Christology. Grant LeMarquand calls this "perhaps the most important single New Testament verse in African exegesis," and it is also much quoted in Asia.[59] The word "life" is not necessarily used in terms of material well-being alone, but that sense is usually present. In a world in which life is so short and uncertain, the words imply an overwhelming promise, and the relevance to prosperity teachings is evident.

Faith gospel believers often cite the short book of the prophet Malachi, a text with a curious history in the canon. In the Jewish tradition, Malachi was simply one of the minor prophets, and the text does not occupy any privileged place. Early Christians, however, were excited by what seemed like explicit messianic prophecies, and they placed the book at the end of what they would call the Old Testament. Malachi was thus presented as the culmination of the Hebrew tradition, which would be fulfilled in Christ. This pivotal role is still more obvious in Protestant Bibles, since Protestants reject the apocryphal or Deutero-canonical books accepted by Catholics. In a Protestant Bible— such as the King James—Malachi is the last book that the reader encounters before turning directly to the gospels. In this context, it becomes a proto-gospel, reminiscent of the far more substantial messianic passages in the book of Isaiah. Zephania Kameeta argues, "The Book of Malachi can rightly be seen as a bridge whereupon we cross, in our faith, from the Old to the New Covenant."[60] As such, Malachi's words carry special modern relevance, whether the issue at hand is liberation theology (Malachi 4:1–2) or the possibility of achieving material blessings in this life.

Once Malachi is given this awesome status, the reader pays special attention to its rules for living, which strongly emphasize giving God what is rightfully His, specifically in tithes and offerings. Christian churches around the world—North and South—use these passages to encourage believers to give according to their means, and ideally, to tithe. Prosperity-oriented churches, however, place special importance on the reciprocal obligations presented in these texts. God's people are sternly forbidden from cheating on offerings—literally, from robbing God—and such behavior brings a curse on individuals and communities. In return for their honest dealings, though, God will fully meet his terms of the covenant: He will "open you the windows of heaven, and pour you out a blessing, that there shall not be room enough to receive it." We encounter such passages repeatedly in accounts of African-Christian practice, especially in Pentecostal and charismatic churches. Evangelist Judy Mbugua reports how wealth made her so overconfident that she became slack in her tithing. The result was a series of disasters, problems, and family illnesses, which ended only when the family resumed their full church offerings. "Since God took me through that lesson, whatever happens, my cheque for tithe is always first."[61]

Problems of Prosperity

At its worst, the gospel of prosperity permits corrupt clergy to get away with virtually anything. Not only can they coerce the faithful to pay their obligations through a kind of scriptural terrorism, but the belief system allows them to excuse malpractice. If the pastor drives a limousine, this is only just recompense for his outstanding faith. And critics must either be lacking in their faith, or else they serve as agents of evil. Elmer Gantry figures exist in all regions, and in all faiths. Euro-American liberals, alarmed at the rise of vast new conservative and orthodox Christian populations in the global South, can point to the "health and wealth" approach to suggest that the emerging Christianity is at its heart shallow and naïve. A U.S. journalist characterizes the message of London-based Nigerian pastor Matthew Ashimolowo as "a blend of Corinthians and Hallmark, gospel truth and pop psychology, rendered in the style of a convention center motivational speech." Recently Ashimolowo's ministry has been hit by scandal, as an official investigation found "serious misconduct and mismanagement" in its financial affairs. "Among benefits he received was a £120,000 birthday party, of which £80,000 went on a Mercedes."[62]

The materialism promoted by prosperity teachings, and attributed to the scriptures, is as troubling to many African and Asian leaders as to their North American counterparts. In Nigeria, journalist Chris Ngwodo writes, "The now prevalent free market capitalist brand of Christianity has as its purveyors, the *nouveau riche* smooth talking prophets of profit peddling a feel good gospel of greed. The competition for the hearts and minds of the poor and the gullible is so intense that self-promotion and marketing is being taken to outrageous heights. With each TV and radio jingle, each banner, poster and handbill, the next anointed man of God struggles to outdo the last by making even more brazen claims. The damage being done to the Christian witness is incalculable." More briefly, the Catholic archbishop of Lagos complains, "The quickest and easiest way to make money in Nigeria is to carry a Bible on Sunday and start preaching." Ghana's chief justice denounces the many churches that serve as "profit-making ventures, feeding on the ignorance and plight of the population. . . . Leaders of some these churches have an exaggerated opinion about themselves and convince their congregation to accept their adulterated word in place of what is in the Bible." Another Ghanaian leader, Baffour Amoa, scoffs at the idea that failure in life results from a lack of faith: "Those who say we are poor through our own fault and guilt speak from ignorance—if they knew anything of our history they wouldn't propound such cheap arguments."[63]

Yet matters are not quite as simple as this account would suggest, nor as bad. While the megachurches and revivals cannot fail to attract attention, especially from visiting journalists, they represent only a small portion of the continuing Christian practice and worship. Nor should we forget that, however sincere their complaints, leaders of old-established churches have a vested interest in painting their prosperity-oriented rivals in the bleakest and most mercenary terms, precisely because they are such successful competitors for the souls of the faithful. In the common parlance, one reason the upstart churches are so hated is that they are such effective sheep stealers.

On the positive side, some megachurches focus primarily on piety rather than prosperity, and most prosperity preachers take care to integrate their teaching into conventional Christian and specifically evangelical frameworks. Many offer forms of deliverance from poverty that are incontestably valuable to their congregations. Firmly convinced of the evils of debt—"debt is like bodily sin"—many charismatic churches teach sternly practical lessons in avoiding debt, forcing believers to acquire practical skills of budgeting and saving. As David Maxwell shows, the deliverance taught by Pentecostal and independent churches often focuses on the resocialization of young males, who are taught values of thrift, fidelity, sobriety, self-restraint, and responsibility, part of what in Latin America has been well termed a "reformation of machismo." The experience of Victorian England and North America suggests that such a reorientation of values can have dramatic effects in reducing poverty, not to mention laying long-term foundations for a working civil society.[64]

Also, many of the prosperity preachers themselves are well aware of the temptations of get-rich-quick teaching, and they urge that material blessings must be used for the good of society. Bishop Oyedepo has said, "I tell people to quit looking for cheap money because it will cheapen your destiny. I tell my congregation that they must learn to live for others. We have been anointed as change agents for Africa. This anointing is not given to you just so you can feed your family—it is to make you a blessing to the world."[65]

A Gospel of Poverty

Furthermore, before dismissing the health-and-wealth tradition as pure materialism, indeed as sub-Christian, we have to understand the wider context of extreme poverty, a world in which it seems impossible to survive without miracles. Just to take Nigeria, a country that abounds in prosperity churches and crusades, consider the city of Lagos, with its fifteen million people. Conditions are at their absolute worst in "dangerous, volatile and unhealthy" sections such as Ajegunle, "Jungle City," which now contains one million residents, with a population density higher than Calcutta. To quote one local activist, "Everyone here wakes up in anger. . . . The frustration of being alive in a society like this is excruciating. People find it very hard and it is getting worse. Day in, day out, poor people from all over Africa arrive in this place, still seeing Lagos as the land of opportunity. . . . There is extortion at every point. Only one in ten people have regular work." "The main growth businesses" in such ghettos are "gangs, and evangelical churches which promise a better life." And one could easily point to similarly desperate sections of Kinshasa, Nairobi, Soweto, and fifty other megacities of the contemporary global South. Even for middle-class believers, it can seem like a miracle when public services operate according to plan, when electricity is available, when paychecks arrive loosely on time. One's fate and one's prosperity are in the hands of God. Observing contemporary South Africa, journalist Roger Cohen writes, "Planning is not for the poor. Things happen; adjustments are made; life of a sort goes on until it ends."[66]

First World residents today can rarely imagine the sense of powerlessness and dependence created by living in a very poor society—though historically, we are not in fact that far removed from such conditions. Throughout the early modern period, European churches and church leaders often had to find spiritual means of responding to plague and pestilence, and some great saints owe their reputations to their conspicuous heroism at such times, their willingness both to visit the sick and to perform great public acts of penance. Epidemics posed a continuing threat until the public health reforms of the mid-nineteenth century, but other threats of cataclysm continued much later. In the 1930s, starvation was a real threat to the poorest in many Western nations, including in the United States, while just sixty years ago, Europeans knew the four horsemen all too well. If matters had worked out only a little differently, if U.S. governments had retreated into isolationism, then post–World War II Europe could have lost tens of millions to famine. That modern

Euro-Americans can regard themselves as so distant from the threat of famine or plague, can afford the luxury of expressing so little awareness of the food supply, represents an amazing act of communal amnesia, a triumph of hope over experience. The fragile nature of First World prosperity is occasionally brought home to us by natural disasters such as Hurricane Katrina, which in 2005 wrecked the city of New Orleans.

Since 2001, Americans have been understandably alarmed at the prospect that terrorists might launch biological or chemical attacks on U.S. soil. Many Africans and Asians, though, are less than startled at the prospect of a society ravaged by epidemics and random violence, deprived of adequate food supplies, unable to trust the drinking water, subject to ever more oppressive policing and internal security. For much of the world's population, such conditions sound fairly normal. As they might respond to such a vision: what else is new? Lacking a sense of the fragility of social and economic arrangements, Euro-Americans can scarcely understand the sense of direct dependence on divine favor that has characterized virtually all human societies before very modern times.

However much observers might attack the prosperity churches—and they rarely lack ammunition to do so—the promise of material blessings does raise provocative questions about more mainstream Christian theologies. Few mainline churches in Europe or North America would dream of promising health and wealth, which they would regard as a vulgarization of the faith. At the same time, though, they do not pursue their critique to what would seem to be the logical course, of offering their congregations an enticing message of "sickness and poverty." Rather, they fully agree with the prosperity churches that health and wealth are desirable goals, but that realistically, such blessings can only be obtained through secular means, through hard work, thrift, wise investment, and access to good medicine. Health-and-wealth churches assuredly exaggerate the potential role of prayer and godly behavior in securing material prosperity, but they might well respond by asking if Euro-American mainline churches allow any serious belief whatever that prayer can shape one's material conditions. Are Christian critics of "prosperity" arguing that faith and prayer are absolutely unconnected from material realities? Why then do most or all incorporate prayers for well-being into their services and liturgies?

In such matters, ordinary African or Asian believers are not too far from the mindset of the biblical worlds they read about, in which there is a strong presumption that God will reward his faithful, in this world as well as the next. Kefa Sempangi describes the expectation that religion must, at least to some extent, cater to people's needs for simple survival. For Africans, he argues, "A religion is true if it *works*, if it meets *all* the needs of the people.

A religion that speaks only to man's soul and not to his body is not true. Africans make no distinction between the spiritual and the physical. . . . If the gospel you are preaching does not speak to human needs, it is useless. It cannot compete with the witch doctor and the gods."[67] Even the book of Job explains that after all his agonies, "the LORD blessed the latter end of Job more than his beginning," pouring upon him material blessings and rich possessions.

For a Northern world that enjoys health and wealth to a degree scarcely imagined by any previous society, it is perilously easy to despise believers who associate divine favor with full stomachs or access to the most meager forms of schooling or health care; who seek miracles in order to flourish, or even survive. The Prosperity Gospel is an inevitable by-product of a church containing so many of the very poorest.

✝ 5 ✝

GOOD AND EVIL

We are all here in this church because we have found healing here. But for this church, the great majority of us here assembled would not be alive today. That is the reason why we are here.

Preacher of the Mosama Disco Christo Church

For many African and Asian Christians, familiarity with the New Testament world extends to their understanding of evil and sickness. As in the early church, much of global South Christianity today is a healing religion par excellence, with a strong belief in the objective existence of evil, and (commonly) a willingness to accept the reality of demons and the diabolical. Biblical texts and passages that the South makes central are seen by many Northern churches as marginal, symbolic, or purely historical in nature.

As remarked earlier, the North-South divide is not absolute, and some Euro-American Christians accept theories of the diabolic and demonic, of supernatural warfare and spiritual healing. Yet most Northern-world Christians share the bemusement, the mockery, with which the more secular-minded regard such manifestations. For post-Enlightenment Christians in the West, the demonic elements in the New Testament mean so little that they are scarcely even an embarrassment anymore. Many Westerners read over such passages and attribute them to a long-departed stage of scientific development. Most Northern readers today would label believers in demons and witchcraft irredeemably premodern, prescientific, and probably preliterate; and such beliefs would cast doubt on believers' claims to an authentic or intelligent religion.

Yet the supernatural approach certainly harks back to the ancient roots of Christianity. To read the gospels is to make the intimate acquaintance of demons and demonic forces. Arguing for a social justice approach to Christianity, Jim Wallis rightly points out that excising references to "the poor" leaves very little of the biblical text intact. But by the same principle, precious little is left of the New Testament after we purge all mentions of angels, demons, and spirits. Shorn of healing and miraculous cures, the four gospels would be a slim pamphlet indeed.[1]

For the earliest followers of Jesus—and presumably for Jesus himself —healing and exorcism were essential components of his proclamation. In his acts of healing, Jesus was not just curing individuals, but trampling diabolical forces underfoot, and the signs and wonders represented visible and material tokens of Christ's victory over very real forces of evil. Leaders of the early church carried on this tradition. One landmark in the history of Trinitarian doctrine is the creed proclaimed by the third-century saint Gregory Thaumaturgus, theologian and mystic: that document is a major source for the Nicene Creed. Yet Gregory's name, "wonder worker," recalls the chief basis for his fame, as a singularly gifted exorcist and healer, who repeatedly overcame demons and pagan deities. In turn, that record of accomplishments in spiritual combat added vastly to the credibility of his Trinitarian doctrines, which he reportedly received in a vision. Among other accomplishments, Gregory was said to be the first individual in history to receive an apparition of the Virgin Mary. Describing the Christian message first brought to Europe and the Roman frontier lands, Peter Brown comments that "Christians worshipped the one high God; but unlike modern post-Enlightenment Christians, who are wary of the notion of a universe crowded with inter-mediary beings, they positively gloried in the closeness of invisible guides and protectors. . . . They did not carry around in their heads the empty skies of [modern European] missionary Christianity."[2]

Under Northern eyes, such demonological readings raise troubling ques-tions about the future of Christianity. Yet a Christian worldview that acknowl-edges supernatural evil does not disqualify itself from active participation in worldly struggles, including movements for far-reaching social and economic transformation. Also, we have to situate emerging Christianity in its social and intellectual context. Whatever their spiritual truth—whatever their fidelity to Christian tradition—supernatural approaches can be valuable in moving societies away from pernicious traditional superstitions. For instance, offer-ing distinctively Christian solutions to witchcraft helps disarm the sometimes bloody practices of anti-witchcraft rituals. In a relatively short time, the new Christian emphasis on prayer and Bible reading defuses the fatalism inherent in a traditional system based on notions such as witchcraft, curses, and the power of ancestors. Instead, Christians are taught to rely on faith, and on the role of the individual, who is no longer a slave to destiny or fate. By treating older notions of spiritual evil seriously, Christians are leading an epochal cultural revolution.

Facing Evil

Overwhelmingly, global South churches teach a firm belief in the existence of evil and in the reality of the devil; and that is especially true of Pentecostal and charismatic churches. The frequent disasters that befall the world's poorer nations give ample opportunity to debate the issue of the roots of evil. To quote Olusegun Obasanjo, "Doubting the existence of the devil or Satan is like doubting the existence of sin. Noticing the influence and the effect of occultism, esotericism and secret cults in our society and particularly in our institutions of higher learning, we can hardly deny the existence of demonic or devilish beings."[3] The views gain significance when we consider their source: since 1999, Obasanjo has been president of Nigeria, one of the two most important countries in Africa.

Similar ideas flourish in the strictly mainstream churches. In 2003, the (Roman Catholic) *African Ecclesial Review* published a special number on "Evil Practices in Africa." After listing the horrors facing the continent—all the wars, massacres, crime, and corruption—the editorial declared that the problems could be tracked back to "narcissistic and irresponsible people who seek at all costs instant wealth and pleasure. Hence, the perpetrators of these evil deeds are agents of the devil."[4]

While human sinfulness can be invoked to explain acts of war, genocide, and ethnic cleansing, traditional notions of evil also explain natural disasters. One test of faith came with the catastrophic tsunami in 2004. Some churches in the region responded in modern and secular form, urging collective action against global warming, but many smaller communities offered supernatural explanations. The leader of one Nigerian independent church, God's Kingdom Society, commented that "the Holy Bible shows that Satan is responsible for the troubles that afflict the world." Citing the book of Job, he argued that the Devil "makes people believe that God is the cause of their ills and thereby influences them to reproach their maker. . . . God does not act without first giving warning to the people and . . . He does not punish the just and unjust together."[5]

If the works of the devil are so easy to discern in such a cosmic act, then it is scarcely surprising that they are so readily traced in everyday matters, in sickness and misfortune. In 1998, Honduras was devastated by Hurricane Mitch, which killed over ten thousand. Generally, Hondurans believed that God sent the storm to punish a nation overwhelmed by corruption, drug trafficking, and witchcraft. However, it was not just the hurricane that attracted such explanations. "Many saw [Hurricane] Mitch as a punishment sent by God because they *commonly* interpret sickness, the loss of a job, and other setbacks as interventions by an angry God."[6]

Pagan Memories

In much of Africa and Asia, the ready attribution of evil to powerful spiritual forces reflects the continuing influence of pagan and animist beliefs, and we must remember what a recent presence Christianity is in these regions. In the lands that would become Nigeria, for instance, just between 1900 and 1970, the Christian share of the population grew from roughly 1 percent to around 44 percent, and overwhelmingly, those new converts came from peoples who had earlier been animists or ethnoreligionists. For Africa as a whole, the religious shift during the twentieth century meant that around one-third of the continental population transferred its allegiance away from native religions or animism to different shades of Christianity. Most African Christians are second- or third-generation members of the faith, so that a lively animist presence is always in evidence. Memories of folk religions also remain strong among Korean and Chinese Christians, most of whom come from families converted over the past half-century. A rich novel such as Han Malsook's *Hymn of the Spirit* suggests how Korean Christianity established itself in a society deeply imbued with Buddhist and shamanistic elements, in which enormous significance was already attached to dreams, visions, and divination. In Latin America, the surging Pentecostal churches of Brazil commonly draw on believers converted from African-rooted faiths such as Umbanda. Around the world, sorcerers, mediums, spirit healers, and other spiritual professionals are familiar figures in everyday life, much as they were in the milieu of the book of Acts. Then as now, a trip to a marketplace might well mean an encounter with a magician claiming to invoke pagan forces.[7]

This pagan inheritance has a complex impact on contemporary Christianity. As we have seen, some Christian thinkers have a highly inclusive view of the older religions, recognizing the presence of God in traditional faiths. Other believers, though, are less tolerant. The mere presence of alternative religions reminiscent of those condemned in the Bible allows some Christians to frame these practices in terms of devil worship, giving credibility to the objective existence of Satanic evil.

Old Testament warnings about the evils of idolatry are reinforced by the periodic exposés of sinister activities by traditional African and Asian religions, with tales of blood cults and human sacrifices. Now, such accounts have to be treated with caution, since modern history is littered with discredited horror stories about pagan atrocities, the tales usually emanating from overenthusiastic missionaries or colonial authorities. On occasion, though, the charges are well substantiated, particularly in the context of the secret societies that have exercised such power across West Africa. In 2004, Nigerian police reported that hundreds of sacrificial killings had occurred in recent years at the pagan shrine of Ogwugwu Okija. Making matters worse, the killings took place in Anambra state, in what was supposedly the bastion of Igbo Christianity.[8]

Such stories stand in contrast to events in North America some years ago, where lurid tales of Satanic cults and ritualistic abuse collapsed in the face of a total lack of material evidence. Just where were all the bodies? In Anambra and elsewhere, in contrast, the bodies were there to be seen. No less a figure than Nigeria's President Obasanjo has written, "There are devilish people who in today's Nigeria believe that human sacrifice and human parts in magical stuff, charms and amulets, can provide them with [anything they want] and without regard for human life. They maim and kill to take parts of human bodies." African Christians celebrated the destruction of the Anambra shrines and their idols, and the bloodthirsty rituals that accompanied them, citing Elijah's victory over the prophets of Baal.[9] Paganism is a reality, and for many Christian churches, so are the forces worshipped by those pagan believers. In this view, demonic forces exist, they exercise pervasive power over human beings, until and unless people opt for the Christian resources that alone can deliver them from evil.

This spiritual-warfare perspective helps explain the depth of fury and alarm expressed in recent sexual controversies within the Anglican communion. When conservative African and Asian clergy invoked the language of the diabolical in these conflicts, they were not just indulging in overheated rhetoric. Reacting to the proposed ordination of a gay bishop in the Church of England, Nigerian primate Akinola proclaimed, "This is an attack on the Church of God—a Satanic attack on God's Church." Speaking of the U.S. Episcopal bishops who refused to approve the ordination of Bishop Gene Robinson, Akinola applauded "the admirable integrity and loyalty of those gallant 45 Bishops of ECUSA who have refused to succumb to the pressure for compromise. In the language of the Bible, they have refused to bow their knees to Baal." Another conservative, southeast Asian primate Datak Yong Ping Chung, similarly portrayed Episcopal liberals as compromising with evil forces. He protested, "The enemy, the devils, try to discount and destroy the church by promoting the so-called critical approach to the Bible."[10] Bowing to idols and serving demons might be familiar enough metaphors in Western society. The imagery has quite different connotations when used in societies in which fertility rituals, animism, and image worship still exist; and in which, moreover, these customs are not seen as quaint parts of the tourist heritage, but as living manifestations of devil worship.

Victory

Pagan religions have left a potent inheritance in the form of widespread beliefs in spirits and spiritual forces that can be manipulated by human beings. Korean Wonsuk Ma writes of "the rich Asian perceptions of the spiritual world. Unlike the western world, many Asian societies hold the fundamental animistic beliefs in one way or another. Malevolent spirits are believed to cause sickness, misfortune, and disturbance especially in dreams. Many of the 'high religions' of Asia also provide a fertile ground for awareness of spiritual beings. This has a direct bearing on the Asian Christian's religious experiences and our interpretation of them." In traditional Korean thought, people attributed much evil to *han* spirits, the angry and bitter ghosts of those who had died unjustly. In Africa, similarly, "the existence of evil ones and enemies is painfully real. Evil spirits, witches and wizards, sorcerers and ill wishers are a constant source of fear and anxiety."[11]

Pagan and primal religions teach the existence of spiritual menaces facing society, but they also provide means to combat those dangers. A crucial flaw of early white missionary activity in Africa and Asia was that it forbade these solutions, whether amulets, fetishes, spells, charms, or ceremonies, since all were conspicuous symbols of pagan practice. At the same time, though, missionaries rarely offered plausible spiritual resources to combat what were still universally seen as pressing menaces. For most missionaries, New Testament stories of healing were interpreted "either as spiritual lessons having little to do with prayer for sick bodies, or as a call to found clinics and hospitals." As Grant LeMarquand comments, "The latter they ought to have done, not neglecting the former."[12] Newer indigenous churches succeeded by taking seriously the danger posed by the demonic and supernatural—indeed, in interpreting these forces firmly in the ancient Christian tradition. They allowed believers the right to bear arms for spiritual self-defense, though protection was now characterized in strictly Christian terms.

The sense of confronting a vast empire of evil does not cause believers to despair, since the Christian message teaches that the powers of good have already triumphed over these forces, through the Incarnation and Resurrection. Christ's victory is epitomized in the cross and crucifixion, themes that are absolutely central to hymns and forms of popular devotion. Jesus defeated death and sin not just in this world, but in any conceivable realm of spirits or ancestors. Indeed, early Christian apologists repeatedly used the evidence of spiritual triumph as a key selling point for the faith. For Justin Martyr or Origen, the truth of Christianity was proved every time an ordinary Christian cast out demons, not through great occult learning, but through prayer and simply invoking the name of Jesus. As Tertullian boasted, "All the authority and power we have over them is from our naming of the name of Christ." In much of today's Christian world, such arguments still ring true. Reading Hebrews, African Catholics learn that Jesus "is superior to the angels and spirits and to any ancestor one might think of; he surpasses in dignity and efficacy all soothsayers and sacrificers." In Korea too, where "the power of the dead is stronger than that of the living . . . the traditional faith of Koreans in the power of ancestors and the influence of the killed for justice is in accord with the Christian faith in the death and resurrection of Jesus."[13]

Biblical descriptions of Jesus' triumph over evil imagine a king dragging his defeated enemies behind him, while rewarding his followers. "Having spoiled principalities and powers, [Christ] made a shew of them openly, triumphing over them in it." "When he ascended, he led captivity captive, and gave gifts unto men." These heroic images still make wonderful sense for anyone accustomed to traditional African or Asian cultures. One hymn from the Transvaal declares,

> Jesus Christ is Conqueror
> By his resurrection he overcame death itself
> By his resurrection he overcame all things
> He overcame magic
> He overcame amulets and charms
> He overcame the darkness of demon possession
> He overcame dread
> When we are with him
> We also conquer.

Such a hymn could easily have been sung by Mediterranean Christians of the first three centuries after Jesus' time. Still more startlingly martial is a hymn of the Ghanaian Afua Kuma:

> If Satan troubles us
> Jesus Christ
> You who are the lion of the grasslands
> You whose claws are sharp
> Will tear out his entrails
> And leave them on the ground
> For the flies to eat.

Victorian hymn writers had little to teach their modern counterparts about utilizing bloody or militaristic imagery.[14]

Loosing the Captives

Ideas of spiritual warfare and deliverance span the globe, in the sense that they are found wherever charismatic churches exist. The doctrine is grounded in a passage from the letter to the Ephesians, "we wrestle not against flesh and blood, but against principalities, against powers, against the rulers of the darkness of this world, against spiritual wickedness in high places." In North America, spiritual warfare theories pervade the popular religious thrillers of

Frank Peretti, in works like *This Present Darkness*. In more psychological form too, the exorcism-derived phrase "Woman thou art loosed!" provides the title for T. D. Jakes's best-selling study of women's recovery from abuse and psychic wounds. In the global North, though, spiritual warfare ideas represent one minority strand of Christian belief and practice, in contrast to their strictly mainstream character in Africa or Asia. In North America, moreover, ideas of exorcism and deliverance appear bizarre or fanatical to outsiders or to secular observers, whereas they fit quite logically into conventional assumptions in many newer churches.[15]

Across Africa and Asia, spiritual warfare is a familiar component of most Christian practice, even among denominations that in the global North would scorn such approaches. The boundaries separating evangelical and charismatic churches are very porous in the global South, so that African and Asian evangelicals demonstrate little of the coolness to "Pentecostal excesses" that marks their North American brethren. Moreover, mainstream liturgical churches (Catholic, Anglican, Lutheran) have adopted at least elements of the spiritual warfare worldview, largely through sincere conviction, but also from the urgent need to compete with Pentecostal, charismatic, and independent congregations. Demonology is thus credible for African and Asian churches, in a way it can scarcely be for most educated Westerners, and so is the idea of exorcism. I once heard a white American Adventist clergyman recount a hair-raising tale of his visit to a packed church service in southern Africa. Though initially startled to see a white face in its midst, the hospitable congregation was delighted to find that the visitor was an ordained pastor. Happy to welcome the new arrival, the church's minister announced that Pastor Smith had come all the way from America to visit them, and that he would be conducting tonight's exorcism. Pastor Smith, needless to say, had no experience whatever of such a practice, and he had to improvise speedily.[16]

The theme of spiritual captivity and release finds expression in many biblical texts. In the New Testament, the critical passage is the words of Jesus announcing his mission as he stands in the Nazareth synagogue. Reading from Isaiah, he applies to himself the words "The Spirit of the Lord is upon me, because he hath anointed me to preach the gospel to the poor; he hath sent me to heal the brokenhearted, to preach deliverance to the captives, and recovering of sight to the blind, to set at liberty them that are bruised, To preach the acceptable year of the Lord."[17] This passage is quoted so often today because it concisely summarizes the message of Jesus as seen by two strands of thought that for Euro-Americans, at least, seem barely compatible, namely deliverance, in the charismatic sense, and liberation, in the view of social activists. As we have seen, though, in much of the global South, these two forms of freeing represent sides of the same coin. Spiritual interpretations apart, the conditions of life for the very poor give enormous appeal to the promise of release from the miseries of everyday life, which are easily conceived as chaining or captivity.

Virtually all the available Bible texts about loosing and release enjoy wide currency. These include the story of the raising of Lazarus, and especially the crowning words of Jesus on seeing the risen man: "Loose him, and let him go." Also popular is the story of the crippled woman, to whom Jesus said, "Woman, thou art loosed from thine infirmity." As a Gikuyu hymn declares, "Woman, are you bound? It is Satan. Jesus is calling you." The church's power to undertake such loosing forms part of the spiritual gifts poured forth upon believers at Pentecost, as described in the book of Acts.[18]

Bible study groups often select passages describing the healing miracles of Jesus, and his interaction with the world of demons and spirits. One much-discussed text is the eighth chapter of the Gospel of Luke, which includes the story of the Gadarene swine, as well as the raising of Jairus's daughter and the healing of the woman with the issue of blood. These stories teach a very material conception of evil. The demons cast out of the possessed man have to go somewhere, and they find a convenient home in the pigs that then hurl themselves to their deaths. Shortly afterward, the woman takes the initiative in seeking healing, by surreptitiously touching Jesus and drawing on his power without his consent, making him seem almost like an electric generating station. Neither case permits the reader to resort to the familiar rationalization of miracles, to understand Jesus as a master interpreter of psychosomatic ailments, or one who boldly ignores ritual taboos. The spirits transferred to the pigs are real, honest-to-Beelzebub demons.

The vision of deliverance as a matter of warfare is usually grounded in the Ephesians passage, which has long been a popular sermon text for African churches. In Korea too, "To Pentecostal believers, prayer is neither a kind of meditation nor cultivation of the character. It is a desperate warfare with demons." To see the martial spirit in operation, we might look at the vastly successful Latin American revivals led by Argentinian Carlos Annacondia. Standing before a packed stadium, the evangelist begins his meetings with a roar of "Oime bien, Satanas!" ("Listen to me, Satan!"), a direct imitation of how Jesus rebuked the demons of his day. Annacondia then exorcises those who come forward for deliverance, before proceeding with the rest of the event.[19]

To illustrate the mainstream character of such beliefs, we can look at the pages of the *African Theological Journal*, a respectable publication based at a Tanzanian Lutheran college. In 2001, the journal published an article entitled "Demon Possession and Exorcism in Mark 1: 21–28," studying the passage in which Jesus meets a possessed man. Jesus casts out the demon, though only after it has acknowledged his divine status. The author of the Tanzanian article gave the scriptural text the kind of close reading that might have appeared in any North American journal, but after analyzing it, the author then applied it precisely to a recent case of his acquaintance. "What happened to the demoniac in Mark 1: 21–28 happens to many demoniacs in Tanzania as it once happened to Esther in 1982." Esther had been possessed for several years by demons who thwarted her desire to attend religious schools, whether Christian or Muslim. Finally, an exorcism was prescribed. "After singing three songs, three texts which narrate demon possession and exorcism, we read one text from each of the first three gospels. The fourth text on which the sermon was based was Mark 1: 21–28." As the exorcism progressed, those present heard demonic voices screaming through Esther's mouth: "We are being burned! We are being burned!" but then "We are going out!" The ceremony was so successful that Esther needed no further intervention, and she remained untroubled many years afterwards. The author concluded, "Exorcism brings both spiritual and bodily or material blessings to the individuals and society. Due to such blessings, the church should see to it that exorcism is done whenever the need arises."[20]

The Lion and the Adder

One ubiquitous text dealing with such matters is Psalm 91, an assertion of strength against various enemies, material and spiritual (see Appendix 2). As early as Jesus' own time, the psalm was interpreted chiefly in demonological terms, and it belonged firmly in the realm of exorcism. This fact adds to the irony when the Devil himself quotes the psalm to Jesus, when he urges him to cast himself from the Temple, knowing that angels will protect the messiah from harm. To compare a modern popular mythology, hearing this demon-scaring citation from such a source is rather like seeing a vampire contentedly waving a crucifix.[21]

Throughout Christian history, the psalm has been invoked for protection. As recently as the mid-nineteenth century, Charles Spurgeon remarked, "A German physician was wont to speak of [Psalm 91] as the best preservative in times of cholera, and in truth, it is a heavenly medicine against plague and pest. He who can live in its spirit will be fearless, even if once again London should become a lazar-house, and the grave be gorged with carcasses."[22] In modern times, the text is much used in the West for defense against secular evils, and it is a favorite among soldiers going into battle. After the attacks of September 11, one could see bumper stickers of U.S. flags with the words "PSALM 91" printed across them. Athletes also cherish its words.

In Christian Africa and Asia, though, the psalm is everywhere, and it is still used for exorcism and spiritual protection, with the written text occasionally serving as a kind of amulet. Emphasizing its Christian relevance are verses promising that the believer will "tread on the lion and the adder," which recalls the miraculous powers over serpents that Jesus promised his disciples. (In various translations, the reptile is a serpent or an asp.) In tropical regions, snakes and other deadly creatures are a far more familiar quantity than in the global North, giving a special relevance to the comparison with diabolical forces, and the assurance that the believer will triumph over them is all the more valued.[23]

The African love affair with Psalm 91 goes back many centuries, to the ancient Coptic churches. St. Antony—the third-century Egyptian founder of monasticism—specifically mentions lions and asps as two forms in which the demons threatened him, and he recited psalms to scatter them. "Coptic legend and iconography took the imagery of these scripture verses much further, legitimating a general discourse of power over demonic fauna. Several Coptic holy men were hailed for their taming or eradication of crocodiles; and one Apa Timothy was recalled specifically as master of a herd of desert antelope. For Apa Poemen, the demons that he and his fellow monks repel are said to be venomous like reptiles."[24]

Modern Africans likewise value the text. This psalm circulates far beyond faith-healing churches such as the Aladura, and it has wide currency among mainstream evangelicals and charismatics—groups that comprehend most African Protestants. On the London-based Voice of Africa radio, Evangelist Ruth declares that "God's Word is filled with promises to deliver His people from terror and destruction (Psalm 91:5). As you live in obedience to Him and confidently rely on His Word, you can rest assured that nothing evil will happen to you, and neither will any sickness or disease come near you (vv. 10–11). God has assigned angels to make sure of it." The Anglican Church of Nigeria lists the psalm as an appropriate text for "birthday or other personal celebrations." In popular culture too, the text appears in the oddest settings. In the celebrated Brazilian crime film City of God, the psalm is heard as a gangster reforms and turns to the church, and we see him passing unharmed through his enemies—in this instance, police detectives and rival criminals.[25]

Psalm 91 becomes all the more important during times of crisis such as the tsunami, when (presumably) the forces of the lion and serpent are at their most active. After the tsunami, the Indian leader of the Gospel for Asia movement declared, "I pray Psalm 91 over this ministry—may God protect and comfort in this great time of need." A member of a Singaporean church wrote of the miraculous preservation of his family from the tsunami that devastated his native Sri Lanka: "I assured my parents that God's favor surrounds our family and that no harm will come to us because our trust is in the blood of Jesus. My parents saw a thousand fall at their side, ten thousand at their right hand but it did NOT come near them. . . . My family became living proof of Psalm 91 in a situation that saw the deaths of tens of thousands."[26]

Among the many miracles attributed to the psalm, we find survival in the midst of the Rwandan massacres. One survivor reported that "[s]he's certain she would not have survived the genocide had a friend not given her a tiny book of Psalms on the eve of the killing and urged her to read Psalm 91. . . . She held the book open over her heart as killers searched a room where she stood in plain sight and could not see her, and again as a guard at a road-block raised a machete over her head that somehow never fell. 'There is no word for that but miracle,' she says."[27] In each case, of course, we ask the obvious theological question, of why the miraculous preservation of one did not extend to the many equally innocent and faithful who perished at the same time.

And It Was Night

A belief in confrontation with dark forces helps explain the practice of vigils and all-night services, which are commonplace throughout African and Asian churches. Now, such meetings might arise for good and practical reasons, for instance because that is when hard-working believers can take time off to gather. In Asia Minor around A.D. 110, Christians met "on a fixed day before dawn." In modern Korea, "the Full Gospel faith stresses the importance of all night prayer, as do all other Korean churches. . . . However, there were often all night prayer meetings during revival movements in the early part of the twentieth century. A majority of revival meetings were held in the evenings, and after the worship service, cry-out prayer continued. When the believers were moved and filled with the Holy Spirit, these meetings continued into an all-night prayer." But night meetings also acquire spiritual dimensions, with the potent symbolism of light and darkness. The appeal of such ideas is easy to understand when we appreciate the genuinely frightening nature of night and darkness in the centuries before the coming of urban lighting systems, and especially the technologies of gas and electricity.[28]

Night vigils are a standard feature of Africa's independent churches, as believers proclaim the powers of light and good at times when the forces of darkness are at their strongest and most pernicious. As Jean Marc Ela writes, "In black Africa, the world of the Night or of the Invisible is perhaps the privileged place in which we must understand the good news of the descent of Jesus into hell (1 Pt 3:19–20) in order to announce liberation to the African menaced by occult power." A centerpiece of Zimbabwean devotional life is the vigil, or *pungwe*, a huge rural gathering of prayer and preaching, praise and preaching, deliberately held through the night to proclaim the victory of Christ and to challenge the potent forces of darkness. As one leader of the movement reported, "Many times, Jesus used to work at night: that is when the alien spirits used to come out."[29]

For American observers, the darkness theme can seem like the worst kind of superstition: surely only children are scared of the dark? But the rhetoric of the *pungwe* movement, to take one example, meshes very well with the New Testament and with some of the subtlest portions of that text. In particular, the image of light and darkness, day and night, runs through the Gospel of John, with night symbolized as the dwelling place of evil. After Jesus identifies Judas as the one who will betray him, he sends him away, initiating the sequence of events that culminate in the crucifixion, the apparent triumph of the forces of evil. The departure of Judas is followed by the single hammer-blow line, *en de nux*, "and it was night." In using such words, the evangelist is doing much more than just establishing a chronology.

Witches

In many parts of the world, the feared forces of darkness include witchcraft. Any observer of African Christianity soon realizes not only that evil forces are seen as threatening realities, but also that human beings are allied to these forces. Under whatever name we choose to describe it, witchcraft is believed to pose a pervasive threat, and that problem has not diminished with time. To the contrary, such beliefs have increased as people seek explanations for the disasters facing Africa, while traditional belief systems have fallen into disarray. Nigerian Samuel Kunhiyop writes of "the modern mass hysteria of belief and practice of witchcraft." In many ways, the sequence of events in modern Africa closely recalls the experience of post-Reformation Europe. As reforming churches, both Protestant and Catholic, struggled to suppress the practices of folk magic, witchcraft fears surged among people who felt deprived of their familiar defenses, and witch panics reached dreadful heights between 1560 and 1640.[30]

Most observers date the upsurge in African witchcraft beliefs, the emergence of the new witchcraft problem, to the years of disillusion that began in the 1970s. Ugandan Fr. Peter Wasswa Mpagi remarks that since that time, "Many sicknesses cannot be cured medically. . . . There is widespread belief in Tanzania and elsewhere of *Wamumiani* who bleed people and sell their blood. In Uganda there are continuous stories about kidnapping, disappearances of children and sacrifices of human victims. In the city, people are worried about how to keep their jobs, and the fear of witchcraft is on the increase." In response to such fears, there has emerged a thriving class of spiritual entrepreneurs, of diviners, witch finders, and hunters.[31] Ghanaian Catholic bishop Peter Sarpong has written, "The phenomenon of devil worship is fast gaining ground [in Africa], competing with some of the barbaric and sadistic practices of some traditional secret societies. . . . Africa needs the Good News . . . to be able to rid itself of the menace of obsession with the spirit world, especially witchcraft and magical beliefs and operation of secret societies and devil worship." Allegedly, clergy themselves are often among the practitioners. According to one recent account, "The Nigerian church is experiencing an unprecedented resurgence of cultic, occult, witch-craft and demonic activities."[32]

People need techniques to protect themselves against these menaces, and if they cannot find these within the church, they will seek help in traditional practices. As one African Catholic bishop complained, his flock practices "rosary in the morning and witchcraft in the afternoon." When a Pan-African Christian Women Alliance gathered in 1989, the witchcraft problem was treated very seriously indeed. According to one presenter, "One sorcerer who was later converted spoke in his testimony of the fact that he was able to put a spell on a whole village by placing a talisman at the source of their sup-ply of drinking water. By doing this he turned the hearts of the people against the word of God."[33] Addressing the Roman Catholic Synod on the Church in Africa in 1994, Nigerian Kathryn Hauwa Hoomkwap commented, "Child-lessness, the fear of evil spirits, witchcraft, are real concerns which are very often laughed at, dismissed as imaginary and non-existent in our Church circle. But, to the suffering African woman, these problems are real." So real are these issues, in fact, that people drift to independent churches where they are taken seriously. "These movements or sects are winning our Catholic women over because they seem to be responding to their real needs." A Cameroonian bishop agreed, "The African Christian is fearful: fear of the environment, fear of the neighbors, fear of sorcerers. Only Jesus Christ can free him."[34]

Churches of all theological shades find abundant biblical resources to address the issue of witchcraft. A friend once described visiting one of the most popular up-and-coming evangelical churches in Ghana. Entering the sanctuary, she saw a huge banner, of the sort that in an American church might proclaim "Love," "Jesus is Lord," or some other inspiring message. In the Ghanaian example, though, the banner quoted Exodus 22, "Thou shalt not suffer a witch to live!" Other texts believed to offer protection and aid to sufferers include the spiritual warfare section of Ephesians 6. So are the psalms that portray the believer under assault from "enemies," here con-ceived as witches or demonic forces. Such is the reading of Psalm 35, "Plead my cause, O Lord, with them that strive with me: fight against them that fight against me."[35] Psalm 31 is another prayer of rescue and refuge, of deliverance from enemies. This has the added advantage that Jesus himself quoted from it, when on the cross he prayed, "into thy hands, I commend my spirit." A verse in the first Epistle of John declares that "there are three that bear witness in earth, the Spirit, and the water, and the blood: and these three agree in one." This passage is used in exorcism rituals that invoke the triple power of the name of Jesus, the blood and the holy spirit. Adding to the aura of this verse, older translations such as the King James link it to the only explicit assertion of Trinitarian doctrine in the whole Bible.[36]

Armed with such weapons, Christians triumphantly boast their victories against the powers of darkness, and most prized in such accounts are stories of witches and pagan priests themselves surrendering their powers. In Uganda, Kefa Sempangi reports his struggles against traditional healers, which culminated when one witch doctor agreed to burn her images and magical tools, initiating a mass conversion among local magicians. "It was a moment of great triumph, a day when Jesus' words took on a new meaning for us all: 'But if I with the finger of God cast out devils, no doubt the kingdom of God is come upon you.'" However, Sempangi stresses that such individual conversions could not of themselves solve the problem: "I began to understand the scope of Satan's kingdom. It was a kingdom of innumerable loyal subjects whose shrines were not only inanimate objects but human beings themselves. No matter how many fetishes we burned and no matter how many witches we converted, we would never reduce the demons"—or at least, not by flesh and blood alone.[37]

In Korea, similar conversion stories are cited as warrants of the truth of Christianity. A typical tale told by supporters of the Full Gospel church recounts how "Bok-hee Lim, who believed in shamanism and strongly denied the Christian faith, finally gave up the life of the shaman because Christians gathered around her neighborhood to pray. She said later, 'Because it was a confrontation between a demigod and the almighty God, the demigod could do nothing but to be defeated in a groggy state without even having a real fight.' Soon, Lim collected all the clothes and equipment that she used for her practice and burned them all. . . . Then, she destroyed the little temple for her god of shamanism in her backyard." Such stories echo the classic biblical stories of confrontations with alien gods, in the book of Acts and elsewhere.[38]

One modern paladin in the struggle against witchcraft is German revivalist Reinhard Bonnke, whose African crusades are strongly oriented to spiritual warfare ideas and techniques. He boasts how "locals brought sacks full of witchcraft items to the crusade grounds for burning each night." One of his supporters remarks, "This is the greatest number of witchcraft items we have ever seen. People surrendered their idols by the sackfull. . . . [W]e started burning the witchcraft items from the second night of the conference, when Reinhard preached on the Blood of Jesus and took authority over the powers of the enemy. The strongholds in the city were demolished and the people released."[39]

Some harrowing accounts of the damage wrought by witches and occultism derive from enthusiastic Christians who themselves claim to have been mighty pagan adepts before their conversion. Such stories at once heighten the magnitude of their sin and the miraculous quality of their subsequent rescue. What are presented as firsthand confessions are felt to give strong validation to popular beliefs about the nature of evil, and the stories have become a thriving genre of religious popular culture. Samuel Kunhiyop complains, "Many Christians can hardly give one story of deliverance from demonic power but can give countless stories of the confessions and power of witches and wizards."[40]

Some of these conversion stories have become best-sellers. The prototype for the modern tale is E. O. Omoobajesu's 1968 book *My Conversion: From a Witch-Doctor to an Evangelist*. Another popular work from the 1980s is Emmanuel Eni's *Delivered from the Powers of Darkness*, allegedly "the true story of the conversion of a great African wizard." Eni's problems began when he married a spirit-woman who changed shape into animal forms, and he was subsequently initiated into a global occult brotherhood headquartered in India. The group sacrificed children and performed disgusting rituals. Such stories gain credibility in West Africa, where well-authenticated secret societies play a central role in traditional culture and where many practice blood rituals; but Eni's accounts become even more spectacular when he draws on the conspiratorial anti-Satanic exposé literature then so popular in North America. Thereafter, Eni claims that his deeds became much worse: "I destroyed lives to the extent that Lucifer became very pleased and made me CHAIRMAN OF THE WIZARDS." Eni's salvation came when he turned to the Assemblies of God Church and, as a new Christian, fought desperately against his former allies.[41]

Healing Words

As in the New Testament world, many Christians in the global South link the struggle against evil forces with the quest for healing in body and mind, seeing both as forms of deliverance. In this emphasis, Christians are undoubtedly following biblical examples, but they are also reflecting attitudes toward healing in their own traditional societies, in which healing is seen in supernatural and ritual contexts.

Across the global South, healing ministries have been critical to the modern expansion of Christianity, much as they were during the conversion of Western Europe following the collapse of the Roman Empire. And today, as then, it is all but impossible to separate healing of the body or mind from spiritual deliverance. In modern China, ordinary Christians demonstrate "a strong expectation that God will intervene in miraculous ways in the daily lives of believers. House church Christians exhibit a firm belief in God's ability and willingness to work miracles in their midst. Their testimonies often refer to God healing the sick, raising the dead, granting special wisdom or direction, communicating through dreams, visions, or prophetic messages, providing boldness for witness, or granting miraculous strength and protection." The faithful declare their openness to the "gifts of the spirit" as promised in first Corinthians; to the blessings of prophecy, miracles, and speaking in tongues.[42]

In Korean Protestant and Pentecostal teaching, too, gospel accounts of miraculous healing are prominent. In a study of leading Korean churches in the early 1980s, "the topic of faith healing, along with other miraculous deeds of Jesus, comprised the most prominent place in their sermons, while ethical or pedagogical themes remained relatively inconspicuous." "Put forth as a demonstration of God's love and power, the miraculous healing in the Bible was advanced by a vast majority of Korean clergy to the level of magical potency."[43]

Healing is an integral part of the narrative of conversion and salvation, and accounts of healing represent a large proportion of literature and testimony among African and Asian Christians. In a tribal community in the Philippines, for instance, an evangelist reports the experience of a new convert: "Very soon, a neighbor quietly asked him if this new God could heal his dying child. Badol laid his hand upon the motionless baby and prayed in the name of Jesus who had given life to her. The next Sunday, the entire family, with the now recovered baby, joined the church. . . . [T]he villagers regularly asked him to pray for the sick, and most of them were healed miraculously. About fifteen years later, everyone in Papasok serves this new God who can heal the sick." But the healing emphasis survives vigorously in more developed communities too. To quote one modern African Catholic, "I look at [Jesus] as a healer, and I think many Africans do. The most powerful image of Jesus is Jesus the healer. He can take away our diseases."[44]

When Christians approach their healing ministry, they have no shortage of scriptural passages from which they can draw. On occasion, the use of biblical texts looks superficial, in the sense that they are added to justify what the groups concerned were going to do anyway. This kind of reading is sometimes described as eisegesis, the determined effort to read one's own meaning into a particular text. We see an example of this in West Africa, among the wave of prophetic and charismatic churches that came to be known as the Aladura. These groups drew heavily on older animist practice, especially in the realm of healing—which is not to impugn their Christian credentials. One such group, Christ Apostolic Church of Yorubaland, uses the water symbolism that was so prevalent in the older Native beliefs of the region. Founder Apostle Joseph Ayodele Babalola claimed that "God gave him the *Omi lye* (Living Water) as a sign for the power of healing. . . . [T]he Lord made the *Omi lye* a clarion to call all people unto Him for Salvation and a healing medium for all illnesses and sicknesses (Isa. 55:1–7)."[45] Though the Isaiah text does indeed refer to waters, the scriptural grounding is retroactive, and the same is true of the wide variety of psalms used almost as spells in such rituals. In one Kenyan church, similarly, elaborate healing rituals use candles, confession, and fasting, which ostensibly draw on the rich color symbolism laid down for the Hebrew tabernacle in Exodus 39: white is holiness, blue is for faith, and so on. Conceivably these ceremonies might represent a sincere attempt to reconstruct ancient Hebrew rituals, but they are just as likely to be older tribal ceremonies dressed in biblical garb. Some Indian Christians use scripture to justify their belief in malevolent spirits. The book of Ecclesiastes declares, "To every thing there is a season. . . . A time to be born, and a time to die," and if someone dies before their allotted time, they will wander the earth until someone takes action to remove them.[46]

Usually, however, the use of healing texts is faithful to the scripture. The passages most often studied and invoked by believers across denominations are the many examples of Jesus' healing ministry. Also popular are the closing verses of Mark chapter 16, in which the faithful are promised spiritual powers; and the tenth chapter of Luke, which includes the commissioning of the seventy disciples and Jesus' declaration that he has seen Satan fall from heaven.

The ever-popular letter of James also provides rules for spiritual healing, instructing believers to seek cure from prayer and anointing by elders of the church.[47] James's influence can be seen in the widespread practice of anointing with oil. This is a trademark of healing churches like the Aladura, for whom healing is and has always been their main raison d'être, but anointing is widely used across denominations. In West Africa's booming Winners Chapel, the text from James is reinforced by a battery of Old Testament passages, and the anointing oil is sometimes credited with miraculous powers. West Africa's Mosama Disco Christo Church offers a concise summary of healing texts in its articles of fundamental belief. After declaring forthrightly "We believe in divine healing," the document lists the classic passages: James 5:14–15; Isaiah 53:4–5; Luke 8:43; Matthew 15:28.[48]

Also widely used in discussion groups and as sermon texts are the Old
Testament accounts of Elijah and Elisha, whose healings and prophecies so
influenced the miracle narratives in the canonical gospels. The resemblances
are especially clear when the Old Testament tales are read in the Septuagint
Greek that would have been familiar to early Christians. In modern Africa, so
popular are these stories—incidents such as the healing of Naaman the Syrian
from leprosy and the raising from the dead of the widow's son—that the two
books of Kings are treated as quasi-gospels. In the Winners Chapel, the tales
of Elijah and Elisha have given rise to a whole new symbolism. As Paul
Gifford comments, "A white handkerchief is called a mantle; every congregation member waves one, and the Man of God blesses it, and imbues it
with double anointing (the reference is to Elisha inheriting the mantle of
Elijah, with its double portion—II Kings 2:11–14)." This "mantle ministry"
implies miraculous powers, and accounts tell of the cloth's use in healing
and in raising the dead. This practice looks like a direct plagiarism from traditional religion—though it does have some biblical warrant. The book of
Acts recounts the miraculous effects of handkerchiefs or clothing touched by
the apostle Paul.[49]

Andrew Walls has pointed out the many resemblances between modern
African Christianity and its ancient precursors, especially in Egypt; and the
frequent use of these healing and miracle texts certainly suggests continuity,
or rather unconscious revival. The Elijah/Elisha sequence was very popular
in early and medieval Mediterranean Christianity, and indeed it did much
to shape the medieval European tradition of hagiography. Early Egyptian
Christians were so enthralled by the figure of Elijah that they attributed
pseudoscriptures to him. As Saint Elias, Elijah has always been a beloved
church patron for Orthodox believers, not to mention a frequent subject
for ikons; and he holds a special place in the hearts of Arab Christians. Across
the Orthodox world, his feast day on July 20 is a major celebration.[50]

But the resemblances between ancient and modern African belief go
beyond a fascination with this one prophet, and we have already noticed
the Egyptian taste for Psalm 91. When modern Africans cite the Lukan passage about the fall of Satan, they are unconsciously echoing Egyptians such
as St. Antony, who used the very same text seventeen hundred years ago to
announce victory over demonic forces. Still today, accounts of African prophets and healers offer many echoes of the deeds of ancient Coptic holy men,
those earlier warriors against spiritual evil. Of course, this does not mean
that religious patterns are shaped by geography or some kind of ineffable
Africanness, but rather that ancient and modern Christians saw themselves
facing many similar issues, in terms of the confrontation with evil, which
manifested itself in the all-too-visible vestiges of paganism. Naturally, they
turned for understanding to a similar range of scriptural texts.[51]

Old and New

The biblical emphasis on healing rings so true to modern believers because it fits precisely into their cultural expectations and the healing traditions of pre-Christian societies. In Korea, popular shamanism had many points in common with the Pentecostal Christianity that would largely supplant it. Shamanism offered emotional services, often under female leadership, and was strongly oriented toward healing and exorcism.[52]

But in both Africa and Asia, the specific techniques of healing often resembled those described in the gospels, giving a distinct local flavor to the New Testament accounts. David Adamo writes, "In the biblical miracle stories we [Africans] found many healing techniques we are accustomed to, such as potent words, touching, prayers, and ordinary water." One African Christian was awed by what a versatile healer Jesus was, and how many familiar techniques he deployed: "And when it comes to healing, he uses so many ways. He can touch you, he can put mud or saliva on your eyes, he can command these spirits. He has all manner of ways; by his word he can even heal at a distance. . . . He can even speak to forces, so is a real miracle-worker." In some traditional societies, converts are shocked to find references to Jesus using methods that they had assumed were peculiar to their own strictly local tradition, as when he cures blindness through a mixture of soil and spittle.[53]

But Jesus is more than merely another healer, even a reputedly successful one, since he combines familiar methods with dramatic spiritual and psychological insight. One scholar tells of a South African group reading John 5:1–14, the miracle of the invalid healed by the pool. These readers find little novel in the healing techniques mentioned—the use of water and prayer—but they are very struck by Jesus' question to the man, "Do you want to be made well?" For the group, this element of faith, of demanding the sick person's full commitment to the healing process, showed Jesus' wisdom and superiority to mere professional healers, whether African or Western. As one group member remarked, "Something he could not do for 38 years was done in less than five seconds. What a surprise! This text is fascinating."[54]

The story of the paralyzed man culminates with a passage noted and debated far more in Africa and Asia than in the contemporary West. After the healing, Jesus instructs his patient, "Behold, thou art made whole: sin no more, lest a worse thing come unto thee." The implication is that sickness is a direct result of sin, perhaps a divine punishment; and this concept is borne out by other passages. In Exodus, God promises that if his people keep his commandments, then "I will put none of these diseases upon thee, which I have brought upon the Egyptians: for I am the LORD that healeth thee."[55] Such texts can be used to support a view that illness results from sin or misbehavior by the individual sufferer, rather than in the universal sense that sickness and death are consequences of the Fall. This is not meant to suggest that such readings are widespread, but they do occur, especially in some smaller independent churches, in which Christian healing practices draw heavily on traditional techniques.

Jesus' superiority to traditional healers gives churches an added weapon in the continuing contest with pagan and primal faiths, to which some Christians resort in times of crisis. As a result, modern preachers and pastors often cite texts against pagan practice that have long fallen out of use in the First World. In Zimbabwe, where traditional healers (*n'anga*) still enjoy a real following, preachers invoke familiar warnings about biblical figures who suffered for their continuing allegiance to pagan worship, especially when that meant trying to peer into the world beyond the grave. They recount the tale of the golden calf; they cite the warnings of Deuteronomy and Isaiah against wizards and mediums. To quote one Malawian preacher, "Instead of relying on God as Hezekiah did, we go to witch doctors to find out who has bewitched us."[56] More practically, Christians use healing texts to denounce pagan spiritual professionals who charge for their services, often exorbitantly. Elisha charged nothing for curing Naaman the Syrian, and an associate who tried to profit from the deal was smitten with leprosy. The message is not that pagan forces cannot help their devotees, but rather that Christians can perform the same tasks more efficiently, and without risking either spiritual or material harm to the sufferer.[57]

Into the Mainstream

Not all African churches offer exorcism and spiritual healing on a routine basis. For many clergy, counseling is the correct response for a person who comes forward reporting being possessed or bewitched. Even in such cases, though, the powerful example of the Bible means that the sufferer's belief system must be treated with total respect, and spiritual intervention must be offered as a last resort.

Having said this, the normality of spiritual healing is in some form accepted across most denominations, including those that in North America would be regarded as strictly mainstream. At a healing revival in Uganda, a woman reported being cured of a spinal complaint. After this event, "a whole stream of people . . . stood up one by one to declare joyfully what Jesus had done for them. They had been dumb, mad or psychologically disturbed; crippled, epileptic, hemorrhaging; they had had cancer, epilepsy and asthma. By turns they declared that they had been healed by prayer and the power of the Lord Jesus. So many people wanted to testify that in the end the parish catechist simply resorted to calling out the afflictions and doing a headcount of those who had been healed." This may sound like the typical currency of charismatic movements the world over, except that this particular example occurred in a Roman Catholic church, through the ministry of an Indian priest, and the initial miracle described took place during the exposition of the Blessed Sacrament.[58]

African Catholics recognize the urgent necessity of accommodating African theories of disease and misfortune within the Christian and biblical scheme. In Zambia in 2004, a church-sponsored Inculturation Task Force issued a practical guide for Christian communities struggling with issues of healing and witchcraft. The booklet offers case studies of perceived supernatural threats that are all too familiar in this society, and that have limitless potential to spawn scandals and conflicts within the Christian community. In one story, a loyal Catholic lady is accused of being a witch and shunned by her community, before they realize that the deaths of which she has been accused result from AIDS. Another case concerns a brother and sister whose families were suffering sickness. After her son died, "the mother became upset and went to the diviner who told her that her brother bathed in some medicines with his wife and children, to ward off the haunt of some disgruntled dead ancestor's spirit, which then in turn killed her only son. Mrs. Lufafa was very angry because, according to her, the brother with five children acted in a very cruel manner by letting the unappeased spirit attack her in this way."[59]

Overall, the pamphlet teaches restraint, tolerance, and humanity, but of necessity, traditional beliefs have to be treated respectfully. Christians need to learn that, while "healing that comes to a sick person through traditional means can truly be God-given," they must exercise great care in avoiding harmful practices. At every point, the cases are assessed from the standpoint of the predictable biblical texts—the Old Testament prohibition on visiting diviners, the healing miracles of Elijah, the spiritual warfare texts in Colossians and Ephesians, and Jesus' speech in the Nazareth synagogue. Congregations are encouraged to discuss these issues and to act out situations arising from them. According to the Catholic-sponsored commentary to the *African Bible*, "As long as a witch doctor is not harming but trying to empower, the Christian faith can integrate the message of healing in its message. Christ himself was a healer; all the Christian sacraments can be seen from the point of view of healing."[60]

Incidentally, this and other contemporary guides to responding to witchcraft and the demonic can be obtained via the Internet, in a remarkable juxtaposition of pre- and postmodern technologies and worldviews. Also on the Internet, we find the website of the respectable and strictly mainstream Anglican Church of Nigeria. This recommends "Bible passages for certain life situations," presenting a deeply religious interpretation of sickness and health. The site asserts:

> Health is natural: Gen. 1:26–31.
> Death or sickness in general originates from sin: Rom. 5:12; 6:23; I Cor. 15:26; Mk. 2:1–5; John 5:14.
> But not every instance of sickness in particular is a direct result of sin: John 8:23; Lk. 13:1–5; Job 1:6–12, 2:1–10.
> Sometimes ill health or suffering may be a trial from God to test our faith: I Peter 1:6, 7; Job.

Several passages are prescribed for "healing through prayer," including the passage from James 5.[61] Used in this proof-text manner, such readings could support the view of faith and prayer as remedies for illness, and we note the inclusion of John 5:14, the tale of the invalid, discussed earlier. Taken in context, though, the church is anxious to present a more sophisticated view of the causes of sin and suffering, and the reader is referred to the passage in Luke in which Jesus explicitly denies that the victims of a disaster provoked their fate through their sins.

From Generation to Generation

Most global South churches believe that evil is an objective reality, and for a surprising number, its power can span generations. Of all the biblical passages that resonate differently in the global South and North, it would be difficult to find a better example than the words of the prophet Ezekiel. Why, asks God, do Israelites repeat the proverb " 'The fathers have eaten sour grapes, and the children's teeth are set on edge'? . . . Behold, all souls are mine; as the soul of the father, so also the soul of the son is mine: the soul that sinneth, it shall die."[62] This passage represents a truly radical principle that emerged in Israel from the seventh and sixth centuries B.C.E., denying collective criminal responsibility for wrongdoing and instead placing the burden on the individual. In the modern world, the idea seems too obvious to be worth stating. Exacting collective revenge against whole families is a token of the bloodiest dictatorial regimes, of Stalin's Russia or Mao's China. What possible religious relevance could such a principle have today?

For many Christians in the global South, though, the idea of ancestral guilt, of curses spanning generations, is anything but a relic of distant antiquity. Perhaps a quarter of the world's people follow religious systems in which one's present condition is thoroughly determined by one's conduct in other lives. In such a setting, the poorest and most oppressed have only themselves to blame for their lot, through the historical burden that they have earned.

It is thus scarcely surprising to find that, in India, the greatest appeal of both Christianity and Islam is to members of the lowest social castes, who find in these religions the ability to cast off the weight of history, ancestry, and accumulated sins. The potential for future growth among these classes is staggering. In India, some two hundred million belong to the untouchable class, the Dalits, who are subject to systematic exploitation and discrimination at least as bad as that inflicted upon African Americans in the segregationist South, or on black South Africans in the apartheid years. Especially since the late nineteenth century, many Dalits have rejected attempts to justify their burdens in terms of the effects of past lives and karma.[63]

Incidentally, given their own bitter experiences of Hinduism, many are troubled by current efforts at interfaith dialogue. They view as simple betrayal the efforts of Euro-American theologians to absorb Hindu philosophies and mystical concepts, which assume the oppressive framework of caste and rebirth. Dalits resent "how, in the name of inculturation, Brahminical categories were being promoted, such as . . . Vedantic and Advaitic concepts in the writings of Bede Griffiths and others associated with the Christian ashram movement . . . and so they rightly asserted that Indian Christian theology was still heavily dominated by the so-called upper castes."[64] Instead, Dalit Christian theology preaches a radical vision of equality founded upon equal birth, a much more sweeping doctrine than mere equality of opportunity.

In Africa, Christianity encounters societies with a resolute belief in ancestral forces, in the effects of sin and ritual transgression carried down through generations. And in contrast to the original European missionaries, contemporary churches take these beliefs very seriously. As a contemporary Ghanaian scholar writes, "[S]alvation in the African context involves not just repentance through the confession of personal sins but also the renunciation of intended and unintended participation in 'demonic' cultural practices, such as rites of passage, and the repudiation of the effects of generational sins and curses upon a person's life." In trying to justify the objective existence of such curses, some contemporary preachers excavate texts dating from long before the time of Ezekiel, especially the divine warning in Exodus 20 that "I, the Lord your God, am a jealous God, punishing the children for the sin of the fathers to the third and fourth generation of those who hate me." Also suggestive is the cry of the Jewish crowd in Matthew, "His blood be on us and upon our children." But whatever the origins of deep-laid afflictions, Christianity also offers the means to solve them, even for individuals whose curses or taboos seem overwhelming. Chinua Achebe's classic novel *Things Fall Apart* tells the story of two ultimate outcasts for whom Christianity is literally the only way of overcoming their status.[65]

Here again, many modern readers can find a relevance in biblical debates that have little meaning for Northern-world Christians. Modern Euro-Americans can only be puzzled by the question asked by Jesus' disciples when they see a man who was born blind: whose fault was this, was it his sin or that of his parents? We know the answer, as Jesus gives it: neither this man nor his parents sinned.[66] In much of the world, though, whether in the first century or the twenty-first, that answer is not obvious, and the biblical principle of individualism and individual responsibility can still startle.

Healing and Wholeness

For many global North Christians, much of the religious thought world of their Third World counterparts looks suspicious. Even if the early Christian tradition accepted notions of the demonic—as it clearly did—surely, we have outgrown these ideas. Should we really fear darkness? Can any sane person in the modern world seriously believe in witchcraft or ancestral curses? The healing emphasis seems dubious, particularly when it is coupled with promises of worldly prosperity. In the worst light, we find all too many continuities with the pre-Christian primal religions.

Assessing religious claims is a risky business, in which even supportive arguments can easily appear as empty rationalizations. Who can assess the benefits of exorcism or spiritual warfare? Who can judge whether "superstitious" beliefs might be spiritually beneficial, or damaging? But one useful solution is to adopt the approach suggested centuries ago by Hugo Grotius, in his formulation of international law, namely, that we should proceed as if God is not a given, *etsi deus non daretur*. An objective observer might or might not accept the existence of the supernatural, but she can, for the sake of argument, assess claims on a purely secular basis. From that perspective, we find that even the seemingly widest cultural gulfs are not necessarily as broad as they appear. Viewed more closely, global South versions of Christianity and Bible interpretation are much less archaic than they might appear, while global North assertions of rationality are more fragile.

The issue of spiritual healing illustrates the point. We seem everywhere to see the consequences of blatant superstition: healing "mantles" and magical oils; psalms and Bible texts used as talismans; pastors and churches profiting from the fears of the sick; people refusing to seek modern medical care where it is available, on the grounds that this would represent a lack of faith. Some healing ministries do indeed bear close resemblance to the classic medicine show. Even if such abuses affected only a small minority of believers, would this not prove that there was something very wrong indeed with the forms of Christianity that have developed in the global South? If this is really the future of the faith, should we not despair?

All the problems cited here do occur, and have occurred, though they need to be kept in context. The great majority of churches work strenuously to suppress fraudulent claims and bogus miracles, and they view alleged miracle healers with great suspicion. In 2004, in a move to limit outrageous claims, the agency that supervises broadcasting in Nigeria issued stern new rules prohibiting the reporting of miracles and healings, except where they are "provable and believable."[67] Most churches, likewise, do not prevent their followers from seeking Western-style medicine where this is available and affordable—two conditions that are all too rarely met. And considered from the strictly secular point of view, it is difficult to see what harm is done by a belief in spiritual healing. What, after all, are the realistic alternatives? Followers of the new churches are no worse off than they would be resorting to traditional healers, and probably far better off in the sense that the churches demand less in terms of payment or sacrifice. Many secular observers would accept that someone who strongly believes he or she is being cured may well benefit from that state of mind, especially when it is reinforced by the presence of a caring and supportive community. The benefits are undeniable when spiritual cures are believed to remove ritual curses or taboos that, without intervention, would cause the sufferer to be shunned by that society.

When all the criticisms are granted, global South churches can make an excellent argument that healing—broadly defined—is central to the New Testament message, so central as to raise serious questions about just what is left after these elements are read out of the New Testament. For most, too, healing is understood not in terms of curing specific ailments, but of offering a holistic, comprehensive treatment of ills, so that we need not be satisfied with the pallid defense that at least such healing need cause no actual harm! As Daniel Chiquete remarks of Latin American Pentecostal churches, "This option is embodied in practice by a Jesus who touches, heals and saves the sick, thus restoring them to physical health, reintegrating them into their society and giving them the chance to develop a spiritual and a family life. In restoring them to health he also gives them back their dignity." Illustrating this theme, the author cites the Marcan parallel to the Luke 8 passage about the woman with the issue of blood: "Daughter, your faith has made you well; go in peace, and be healed of your disease." Canon John Kanyikwa, a strictly mainstream leader of African Anglicanism, uses the Markan account of the blind beggar Bartimaeus, who cries out, "Jesus have mercy on me." For Kanyikwa, this represents the cry of modern believers for healing of their ills, physical, mental, and spiritual.[68] From such a viewpoint, Northern-world resistance to ideas of a healing mission can readily be criticized as a stubborn refusal to acknowledge the plain lessons of scripture.

Critically, too, faith in healing generally does not become a simple test of God's existence or intent, and the vast majority of Southern-world Christians know perfectly well that in many instances, the faithful and devout will continue to suffer. In explaining this mystery, readers turn to such familiar texts as the book of Job, which was cited in the Nigerian Anglican source noted earlier. Others turn to texts that promise a wider meaning to suffering, beyond what our minds can currently comprehend. For Latin American Pentecostals, the familiar text in such settings is "We know that all things work together for good for those who love God."[69]

Religion and the Decline of Magic

Also, precedents from early modern Europe and America suggest that present conditions might provide the precursors for a wider acceptance of modern science and healing techniques. Current Christian practices that look like concessions to superstition might actually be the best way of channeling and controlling those beliefs, and of eradicating genuinely harmful customs.

A parallel comes to mind in Keith Thomas's classic study *Religion and the Decline of Magic*, which traces the decline of witchcraft, magic, and traditional superstitions in early modern England.[70] As in the world portrayed by Thomas, contemporary African churches proclaim a belief in supernatural manipulation, but also warn against an unhealthy obsession with such forces. While struggles against demons and witches do occur, these activities must be tightly regulated and brought under church control, and carefully distinguished from vulgar superstitions. Nigerian evangelical Samuel Olarewaju warns believers against "finding a demon under every bush." Samuel Kunhiyop agrees that "Christians generally are prone to provide worldly standards and demonic explanations to the questions of evil rather than biblical and theological explanations. Consequently though we claim to be Christians we are quick to suspect witchcraft rather than to recognize Christ's power over our lives. We therefore cling to witchcraft which satisfies our desire to find answers to our questions." Believers must learn the primary truth that "the Christian has victory in Christ over witchcraft and all its divergent forces." Instead of elaborate semipagan rituals, Olarewaju asserts, "The biblical way to challenge demonic assault is the authority of the name of Jesus."[71]

Resolute faith in the supremacy of the church and the decisive victory of Christ allows believers a degree of confidence that was never available in traditional thought worlds. By such means, in fact, they can achieve an undeniably authentic form of "deliverance." For instance, many African cultures retain elaborate widowhood rituals that can humiliate the women concerned, but families think these customs are essential if the shade of the dead man is not to be offended and provoked to inflict harm. For Christians, though, such rituals are neither necessary nor acceptable. As Ghanaian scholar Juliana Senavoe wrote, "Scripture teaches that any haunting spirit is of the demonic

realm. Jesus by his death and resurrection has triumphed over all principalities and powers and is therefore able to offer perfect protection against any
of them on behalf of those who seek refuge in him." Her research "discovered
a strong link between a personal faith in Jesus Christ and the reduction or
complete absence of fear of forces of evil." In Africa, such a "complete
absence" represents a near-miracle in itself.[72]

While a Euro-American audience might be appalled to think that an
African church preached a belief in witchcraft, the practical consequences of
this teaching in a particular society might be beneficial. In traditional religions, when people think they have no alternative to violence, anti-witchcraft
panics can kill thousands of innocent people. Rather than have desperate
people resorting to such tactics, it is clearly better to have them feel confident
in the protections offered by churches, through prayer and exorcism. Bringing
witchcraft within the ambit of formal religious structures might be the most
effective way of controlling and, ideally, subduing the belief system.

When Christians boast that their faith frees believers from fear, they are
making a profound claim, and one that can easily be substantiated. A society
that no longer believes itself subject to fatalism and occult manipulation is
one that has experienced a real cultural and intellectual revolution, an epochal
change that is the necessary precondition for any later growth. People thus
freed are ready to accept new challenges.

The Triumph of Reason

Nor should we assume that advanced modern nations are as free of superstition as many like to believe, whether indeed their skies are as empty as some
observers claim. Americans and Europeans are unusual in their assumption
that modernity and technology are wholly founded on secular values. If we
look at the world's most progressive and fast-growing economies, that conclusion is far from given. Indians would no more think of beginning a high-
tech venture without a priestly blessing than would the Japanese, and figures
of the god Ganesha grace many of India's thriving IT offices. Sophisticated
Chinese corporate warriors pay careful heed to the mystical arts of feng shui
and are deeply aware of the power of auspicious dates and numbers. In both
Hindu and Buddhist cultures, astrology continues to influence policy, even in
technologically advanced communities.

And on closer examination, perhaps Euro-American proclamations of
scientific objectivity are not quite as genuine as they appear. In the 1930s,
Leon Trotsky remarked with disgust on the failure of modern technology to
root out supernatural beliefs, and he would be scarcely less appalled today:
"Today, not only in peasant homes but also in city skyscrapers, there lives
alongside of the twentieth century the tenth or the thirteenth. A hundred

million people use electricity and still believe in the magic power of signs and exorcisms. The Pope of Rome broadcasts over the radio about the miraculous transformation of water into wine. Movie stars go to mediums. Aviators who pilot miraculous mechanisms created by man's genius wear amulets on their sweaters. What inexhaustible reserves they possess of darkness, ignorance, and savagery!" And he was writing long before the arrival of the Internet.

Viewed at the most rationalistic level, the human mind is hard-wired to interpret happenings in supernatural ways, to seek causality and agency in the natural world. We plead and argue with cars and computers. We also look for significance, and (despite all evidences to the contrary) we find it. After September 11, it was dismaying to watch the upsurge of myths concerning the numerical significance of the event. According to a growing body of urban legend, transmitted verbally and electronically, the whole disaster was surrounded by omens and auguries, by arcane numerological patterns. The twin towers of the World Trade Center physically resembled the number eleven; the individual figures in 9–11 add up to 11; the first aircraft to hit the World Trade Center was American Airlines Flight 11 from Boston; and so on. People clearly felt that these correspondences were of incalculable importance. Individuals educated and articulate enough to construct sophisticated websites used them to promulgate ludicrous conspiracy theories blaming the disaster on any number of sinister dark forces, beside which demons seem almost plausible. In terms of healing, too, current laws permit millions of Americans to seek out alternative medical approaches that range from the somewhat plausible to the comically bogus.

Nor can we ignore the recent outbreak of what can only be called a witchcraft panic in the United States and other ostensibly secular societies. In the decade after 1984, virtually every significant U.S. media outlet published or broadcast stories giving credit to ludicrous claims about the activities of Satanist gangs and murder rings on American soil, and the mass ritual abuse of small children. Therapists who led victims to "recover" memories of such atrocities came to constitute a whole profession, which preyed on the irrational fears of tens of thousands, using techniques that verged on the shamanistic. During therapy, alleged experts in multiple personality disorder evoked "alters," the suppressed alternative identities of their patients, who knew nothing of the amazing abilities and characteristics reputedly possessed by these secret shards of their minds. Nothing apart from the rhetoric and pseudoscientific terminology distinguished such alters from the shrieking demons of first-century Palestine. Victims of ritual abuse were often reported to be the offspring of multigenerational Satanic cults, bearers of what we might call ancestral curses. Hundreds of innocent individuals were caught up in trials arising from the Satanism scare, usually involving charges of mass or ritualized child abuse, and a few remain incarcerated to this day.[73] Moreover, the American panic developed offshoots in every English-speaking nation, as well as in France and the Netherlands. To date, none of the Satanic charges has been substantiated. Only when Euro-American media, law enforcement agencies, and therapeutic professions have begun to acknowledge their own scandalous misbehavior in these affairs can they plausibly criticize Africans or Asians for credulity.

Western society possesses an ineradicable substratum of irrationality and ritualistic behavior, which accounts for the persistent quest for solutions in cults and fringe religions, fads and superstitions. What separates us from our medieval ancestors is that mainstream religions no longer deign to offer formal channels for such impulses within the framework of faith, leaving the door open to fads, cults, and mountebanks. African churches may be more realistic in their holistic approach to human religious impulses.

Even in the matter of "ancestral evil," Northern and Southern worlds are perhaps not as different as they initially appear. Individual responsibility is deeply embedded within our laws, but less so, perhaps, in political attitudes. Much social debate in the United States ultimately concerns the correct attitude toward collective historical responsibility for present-day failings, especially in racial matters. As many have pointed out, individuals do not begin at a common starting line, since their life chances are so conditioned by the historical evils of slavery, segregation, and discrimination; and any decent government must adapt its policies to the position of various groups. As one of Faulkner's characters observed, the past is never dead: it's not even past.

Also, through much modern history, the global North accepted deeply hereditarian views, which found notorious expression in eugenics. While such ideas are discredited today, modern advances in genetics once more promise to make heredity and ancestry critical themes in social debate. Future historians might regard the second half of the twentieth century as an atypical and possibly eccentric period, in its widespread downplaying of hereditary factors in the making of personality. None of these attitudes necessarily have any religious dimension; but the more we appreciate our covert hereditarianism, the more radical seems the biblical vision of the clean slate.

Though many Southern-world Christians believe thoroughly in ideas of spiritual warfare and healing, that does not of itself imply an otherworldly orientation, in the sense of a reluctance to become involved in secular conflicts. Quite the contrary, a core belief in the demonic shapes attitudes toward the secular, and it often motivates passionate involvement. The secular world is not necessarily in the throes of evil, but if secular values challenge or endanger the church, an easy explanation lies at hand: the world serves the Devil, and it is attacking Christ's church.

PERSECUTION AND VINDICATION

They shall deliver you up to councils; and in the synagogues ye shall be beaten: and ye shall be brought before rulers and kings for my sake.

Mark 13:9–11

Remember that the Church is an anvil that has worn out many a hammer.

Theodore Beza

The New Testament portrays persecution as a likely if not inevitable consequence of Christian belief. In Mark's Gospel, Jesus warns his followers of bleak times yet to come, warns about *when* they lead you before a court, not *if*. Most Western readers see in such passages only historical references to long-gone times of persecution. These prophecies, after all, belong to a time when expulsion from the synagogues was a nightmare to be dreaded. In order to make such warnings relevant today, we have to imagine an End Times scenario after the Rapture and the coming of the Antichrist, as portrayed in the fantastic novels of Tim LaHaye and Jerry Jenkins.[1]

In contrast, persecution is a quite real prospect for much of the new Christianity, and martyrdom is both a recent and a continuing reality for many African and Asian churches. All too often, secular ideologies appear false and destructive; their claims to provide growth and improvement are farcically inaccurate; and they sometimes undertake bloody repression. Even when states are not actively homicidal, the common assumption—in the twenty-first century, as in the first—is that the state is a hostile institution, and that secular society must be seen as enemy territory, in which believers tread at their peril. Christians are rarely wise to put their faith in princes or presidents.

Because of their modern historical experience, many Southern Christians easily identify with the profoundly antistate and separatist texts in the New Testament produced by early believers living within the Roman Empire, who themselves faced the danger of imminent persecution. Such diffidence—to say the least—about the secular world contrasts sharply with attitudes in the global North. If global South believers are accused of "supernaturalism," we might well ask what grounds they have for putting their trust in developments in this unjust world.

Of course, the Bible lends itself to a great many political interpretations, and visions of martyrdom and persecution are by no means the only themes that can be found. In different circumstances, modern Christians can find lessons about submission to authority, about the reform of the state, about democratization and human rights. In every case, though, the Bible offers global South Christians a rich fund of texts and ideas, which shape political conduct and public life in ways that often recall the historical experience of Europe and North America.

The Powers That Be

However they interpret the passage, Christians debating political involvement must deal with the stern words of the apostle Paul in Romans chapter 13: "Let every soul be subject unto the higher powers. . . . [T]he powers that be are ordained of God." This injunction is all the more remarkable since it was written at a time of brutal repression, by one who would himself fall victim to Roman imperial power; and yet there the words stand. In the modern West, obedience to state authority is rarely an issue, however much particular churches might criticize secular laws over issues such as abortion and gay marriage. Mainstream American and European churches accept the governments of their respective nations as legitimate and representative, founded as they are on popular will, expressed through the democratic process. The situation is radically different in much of the global South, especially in Africa and Asia. While churches preach the virtues of godly rule, and advocate righteous states on the lines of the Old Testament, bitter experience indicates that few such models exist presently. To the contrary, many existing states are characterized by dictatorship and corruption.

Religious violence and persecution have been persistent themes in the history of the churches of the global South. Lengthy persecutions of Korean Catholics culminated in an orgy of killing in the post–1866 decade, when perhaps eight thousand perished; and North Korea's post–1945 Communist regime slaughtered thousands more. In Uganda, where Christianity was introduced only in the 1870s, many famous martyrs have perished in struggles against pagan kings or secular dictatorships, and many countries have their own litanies of neomartyrs. Between 2000 and 2005, violence between Muslims and Christians in just one Nigerian province killed or expelled over fifty thousand people, mainly Christian.[2] Across Africa, repression by secular states often includes an incidental religious element because of the strong Muslim tradition in the armed forces: this predominance recalls the preference of colonial powers for Muslim "warrior races." Soldiers serving dictatorships tend disproportionately to be Muslim, and their critics and opponents are often Christian clergy.

And for every act of martyrdom, there are thousands of acts of bullying or discrimination. In India, for instance, successive governments have tried to assist Dalits by granting jobs and set-asides, in a kind of affirmative action system, but there is a major catch. These plums are available only for those who remain officially Hindu and who continue to accept their caste status. A lower-caste Hindu who accepts Christianity thus forfeits all these privileges, and likely renounces any hope of dragging his family out of penury.

The notion of being brought into a court to answer for one's faith is no mere End Times fantasy for Christians in Nigeria or Sudan, India or China, Indonesia or Egypt. In addition to interreligious violence, Christians have suffered at the hands of secular states, which might be notionally Christian. Across Central America, the violence and civil wars of the 1980s killed thousands of believers, including prominent clergy. Such situations pose real, practical difficulties for the doctrine of Christian submission. Christians living under repressive Muslim regimes—as in the sharia law states of northern Nigeria—ask seriously whether the words of Romans 13 should apply to them, and at what point Christian submission should give place to the martial spirit of the Old Testament.[3]

The Blood of Martyrs

When Euro-American Christians hear the word "martyr," the images that come to mind have an ancient air, perhaps white-clad men or women facing lions in an arena reminiscent of the film *Gladiator*. The connotations for modern African and Asian Christians are quite different and, of course, contemporary. Not long ago, the Kenya-based Pauline Publications produced its sumptuous *African Bible*, which applies the scriptural text to contemporary African conditions. The cover portrays what at first sight looks like a Maltese cross design, but the underlying story is rather more complex. The design "is based on metal crosses made by Philip Makuei, of the village of Jalé in Bor area, southern Sudan. . . . One day, searching for metal to use in his craft of mending canoes, he discovered that the gas tank of the MiG fighter which had crashed nearby provided metal that could be easily worked." He took special delight in transforming the scrap metal into crosses. "The area had experienced bombing from such MiGs as the one Philip used for his crosses. Some people have seen in the cross the representation of four MiG fighters colliding—the emblems of death being transformed into the emblem of life."[4] For a global North Christian, the word "martyrdom" implies a cinematic lion;

for an African, it suggests a jet fighter in the service of a strictly contemporary regime.

Biblical images of martyrdom and innocent suffering are all the more relevant in societies with living memories of sacrificial traditions. Following the murder of Uganda's Anglican archbishop Janani Luwum in 1977, friends and followers gathered to commemorate him, although Idi Amin's regime had not returned his body. Their minds soon turned to the Bible's ultimate act of martyrdom, the death of Christ. "Then our eyes fell on the empty grave, a gaping hole in the earth. The words of the angel to the two women seeking Jesus' body flashed into our minds, 'Why do you seek the living among the dead?' Namirembe hill resounded with the song that the *Balokole* [revivalists] have taken as their own, *Tukutendereza Yesu*:

> Glory glory hallelujah
> Glory glory hallelujah
> Oh the cleansing blood has reached me
> Glory glory to the Lamb.

We came away from the service praising, healed by the revelation of the empty grave. We greeted each other using the words of the old Easter greeting, 'Christ is risen!' 'He is risen indeed.'"[5]

The Ugandan persecutions produced many stories of martyrdom, which often reflect the theme of crucifixion and the believer's death to this world. One instance in particular has been much recounted in sermons around the world. Kefa Sempangi tells how, after long evading Amin's forces, he eventually met five of the dictator's thugs, who were intending to kill him. Sempangi told them, "I do not need to plead my own cause. . . . I am a dead man already. My life is dead and hidden with Christ. It is your lives that are in danger, you are dead in your sins. I will pray to God that after you have killed me, He will spare you from eternal destruction." To his astonishment, the assassins not only spared his life, but asked him to pray for them.[6]

The crucifixion story is so well known that it can be referenced subtly. In one moving incident in 1970s Brazil, military authorities refused to release the body of a young demonstrator killed in street protests. At a mass meeting, Catholic cardinal Paolo Arns read the story of how, after the crucifixion, Pilate granted Jesus' body to Joseph of Arimathea, who took it for burial. The cardinal read the words "With Pilate's permission, he came and took the body away" and was then silent. There was no need to say more: a pagan tyrant showed mercy, while a modern Christian state did not. The government was shamed into granting the family's request for the body.[7]

Other biblical passages provide a framework for understanding acts of persecution and martyrdom. Beyond the gospels, believers read the stories of Elijah, who resisted a regime that was at once a political tyranny and a sponsor of evil pagan religion. The association of paganism and despotism also marks two other critical sources of political analysis, namely the book of Revelation—of which more later—and Daniel. In both cases, modern conditions echo the circumstances in which the books were written, especially the systematic persecution that demanded the use of coded language. Living in times of fierce religious repression, the authors of both Daniel and Revelation set their stories in distant historical periods, or exotic locales, so that the real-life Rome became the apocalyptic Babylon. If challenged today, in hostile environments such as Pakistan or China, Christians can similarly assert that they are not discussing sedition, but merely studying Bible texts written thousands of years ago, which have no contemporary application. In the Coptic Church, which has often encountered violence from Muslim overlords, the story of Daniel in the lions' den is taken as one such covert account of martyrdom and resistance, by which believers learn to give thanks even in the fiery furnace.

Biblical images of martyrdom and the suffering of the righteous shape interpretations of secular political conflicts. Images of the devil and hell are common during times of persecution or armed conflict, especially when other religions are involved. This need not imply that those other religions are themselves evil or diabolical, but rather that they have become tools of evil. Following the savage Muslim/Christian rioting of 2003, the Anglican bishop of Jos in Nigeria remarked, "Only God can help us now. In September [2001] . . . I said that Satan had unleashed hell on us. I was wrong. What he did then was to release only a sting of hell. Now we are having some form of a blast of hell." The persecution of Christians in southern Sudan has often been termed "hell on earth," and not just in the conventional Western sense of an extremely bloody or chaotic situation. Responding to the parlous situation in the Congo, theologian Musiande Kasali has urged, "We need Christian leaders who will serve God's reign. Surely we have seen enough of Satan's hand in our land." Such writers often have cause to recall the warning in the letter to the Ephesians, "We wrestle not against flesh and blood."[8]

Liberation

The sense of polarization between Christianity and the secular order leads believers to different responses, different means of applying the Bible to their own particular circumstances. Perhaps the most familiar for North Americans is the liberation theology that emerged in Latin America in the 1960s, and that later inspired activism in southern Africa during the struggles against apartheid. In this view, Christians are required to struggle against unjust social and political regimes, which should be replaced with a just order.

Throughout Christian history, believers have used Bible texts to justify every possible shade of political activism, including revolutionary radicalism. The most famous anthem of the American civil war, "John Brown's Body," sews together a number of prophetic and apocalyptic texts. As Christianity spread beyond Europe and North America, the Bible often provided resources for revolutionary militancy, sometimes by offering texts that could be safely explored and discussed at times when explicitly political materials attracted official repression. In the China of the 1940s, novelist Mao Dun used Bible stories as a coded means of denouncing the rightist Kuomintang authorities under whom he lived. In "The Death of Jesus" (1945), he systematically portrayed Jesus and his followers as ancient predecessors of the persecuted left of modern China, with the Kuomintang as the scribes and Pharisees, the brood of vipers who persecuted the saints. The allegory draws on Isaiah to sketch a cataclysmic future after which the peasants would triumph and beat their swords into plowshares.[9]

One of the texts most used for radical ends is the Epistle of James, which expresses such outrage at social injustice and exploitation. In the English-speaking world, James has inspired radicals and socialists: Victorian leftists dared reactionary parsons to preach sermons on James's cry, "Go to now, ye rich men, weep and howl for your miseries that shall come upon you!" The letter has all the more impact in societies in which the authorities keep a close watch on seditious materials. As Costa Rican theologian Elsa Támez writes, "If the Letter of James were sent to the Christian communities of certain countries that suffer from violence and exploitation, it would very possibly be intercepted by government security agencies."[10] Some passages could well be taken as signs of "Marxist-Leninist infiltration of the churches"! Reading the epistle had practical consequences. A key moment in the political history of African Christianity was the 1915 revolt led by John Chilembwe in what is now Malawi. This was an early manifestation of religious-based African nationalism, and the rebels cited the fifth chapter of James as justification for their action. The epistle continues to inspire activism worldwide.[11]

In the 1960s, leftist Roman Catholic scholars in Latin America evolved what became known as liberation theology, which rooted itself firmly in the Bible. Some of the readings were obvious enough: any reader can appreciate how easily an oppressed people can identify itself with the Children of Israel enslaved by Pharaoh, and can envisage a deliverance from that tyranny, either through literal escape or else through a revolutionary overthrow of the social and political order. As Argentine scholar Néstor Míguez writes, activists identified a selection of "'liberating texts,' that were quoted over and over: Exodus, excerpts of the Deuteronomistic history, some prophets like Amos, Isaiah, a selection of Psalms, the synoptic Gospels and the first chapters of Acts, James and, occasionally, Revelation read as an anti-imperialistic manifesto. These became the canon within the canon." Rene Krüger singles out the Gospel of Luke and the Letter of James as "the outstanding examples of deeply rooted social message" directly relevant to the poor of Latin America. The Magnificat "presents God's option for the humble and God's inversion of the relationship between power and property as reflecting God's mercy and promises." Even the book of Nahum, which celebrates the imminent fall of wealthy, oppressive Nineveh, readily translates into a prophetic denunciation of the United States.[12]

The choice of texts was associated with a particular style of reading the Bible, which gave the poor a definitive voice in issues of interpretation. In some cases, this approach becomes what Míguez has termed the "fundamentalism of the left." According to this stance, if in fact God dwells among the poor—a basic tenet of liberation theology—then the interpretations of the Bible presented by the poor must always trump those of accredited scholars. As Míguez writes, "The Bible was 'the memories of the poor'; it was considered as coming totally from below, from the experience of the destitute, where God dwells. So, the texts could only be interpreted in that sense, and many biblical passages were forced to talk in that direction. The Bible was entirely the 'book of the people,' ideologically captured by the powerful and conquerors, but now the poor and powerless were recovering their own heritage, and bringing back the true meaning of the text." Justifying this approach, activists cited the prayer in which Jesus himself thanked his Father for revealing to infants what he concealed from the wise and educated.[13] To adapt the political maxim, *vox populi* really was *vox Dei*.

The great monument to this populist approach is the famous collection of transcripts of discussions published as *The Gospel in Soletiname* (1975). These volumes record Bible studies held under the auspices of liberation theologian Ernesto Cardenal, at a radical settlement that operated in pre-revolutionary Nicaragua. The book, which attracted worldwide attention, aspired to show how ordinary readers were reclaiming the Bible for the poor and restating its subversive message.[14] As Míguez noted, the biblical interpretations that emerged from these communal sessions were presented as—if not infallible—at least authentic and incontestable voices of the masses, who represented the heroes of both the Christian story and the Marxist historical narrative.

Voices of Resistance

Latin American liberationism influenced other movements across the Third World. Such movements were reinforced by the work of North American and European critics exploring the historical setting of the gospels, and understanding the world of Jesus in its political and colonial setting. These scholars see the Judea of Jesus' time as an oppressed colony under a highly repressive and exploitative Roman order, which moderns freely compare to the position of contemporary Latin American and African societies.[15]

The activist "canon within the canon" is diverse. Often cited is Jesus' "Nazareth Manifesto," his declaration in the synagogue that he has come to preach the gospel to the poor. This text provides the clearest basis for what the Catholic Church terms the preferential option for the poor. But many of Jesus' sayings lend themselves to these purposes. In his novel *Petals of Blood,* Ngugi wa Thiong'o cites Jesus' condemnation of those who fail to engage in social and political activism: "Depart from me, you accursed, for I was hungry and you gave me no food, I was thirsty and you gave me no drink." Ngugi uses the text to justify the Kenyan Mau Mau insurrection of the 1950s. Namibian author Zephania Kameeta presents a series of sermons and paraphrased texts that grow from that nation's struggle against South African occupation. Kameeta rewrites the first psalm, for instance, as

> Happy are those who reject the evil advice of tyrants
> Who do not follow the example of sellouts
> And are not resigned to live as slaves.

To the familiar sequence of liberation texts, he adds the Magnificat, and also the texts of Jeremiah: "See, I have this day set thee over the nations and over the kingdoms, to root out, and to pull down, and to destroy, and to throw down, to build, and to plant." Other African theologians went further, not just seeking favorable texts, but challenging and confronting those passages that seemed to justify repression, to purge "the oppressor in the text."[16]

Visions of God as liberator had a special power in South Korea, where the swiftly expanding Christianity of the 1970s and 1980s ran afoul of a military dictatorship with a grim human rights record. In response, theologians evolved their own distinctive form of liberationism in the form of *minjung* thought, which gave the primary place to the common people. Christianity exalted the poor and weak—the *minjung.* As Korean pastor Park Jae Soon declares, "Jesus, the suffering servant, in his death on the cross, shows his deep unity with *Minjung.* His cry on the cross . . . represents the screams of *Minjung* ever coming out of the bottom of history."[17]

These ideas drew on the tale of Exodus and on the prophetic books. Cyris Heesuk Moon writes that in 1945, Koreans "finally were liberated from the rule of the Japanese emperor who, like Pharaoh, had exploited them to the utmost. Thus, the Exodus Model parallels the Korean experience in many ways. The *minjung* of Korea, like the Hebrews, had to assume responsibility and strengthen their awareness of the depths of their bondage in order to rise up against the system in rebellion." Moon annotates a Sunday school lesson from the occupation years thus: "Exodus is the book of the miracle of God's liberation of the people of Israel from the power of Pharaoh [the Japanese emperor]."[18]

Dalits

Another manifestation of liberationism developed in India during the 1980s, in the form of Dalit theology. Though not as familiar to Americans as its Latin-American counterpart, this theology potentially affects a sizable population. India has between twenty-five and fifty million Christians, a small proportion of the country's vast population, yet in absolute terms this figure is comparable to most large European nations; and the number of Indian Christians is also likely to grow in coming decades. Christians draw their numbers disproportionately from people of the lowest caste. Probably 70 percent of Indian Christians are Dalits, though they are gravely underrepresented in positions of church leadership. Read from a Dalit perspective, the Christian gospels are an astonishing document, as Jesus systematically flouts restrictions, taboos, and eating rules powerfully reminiscent of modern Hindu practice. In Jesus' time, as today, the critical divisions in society involve the people or groups with whom one is allowed to eat. His preference for "the poor and the marginalized, tax-collectors, prostitutes and lepers, . . . portrays Jesus as God incarnated as a Dalit." Like the *minjung*, Dalits are the "lost sheep" to whose salvation Jesus' mission was particularly devoted.[19]

At every stage, Jesus does things that offend the elites of his day, the scribes and Pharisees, the people whom modern Indian readers identify as people of the highest castes. These are the ones who ask, "How is it that he eateth and drinketh with publicans and sinners?" From his birth, Jesus breaks caste rules. He is conceived outside wedlock and brought up in the despised, marginal land of Galilee. As Dhyanchand Carr remarks, "In this capacity he represents along with Mary all those who are made to bear the blame of being 'immoral' by the hypocrites and snobs of the world." As an adult, Jesus proclaims liberation for the oppressed in the Nazareth Manifesto, an act that literally gets him chased from the synagogue and threatened with lynching. His gospel is directed to Galileans around the world, "a paradigm of all oppressed, marginalized and stigmatized people." Jesus taught "a gospel of the last and the least of human history and not of the rich and the powerful."[20]

Perhaps only a society in which wealth and power are so intimately tied to religious and ritual status can appreciate the authentic social radicalism of the earliest Jesus movement, or the direct physical risks entailed in membership.

This perspective allows Dalit readers to identify with the denunciations of corrupt elites from the Old Testament prophets, especially Isaiah. And as some Dalits today agitate for the right to pray and worship in Hindu temples —at the risk of their lives—Dalit Christians naturally relish Jesus' cleansing of the Jewish Temple of his day. This sense of identification with Jesus reaches its height in the story of the crucifixion, which exalts humility and submission, and proclaims the victory of service over privilege.[21] Elsewhere too, the vision of Jesus as the product of a despised, marginal land appeals to Christians from colonized or tribal communities. Asian theologians write at length about the plight of "the *minjung* of Korea, the Burakim of Japan, the aboriginals of Australia, the Dalits, Adi Vasis or tribals of India, the Maoris of New Zealand, the Oranges of Malaysia, the First Nations of Canada, the national minorities of the Philippines." An Anglican bishop of native Maori origin wholeheartedly identifies with the ridicule inflicted on Jesus for his Galilean background: "Maori continue to be treated as foreigners in their own land. Maori are treated with suspicion and still bear the stigma of being labeled as heathens, natives and cannibals. . . . The crucifixion of Jesus symbolized Maori suffering." For such readers, as for the Dalits, the triumph of Jesus holds out the promise of victory for the marginalized.[22]

The Joshua Syndrome

Sometimes the closeness of identification with biblical settings raises a real dilemma for modern readers. Most global South nations with large Christian populations have recent memories of colonialism and imperialism, usually enduring up to the last forty or fifty years, and these experiences have largely shaped the political narratives of those societies. The recently colonized easily identify with the sufferings of Hebrews under oppressive foreign rulers, whether Babylonian or Assyrian, Greek or Roman. At the same time, though, tales of Hebrew victories and advances can read sourly in such societies, where many Christians identify with the defeated and massacred Canaanites, rather than the triumphant followers of Moses and Joshua. Such linkages become more commonplace when—as in South Africa—white settlers themselves invoked the conquest of Canaan in order to justify their own occupations of native lands. Zimbabwean Dora Mbuwayesango writes, "The book of Joshua appears to be a blueprint for the colonization of southern Africa. . . . [Joshua] is one of the most troubling books in the Bible."[23]

In the modern world, moreover, the name Israel connotes an advanced Western state locked in seemingly endless struggle with a dispossessed "native" population. South African Anglican archbishop Desmond Tutu has explicitly compared Israel's treatment of the Palestinians with the apartheid system that endured for so long in his own country. One Taiwanese Christian scholar suggests that in the light of the modern Israeli-Palestinian conflict, we had better understand "that the stories about ethnic and land wars in [the Old Testament] are just one-sidedly told by the Jewish rulers and documented by their royal scribes at the expense of the ruled—the Palestinian ancestors. For Jews to enter the 'promised land' is a 'holy war' while for Palestinians it is blood and tears."[24]

In some ways, then, identifying with the biblical setting can pose real problems for understanding the narrative in the ways it was intended. Native American scholar Robert Alan Warrior wrote an essay with the evocative subtitle "Canaanites, Cowboys and Indians," suggesting how some indigenous peoples sympathize with the conquered and occupied, and are duly suspicious of settler claims to divine authorization. That sensitivity is certainly found among the tribal and indigenous peoples who have responded so warmly to the Christian message around the world, among the Indian peoples of Latin America and the tribal minorities of the Indian subcontinent and southeast Asia.[25] Through history, such groups have been driven onto marginal lands, by state mechanisms that remain firmly in the hand of dominant ethnic and religious groups.

For such communities, reading about the conquest of Canaan can be a wrenching experience. Jione Havea records the experience of Bible reading in a South Pacific community. In one session, the reading was Numbers chapter 32, a typical story of conquest and dispossession, followed by the settlement of new colonists on appropriated land. As Havea remarks, such a passage "is painful for natives who have witnessed and suffered the kind of violence described in this story." They respond with "a cry of despair . . . as they hear the stories of the natives of Transjordan, a people whose land was conquered and whose cities, towns and villages were totally destroyed." Havea continues, "The indigenous peoples of the earth all too rarely shout a joyous cry. No joyous cry for the inhabitants of the kingdom of King Sihon of the Amorites or the kingdom of King Og of Bashan, or of Gilead . . . who had the bad fortune of having a land that the Reubenites and the Gadites deemed 'good for cattle.'"[26]

The notion that exodus and liberation are founded on seizing someone else's land gives the Bible a double-edged quality. To quote the general secretary of the Philippine National Council of Churches, "Land grabbing that leads to landlessness is the major problem of the national minorities. Because the land gives life to the national minorities, it is held sacred. Because the land sustains the national minorities, they cannot make claims to it. Instead, it is the land that claims them. And so land cannot be parceled out to a person or a group. It cannot be titled out to one and passed on to another as one would do a piece of property. Land is to be shared by all." To counter the warrants for expansion offered to Joshua, she would rather stress the defense of Naboth, who refused to sell the king the vineyard that was his ancestral land. Even at the risk of his death, Naboth flatly declared, "The LORD forbid that I should give you the inheritance of my fathers." Ahab's evil wife Jezebel then forged evidence that would lead to Naboth's execution, and with Naboth out of the way, the state illicitly acquired his land. Ultimately, God vindicated Naboth's resistance, to the extent that the king and his queen, Jezebel, met awful deaths. Others too have found a strong defense of native land rights in this passage. In the 1970s, the white South African regime deported millions of black residents to their supposed "homelands," a policy justified by the Afrikaaner claim to a special divine mandate to the land, based on their Old Testament–inspired covenant theology. Recalling these events, Archbishop Desmond Tutu asks, "When confronting the iniquity of forced removals of black people, was not the story of Naboth's vineyard perfectly tailor-made for castigating official injustice and oppression?" Once again, Naboth confronted Joshua.[27]

Other biblical accounts of conquest and massacre read worryingly in the context of modern imperialism and military conflict. Reading a Deuteronomistic passage about clearing away the previously settled peoples of Canaan, Mercedes Garcia Bachmann comments, "From our perspective in Argentina, we intensely dislike the passage's militaristic tone," which so readily lends itself to justifying modern imperialism. Criticizing U.S. policy in the aftermath of September 11, Korean scholar Noh Jong Sun argues, "There seems to be a danger of the 'Joshua Syndrome,' the psychiatric identification with Joshua of Old Testament era. People in power, formerly strangers from Europe in Americas, over against the Native Americans, seem to have some illusion that they are Joshua in the 21st century, with full legitimacy given by God of the Hebrew Tribes to conquer the land and kill 12,000 people in Ai. Strangers sometimes become the oppressive powers against the natives." Such attacks on Western visions of manifest destiny proliferated after the first Gulf War of 1991, and still more so during the current Iraq war.[28]

Such readings do not represent any kind of majority opinion for global South churches, many of which view their story very much in the standard Old Testament pattern and see themselves as the new Hebrews; but it is by no means rare for modern readers to see themselves in the position of the dispossessed rather than the conquerors. Not only can they identify with the circumstances of the biblical world, but in this instance, they understand it all too well.

The Great Disappointment

In their various forms, liberationist readings enjoy worldwide currency today, and the great age of Dalit theology may still lie in the future. In Latin America, though, the movement has experienced many disappointments over the past quarter-century. Under Pope John Paul II, the Vatican made every effort to suppress what the hierarchy viewed as Marxist penetration within the church. But certain forms of liberationism also suffered from serious internal contradictions. Though biblical denunciations of injustice lend themselves to radical political readings, interpreters differ widely on the political outcomes they find in the text. Some liberation theologians suggested that, especially in its Latin American homelands, oppression could be ended by political action, through the operations of an activist secular state. This approach led the movement into a perilously close interaction with Marxism. Such a political framework was multiply risky, because an optimistic view of the potential of state power neglected Christian insights about the pervasive effects of original sin and human corruptibility. Religious-based activists sometimes wrote in exactly the same mode as secular radicals, though with biblical references thrown in.

In practice, this overoptimism often led Christian writers to idealize or excuse regimes speaking the language of the left. Liberationist writings of the 1970s and 1980s were prone to romanticize gruesome dictatorships such as Castro's Cuba and Sandinista Nicaragua. Meanwhile, moderate scholars affected to take seriously the claims to Christian statesmanship of various African dictators or presidents-for-life, especially Zambia's Kenneth Kaunda and Tanzania's Julius Nyerere. Looking back at the liberationist writings of these years, the critiques of social injustice still carry weight, but authors discredit themselves by the political models they hold out as solutions. In 1998, the World Council of Churches, a body long committed to liberation movements in Africa, celebrated its fiftieth anniversary as a guest of tyrannical Zimbabwean president Robert Mugabe.[29]

As Marxism crumbled globally—and the apartheid crisis was resolved in southern Africa—the more utopian forms of liberation theology seemed increasingly obsolete. Since the 1970s, the combined forces of globalization and economic liberalism have reduced the incidence of worldwide poverty with a speed and efficiency beyond what even the most radical socialist theorists ever dreamed possible. As Ernesto Cardenal admitted in 1999, "Capitalism won. Period. What more can be said?" Moreover, the old-established churches in which activist liberation theologies flourished lost support while newer Pentecostal and evangelical churches grew at their expense, during the charismatic revival that constitutes one of the most significant developments in modern Christian history. In Latin America, the Roman Catholic Church suffered mass defections to the Pentecostals. In Africa, the losers were mainline Protestant denominations affiliated with the World Council of Churches, groups such as the Methodists and Presbyterians.[30]

Newer churches were commonly suspicious of overt political involvement. Writing of Kenya—though the description has wider application—John Lonsdale remarks that for charismatics or conservative evangelicals, "the nature of secular governance seems to be largely immaterial to personal salvation. Indeed, insofar as they comment on politics at all, they would say it is the conviction of personal salvation in the country's rulers, rather than their respect for democratic rights and procedures, that is the only sure recipe for honest and just government. These churches quote more from the Old Testament than from the New. They recall stories of how God rewarded or punished Israel's rulers according to their obedience or disobedience to Him, not according to their adherence or otherwise to democratic procedure and the will of the people." This does not mean that evangelicals are apolitical, but as we will see, they are concerned more with creating a righteous political order than with effecting far-reaching economic restructuring.[31]

Radical theologians who had placed their hopes in socialist utopianism entered a long period of disarray and disappointment. Most did not renounce their commitments, but rather turned to other biblical traditions to learn how to confront what they saw as the lies and illusions of globalization. Some found hope in the wisdom genre, which, while less sensational in its imagery than apocalyptic, likewise teaches strategies for survival in times of exploitation and oppression. In both Asia and Latin America, Ecclesiastes has acquired a following among those who thirty years ago would have been drawn to radical political activism, but who now realized the futility of such efforts. In wisdom, they find the philosophical strength they need to assure their endurance. By exposing the illusions underlying modern society, with its deceptive façade of advertising and mass media, Ecclesiastes offers strategies by which Christians can withstand "contemporary technocratic culture." Mercedes Garcia Bachmann notes that "Qoheleth's approach to what was the empire propaganda of the time ('new' = 'better') seems to be . . . timely." In the weary words of Elsa Támez, the book was written for times "when horizons are closing in and the present becomes a hard master, demanding sacrifice and suppressing dreams." In east Asia too, John Mansford Prior comments, "Precisely these struggling base communities are finding in Ecclesiastes both the skepticism they require to face the all-enveloping global market and the rootedness they need as their precarious cultures are buffeted by rapid change."[32]

Saving the State

Post–1990 political shifts caused many Christian leaders not to abandon the political realm, but rather to shift their emphasis. Believers still turned to biblical calls for justice, which were all the more telling given the continuing economic despair in parts of the global South, but they were less inclined to dream of millenarian economic solutions. Indeed, the loss of faith in states and secular power—and loss of capacity to effect change through state socialism —actually enhanced the prestige and influence of churches and Christian leaders, who found themselves playing a pivotal role in their societies.

The experience of post-independence Africa illustrates the churches' growing political role. The new regimes that came to power in the aftermath of colonialism usually defined themselves as secular, nationalist, and (in a broad sense) socialist; and their commitment to modernization made them enemies of most manifestations of traditional religion. As hopes of modernization failed, so did the associated ideologies and the attendant rhetoric. The time soon came when it was simply no longer plausible to blame all the problems of the new societies on the colonial heritage. The systematic failures of secular politics were exemplified by the agonizing sequence of military regimes and kleptocracies in most countries, as well as the pervasive corruption. In the forty years following independence in 1960, Nigerian regimes squandered or misappropriated over $200 billion, potentially enough to have raised the country's standard of living to European levels. Africans remarked cynically on the powerful emerging tribe of the *waBenzis*, the utterly corrupt rulers whose most prized possession was a stretch armored Mercedes-Benz S600L. And while secular ideologies crumbled, millions turned instead to religious beliefs that challenged the whole basis of the secular state.[33]

Similar changes occurred elsewhere. In the Middle East, once-intoxicating ideologies such as Nasserism and Ba'athism confronted the overwhelming challenge of resurgent Islam. In Latin America too, Pentecostal churches filled the void left by states unable to cope with globalization and explosive urbanization. Around the world, religious activism promoted social and political structures far more effective than anything the secular states had achieved, and less tainted by corruption.

States fail; churches flourish. And the bishops and pastors who lead these churches gain added power from their record of standing firm against egregious violations of human rights. Across the global South, it has commonly been church leaders who most visibly struggle for reform, democratization, and human rights; who most publicly denounce tyranny, at whatever risk to their personal safety. Churches of many denominations were indispensable to the resistance against dictatorship in the Philippines and South

Korea, in Brazil and South Africa. Some legendary leaders include Oscar Romero in El Salvador, Desmond Tutu in South Africa, and Jaime Sin in the Philippines. Others, such as Liberia's Archbishop Michael Kpakala Francis, are less celebrated but no less heroic. The Catholic archbishop of Bulawayo, Pius Ncube, has proved such a dauntless opponent of Zimbabwe's Mugabe regime that many marvel at his continued survival.[34]

The role of the clergy as defender against tyranny harks back to European medieval precedent. Then as now, governments without qualms about killing or jailing lay opponents felt they had to act cautiously against venerated clergy, especially when those clergy served a well-connected supranational organization. Churches with deep-inlaid theories of martyrdom and sacrifice are all too likely to turn their fallen leaders into unconquerable symbols. Just as the medieval church sanctified Archbishop Thomas Becket, so modern Africans remember Janani Luwum, and Latin Americans recall Oscar Romero. Partly to deter regime forces, Archbishop Ncube decorates his cathedral with portraits of Romero and Martin Luther King Jr. and cites Tutu and Luwum as his special heroes. At the same time, even the bravest bishops and cardinals know they have to walk carefully for fear of provoking a tyrant to open persecution.

Interesting Sermons

In upholding the democratic process, Christian activists have drawn on many of the familiar texts espoused by the liberation theologians, but they also apply others seemingly more conservative in tone. Biblical attacks are particularly lethal when church leaders deploy against left-leaning native elites the very same texts that liberation movements had earlier used against colonial authorities. Archbishop Ncube freely uses the Exodus narrative, with Mugabe cast as Pharaoh: "The Israelites prayed to God to deliver them from Egypt —from Pharaoh, who was an oppressor. And so we also ask that God may deliver us and take this man away." An admiring journalistic account described Ncube finding in his Bible Luke 4:18 and commenting, "Free the oppressed. This is our calling." As his sermons represent the freest and most outspoken expressions of opposition in the nation, government agents closely monitor all his sermons, presumably with a close eye on their political implications. In such a modern repressive regime, secret police forces have to be skilled in biblical hermeneutics.[35]

Often, religious leaders using biblical texts against oppression or extortion do not necessarily refer to a named individual or party. Grounding an argument in scripture allows subversive doctrines to be deployed without provoking the direct confrontations that might arise from less surreptitious approaches. During the dreadful regime of Nigerian dictator Sani Abacha in the 1990s, the nation's Christians turned to James, and to the prophetic words of Amos, who similarly denounced wealth and corruption.

A consummate master of this semicovert resistance technique was Kenya's Anglican leader David Gitari, who is nowhere near as well known as South Africa's Desmond Tutu, but who is no less significant or courageous a moral leader. Though Gitari's Anglican Church enjoys great prestige in Kenya, it represents only a small minority of Christians. Nevertheless, his masterful use of scripture for political ends illustrates just how powerful this kind of biblically based politics can be. From 1975 through 1990, he served as bishop of the diocese of Mount Kenya East, and from 1996 through 2002 he was archbishop of the whole Kenyan church. Through most of Gitari's episcopal career, Kenya was led by the authoritarian Daniel Arap Moi, who presided over a corrupt and occasionally lethal regime, the opponents of which tended to die mysteriously. Though Gitari survived, his house was assaulted by members of the ruling party, he was heckled and jostled by the party faithful, and, like Ncube, his life seemed to be in grave danger. Gitari first came to notice in 1975 when a prominent reformer within the governing party was murdered. Commissioned to deliver a series of radio talks to the nation, Gitari chose as his text the story of Cain and Abel, ruminating on violence as a curse gnawing at a nation. "Today, God is asking Kenyans, 'Where is your brother J. M. Kariuki?' And those who assassinated him or planned his assassination are saying, 'Am I my brother's keeper?'" Following another assassination, in 1987, the bishop preached a sermon entitled "Cain Strikes Again."[36]

Through the 1980s, Gitari preached on a series of incendiary texts, usually introducing them with the innocent-sounding note that his audience would find a text "interesting." He made a point of publishing these ruminations, not through an author's vanity, but rather as a means of making them nationally available. When Kenya became a one-party state in 1982, Gitari found "interesting" the book of Esther, in which the advice of evil counselors led the Persians to pass a disastrous law that could not be repealed. Kenyans, he noted, were under no such restraints and could reverse tyrannical or foolish laws. Gitari's message to Kenyan leaders—and to the military—repeated the words of Esther: "And who knows but that you have come to your royal position for such a time as this? Only do not keep silent."[37]

Other texts favored by Gitari included the Beatitudes, especially "Blessed are the peacemakers." His point was that dictators and exploiters create conflict rather than peace, while failing to oppose unjust rulers contributed nothing to true peace or justice. Gitari drew particularly on that apocalyptic favorite, the book of Daniel, which had the added advantage of sharing a name with the president. The biblical Daniel was a loyal man attempting to serve his country and to tell the truth, without compromising his loyalty to God. The consequence, though, is that he provokes the wrath of corrupt courtiers and sycophants. Speaking as Moi was attempting an outrageous restructuring of electoral law, Gitari preached that "Daniel was in effect telling the king [that] when the constitution is fundamentally changed so as to interfere with a fundamental human right . . . that new law can be disobeyed." As so often in modern Africa, Daniel becomes an image of the righteous man in politics, who stands steadfast against the threats of a corrupt state.[38]

When security forces brazenly attacked prodemocracy activists gathered at Nairobi's cathedral, Gitari abandoned the thin disguise offered by biblical analogies and used Daniel to launch an outright prophetic condemnation: "Moi allowed the All Saints Cathedral to be defiled. . . . That is enough to bring down divine wrath on him, as the writing appeared on the wall when King Belsassar defiled the holy vessels in the Book of Daniel. I am no prophet nor a son of a prophet, but I told Moi myself that his days are numbered and his kingdom will crumble if he refuses to repent and accept constitutional changes." The line about the "son of a prophet" is taken from the book of Amos, in a passage that warns of the destruction of the land should its people fail to repent.[39] Amos, not surprisingly, was also a favorite of Martin Luther King Jr.

The Lord Is My Shepherd

Confronted with tyrannical rule, Christians can turn to any number of biblical texts. Throughout the New Testament, passages advise believers to keep the state at arm's length, while ideas of election and separation from the ungodly have encouraged various forms of physical segregation from mainstream society. Apart from the obvious Old Testament examples—Abraham leaving his homeland, the Hebrews leaving Egypt—New Testament texts reinforce the message. In Revelation, believers are told to "come out from her [Babylon], my people." Christians are told, "Therefore come out from them, and be separate from them," to become "a peculiar people." The modern spread of evangelical Christianity in parts of Latin America has caused clashes that have driven believers from their homes, sometimes to build biblically based new settlements, to found "New Jerusalems" or "New Israels." Again recalling events in Europe centuries ago, believers spurn customs and traditions believed to be pagan, creating radical new definitions of community and fellowship.[40]

Some prophetic texts can make modern Christians sound like radical Islamists in their fierce opposition to a state based on mere human authority. The resemblances are not surprising, since both are ultimately drawing on a common Hebrew tradition, in which earthly rulers exist at God's pleasure and can forfeit this authority if they abuse their power. That is the spirit of the text of Amos suggested by Gitari. Congolese scholar Katho Bungishabaku discusses Jeremiah 22, one of many Old Testament passages in which a prophet threatens ruin to the king or state that does not give justice and protect the weak. Looking at modern Africa—including most "Christian" nations—he describes dictatorships and cults of personality as outright idolatry. He continues: "God has been killed so that our leaders may take his seat. . . . [Any] kind of abuse of power is rebellion against the One who is the source of all power. . . . There is a need to desacralize human power in Africa by presenting an alternative: the power of God." Such words read almost like a text from Muslim Salafists. Illustrating the similarity of rhetoric, if not of actions, we recall the assassin of Egypt's President Anwar Sadat boasting, "I have killed Pharaoh!"[41]

Looking at biblical texts concerning persecution and attitudes toward the state, few Westerners would think to build upon the numerous passages concerning shepherds. Most Western Christians know the New Testament passages in which Jesus is the shepherd and believers his flock, and the resulting image is romantic or sentimental. This language conjures up a literally "pastoral" scene, perhaps orchestrated to Bach's "Where Sheep May Safely Graze." But societies in which people care for domestic livestock understand the role of the shepherd in terms of performing duties of care and protection with a proper sense of responsibility. They readily understand the role of the shepherd in political terms, and the image of the shepherd king goes far back in Near Eastern tradition: we think of King David. In turn, this analogy gives rise to the Old Testament passages condemning as wicked shepherds those rulers and priests who exploit and betray their people.[42]

One "shepherd" text read in political ways is Ezekiel 34, a harangue against the corrupt "shepherds of Israel." Kenya-based theologian Hannah W. Kinoti remarks that "God's word through the prophet Ezekiel, in which the leaders of Israel are depicted as wicked shepherds who defraud and destroy the sheep (Ez 34) is so graphically true of leadership in Africa today that the people have to say 'Yes, the lord is my shepherd, nobody else.' " One version of her essay was entitled "In the Valley of the Shadow of Idi Amin." To quote a modern African Bible commentary, "The image of the shepherd referred to the kings but it also refers to all people entrusted with the task of leadership." When shepherds failed, the sheep were scattered, "in this context the exiles, and in our present situation the refugees."[43]

David Gitari deployed Ezekiel 34 during Kenya's growing political crisis of the early 1990s. In 1991, he preached a sermon entitled, encouragingly, "You are doomed, you shepherds of Israel!" Gitari addressed the call to "shepherds," to "teachers and heads of schools, . . . chairmen of farmers cooperatives, village and market leaders, assistant chiefs, District officers, District Commissioners, provisional Commissioners, and even the Head of State." In a throwaway tone, he added the president to his list, as if as an afterthought. The sermon then illustrated grotesque examples of failure and betrayal by shepherds—by ministers and party officials—as well as by corruption and self-enrichment, or the abuse of prisoners and rivals. But there was hope: "How wonderful it is to know that God cannot leave his sheep to be exploited forever, because the sheep belong to him."[44]

Gitari would often return to the shepherd theme. When the government sought to restrict voting rights, he preached on Matthew 9, which tells of Jesus' compassion for those who "fainted, and were scattered abroad, as sheep having no shepherd." And while using Ezekiel 34 as a lesson in how not to govern, he presented the image of the Good Shepherd as a model of correct behavior—a model, of course, that few contemporary leaders seemed to fulfill. The passage in question is so well known in Africa because it immediately follows the much-quoted verse 10:10, in which Jesus promises his followers life in abundance. Preaching to a gathering that included many politicians, Gitari concluded, "Go to parliament and be a good shepherd."[45]

When all earthly shepherds have failed, one turns to the truly radical statement of reliance on God alone, in Psalm 23, "The Lord is my shepherd." At its face value, the psalm is associated with death, and it is widely used as a funeral text—making it somewhat odd that British Commonwealth nations so often employ it at weddings. So common have these conventional uses been that the words have been tarnished by familiarity. Hearing the opening words at a funeral, a character in a recent American novel despairs, "as if these weren't the most rote, all-purpose public school stanzas in the entire Bible!" But the scripture is popular across Christian Africa. The Ewe people of Ghana are "deeply attached" to "the Shepherd of Psalm 23 and the Good Shepherd of John 10. They pray or recite Psalm 23 in any life-threatening situation and find consolation in it." Recalling his time tending sheep in his childhood, the great theologian John Mbiti wrote, "As I went about in my youth looking after these animals, little did I realize that the gospel was right there in front of me."[46]

Global South Christians use Psalm 23 in familiar devotional ways, but they also understand it as a stark rejection of unjust secular authority. Cyris H. S. Moon reports its popularity among Koreans living under a savage Japanese occupation: "Christians in Korea silently wished for their God to intervene and to make them the subjects of their own destiny, living in restored relationships with their enemies in the presence of their God." He quotes the psalm thus, with parenthetical comments: "Even though I walk through the valley of the shadow of death [Japanese Imperial Government], I will fear no evil. . . . Thou preparest a table before me in the presence of mine enemies [i.e., Japan]."[47] Namibia's Zephania Kameeta offers this modern adaptation of the text:

> The Lord is my shepherd I have everything I need
> He lets me see a country of justice and peace
> And directs my steps towards his land

Ugandan poet Timothy Wangusa has written an effective parody of the psalm, "The state is my shepherd," the point of course being that the state, as so often, is seeking to replace God.[48]

To declare "The Lord is my shepherd" is to deny the claims of worldly seekers of that status, possibly a throwback to the sense in which shepherd imagery was originally presented by Jesus and his first followers. It is as if the believer is proclaiming to unjust rulers, "The Lord is my Shepherd—you aren't." The psalm serves a purpose closely akin to the Muslim declaration "*Allahu akbar*!" Though famous (or notorious) as a battle cry, this phrase also contains a weighty theology. Whatever goals the world sets forward, God is greater; whatever power is claimed by earthly authority, God is greater. For Christians too, Psalm 23 carries the message that God alone has the authority to shepherd his people.

Adding to the power of the psalm, the evils that it condemns are at once political and spiritual, forces of tyranny and of the devil. Besides its political role, the Psalm 23 is much used in services of healing, exorcism, and deliverance. In his description of Ghanaian Pentecostalism, J. K. Asamoah-Gyadu writes, "It is thus a deep affirmation of charismatic theology when at the close of services members repeat the words of Psalm 23:6: 'Surely, goodness and mercy shall follow me all the days of my life, and I will dwell in the house of the Lord forever.'" He records a confrontation with pagan forces, at the climax of which he delivers a woman from her possession by a river goddess: "[With] a few of my elders, we sang some hymns, I prayed and then read Psalm 23. At the end of these prayers, the priestess had become sober."[49] Oppression in this world and the supernatural are closely allied.

Defending the Land

In addition to their struggles for human rights, African churches in particular have demonstrated a keen awareness of threats to the environment and the urgent need for activism. As we have seen, John Mbiti urged African Christians to develop their theology of the land, and in some areas, environmental consciousness has become highly developed. For African independent churches, key texts include the passages asserting Christ's dominance over the entire earth. In the much-heard ending of the Gospel of Matthew, the risen Jesus declares, "All authority in heaven and earth has been given to me." Also cited is Colossians 1:17: "And he is before all things, and by him all things consist." If Christ is the overlord of all Creation, his followers have an absolute duty to protect it. The Shembe Church, for instance, strictly forbids killing any animals, including snakes; and followers are not permitted to keep dogs lest they succumb to the temptation to hunt.

Christian-based ecological movements have thrived in Zimbabwe. European missionary Martinus Daneel worked closely with local churches to form organizations such as the Association of African Earth-Keeping Churches and the Zimbabwean Institute of Religious Research and Ecological Conservation (ZIRRCON). In a typical ceremony, "some 50 bishops of various African independent Christian churches . . . sprinkled holy water on ground that was soon to welcome tree saplings. Bishop Mutikizizi, tall and elegant in a scarlet robe and light blue cape, white scarf and six pointed crown of scarlet cloth and sequins, offered communion to the villagers and simultaneously blessed the tiny saplings they held in their hands." When villagers confess their sins, they are encouraged to include offenses against the land: "One woman nursing a baby says 'I've cut a living tree without planting one to replace it.' An old man admits to clearing natural vegetation in order to grow crops on river banks. Another man confesses 'I failed to manage contours on steep land.'" However far such activities may be from the liberation theology of the 1970s, they potentially represent an important force for social change.[50]

Again, Archbishop Gitari used his preaching to defend environmental causes. In 1991, he responded to a scandalous land grab in which local politicians had secured a grant of public land, a mountain of natural beauty and environmental importance. Gitari's text on this occasion referred to "one of the most *interesting* dramas in the Bible," the conflict between King Ahab and the peasant Naboth.

The lessons of the sermon—"Was there no Naboth to say no?"—are painfully relevant to the immediate circumstances of the land grant, but as in all of Gitari's preaching, a biblically literate readership sees additional layers. When Naboth refused to sell the land of his fathers, he responded much as Kenyans and other Africans did to European demands that they give up their ancestral holdings, so that Gitari is effectively identifying the Kenyan government with colonial oppressors. The land grant went to two local party officials, while Naboth was convicted on the evidence of two "scoundrels." We also recall the two false witnesses whose evidence led Christ to his execution (Matthew 26:60). Jezebel, moreover, through her patronage of the prophets of Baal, symbolizes paganism, and the book of Revelation uses her name to label a sinister heretic. Jezebel was also the mortal enemy of Elijah, who prefigures Christ. A simple act of graft or land theft now acquires apocalyptic and even diabolical dimensions, and these allusions do not begin to exhaust the implications offered by Gitari, who makes the story of Naboth "interesting" indeed.[51]

By These Words We Are Comforted

But for all the popularity of other texts, the main biblical assertion of God's supremacy over an evil secular world is clearly that found in Revelation, with its florid imagery that has for so long made it a source of inspiration to artists. Revelation is difficult for Christian readers to avoid, not least because its conventional position at the end of the New Testament seems to give it the status of a conclusion and summary to the whole work. At the same time, the book has fared poorly among Northern mainline believers, who are puzzled or alienated by the violence of its apocalyptic and ferocious moralism, not to mention the book's stern rejection of sexuality. In modern America, apocalyptic suggests to many the thought world of cult compounds and armed militias.

Apocalyptic is such a common theme in religions worldwide that it seems almost hardwired into our consciousness and our belief systems. For all human beings, radical and fundamental changes in life can demand a period of crisis marked by agony and blood—we think of the moments of birth and death—and we project these ideas to the cosmic scale. In the global South, however, the biblical account of Revelation exercises an immense fascination across the political spectrum. Given its portrayal of secular states as deceptive, evil persecutors, and cities as the seats of demonic forces, the book's appeal requires little explanation. For many, on both left and right, it reads like a political science textbook. From a liberationist perspective, Brazilian scholar Gilberto da Silva Gorgulho remarks, "The Book of Revelation is the favorite book of our popular communities. Here they find the encouragement they need in their struggle and a criterion for the interpretation of official persecution in our society. . . . The meaning of the church in history is rooted in the witness of the gospel before the state imperialism that destroys the people's life, looming as an idol and caricature of the Holy Trinity."[52]

Revelation is eminently suitable for a society that lives constantly with disasters and violence. Churches in Sudan, subject to decades-long mass martyrdom, read Revelation for its promise that whatever may ensue in this world, God's justice will ultimately prevail. Such a message was no less newsworthy for Ugandan Christians in the 1970s, in the years of the Amin dictatorship. At one point, the small Redeemed Church faced imminent persecution and likely extermination. Its followers naturally turned to Revelation to make sense of their plight, and in one service, they read this passage: "And when they shall have finished their testimony, the Beast that ascendeth out of the bottomless pit shall make war against them, and shall overcome them, and kill them." The preacher continued, "By these words we are comforted." The "comfort" in such nightmare images might seem slight indeed, except that now the listeners have been reminded of two things. They understand the diabolical nature of the Amin regime, and by the same token, they also know the end of the story, that the Beast will be annihilated. A church leader, Kefa Sempangi, reports meeting one of Amin's Nubian assassins and torturers, who claimed to have slaughtered two hundred people. The man was converted when he read John 8:44, "Ye are of your father the devil," and he realized that in working for Amin, he had been serving Satan.[53]

The message of Revelation is simple: however overwhelming the world's evils might seem, God has triumphed and will triumph. In China, Christians turned to Revelation for hope during times of persecution, above all during the phantasmagoric horrors of the Cultural Revolution. According to K. K. Yeo, "By means of the motifs of visionary transportation to heaven, visions of God's throne room in heaven, angelic mediators of revelation, symbolic visions of political powers, coming judgment, and new creation, Chinese Christians see the final destiny of this despaired world in the transcendent divine purpose. . . . It is the hope portrayed in the Book of Revelation that sustains Chinese Christians to endure to the end."[54]

Latin American liberation theologians have also seen their story in apocalyptic literature. When in 1990 the defeat of the Nicaraguan Sandinistas crushed revolutionary hopes in Central America, prominent radical scholars contributed to a special "apocalyptic" number of the journal *Revista de Interpretación Bíblica Latinoamericana*, addressing not just Revelation but also texts such as Mark 13, Thessalonians, and Daniel 7. Editor Pablo Richard remarked, "Apocalyptic rises in periods of persecution to stir the hopes of the people of God. . . . Apocalyptic declares the judgment of God that puts an end to the crisis that the people suffer, and announces the imminent arrival of the kingdom of God in history; apocalyptic uncovers the reality of God in history which is the reality of God's poor; apocalyptic is the moment of truth and justice. . . . [A]pocalyptic is the hope of the oppressed." According to another contributor, "The church's function, in any Christian community, is to denounce the sinister intentions of any system claiming total hegemony through the imposition of an economic system that assumes the nature of idolatry." Throughout, the authors leave no doubt about the identification between the monstrous Roman power described in Revelation and the contemporary imperialist United States.[55]

Elsewhere, too, Revelation speaks plausibly to a modern audience. The modern development of apocalyptic theology reached new heights in the South African churches of the 1980s, when government opponents portrayed the apartheid regime, and its religious allies, according to the most harrowing texts of Revelation. Preaching at the funeral of civilians killed by South African authorities, Desmond Tutu chose as his text Revelation 6, in which the martyrs cry out, "Lord, how long?" So burningly relevant were such texts that, as Tutu remarks, they "seemed then to have been written with our particular situation in mind." Though the government exercised a draconian censorship, they had missed such incendiary items as Revelation: "the book they should have banned was the Bible."[56]

In the famous Kairos document of 1985, a group of influential theologians agreed that the white-dominated South African state was worse than a mere dictatorship. The government served "the god of superior weapons who conquered those who were armed with nothing but spears. It is the god of the casspirs and hippos [military vehicles], the god of teargas, rubber bullets, sjamboks [whips], prison cells and death sentences. Here is a god who exalts the proud and humbles the poor—the very opposite of the God of the Bible who 'scatters the proud of heart, pulls down the mighty from their thrones and exalts the humble' (Lk 1:51–52). From a theological point of view the opposite of the God of the Bible is the devil, Satan. The god of the South African State is not merely an idol or false god, it is the devil disguised as Almighty God—the Antichrist."[57]

For the churches, the struggle against apartheid had a powerfully religious character, almost amounting to a crusade, and Christians needed to move beyond the submission enjoined by Romans 13. The Kairos document proceeds: "God does not demand obedience to oppressive rulers. . . . The Jews and later the Christians did not believe that their imperial overlords, the Egyptians, the Babylonians, the Greeks or the Romans, had some kind of divine right to rule them and oppress them. These empires were the beasts described in the Book of Daniel and the Book of Revelation. God allowed them to rule for a while but he did not approve of what they did."

Though other global South crises and confrontations fail to stir the Western media as much as South Africa did, apocalyptic visions still shape African Christianity. One Ghanaian author notes, "In Africa today there are still marks of the 'Beast'—pain and suffering arising from ethnic conflicts and civil wars, corruption in high places which results in unnecessary deaths on our roads, political assassinations, high increase in crime on our streets, extreme poverty and hunger which dehumanizes many Africans." But Revelation exercises a widespread influence, and passages and images from it appear in the oddest contexts. Even launching a routine church committee meeting in Nigeria, one naturally uses a weighty and quite threatening text from Revelation: "The biannual meeting of the Standing Committee of the Church of Nigeria kicks off Tuesday this week in Maiduguri with the theme, 'I know your works' (Rev. 2 and 3)."[58]

Related texts from the gospels are also popular: A sermon from Malawi uses as its text Luke 21, the "little apocalypse," with its warnings of wars and disasters to come. "Haven't you heard of wars in many parts of the world? Think of what happened in Rwanda and Burundi. What about Iraq and Liberia? . . . [A]re you not convinced that all these conflicts between nations are only taking place to fulfill what Jesus spoke to the disciples many years ago? We have heard of many people shedding their blood in South Africa, Burundi and Rwanda. We have heard of diseases like AIDS, Ebola and tuberculosis claiming many lives. All these, brethren, are signs which indicate to you and me that time has gone. We are now living in injury time like in a football match. Any time from now, brethren, Jesus is coming to take his faithful with him to God's Kingdom." Kenya's independent churches tell their members to be neither surprised nor discouraged by political persecution. They should turn to their Bibles, to Revelation chapter 3, and to Luke's little apocalypse. There, they will find infallibly prophesied both the coming of persecution and the promise of immortality to those who keep their faith unto the end.[59]

Texts for Democracy

So ferocious, in fact, are these biblically based rejections of secular authority that at times, it seems difficult to believe that churches might reconcile themselves to supporting a state. In fact, as in early modern Europe, churches find little difficulty in exhorting believers to obedience, with the proviso that in case of conflict, the battery of apocalyptic texts remains in reserve. Through their denunciations of tyrants and dictators, Gitari and his counterparts are asserting the proper values needed for a just ruler. More difficult, of course, is the creation of a political order not dependent on the individual whims of a king or president, but here too, churches have used biblical texts to present a democratic political vision. Philippine cardinal Jaime Sin—nemesis of the dictatorial Marcos family—proclaimed that "politics without Christ is the greatest scourge of our nation" and sought to shape political affairs according to that vision. Today, the Christians of the People's Republic of China face an awesome challenge in trying to promote democratic government and human rights within that nation, though their ideas have the potential to win real influence. Christian theories of servant leadership, of the last being first, carry special weight in a society where the prevailing Communist ideology has long preached such a notional message of official humility, while glaringly failing to live up to it. In this setting, texts such as the Christological hymn in Philippians, about Christ's self-emptying and self-denial, bear a special political relevance. So, of course, do Christian ideas of the value of the individual.[60]

Biblical creativity was much in demand in the 1980s and 1990s, when many nations across Africa, Asia, and Latin America were undergoing a transition to democracy after long periods of dictatorship or political oppression. And in most instances, churches and church-based activists served as the key figures in promoting such transitions. In Malawi, for example, the Catholic Church did much to foster democracy following the end of the long Banda dictatorship in the 1990s. In formulating the goals of the political order, church leaders used both the Bible and African proverbs to urge the importance of social cooperation for the common good. During the transition period, many sermon texts were drawn from the historical books of the Old Testament, from Judges through 2 Kings, which stress how the conduct of the ruler affected the health of the state. Only by obeying God and promoting justice did the Hebrew nation achieve stability and wealth among its hostile neighbors.[61]

These texts have a wide currency in African political thought, much as they did in the European Middle Ages. Congolese scholar Fidele Ugira Kwasi writes, "The Book of Judges has much to teach to us in sub-Sahara Africa regarding how to emerge from four decades of chaotic political and economic transition." Then as now, clans, tribes, and peoples need to unite in common obedience to God, common loyalty to shared national narratives, and a recognition of one another's value. Also influential in the Malawian case was the book of Daniel, which describes how God intervened dramatically in history to save his people.[62]

From the New Testament, the most valuable passages were the Pauline texts on the body and how different parts worked together for the good of the whole. As happens so often in African church life, the critical text proved to be the letter to the Ephesians, a text that is so often mined for materials for church government, no less than for its words on spiritual warfare. In this context, though, the key passage was drawn from chapter 4: "From him the whole body, joined and held together by every supporting ligament, grows and builds itself up in love, as each part does its work." In a Western context, such words might seem to be a generic exhortation to unity, but they read very differently in an African nation with deep ethnic and regional division.[63] Malawi alone has perhaps thirty-five ethnolinguistic groups, and fourteen major languages are spoken. A call for national harmony may sound bland in the United States: in Rwanda or Congo, Sri Lanka or Indonesia, it is almost a millenarian dream.

Also recalling medieval precedent has been the heroic work of church leaders in promoting reconciliation in the aftermath of conflict, war, and repression. Though the idea of forgiveness is basic to Christian thought, the theme plays strikingly little role in modern activism in the global North. Through the early modern period, though, European churches had often been active in persuading groups and individuals to accept reconciliation, to forgive their enemies and abandon grievances that could promote destructive vendettas. This policy has been revived in modern Africa, most spectacularly in the Truth and Reconciliation movement sponsored by the South African churches and implemented in the influential commission that brought together former deadly enemies. Through the powerful cultural example set by South Africa, similar ideas might well influence other African nations as they emerge from various forms of political disaster. Such a reconciliation policy would also contribute mightily to achieving unity between ethnic groups and regions.[64]

In a democratic setting, churches face issues quite different from those encountered under a dictatorship. As Terence Ranger observes, even something like the Kairos document was "too 'theologically thin' to provide guidance on how to go on being prophetic in majority rule South Africa."[65] Or as Desmond Tutu remarked, following the democratic transition in that nation, "It is easy to be against. It is not nearly so easy to be clear about what we are *for*." Prophetic denunciation might be appropriate in the face of naked violence and persecution, but matters change when a state can plausibly claim to express the will of a democratic majority. In such a situation, churches must be more willing to follow the principles of obedience to established authorities laid down in Romans chapter 13.

Church leaders also face the practical difficulty that their wishes might run contrary to those of other groups, people of other faiths or of none, who might pass laws that Christians find unpalatable. In contemporary Brazil, for instance, the thriving Protestant and Pentecostal churches often debate their role under a democratic government to which they feel largely sympathetic. The Assemblies of God state, "The Church respects all constituted authority and teaches its members to be faithful fulfillers of their duties, and to obey the laws of the country. The Church collaborates with the authorities by restoring lives through the preaching of the Word of God. . . . Obedience and submission to the authorities are commandments of God. Romans 13:1–7. (The Church obeys the laws of the country provided these are not contrary to the laws of God, Acts 4:19, Acts 5:29)." The final clause deserves closer examination, since the quote from Acts seems to advise selective resistance: "We must obey God rather than men." The sensitive areas are what in the United States might be termed fronts in the culture war, matters such as abortion, homosexuality, and euthanasia. In such matters, the church "shall exercise a critical function, of vigilance (Ez. 33:7), of a Nation's conscience." In the text in question, God instructs a prophet to keep watch over the nation, to serve as "a watchman unto the house of Israel." Once again, the prophecies of Ezekiel offer a model for approaching secular rule, for ensuring that "shepherds" remain true to their trust.[66]

Trusting the State

The obvious nervousness about secular states helps explain Southern churches' conservative attitudes toward authority in moral matters. This has been illustrated during the recent sexuality conflicts within the Protestant churches. However much they may aspire to be countercultural, most larger churches in Europe and North America do in fact respect secular notions of progress and social liberalization. As North American churches have discussed issues of gender and sexuality, debates have been largely fueled by the changing mores of the mainstream secular society. Pressure to change traditional church teachings has not come from new textual discoveries by biblical scholars, nor by new insights from academic theologians, but from observing and accommodating the changing secular environment. Awareness of changes in secular life pushed mainline Protestant churches to ordain women clergy during the 1970s and to liberalize their attitudes to homosexuality over the past decade.

The liberal view holds that churches must reform to accommodate what U.S. Chief Justice Earl Warren famously characterized as "the evolving standards of decency that mark the progress of a maturing society." For liberal Western Christians, these evolving standards constitute a source of authority quite as powerful as those orthodox values of tradition and scripture, and sometimes more demanding. Americans generally accept that the changes in secular values over the past few decades really do represent a story of progress. While there is ample room for controversy over issues such as abortion and gay rights, all but a tiny minority accept and laud the changes in the status of racial minorities and of women.

For Americans, secular states and their courts have been associated with many changes that are unquestionably good: the secular narrative of progress remains plausible. As we have seen, though, in much of the global South, that is simply not the case. Against this background, we can understand the puzzlement of African and Asian church leaders when Americans and Europeans argue that the church and its process of Bible interpretation should keep in tune with secular values. In their experience, such conformity is a recipe for ruin. The conflict is well illustrated by events in the Lutheran churches, in which, as we have seen, European conservatives turned to Kenyan bishop

Walter Obare for protection against their liberalizing superiors. When Bishop Obare attacked the Swedish Lutheran leadership, he focused not on specific policies or attitudes, but on what he saw as the Europeans' slavish following of secular values and of the state. Citing Psalm 118, he asserted, "It is better to take refuge in the Lord than to trust in man. It is better to take refuge in the Lord than to trust in princes."[67]

For the newer churches, biblical language and models provide the framework for political engagement. While this is true of "high" politics and national affairs, Christian thought also shapes the social issues that have increasingly come to prominence, in matters of gender and sexuality. And just as the Bible lends itself to different shades of politics, left and right, so it can be used to promote a striking range of causes in gender matters, to the point of providing the foundation for an influential Christian feminism.

WOMEN AND MEN

Charismatic renewal, conflict with demons, and the liberation of women are other fruits bearing directly on the churches' mission in Zimbabwe.

Titus Presler

At one of Zimbabwe's night vigils, a woman preacher drew extraordinary lessons from an unpromising text, the story of Jesus ordering his disciples to untie a donkey for his entry into Jerusalem. She applied the passage directly to the experience of African women: "I have seen that we are that donkey spoken of by the Lord. . . . Let us give thanks for this time we were given, the time in which we were blessed. We were not objects. . . . We were not human beings. . . . Some were even sold. To be married to a man—to be sold! . . . But with the coming of Jesus, we were set free. . . . We were made righteous by Jesus, mothers." Another woman agreed: "I heard another woman give an example of a donkey that was set free. In coming here to Maronda Mashanu I also have been set free. Thank you, people of God!"[1]

This story illustrates themes that we find across much of the global South, namely that women find in the new churches the power to speak and often to lead, and that Christianity is transforming women's role and aspirations. In a sense, it is almost too easy to find material on women's role in these churches, since feminist theologians contribute such a sizable proportion of the literature on Third World Christianity easily available in North America. As a corrective to such writing, it is helpful to recall the quite conservative positions still held by many ordinary church leaders. But even when we take a more balanced view, the impact of Christianity on women's lives remains impressive, extending well beyond academic or intellectual ranks to the ordinary women of the sort who preach at the *pungwe*.

Women play a central role in Southern Christian denominations, whether or not they are formally ordained. They commonly constitute the most important converts and the critical forces making for the conversion of family or of significant others. Women's organizations and fellowships, such as the Mothers' Unions, represent critical structures for lay participation within the churches and allow women's voices to be heard in the wider society. So do prayer fellowships and cells, which can be so independent as to unnerve official church hierarchies. Female believers look to the churches for an affirmation of their roles and their interests, and they naturally seek justification in the scriptures, which provide a vocabulary for public debate. Some texts—like the story of the donkey—have to be tortured in order to yield the desired meaning, though given the pervasive interest in deliverance, any passage that can be linked, however tenuously, to "loosing" is too good to be ignored. With other texts, though, liberating interpretations are readily found. But throughout this process, literalist readings that may appear conservative in terms of their approach to scriptural authority in practice have consequences that are socially progressive, if not revolutionary.[2]

Far Above Rubies

It would be misleading to claim that the growth of Christianity has had only liberating effects for women, as biblical texts are sometimes used to reinforce traditional values. So abundant are such examples, in fact, that we might initially assume that the rise of Christianity bodes little good for African and Asian women. Korean Christian feminist Hyun Kyung Chung has remarked, "I want to put a warning sign on a Bible just like tobacco companies put them on their cigarette packs. The label should say that without guidance, this book can lead to various side effects, such as mental illness, cancer, rape, genocide, murder and a slavery system. And that it's especially dangerous to the mental health of pregnant women."[3]

The newer churches have arisen in societies with conservative notions of gender roles, and they naturally gravitate to Bible passages that support these ideas. Read selectively, the letters of Paul are a goldmine for such purposes, supporting a conservative model of the good woman, submissive, pious, and unquestioning. Traditional readings predominate in the burgeoning Protestant and Pentecostal churches of Korea, where the ideal social roles presented in sermons sound strikingly like Confucian worldviews. Popular verses include "Wives, be subject to your husbands as you are to the Lord," a text that is commonly used in wedding ceremonies. Even the Book of Ruth—potentially a promising feminist text—lends itself to traditionalist readings, with the devoted love of Ruth for Naomi used as a model of the proper submission that a daughter-in-law must show to her mother-in-law. Korean preachers urge children to be no less devoted to their parents and elders. One modern critic has argued, scathingly, that "from a feminist perspective, the quantitative growth of the Korean Church is in inverse proportion to its qualitative development. . . . In the pursuit of patriarchal culture and social structure, the Confucian men and the most conservative Christians were on the same boat."[4]

Biblical texts regulate and constrain women's roles within the churches, especially in the matter of ordination or leadership. Again, Paul is commonly cited as the authority for such exclusion, particularly the severe words directed against female authority in 1 Timothy. One such passage enjoys wide currency: "Let the women learn in silence with all subjection. But I suffer not a woman to teach, nor to usurp authority over the man, but to be in silence. . . . Notwithstanding she shall be saved in childbearing if they continue in faith and charity and holiness with sobriety." In 1 Corinthians, meanwhile, we find the command "Let your women keep silence in the churches. . . . [They] are commanded to be under obedience." As we have seen, the scholarly debate over whether Paul actually wrote such texts has little impact on the authority granted to the words. From a conservative perspective, the fact that Mary "sat at Jesus' feet, and heard his word" indicates the correct role for modern Korean women: "To listen to Jesus means to study the Bible with the pastor."[5]

In Africa too, submission texts fit naturally into traditional values, especially in determining gender roles within marriage. Older values are expressed in proverbial wisdom, in folk talk that condemns pushy women who seek equality with husbands or who rebel against polygamy; and often, the Bible is used to reinforce these deeply conservative lessons. Wifely obedience is prescribed in the submission verse in Ephesians 5, together with other, more plausibly Pauline instructions in 1 Corinthians. In the words of Madipoane Masenya, African women find themselves "trapped between two canons," pre-Christian and Christian. Followed literally, these texts of submission urge women not to refuse their husband's sexual demands and not to seek divorce. Such policies become actively dangerous at a time when AIDS is such a threat.[6]

Societies that find themselves so comfortably at home in the Patriarchal narratives of Genesis identify easily with biblical gender roles and expectations. As theologian Mercy Oduyoye remarks, "Instead of promoting a new style of life appropriate to a people who are living with God 'who has made all things new,' the church in Africa continues to use the Hebrew scriptures and the epistles of St Paul to reinforce the norms of traditional religion and culture." Worse, missionary Christianity looked askance at the spiritual roles that women had played in traditional communities. To quote Kenyan Anne Nasimiyu-Wasike, "Traditionally African women were religious leaders e.g. prophets, mediums, seers, diviners, medicine persons and priests. As religious leaders they were respected and treated in the same way they treated the male religious leaders." As part of the struggle against paganism, however, "The African woman lost the power she had in the religious sphere."[7]

A typical sermon on gender roles in a Malawian independent church reinforced this message through the stories of biblical women. The preacher asserted that "God likes humble women for the kingdom of heaven is theirs. We have heard of beautiful ladies in the Bible who were submissive to their husbands. Women like Sarah, Rebeccah, Milcah, and Mary the mother of Jesus, all ladies, but they were obedient to their husbands." At the other extreme, the Bible offers plenty of awful warnings, not least in Eve and Delilah: "Let us not allow Satan to lead us astray. Samson was led astray by a woman." As in Korea, the book of Ruth is much used for these ends. For Nigerian Tokunboh Adeyemo, all African women should become "women of excellence" like Ruth, faithful, hardworking and morally pure.[8]

This vision is stated perfectly in the portrait of the diligent Good Wife in Proverbs. As we have seen, proverbs have an enduring appeal to African churches, and this passage in particular allegedly stems from a woman of royal blood. The text is much used by writers on the place of women in modern African churches, often by women themselves. One author, Rosemary Mumbi, cites it as a solution to the problem of battering and domestic violence. A woman who lives up to this ideal "has a sense of her self esteem and she is living a full contented life in her Lord and Master through obeying him. In my opinion there would be no need to be a battered wife in normal circumstances."[9]

The practical impact of such texts can often be seen. In Kenya, Catherine Dolan argues that the postcolonial state has deliberately exploited biblically based gender roles to keep women trapped in an arduous household production system. She describes a typical village gathering at which "the chief quoted biblical texts to emphasize the importance of female submission. The women remained silent through the sermons exalting motherhood, domesticity and Christianity." In this setting, women's dissent or social unrest is commonly associated with witchcraft or occult misdeeds, with all the additional scriptural condemnations that involves.[10]

Biblical examples can be cited to justify controversial modern-day customs, including child marriage. As Musimbi Kanyoro writes, "African women notice the age gap in the marriage between Boaz and Ruth. This is an issue of concern when related to child marriages and the sexual abuse of women by men in power. . . . What if this biblical story is used as a justification by African families who marry their young girls to old men?" Reading about the attitudes to childlessness found in the stories of Abraham and Isaac, Africans find support for their traditional opinions about the horror of barrenness.

The Bible too, it seems, views the bearing of male children as a woman's highest goal. One modern feminist remarks that such passages constitute "a major endorsement of the oppression of women in Zimbabwe."[11]

Overenthusiastic adoptions of Hebrew customs lead to other abuses. White missionaries in Africa were implacably opposed to polygamy, demanding that converts renounce plural wives. Generally, monogamy enhanced the role of women. From the end of the nineteenth century, though, some new independent churches allowed polygamy, usually claiming either an Old Testament warrant or a special prophetic revelation. Prophet William Wadé Harris traveled with a group of women who were probably his wives. After the end of colonialism, respect for the principle of inculturation made other churches reluctant to condemn polygamous independents, and the custom survives today among some important congregations, including South Africa's Shembe Church. While AICs have increasingly moved away from polygamy, they have been slow to impose a total prohibition, even among church leaders. For instance, while the Nigeria-based Celestial Church of Christ has now banned polygamy among its clergy, it allows pastors ordained before the new ruling to retain their wives. The failure to enforce monogamy represents a significant compromise with pre-Christian custom.[12]

The African affinity for the Old Testament justifies other harmful reversions to older practices. Some contemporary independent churches combine local tradition with Hebrew laws to create a ritual code in which menstruating women are excluded from church functions, and even from attending worship. Concerns about ritual impurity often form the grounds, explicit or implicit, on which women are excluded from ordination. In some societies, biblical texts justify female circumcision, a practice far more intrusive and dangerous than its male counterpart. In parts of north and east Africa, though, female circumcision remains commonplace, even among Christians, to the horror of most church leaders. Some independent churches justify the practice with reference to the words of Paul—this time from 1 Corinthians: "Circumcision is nothing, and uncircumcision is nothing."[13] However critically many modern Christians view Paul and his role in the development of Christianity, he can scarcely be blamed for the twisting of his words in such a matter.

Women's Voices

Such a catalogue of readings makes Christianity seem like a purely repressive force, a new supernatural justification for the most reactionary patriarchal attitudes. Yet at every step, the fact that patriarchal readings are countered or criticized by African or Asian feminists themselves reminds us of the existence of a greater variety of voices and opinions than might at first seem likely. In the 1970s, women scholars and activists formed part of the larger movement of Third World–oriented Bible study and liberation theology, which in 1976 found a focus in EATWOT, the Ecumenical Association of Third World Theologians. Within a few years, though, this organization faced its own feminist insurgency, as women realized "that although their male counterparts were progressive theologians, they were gender-blind, not only in their theologizing but in their attitudes and behavior." Thereafter, women's groups and caucuses promoted feminist-oriented studies, with scholars based in either academic institutions or international church bodies.[14]

Over the past two decades, women scholars have been among the most visible figures in Bible interpretation in the global South. African Christianity has produced such acute women thinkers and activists as Mercy Oduyoye and Musimbi Kanyoro. Nigerian theologian Teresa Okure is a Catholic sister, one of many African religious who write at length about women's concerns. So is active feminist Anne Nasimiyu-Wasike. (Recalling the situation of her Northern-world counterparts, she has faced reprimand from her bishop after advocating a right to legal abortion.)[15] By the end of the 1980s, African women scholars and activists had convened the Circle of Concerned African Women Theologians, CCAWT. This network seeks to build a new African feminism that, while drawing on Euro-American theory and scholarship, constantly seeks African applications.[16]

Such scholars read the familiar texts, though now with a fresh range of questions for discussion by women's study groups. On Ruth, to take one example, Kanyoro suggests these unexplored themes: "Was Naomi's return to Bethlehem liberating? Whom did it liberate, and why? Did the women really have the open choices that they are credited with? Did Naomi and Ruth choose each other, or did circumstances of vulnerability put them together? Without a husband and sons, what could Naomi have done in Moab?" Madipoane Masenya praises the book of Ruth for the issues it confronts: how Ruth "refused to succumb to the societal definitions of womanhood in her time . . . [c]hallenging the idolization of marriage." Feminist thinkers interact with the liberation theologians who enjoyed particular influence during the long struggles in southern Africa. Like them, feminist Bible readers seek overtly political role models for women. Fruitful texts include the book of Esther and the story of Deborah in Judges, though the Magnificat may be the text most cited by Catholic and Protestant theologians alike.[17]

Asian women's theology has been another lively intellectual field. Korean Hyun Kyung (she prefers not to use the patriarchal surname "Chung") is probably the Asian theologian best known in the West, due to her spectacular performance at the 1991 meeting of the World Council of Churches in Canberra. In "a radical theologizing attempt" that many denounced as syncretism, she led Korean and Australian Aboriginal dancers in a ritual dance designed to appease the restless *han* spirits killed unjustly through history, by imperialism and patriarchy. "These *Han*-ridden spirits in our people's history have been agents through whom the Holy Spirit has spoken Her compassion and wisdom for life." As this declaration suggests, she also presented the Holy Spirit in feminine form. She urges that Korean churches "stop trying to put on the corset of social standards and values that are 2,000 years old to modern Korean women."[18]

Hyun Kyung represents an extreme position within Korean Christianity, but her career reminds us of the diversity over gender matters in that country and others—amazingly so, given the conservative slant of many churches. Just to take the Korean example, Christianity has a distinguished record of promoting women's activism and political consciousness, dating back to the Protestant missions of the late nineteenth century. From the 1970s onward, Christian-inspired feminist groups agitated for political reform during the years of military dictatorship. One distinguished representative is Christian academic Myung Sook Han, whose visible role in antigovernment protests earned her a prison term in the late 1970s. In the 1980s, she chaired the progressive and prolabor Korea Women's Association United. After democracy was established, she became South Korea's first minister of gender equality. Other Asian nations have produced prominent women leaders who contradict the conservative stereotype. Asia's only predominantly Christian nation is the Philippines, which since 1986 has had two women presidents, both of whom worked closely with the Catholic hierarchy. That is two more women leaders than the United States has had.[19]

Women's Reformation

It is not surprising to find such records of public achievement among highly educated women from prosperous families. Nor is it remarkable that feminist approaches are so well represented amongst academics, who, as we have seen, belong to a global community of scholarship. But as we noted in the first chapter, we might ask how well the work of such scholars represents the thought and lived experience of ordinary Christians. Groups like the CCAWT are avowedly dedicated to social activism, and they focus their attention on texts and approaches that can plausibly contribute to this end. Also, their thought has been permeated by Western feminism, which shapes the questions they ask and the methods they apply, perhaps leading them to conclusions far more radical than those of the less educated. They are much more likely to explore readings that promote women's political consciousness than (say) themes of spiritual warfare, though ordinary church members might be more interested in the latter. In the U.S. context, similarly, an immense gulf separates the domain of academic theologians and Bible scholars from the customary thought world of ordinary church members, even the highly literate.

Yet we need not consign such feminist readings to an ivory tower. While we should be cautious about assuming that academic writings are reflecting popular opinion, a great deal of evidence does indicate the explosive impact of Christianity, and particularly of Bible reading, on the women of African and Asian churches. At the grassroots level, among the poor and barely educated, the rise of Christianity has, in an amazingly short time, effected dramatic changes in gender attitudes. In the long run, the greatest change might be the new emphasis on faithful monogamous marriage and on new concepts of masculinity, the "reformation of machismo" that is proceeding apace despite the vestiges of polygamy that remain in some independent churches. Though studied most closely in Latin America, the spread of "Victorian" values of thrift and chastity should be excellent news for Christian women around the world.

The fact of reading as such also carries great weight. In a neoliterate community, access to the Bible betokens power and status, and there is no reason why this gift should be confined to traditional elites. Quite the contrary, if traditional forms of ritual power were expressed in oral culture, and were commonly exercised by older men, then women—and young people of both sexes—have most to gain by achieving literacy. The more conspicuous one's knowledge of the scriptures, the greater one's claim to spiritual status. Eliza Kent describes Protestant worship services in south India. As in many North American churches, a preacher will cite a critical verse or proof text, and the congregation will then refer quickly to it in the Bibles they carry. In global South churches, though, the mere ability to find passages quickly and efficiently gives real prestige. "At each reference to a Biblical verse, there is a pregnant pause and a flurry of hands passing over the pages of Bibles until one voice shouts out the content of the verse—demonstrating in one stroke her (or less frequently, his) facility with the Bible, level of literacy, and command of the formal written Tamil in which the Tamil Bible is composed." Conversely, inability to find a verse—or even to locate the book of Psalms—demonstrates that a person is not a regular churchgoer, or is not serious about Christian commitment. Kent herself notes that her failure in this regard marked her as a "woefully inadequate representative of American Christianity," far inferior in that respect to the Indian woman who clearly regarded finding Psalms as a trivial chore. Evangelicals in the United States have long trained children in sword drill, the rapid location of Bible texts—hence the bloodcurdling cries of "Draw swords!" one hears directed at classes of very small children. But in global South churches, the sword metaphor is very apt: knowledge of the Bible can be an effective weapon for asserting status.[20]

Pastors

Critically important in this process has been the spread of charismatic forms of prayer and worship, so that changes are not confined to what are usually regarded as socially liberal churches. In the epigraph to this chapter, I quoted a sentence from the work of Titus Presler, a juxtaposition of themes that should stop an American reader in his or her tracks. However rarely we think of feminism and exorcism in the same context, the linkages are not as bizarre as they might appear. Charismatic worship, after all, places great weight on individual inspiration and prophetic gifts, and experience has shown that the Spirit alights where it wills, on women and men, young and old. And if that leads to women's taking a direct and active role in ministry, so be it.[21]

This democratization is evident in the countless stories of healing and exorcism that are so characteristic of charismatic churches across Africa and Asia. From China comes a story that is quite unexceptional in its character, yet radical in its implications. A male pastor told how a woman was terrified of a monstrous ghostly presence in her house, apparently of a demonic nature. "After she had become a believer, two sisters in the Lord went home with her, because she was too afraid to go alone," and through prayer and exorcism, the women cast out the demon so that it never returned. The woman's health and confidence were restored, and her life improved vastly. As the European author recording the tale notes, what matters here is less the reality of the demon or the exorcism, but the implications for authority in the church. The role of the pastor is confined to reporting approvingly what a group of lay-women had done, spontaneously, and without any clerical authority or male assistance. In such a theological tradition, the notion of Christ's being present "where two or three are gathered together" applies regardless of gender.[22]

Again illustrating the gender-blind nature of charisma is the story of Margaret Wanjiru, founder of Kenya's "Jesus is Alive" ministries. Her story is in many ways a familiar example of the experiences of ordinary African women, with a teenage pregnancy and early encounters with witchcraft. Unlike most women, however, she felt herself filled with a prophetic gift, as she was inspired by Nehemiah and the Virgin Mary—an intriguing combination. During a vision lasting several hours, God spoke to her: "I chose Mary because she was God-fearing and humble. Because you are obedient and humble I will send you to restore my church. . . . Africa shall be saved!" The reference is to the Magnificat, but with a significant twist. Mary, like all good women, is to be "obedient and humble," but having passed that test, she is divinely licensed to preach and prophesy, to mobilize and agitate.[23]

Given the literalist bent of many African and Asian churches, one would think that the injunctions against female ministry in 1 Timothy would prevent the career of a Margaret Wanjiru, or of her many counterparts, both prophetic and clerical. Yet her experience indicates a common feature of literalist approaches to the Bible, namely that the text offers a variety of possible approaches to a matter, leaving much latitude to the individual guided by prophetic or charismatic experience. When asked about biblical limitations on women's role, one woman leader of an AIC who had proclaimed herself a bishop is reported to have commented, succinctly, that "she respects the authority of the Bible. She is also very open to God's continued revelation."[24]

Global South women have been creative in finding scriptural bases for active ministries. Some radical feminists follow their North American counterparts in claiming that the canonical scripture has been censored to suppress women's role in the early church. Hyun Kyung argues that "Mary Magdalene was performing a funerary rite when she poured oil on Jesus's feet. Some feminist scholars argue that she was a priestess, because the funerary rite was conducted only among the priests at the time of Jesus. Gnosticism, which supports those ideas more clearly, was excluded from the Gospels. . . . [The] Bible was written by the ones who triumphed and advocated their views, just like many other history books."[25]

But even when we remain strictly within the limits of the text, some relevant passages are hard to miss. As Indian Lutheran scholar Monica Melanchthon notes, "Over and over again, the great truths about Jesus are revealed to and accepted by women." Though the gospel accounts of the resurrection differ substantially, all agree that women were first to receive news of the event, and these texts offer rich pickings for advocates of women's clerical role. Seeking to recover the role of women in Jesus' message, Sister Nasimiyu-Wasike writes, "In the New Testament, Jesus broke the male-dominated attitudes of his day and reached out to women. The Christian story in the four Gospels asserts that a group of women were the first people to receive the news of the Easter announcement of the Resurrection. Women seem to have been the financial supporters of the apostolic band, and were primary leaders in Paul's embryonic church."[26]

Independent churches commonly cite the great commandment from the end of Matthew's Gospel, asserting Christ's power over the world and his Great Commission to make disciples of all nations. Women clergy, however, encourage readers to look just a few verses earlier in the same chapter, to a point in the story at which women have received the gospel, before the male disciples. As Nyambura Njoroge writes, "Like the women at the empty tomb, we must discover the risen Christ, worship him, talk with him and take his command seriously: 'Do not be afraid; go and tell my brothers to go to Galilee, there they will see me' (Matt. 28:10)." Njoroge herself is the first woman to be ordained by the Presbyterian Church of East Africa. Presler quotes a (male)

Zimbabwean cleric who comments, with some embarrassment, on the lack of women preachers at a vigil: "The women are the ones who were the first to see Jesus. They ran to the grave. We followed later. The word began with the women. They were supposed to open the meeting."[27]

Questions about female leadership matter, since women have long been prominent in many of the independent churches. If not as patriarchs (a title that some churches preserve), they exercise authority as the venerated wives of founders, as prophets or potent charismatic leaders. Africa has a vibrant tradition of women prophets, including such fiery leaders as Alice Lenshina, founder of a church and prolific author of vernacular hymns. Naturally, then, even churches that officially cite St. Paul's alleged rules of exclusion find room for female authority, by citing such biblical leaders as Deborah.[28]

As we have seen, women's groups have been inventive in approaching the scriptures in their own terms, in ways that work well in oral cultures. Indeed, the very fact of living in such a culture gives special meaning to some scriptural passages that Westerners might not notice. For South Asian Christians, the vision of Mary sitting, listening, at Jesus' feet immediately places her in the role of the pupil of a teacher or guru—in fact, of a disciple receiving privileged teaching.[29] Based on this insight, it is difficult to avoid follow-up questions about women's role in ministry.

The familiar range of woman-oriented texts helps defuse other forms of opposition to female church leadership. One common argument heard in African churches is that women are ritually unsuited to clerical status because of their biological circumstances: how can a woman preside at the altar while menstruating or pregnant? In responding to such objections, Musimbi Kanyoro again cites the Magnificat: "Mary, the mother of Jesus, out of joy in her pregnancy praised the Lord, her spirit was rejoicing in God her savior. And what is more beautiful than the sight of a pregnant woman? . . . How can the sight of a pregnant woman at the altar be shameful before God? If I was a pastor, that would be the moment I would be at my best."[30]

Woman, Arise

For Euro-American readers, matters of ministry and ordination naturally take primacy of place in understanding women's role in the churches. In Africa or Asia, though, other issues come to the fore in women's readings of the Bible. One of the most discussed collections of texts is the sequence of miracle stories of Luke 8, which is central to understandings of healing and exorcism; however, African women scholars, and many ordinary readers, read the chapter for its determined women characters and find in it an enlightening vision of social change.

For Western readers, the woman with the issue of blood suffers from a tragic medical condition. For many African societies, she is tarnished by ritual contamination, which makes her initiative in seeking out Jesus all the more inspiring. That story then leads directly to the miracle in which Jesus raises from the dead the daughter of Jairus, the leader of the synagogue. In one study in South Africa, Zulu women were asked to respond to the parallel passages as presented in Mark's Gospel (5:21–6:1), and readers strongly identified with the healed woman. They found Jesus' flouting of blood taboos all the more relevant since the local independent churches maintain such negative attitudes to menstruation. Gikuyu women immediately identified with the woman with the issue of blood, whose condition was "very real to the women who developed problems as a result of female circumcision." These readers noted "the attention and care that Jesus gave to women who were in oppressive and desperate situations."[31]

Other readings were surprising to Northern eyes. Western feminist readers sometimes see Jairus's daughter as oppressed because she is described only according to her relationship with her dominant male relative. For Zulu women, though, this description gave her place and status, while the lack of any name or family relationship of the hemorrhaging woman was far more distressing: "This was a far greater sorrow."[32]

Teresa Okure describes Luke's account as "a cherished passage" for African women, and Jesus' words to the girl are often echoed in Christian feminist writing. Okure continues, "As African women we are traditionally expected in most of our cultures to be dependent. So far we, like Jairus' daughter, have largely depended on others to speak for us and present our plight and needs before the world." Through Jesus, the sleep of silence ends. "Arise, Daughter" became the founding text, and the rallying cry, for the initial meeting of the CCAWT. A collection of essays from the group is titled *The Will to Arise*, while a more recent African study about recovery from incest and abuse is titled *Little Girl, Arise!* Other women authors use the Aramaic words attributed to Jesus in the parallel passage in Mark, *Talitha cum.* If anyone challenges women's rights to advance and arise, they are answered by Jesus himself, and in one of the rare instances in which his actual words are preserved in the original tongue. For feminist theologians such as Musa Dube, *Talitha cum* becomes a call to Christian activism and resistance.[33]

Reading Critically

Even the ideology of the loyally Christian "good wife" quietly reading her Bible may carry within it the seeds of sedition. In the Kenyan societies described by Dolan, male elites are desperately concerned about any signs of independent female organization, so the good wife is expected to be the pious creature from Proverbs, raising her children in godly ways and studying the Bible. As a result, the Kenyan women she studies devote much time to religious life, to pursuing evangelical and born-again religious styles. They "have also diverted their labor to church groups, and appropriated Christian norms of femininity in court cases to promote their own interests."[34]

But leaving women to pursue domestic piety through Bible reading is like forbidding a restive population to carry weapons, while giving them unrestricted access to gasoline and matches. Pursuing biblical passages relevant to women often produces innovative readings, sometimes by taking the simple step of placing a scriptural text in context, rather than simply reciting an isolated verse. The much-quoted passage in Ephesians 5 certainly does command women to obey their husbands, but as part of an extended argument that actually places more burdens and responsibilities on men, so that both sexes are mutually "submitting yourselves one to another." The more familiar a section of the Bible becomes through frequent quotation, the more impact one has by giving a startlingly different slant on the same passage. Mercy Oduyoye recounts, "When an eminent Nigerian lawyer was invited to speak about the legal rights of women, she quoted the Bible, interpreting Ephesians 5:28–31. She instructed preachers to: 'Place emphasis on love, honor and care . . . rather than subjugation, for love means security for both parties—in love there is no loss of face.'"[35] The reading gains power precisely because the adjacent passage is so often quoted to the opposite purpose.

Other readings are used to criticize the exploitation of women. Jesus' words about the poor widow giving to the Temple treasury her tiny donation, the widow's mite, can infuriate modern African woman readers, who see parallels to poor women forced to donate their tithes to greedy male clergy, even when families lack basic necessities.[36]

Often, a topic is important not because of how it is treated in the Bible, but rather because it appears in that text in the first place. In a new Christian society, the Bible becomes *our* book, *our* history, so that subjects mentioned in the text cannot be dismissed as alien or exotic. The fact that an issue is mentioned in scripture permits it to be addressed and debated in ways it could not be if it was being imported as "the latest Western thinking." One early example of confronting the unspeakable involved female circumcision. Njoroge describes how this suddenly became a divisive controversy in the Kenya of the 1920s, after the appearance of the vernacular Bible. "The Gikuyu women pored over the Bible themselves, then told and retold those stories to others." Based on these reflections, the women discovered that God had indeed commanded Abraham and other men to be circumcised, but not Sarah or any woman. "The women strongly concluded that it is biblically correct to circumcise men but not women." Following these discussions, Christian women formed a guild, the Council of the Shield, Kiama Kia Ngo, to defend their own daughters against circumcision. To understand the radical nature of this step, we have to recall the central importance of circumcision for defining femininity, sexual morality, and adulthood. This was in short a biblically fuelled social revolution.[37]

Women's groups also discuss ideas that might be considered too subversive or indecent for the mainstream society. Njoroge, for instance, uses the Johannine text of the woman taken in adultery to comment on popular attitudes to female sexuality. She remarks, "Like the scribes and Pharisees, it is common practice in the African church to condemn women for sexual immorality as if there were no men involved." Jesus, however, shows no patience with this approach and instead chooses to condemn the condemners. In an Indian context, feminist readers use the Song of Songs to promote discussion of sexuality and particularly women's sexuality, suggesting much more equitable roles for women than the conventional images of submission derived from the early chapters of Genesis. To quote Melanchthon, "Song of Songs uplifts female sexual desire as something to be granted legitimacy."[38]

Other Bible readings legitimize concern over sexual exploitation. Gerald West tells of a community reading the harrowing tale of Tamar, who is raped by her own brother Amnon. The responses to the passage would amaze an American readership well accustomed to discussions of rape and sexual abuse. In the South African context, though, the story comes as a shock. The first response is anger, that church leaders have not previously publicized such texts; but then there is relief. Finally, with the biblical example at hand, the community can actually discuss problems of rape, incest, and abuse that had hitherto been off-limits. One might see in such an account the limits imposed by scriptural literalism, namely that abuse can only be explored when it is explicitly legitimized by a Bible passage. But the consequences of the discovery are immense. Once these matters are brought into public view, participants can never forget that the questions have been raised, and it is difficult to restore them to the realm of decent silence. The genie cannot be put back in the bottle, nor can the text be returned to the book on the shelf.[39]

Women and the Plague

In contemporary Africa, the AIDS crisis has called forth widespread Christian activism, most powerfully by allowing the issue to be discussed publicly. The Christian response to AIDS has been controversial, raising questions about the Catholic reluctance to approve condom use, and the idealistic stress of many churches on abstinence and constant chastity. Some see a Christian-inspired response such as that of the Ugandan government as highly successful, while secular-minded critics dismiss chastity programs as unrealistic or actively destructive. In some isolated instances, biblical readings have undoubtedly caused harm. One pernicious example is the use of Deuteronomy 8:15–16, a text urging believers to trust in God so that he will protect them from poisonous snakes. This passage allegedly teaches believers that, since they are under divine protection, they should not even take precautions against AIDS.[40]

More commonly, though, biblical readings serve to arouse awareness of the threat posed by disease in general, and AIDS in particular. As Musa Dube writes, the scenes in Luke 8 are all too familiar for a contemporary African, who sees in the gospel account almost an unfolding documentary: "Patients who have been sick for a long time—patients who have spent all they had searching for healing strike us, but instead of getting better, they get worse. We are struck by the presence of physicians who have attended patients, received their money but could not heal them. Sick and dying young people strike us. Desperate parents, who are trying to find healing for their children, strike us. Those who are weeping aloud for their dead children strike us." Social oppression and gender prejudice aggravate the harm done by the dreadful epidemic. In such a world, the only hope to be found is in the encounter with Jesus, who healed other incurable ailments such as leprosy.[41]

Adding to the lethal impact of AIDS is the pervasive cultural secrecy surrounding the disease, all the more so given the idea of tainted blood in societies in which blood carries so many ritual associations. Individuals and families thus refuse to admit they have the disease. Apart from an obvious human reluctance to confront disaster, traditionally oriented communities may be tightly limited in the topics that they regard as fit for discussion, especially by women or social inferiors. In this context, clergy make an enormous contribution simply by admitting that they carry HIV, which must not be seen as a divine punishment: AIDS is not a sinners' disease. As one afflicted pastor announced, "There is no holy HIV; anybody can get HIV."[42]

South African scholar Beverley Haddad reports how in some cases, biblical texts can help overcome the special cultural taboos affecting women. In one instance, she was reading with a group of poor and largely illiterate women Mark's account of the woman with the issue of blood. She writes, "In Nxamalala the first opportunity to discuss AIDS opened up unexpectedly during a Bible study discussion. . . . I asked the question as to how the story could be the same for us women today?" To her surprise, one woman cited Ingculazi (AIDS): "AIDS is comparable to this because it is incurable. That means that the doctors fail to cure it, it eats you till you die." The discussion continues, within a group that offers safe territory for women to address delicate and unspeakable issues. The group concludes that, "in situations of blood diseases, it is the power of God that also runs in their veins which enables them to have life in the face of these diseases that bring death."[43]

Other readers look to the passage in Luke in which a "woman of the city" anoints Jesus' feet and dries them with her hair. Though the precise nature of her sin is unspecified, it is commonly assumed to be sexual, making her the "anointing prostitute." The message for contemporary Christians is that Jesus was prepared to love and to mix with sexual sinners, and that willingness and acceptance should provide a template for African churches dealing with AIDS sufferers.[44] Since Jesus lived in a world like ours, and faced the same situations and the same crises, his actions become still more authoritative as a guide for modern readers.

Honoring Widows

Disease, rape, and sexual exploitation might be universal themes, but many of the biblical issues that stir contemporary debate are specific to Africa or Asia. To take one example, the New Testament preserves memories of a time when the proper role of widows was a very divisive matter for the young churches. In Acts, the question of charity to widows divided Greek and Hebrew believers. The first letter to Timothy lays down rules for deciding which widows are truly deserving and which, to use a modern term, are welfare cheats: "Honor widows that are widows indeed."[45]

In the United States, these texts are of only historical interest, recording ancient church debates. In Christianizing societies in Africa, in contrast, passages about protecting widows are literally matters of life and death. Across much of southern Africa, the traditional assumption was that the family and its property belonged to the husband, and beyond that, to his family. Today when a man dies, his relatives are likely to descend on the home, stripping virtually all moveable goods and leaving the widow and children in penury, the justification being that the woman will find a new home through remarriage. Such a situation, always heartrending, becomes devastating in societies already facing ruin through AIDS, in which the seizure of family property becomes a zero-sum gender war, targeted against the poorest and most vulnerable.

In many traditional cultures, too, widowhood demands certain rituals. In some African societies, these can include intercourse between the widow and the brother of her late husband, in order to exorcise the dead man's spirit and to prevent curses that could wreck the community. Apart from its humiliating quality, "sexual cleansing" is a deeply dangerous prospect when HIV is so prevalent. Widows labor under other burdens that can amount almost to a kind of social death. One African Lutheran remarks, "When a woman is widowed, . . . not only do churches and society fail to care for her needs, but in some of the churches, widows are actually required to give up their church positions." Other traditional societies, notably in India, can treat the poor widow as a virtual member of the living dead. Dalit activist Udit Raj complains, "For a Hindu priest, a leper, a beggar and a widow are hateful objects who need to be punished because of the 'curse of their past life.'" The multiple forms of humiliation suffered by Dalit widows amount to absolute social exclusion.[46]

Widowhood ranks among the most pressing women's rights concerns in many parts of Africa and Asia. Catholic activist Kathryn Hoomkwap describes this as "one burning issue which is of great concern to the African women." "The threat of the disintegration of the family institution calls for the Church in Africa to take a firm stand on issues, such as traditional widowhood rites and family inheritance. These are issues which frustrate the widow and expose her life and those of her children to many dangers. . . . [T]he Catholic widow is always subjected to the rough treatment of customary law, since the Church in Africa has never officially addressed this problem." The injustice of the situation facing Christian women is all the more glaring since Islamic law gives widows detailed legal protections.[47]

Respect for widows is a survival issue, and scriptural passages that North American eyes flit over become burningly relevant. Again, Ruth provides a manual for family responsibility, as Boaz performs his duty of marrying a bereaved kinswoman. Still more radical, though, for a society in which the woman remains tied to her husband's clan even after he dies, is the New Testament notion of "till death do us part." So is the scriptural foundation for this offered by Paul's letter to the Romans: "if the husband be dead, she is loosed from the law of her husband." In the West, Romans 7:2 is scarcely a well-known scriptural text; it is not a reference that enthusiastic evangelists wave on placards at sports stadiums. Yet in a global context, this verse may be a truly revolutionary warrant for change. While not addressing vital issues of family property, the Pauline principle does amount to a declaration of women's freedom from burdensome clan and ritual obligations.

Occasional references to widows as proper recipients of charity also take on a new light. Some are drawn from the quasi-gospel in 1 and 2 Kings, the miracle tales of Elijah and Elisha. In one story, Elijah is sent to Zarephath, where he finds a widow whose poverty is about to reduce her and her children to debt slavery. Elijah, though, saves the family by miraculously providing endless supplies of meal and oil. In East Africa, this tale has inspired the creation of guilds and fellowships to support women. In the Epistle of James, one sign of true religion is "[t]o visit the fatherless and widows in their affliction." A modern African scholar comments, "The biblical injunction of

James 1:27 should spur a thriving ministry of visitation with gifts, prayers and other helps to the widow far more than the occasional visits made to them on specific feast days during the year." Nigerian scholar Daisy Nwachuku writes, "The New Testament injunction of 1 Timothy 5:9–14, followed by the church in its pastoral ministry, provides a molested widow with a refuge and an emotional support in defense of her faith and her action." In short, she concludes, "the African Christian widow is a 'person' whole and worthy of dignity despite her grief stricken situation."[48]

Outsiders

The Bible has a liberating potential for a traditional society, especially in matters of family and personal relationship. Yet for all the specific rules and formulae that can be found in scripture—for instance, about widowhood—the most powerful theme that recurs in the text concerns outsiders, those rejected by the world, for whom is reserved the special place at the divine banquet. God makes nations and breaks them. He chooses those whom the world rejects. The Old Testament is one such story of making and election; the gospels tell how Jesus went to people who were at best at the fringes of society. In his initial sermon in the Nazareth synagogue, Jesus used the stories of Elijah and Elisha to justify a mission beyond the frontiers of Israel, whether defined culturally or geographically. Though Israel in those times of famine had plenty of poor and sick, Elijah was sent only to Zarephath, "a city of Sidon, unto a woman that was a widow. And many lepers were in Israel in the time of [Elisha] the prophet; and none of them was cleansed, saving Naaman the Syrian." The broader story of the New Testament is how God expanded the idea of chosenness beyond its accepted limits.[49]

As we have seen, all these miracle stories have a multiple resonance in African and Asian churches, especially for their healing themes. The passages also hold immense promise for people traditionally excluded from their societies or reduced to subordinate roles—especially women. Conversely, all serve as warnings for anyone unwise to consider him- or herself secure in God's favor. At one Zimbabwean *pungwe*, a minister recounted the story of Rahab, the harlot of Jericho, as described in the book of Joshua, as well as the story of Cornelius the centurion, in Acts. These "were people who feared God even though they were outside God's covenant with Israel. He concluded that if God can save such strangers to Israel's faith, Christians attending the *pungwe* should not be complacent in thinking that mere self-identification as Christians, without transformation of life, would save them." The reference to Rahab is doubly interesting, since the story is recounted only twice in the New Testament, both times in books that have a particular appeal to African

Christians, namely Hebrews and the letter of James. The context suggests that the preacher was citing James, who says that Rahab was saved by her deeds rather than, as in Hebrews, by her faith. But whatever the scriptural source, the story teaches that God chooses whom He wills and is prepared to go outside conventional social or religious hierarchies.[50]

In a sense, women outsiders stand at the very beginning of the Christian story. Even in the genealogy that Matthew provides for Jesus, which occupies the first page of the conventional New Testament, his ancestry is traced through women whose record was distinctly not that of the standard good wife. This point has often been noticed by mainstream church authorities, whom one would rarely accuse of feminism. As Egypt's Coptic Pope Shenouda notes, the genealogy "mentioned adulterous women like Tamar, Rahab, the wife of Uriah the Hittite, and Ruth who is a woman of a foreign race (a Moabite, one despised by the Israelites)." Rahab was a prostitute, and Tamar played one, while according to some interpretations, Bathsheba, the wife of Uriah, seduced King David. And at the end of the genealogy, the evangelist records that Mary was found to be pregnant during her engagement. Following ancient tradition, Pope Shenouda observed that such a list directly challenged pride in family and ancestry, a fundamental pillar of most African and Asian societies. "The evangelist wanted to annihilate the haughtiness of the Jews who boast about their grandfathers. . . . When the evangelist registered the genealogy of Christ, he mentioned those sinful women, because it is impossible for any of us to be virtuous by the virtue of his grandfathers, or to be wicked by the vice of his grandfathers."[51]

The radical nature of this idea might be difficult to appreciate in a democratic society that at least pays lip service to the idea of equality, of people beginning life with chances of success not constrained by family, clan, and ancestry. But African and Asian writers stress the theme of trampling traditional restrictions. In the New Testament, they note that Jesus gives his attention to the multiply rejected, especially among women. As a contemporary African woman writer observes, "Jesus responded to all who came to him. He commended the woman with the alabaster box of ointment. He praised the faith of the woman who touched the hem of his garment as he praised the faith of the Roman centurion. He spoke to the woman of Samaria. I have no doubt but that he commends every African woman who humbly turns to him for help."[52]

It was not just in ancient Palestine that Jesus' interaction with the Samaritan woman at the well would have crossed accepted boundaries, or that the woman's active participation in dialogue seemed daring. Udit Raj—a Dalit, and himself a Buddhist—notes, "Born as a higher caste Jew, in the ancestral and kingly clan of David, Jesus did not have any hesitation to take water from a Samaritan woman, an outcaste woman—which gives a notion that there is no caste or creed before the might of thirst and hunger." Indian writer Rekha Chennattu makes her a role model for modern Christians: "The story of the Samaritan woman could empower Indian women to awaken their dormant spiritual energy, the life-giving force. . . . This awakening is needed for women to look at their presence and mission in the Church from a new perspective." Sister Chennattu's account of the Samaritan woman sounds like a frank plea for enhancing women's role in the Catholic ministry. Writing in a Philippine magazine, she finds the woman "remarkable for her openness, conviction, initiative and decisive action. . . . She is not depicted as a passive receiver, accepting unquestioningly all that is said by Jesus. Her theological background, personal interests and spontaneous appropriation of the role of an apostle to bear witness to Jesus in the city are very outstanding and significant."[53]

The case of the Samaritan woman suggests Jesus' willingness to violate traditional rules about gender, but also, like Ruth, it generates discussion about solidarity across tribal and ethnic boundaries. Repeatedly, such outsider texts focus on interactions with women, a point that carries added weight in societies in which strict rules limit contacts between the sexes.[54]

Another popular passage concerns the Syro-Phoenician woman, alternatively the woman of Canaan, who begged Jesus to heal her possessed daughter. For many Christians, the story contains one of the most difficult accounts of Jesus, who initially seems to treat the Gentile woman with contempt. Yet African and Asian readers find their way past this aspect of the story, to see Jesus reaching out to a foreigner, a woman, the despised. Responding to this story, Kosuke Koyama stresses how the participants are brought together by common human emotions, such as maternal love, which straddle cultural and ethnic divisions. "The beginning of faith must contain some universally valid and relevant factor which can erase religious, cultural and political demarcations. Otherwise, how can a gentile woman sincerely come to Jesus Christ, an Israelite? Otherwise, how can the peoples of Hong Kong, Tokyo, Bangkok and Djakarta come to Jesus Christ, a Palestinian Jew?"[55] It is especially from the texts dealing with women that readers discover the full radicalism of the Christian message.

Beyond any single text, the Bible as a whole offers ample ammunition for the use of outsiders, and for the dismay of the established and comfortable. As David Martin famously described in his study of global South churches, Pentecostalism gives the right and duty to speak to those never before deemed worthy, on grounds of class, race, and gender. Now, though, in the new dispensation, outsiders receive tongues of fire. The same observation can be applied across denominational frontiers.

NORTH AND SOUTH

He hath put down the mighty from their seats, and exalted them of low degree. He hath filled the hungry with good things; and the rich he hath sent empty away.

Luke 1:52–53

The impact of the Bible in the global South must raise questions for European and American Christians, questions that are at once exhilarating and disturbing. Nobody is suggesting that in order to recreate this experience, this excitement, Christians need to return to a social order reminiscent of the first-century Mediterranean—still less to renounce modern medicine. But we can reasonably ask whether the emerging Christian traditions of the Two-Thirds World have recaptured themes and trends in Christianity that the older churches have forgotten, and if so, what we can learn from their insights. Let us assume that this contrast is accurate, that the Bible speaks to many global South churches in ways it cannot communicate with modern Europeans or North Americans. What can, or should, be done about that cultural gap? For anyone accustomed to living in the environment of "Western Christianity," the critical question must be to determine what is the authentic religious content, and what is cultural baggage. What, in short, is Christianity, and what is merely Western?

New Eyes

Looking at a familiar book through fresh eyes can be an unsettling experience. Take the case of the English bishop John W. Colenso, who in 1862 published a work that created a religious and intellectual scandal quite comparable in its day to the writings of Charles Darwin. In *The Pentateuch and the Book of Joshua Critically Examined*, Colenso used current scholarship in history, geology, and mathematics to argue that while the "books of Moses" might give us "revelations of the Divine Will and character," nevertheless they "can-not be regarded as historically true." Though Colenso's doubts about biblical literalism had been developing for some years, his encounters in southern Africa forced his decisive break with tradition. Meeting Zulu cultures, Colenso could not believe that unbaptised pagans were automatically consigned to hellfire, nor that polygamy was necessarily a harmful institution in that particular setting.[1]

But it was his exchanges with Zulu converts about the truth of the Bible that radicalized his thinking. Colenso spent long hours responding to the searching questions posed by his assistant William Ngidi. Hearing the story of Noah, Ngidi asked, "Is all that true? Do you really believe that all this happened thus—that all the beasts, and birds, and creeping things upon the earth, large and small, from hot countries and cold, came thus by pairs, and entered into the ark with Noah? And did Noah gather food for them *all*, for the beasts and birds of prey, as well as the rest?" Colenso could not think of an easy answer: "My heart answered in the words of the Prophet, 'Shall a man speak lies in the Name of the Lord?' (Zech. 13.3). I dared not do so." And other problems arose. It was "a sifting process for the opinions of any teacher, who feels the deep moral obligation of answering truly, and faithfully, and unreservedly, his fellow-man, looking up to him for light and guidance, and asking, 'Are you sure of this?' 'Do you believe this?' 'Do you really believe that?' "[2] Victorian observers were bemused by the thought that a learned bishop might have been shaken in his faith by the questions of a mere African, and the story inspired a limerick:

A bishop there was of Natal
Who took a Zulu for a pal
Said the Native "Look 'ere,
Ain't the Pentateuch queer?"
Which converted the Lord of Natal.

Many other missionaries have met similar questions, in that age and since. Not all have responded with Colenso's rigorous honesty.

Colenso's story reminds us of the cultural trappings we bring to any text. As the famous phrase has it, we see things not as they are but as we are. If I had not believed it, I would not have seen it with my own eyes. New Christian converts, coming from a society in which the Bible is not part of the familiar intellectual landscape, have a striking capacity to see things that are not obvi-ous to those bred in the tradition. To take another African example, Akiki Nyabongo recalls the agony of a white missionary who tried to teach the Bible to teenage boys in the emerging Christian society of Buganda at the end of the nineteenth century. In these early years of evangelism, the boys challenged many aspects of the story. Did a whale really swallow Jonah? If Adam and Eve had just two sons, how did those young men find their wives? A class consensus found it likely that Joseph was the literal father of Jesus. If the Virgin Birth was such a critical doctrine, why was it not mentioned in the Gospels of Mark or John? The missionary replied, "John made it more symbolical, but it is still true. Mark left it for the others to tell." The troublesome boy Mujungu, the pupil from hell, taunted, "Probably because he didn't believe it."[3]

Old Questions

Clergy from the long-established Christian cultures of Europe were so used to dealing with such issues that most no longer considered them problematic, if they noticed the difficulties at all. The missionary was so familiar with the four gospels that he unconsciously blended them together into a harmonized Life of Jesus, which glided over the differences. Never having needed to explain the apparent inconsistencies, he had never troubled to formulate an effective apologia. Members of new Christian communities, in contrast, come to the Bible with different assumptions, arising from their own cultures and experiences, and ask different questions. Sometimes, the issues they are exploring have no direct parallels in the West: we think of the Gikuyu women of the early twentieth century searching the scriptures to learn whether God ever authorized female circumcision. Often, though, the questions believers are asking prove to be faithful to the spirit of the societies that produced the Bible, and to the spirit of the early Christian centuries. These are not just good questions, they are the same questions that agitated the early church.

Looking at the readings of the Bible in the global South, we might be awed at the resemblances across the ages, between African and Asian Christianity today and its predecessors many centuries ago. Using the term in the positive sense, African and Asian churches claim a primitive quality, a fidelity to the earliest traditions of the church, and sober scholars of these contemporary versions of the faith note the close resemblances to the Christianity of the ancient Mediterranean. Andrew Walls remarks that what we know of the pre–fourth century church "reveals many of the concerns African churches have today, from distinguishing between true and false prophets to deciding what should happen to church members who behave badly. Even the literary forms are often similar. . . . Africans have a need to understand how God was at work among their own traditions." The resemblances could be extended substantially, and in most cases, applied to contemporary Asian churches. And the continuities and parallels that give global South Christianity such an archaic feel involve precisely the matters that make early Christianity such an alien world for the global North.[4]

Sometimes, these resemblances are literary or cultural, in the sense that ancient images can have a meaning today in some parts of the world but not others. If we are familiar with African Christianity, say, we can appreciate many biblical themes that might otherwise escape us, such as the images of spiritual wealth and poverty—themes such as food and famine, water and thirst, and the centrality of the harvest. Such images give a literary power to the biblical text, but also tell modern believers in the global South that the scripture comes from a world familiar to them, that it is speaking their language.

Other continuities, though, are more substantial, going well beyond just the feel of the text. These issues include debates over the nature of sacrifice and the relationship of the Old Testament to the New. Global South churches can also find abundant scriptural justification for their concern with the forces of spiritual evil. The New Testament describes a world of demons and exorcisms, angels and healings. Colenso faced problems arising from these passages too. As a missionary, he was supposed to denounce witchcraft beliefs as well as polygamy, but with his knowledge of the Bible, he was too honest to do so. "How is it possible to teach the Zulus to cast off their super-stitious belief in witchcraft, if they are required to believe that all the stories of sorcery and demonology which they find in the Bible . . . are infallibly and divinely true. . . . I, for one, cannot do this." So should the missionary reject the biblical stories of the demonic before preaching against witchcraft? Or should he accept both realities? The same questions arise for Korean theologians addressing popular beliefs in *han* spirits.[5]

In other areas too, the Christianity of Africa and Asia operates in a thought world closely congruent with the early or medieval forms of the faith. Societies with a potent sense of the communal and collective can appreciate the Old Testament notion of national righteousness and national sin, ideas that can justify harsh moral legislation but that also encourage prophetic visions of social justice. A world of biting poverty and endemic disaster understands the transience of human life—and equally, of states. Societies that know the threat of persecution, that have experienced anti-Christian violence in living memory, feel a strong affinity to the sections of the Bible that regard the secu-lar state coldly, that present suffering as the likely lot of the Christian in this life. In such communities, apocalyptic literature—especially the book of Revelation—has a near-documentary relevance.

What Americans customarily think of as Christianity is, often, a specific manifestation of the faith that operates in the post-Enlightenment West. Ideas that might appear natural to the religion may not seem so elsewhere. For many Christians outside the West, it is not obvious that religion should be an individual or privatized matter; that church and state be separate; that secular values predominate in some spheres of life; or that scriptures be evaluated according to the canons of historical scholarship.

Looking at such a catalogue, we might well think of another religious tradition that appears so alarmingly different from conventional Euro-American assumptions, namely Islam. So stark are the apparent differences between Christianity and Islam that some evangelicals debate passionately whether Muslims actually worship the same God as Christians. As we have seen, though, the lived Christianity of Africa and Asia shares many assumptions with Islam, and in some matters, can be closer to Islam than to the Christianity of the advanced West. Some of the features of Islam that seem strangest to Euro-Americans in fact stem from older forms of Middle Eastern Christianity: even the fasting season of Ramadan derives from the strict Lenten discipline of the Syrian churches.

So many of the apparent differences between the two faiths arise from making a false comparison, between the privatized Christianity of a largely prosperous post-Enlightenment West, and the collective and tradition-minded Islam of overwhelmingly poor nations in Africa and Asia. Many of the contrasts reflect the cultures in which the two religions exist, rather than any intrinsic qualities of the faiths themselves. If we compare rich Christians with poor Muslims, of course they seem to inhabit different universes, and the differences are still more acute if we compare older Western Christians with young Afro-Asian Muslims. As Euro-Americans struggle to understand the Islam that represents such a vital political force, they could do worse than to try first to appreciate the global South Christianity, with which so many share a common history and language.

Old Readings

To illustrate the extent of the global divide within Christianity, I offer an exercise in cross-cultural understanding. For a North-American Christian, it can be a surprising and humbling experience to read parts of the Bible and to try to understand how they might be read in communities elsewhere in the world. Throughout, we need to think communally rather than individually. We must also abandon, however temporarily, familiar distinctions between secular and supernatural dimensions. And often, we must adjust our attitudes to the relationship between Old and New Testaments.

Any number of texts, then, offer surprises. Read Ruth, for instance, and imagine what it has to say in a hungry society threatened by war and social disruption. Understand the exultant release that awaits a reader in a society weighed down by ideas of ancestral curses, a reader who discovers the liberating texts about individual responsibility in the book of Ezekiel. Read Psalm

23 as a political tract, a rejection of unjust secular authority. Imagine a society terrorized by a dictatorial regime dedicated to suppressing the church, and read Revelation: understand the core message that whatever evils the world may produce, God will triumph. Or again, read Revelation with the eyes of rural believers in a rapidly modernizing society, trying to comprehend the inchoate brutality of the megalopolis. Read Hebrews, and think of its doctrines of priesthood and atonement as they might be understood in a country with a living tradition of animal sacrifice. Apply the Bible's many passages about the suffering of children to the real-world horrors facing the youth of the Congo, Uganda, Brazil, or other countries that before too long will be among the world's largest Christian countries.

Read in this way, the letter of James is eye-opening. Imagine reading it in a world in which your life is so short and perilous that it truly seems like a passing mist: what implications does that transience hold for everyday behavior? See the letter as a manual for a society in which Christianity is new and people are seeking practical rules for Christian living. And in that text, and many others, understand the references to widows not as the ancient history of social welfare systems but as radical responses to present-day problems affecting millions of women worldwide. As a difficult test for Northern-world Christians, try reading two almost adjacent passages in James, one condemning the rich, the other prescribing anointing and prayer for healing, and see both texts, "radical" and "charismatic," as integral portions of a common liberating message. Think of the numerous forms of captivity entrapping a poor inhabitant of a Third World nation—economic, social, environmental, spiritual—and appreciate the promise of liberation and loosing presented in Jesus' inaugural sermon in the Nazareth synagogue. Understand the appeal of this message in a society in which "the frustration of being alive . . . is excruciating."

When reading almost any part of the gospels, think how Jesus' actions might strike a community that cares deeply about caste and ritual purity, and where violating such laws might cost you your life. Think of them in the context of India. Read the accounts of Jesus interacting so warmly with the multiply rejected—in many societies worldwide, the story of the Samaritan woman at the well can still startle. Or go to the eighth chapter of Luke as a template for Christian healing and a reaffirmation of the power of good over evil. Or take one verse, namely John 10:10, in which Jesus promises abundant life, and think of the bewildering implications for a desperately poor society so obviously lacking in any prospect of abundance, or indeed, of any certainty of life.

Now recognize that these kinds of readings, adapted to local circumstances, are quite characteristic for millions of Christians around the world. Arguably, in terms of raw numbers, such readings represent the normal way in which Christians read the Bible in the early twenty-first century.

Other Worlds

A reading exercise of this kind is multiply useful. As in Colenso's day, bringing fresh eyes to the text suggests new ways of reading that can immeasurably enrich the modern encounter with the Bible, to find things that one never noticed before. Arguably, too, it may give a better sense of the original spirit in which the biblical books were written and read than can any number of scholarly commentaries.

But reading in this way must also remind us of the enormous cultural differences that separate the modern American or European reader from the biblical world and also, arguably, from the earliest environment of Christianity. As many African and Asian readers appreciate, the New Testament worldview was in fact based on the struggle against forces of evil, a cosmic vision that most Americans can no longer accept with any degree of fidelity. Modern optimism means that angels remain quite acceptable to popular belief, while giving credence to demons raises doubts about one's sanity.

Paradoxically, of course, the rhetoric of evil retains its currency among those who would have no patience for references to the Satanic or demonic. Quite rational Americans and Europeans see no difficulty in speaking the language of evil, whether the subject is genocide or terrorism, the atrocities of Nazis or of Communists. Even liberal Europeans who scoff at the moralistic commonplaces of U.S. politics surely remember that their societies are only sixty or seventy years removed from the most egregious acts of mass murder and destruction in human history, committed on their territories and in their cities. But is it possible to speak of evil without some kind of supernatural dimension, some sense of a profound violation of absolute or divine law? Surely, though, it is wildly improbable that modern Northern-world Christians —the mainline denominations, at least—might accept a belief in the demonic or in spiritual warfare, even as metaphors. Yet the further Christianity moves from ideas of evil, the less intelligible doctrines such as salvation and redemption become: salvation or redemption from what?

Nowhere is the North-South gulf more evident than in matters of healing, which is so central to the Christian gospels. The Northern world, however, has developed a professional and scientific model of medicine that has probably contributed more to the spread of secular values than all the insights and discoveries concerning the age of the earth and its place in the universe, or the story of human evolution. Louis Pasteur and Alexander Fleming may have altered attitudes to the role of religion far more than Galileo and Darwin. In the twentieth century, too, mainstream Western Christians came to accept wholeheartedly secular treatments for diseases of the mind or psyche.

Of course, ideas of healing and spiritual warfare are familiar to some denominations, but they remain suspect to most. When it was revealed that the U.S. Roman Catholic Church had responded to clergy sex scandals by recommending that offenders undergo treatment through prayer and spiritual regimens, even most Catholics scoffed at the church's dereliction of duty. As all rational people knew, only secular therapists and psychologists could meet the needs of either offenders or victims, and the church had a moral obligation to pay for these services. Not only could the church make no impact on bodily ills such as pneumonia or tuberculosis, but it had no worthwhile spiritual resources with which to respond to depression, addiction or delusion. The mere thought that such an approach might seriously be applied was mocked as "Pray and it will go away." Mainline churches may offer healing services, or pray for a patient's recovery, but direct religious intervention is rarely in prospect. How many seminaries, even those with conservative or evangelical leanings, offer courses on spiritual healing, leave alone exorcism? For most Europeans and Americans, healing is a secular, medical function, and has long been so.

The Real Bible

The differences between old and new Christianities, as manifested in their approaches to the Bible, must make us wonder about the future of the faith. It is easy to romanticize the rising Christianity of Africa and Asia. An evangelical or Pentecostal observer rejoices at the resurgence of primitive Christianity, and in such swelling numbers. In this apocalyptic vision, the authentic biblically based faith of the global South contrasts with the decayed liberalizing religion of North America and Europe. "Southerners" are true to their Bibles; they follow biblical authority; they practice a religion that seems derived straight from the book of Acts and withstand the Northern currents of sexual hedonism and moral relativism. While the global South continues its burning romance with the Bible as traditionally understood, the growing distance of the biblical worldview from the social and economic realities of the North drives Americans and Europeans to more esoteric types of religion ever further removed from traditional Christianity.

The nascent schism extends to the scriptures that are seen as authoritative. Americans and Europeans have shown a passionate interest in alternative scriptures, as suggested by the sales of rediscovered Gnostic scriptures such as the Gospels of Mary, of Thomas, and of Judas, as well as the furor over Dan Brown's Da Vinci Code. The attention paid to various hidden gospels suggests a deep public interest in Jesus and Christianity, but also indicates a sense that these vital matters cannot truly be approached through such flawed and mundane texts as the canonical gospels. Readers seem to be asking, is that really *all*? In Africa and Asia, on the other hand, the process of discovering the text is still under way, and the awe and excitement continue. (While some Third-World theologians have expressed interest in apocryphal texts such as Thomas, such interest is distinctly marginal.) The contrast seems worrying: new orthodox churches hew to authentic scripture; old churches fall prey to liberalism and succumb to fiction and speculation.

The North-South contrast naturally appeals to Southern churches themselves, anxious to assert their independence from Europe and North America, and to prove that they are neither vestiges of colonialism nor puppets of Western globalization. The idea of Southern authenticity also lends itself to conservative political conclusions. If in fact Christians of the South are following the footsteps of the earliest believers, while Euro-Americans have systematically compromised with liberalism and secular scholarship, then rising churches claim not just greater numbers, but greater access to truth, much to the delight of beleaguered Northern-world conservatives. As an old joke has it, we are both going about the Lord's work, you in your way, I in His. The practical consequences are all too clear if we contrast the teeming congregations of Africa and Asia with the empty churches of post-Christian Europe. In the words of the Magnificat, God has filled the hungry with good things and sent the rich away empty.

Too Good to Be True?

However enticing for many, this vision has many problems. African church leaders themselves are quick to point out negative aspects of that continent's triumphal embrace of Christianity. Writing in response to the millennial excitement about Christian growth as the world approached the year 2000, South African theologian Tinyiko Maluleke presented a stern call for humility. In an article entitled "What if We Are Mistaken about the Bible and Christianity in Africa?" he pointed to such sobering developments as the role of Christians in the Rwandan genocide and the apparent mass cult suicide of an Ugandan Christian sect. (In retrospect, the latter incident was more probably a massacre by external forces than a suicide by deluded fanatics.) Other observers raise concern about the spread of Prosperity Gospel teachings and quote the phrase that Christian growth in Africa is "a mile wide and an inch deep." Similar criticisms have been raised about Asian conditions, for instance about the cultish quality of some successful denominations.[6]

Now, each of these arguments can be countered effectively. If Christianity is only an inch deep, whether in Africa or Asia, it is puzzling why so many should be willing to risk death or suffering to defend their faith, and why so many Hindus and Muslims would endanger their lives and fortunes by converting to Christianity. Nor need scandals and excesses stunt church growth in the long term. No religious tradition in any historical period entirely lacks such excesses, and the early Christian church was no exception to that rule. We certainly do not have to replace triumphalism with overpessimism, but such observations do offer a salutary warning against romanticizing the newer Christian churches.

Yet even if it is correct, this image of global South Christianity as "authentic"—even as the one true manifestation of faith—is anything but good news for the religion as a whole. Assuredly, the growth of Christianity over the past century gives powerful testimony to the flexibility and endurance of the religion, its power to adapt to very different social and political circumstances, and also to the capacity of the Bible to serve as a fundamental religious text. But does that flexibility have limits? Can the Bible be read in a socially advanced society with anything like the immediacy that it offers in a community less blessed with a large service sector and abundant information technology, in which poverty and powerlessness naturally encourage supernatural worldviews? If not, perhaps spiritual seekers in the "advanced" world are doomed to seek religious sustenance in spurious or overhyped pseudo-scriptures, or dig once more in the exhausted vein of the Gnostic gospels, while the authentic Bible is left for the world's poor and uneducated. Is traditional, biblically oriented Christianity, evangelical or otherwise, destined to disappear with economic growth and maturation? Briefly, is there an equation between Christianity and underdevelopment?

The fact that so much of contemporary African and Asian Christianity finds the world of the New Testament so congenial might boost the familiar sociological argument about secularization. Briefly, it is a common assumption that poorer societies are much more strongly and pervasively religious than rich ones. Some might claim, then, that the kind of Bible-based Christianity we see in Asia and Africa works well because of its premodern or prescientific setting, but that it will in turn find itself displaced by economic development. Under the impact of modernity, individualism, privatization, and the rise of a scientific worldview, older styles of Christianity lose relevance. According to classic theories of secularization, this is what happened in modern Europe, and the same processes will befall African and Asian churches when those societies too experience Western-style development, when GNP per capita reaches a certain level, when modern hospitals fulfill the need for healing, when people feel confidence in the stability of their society. We would then be proclaiming the death of God, or at least a God who responds to prayer, who intervenes in any kind of traditional sense. In the words of Dietrich Bonhoeffer, humanity reaches a "coming of age," a time when "God is teaching us that we must live as men who can get along very well without Him. . . . The God who makes us live in this world without using Him as a working hypothesis is the God before whom we are ever standing."[7]

Fortunately for Christian believers, the secularization model has many flaws. It works wonderfully well in Western Europe, where Christian loyalties and Christian numbers really are in decline, but woefully badly in the United States, where Christian churches continue to grow and flourish in the world's most advanced economy. Some of the most successful U.S. movements are also conservative, evangelical, or Pentecostal, exactly the sort of groups that should in theory have been hardest hit by modernization. The (Pentecostal) Assemblies of God church is growing fast, as are long-established groups such as the Seventh Day Adventists and flourishing charismatic upstarts such as Calvary Chapel and the Vineyard. Some of the most successful congregations are evangelical and charismatic megachurches, which have grown rapidly in recent years. Counting congregations with two thousand or more weekly worshipers, the number of such churches has grown from fifty in 1980 to a thousand today, with a concentration in southern and western states. Often, such churches appeal to affluent and educated believers, who are far removed from stereotypes of evangelicals as ignorant fundamentalists. Around a quarter of Americans accept the label "evangelical," while many Catholics also accept traditional interpretations of the Christian faith. This hardly sounds like a society that can get along very well without God. The Christianity of the global North is neither as exhausted nor as compromised as its critics charge.[8]

Similarly, by no means all the modern Christian growth in the global South is associated with dire poverty. While Christianity assuredly flourishes in circumstances of poverty and persecution, that is not its only favorable environment. Christianity obviously reaches other audiences besides the poor and demon-ridden. In Pacific Rim nations, particularly, the faith appeals to many professional and upwardly mobile groups. In China, it is precisely the linkage with modernity that gives Christianity its initial appeal for aspiring professionals and intellectuals. In practice, economic development and the growth of science and medicine need not imply any dilution of Christian belief or practice, and Africans deeply resent any charge that their faith is primarily shaped by poverty or a "primitive" worldview. Nigerian Catholic archbishop John Onaiyekan of Abuja mocks the Western idea that "once the Africans get out of their huts and get some education, they'll think like us." He rather suggests that "as Africa's self-confidence and development levels grow, it will become bolder about asserting its moral vision on the global stage."[9] Like any healthy institution, Christianity develops over time, though without necessarily compromising its core beliefs.

Still, the secularization issue should make us think carefully about the cultural contexts of different forms of Christianity, and the extent to which "primitive" features of Christian thought might actually arise from stages of social development. To take a minor but obvious example, the Bible's rural and farming metaphors will have ever less relevance to African and Asian Christians as the process of urbanization continues and accelerates in coming decades. That does not mean that Christians in those regions will be any less faithful, or less conservative, but in matters small and great, they might well lose the easy sense of identification with the biblical world. In an ideal future, the parlous circumstances of the book of Ruth should become as alien to global South Christians as they have to most Europeans and Americans.

Reading from the South

Obviously, then, I am not suggesting that North-South differences herald the demise of Christianity, in either the short or long term. Even so, Northern-world audiences can still profit immensely from the insights of newer churches. While we cannot reproduce the cultural circumstances that shape their religious attitudes, we can still rediscover different ways of reading texts both familiar and not so familiar. "Reading from the South" can help free biblical passages and even whole genres from the associations they have acquired from our own historical inheritance.

Perhaps most important, the experience of the emerging churches must make us rethink the role of the Old Testament. That collection of books is undeniably the Hebrew Bible, the Jewish Bible, but it is also the Old Testament, the root system without which the New Testament and the whole Christian tradition make no sense whatever. Southern readings can help us exorcize the stubborn ghost of Marcion, a task that Christian churches need to repeat with some regularity.

In the process, we can rediscover quite ancient means of responding to suffering or calamity. To take a potent example, the events of September 11, 2001, precipitated a moral and spiritual crisis for many Americans, including Christians, who struggled to understand why God should have permitted such evil. Yet several different biblical genres seek to explain such tragedies, including the wisdom tradition, which reminds us of the transience of life and of nations, and the lamentation literature. Most relevant of all is the apocalyptic perspective, which has as its central theme the triumph over evil. For most mainline churches, though, references to apocalyptic literature at such a time would be an embarrassment, because of how closely Daniel and Revelation have become associated with specific timetables of end-times events and with attempts to identify key characters. Drawing on apocalyptic would almost assume identifying Osama bin Ladin with the Antichrist, or labeling the whole religion of Islam as Satanic, while the warfare imagery can read painfully. Yet African and Asian readings make clear that apocalyptic need involve no such specific references, which detract from the fundamental promise of hope: by these words are we comforted. Even excluding catastrophic violence and terrorism, wisdom, lamentation, and apocalyptic all offer rich resources for contemporary Northern-world believers across the ecclesiastical spectrum.[10]

Though many such themes come to mind, the most significant might be that of healing. For mainline Christians in the global North, not only should churches have no significant role in medicine, but any suggestion that they should summons disreputable images of fraudulent faith healing. The backwoods preacher putting his hand on a sick person and commanding "Heal!" —in a suitably caricatured Southern accent—is a comic stereotype. But we should not exaggerate the supposed dichotomy between religion and "real" healing. The worst offense committed by global North Christians is not that they use conventional medicine, but that so few recognize its spiritual dimensions. If one proclaims Christ as the divine Wisdom, views the Spirit as the presence of God in the world, then we should acknowledge the divinely inspired inquisitiveness and creativity that gave rise to anesthesia and antisepsis, to chemotherapy and cataract surgery. The scientific imagination is —or should be—a religious impulse.

Moreover, the healthier Euro-Americans become in their bodies, the more discomforted or dis-eased they feel in their minds and emotions. Some recent studies suggest that over a half of Americans will, at some point in their lives, suffer from a disorder that will be categorized as mental illness and that will lead them to seek help from psychiatry, from forms of therapy and counseling. In various ways, most of these forms of mind cure make far-reaching assumptions about the nature of the human mind, about character and relationships, which are as much based on faith and ideology as any overtly religious doctrine. This is a natural area for mainline Christianity to rediscover a core healing mission. In the process, they can offer distinctive resources for holistic approaches to mind and body, and speak of the role of forgiveness and reconciliation in social and psychological well-being. Christian-oriented therapy and counseling already represent substantial ventures, but they could yet form a more integrated component of mainstream churches. Here, especially, North and South might yet find common ground.

Thick and Clear

Quite probably, the story of Christianity over the coming decades will be marked by new schisms that broadly follow the North-South division,

conflicts for which the present Anglican/Episcopalian rift provides a sour
foretaste. In fact, understanding the divergent attitudes to biblical worldviews
goes far to explaining the animus on both sides. Unless both North and South,
liberals and conservatives, make a heroic effort to understand the language
of their opponents, and the historical and cultural values in which it is based,
schisms are all but certain. We can also predict with fair confidence the
rhetorical approaches of both sides, as Northern liberals denounce intolerant
fundamentalism, while Southern churches assert fealty to biblical foundations.
The word "primitive" will be freely thrown around, though with radically
different meanings. In themselves, such splits are not necessarily to be dreaded:
cultural differences often have fragmented Christian congregations in the
past, and they will do so again. For present purposes, also, it is far beyond my
predictive powers to imagine which side might have the better case.

Yet having said this, the issue of a religion's "authenticity" needs to be
considered carefully. To say that a faith identifies strongly with the biblical
worldview or can claim a fidelity to the Christian message does not mean
that other varieties of the faith in other societies are any less Christian. The
notion that any one pattern of Christianity is uniquely authentic is tenuous.
However far back we look in Christian history, we always find very diverse
patterns of belief and worship, not to mention attitudes to the scriptures.
Even in the first 150 years or so after the time of Jesus, philosophical and
mystical forms of the faith coexisted alongside charismatic and prophetic
versions, and it is difficult to classify any strand as truer to original doctrine.
This is especially apparent if we read not just the New Testament but also the
Apostolic Fathers, and other early texts that the Great Church accepted as
orthodox. To appreciate the diversity of early Christianity does not require
venturing into the arcane territories of Gnosticism.

In later times, too, the religion developed many faces. Over the centuries,
Christians and their churches have been liturgical and spontaneous, clerical
and individualistic, institutional and populist, militarist and pacifist, world-
affirming and world-denying, mystical and dogmatic, scholarly and anti-
intellectual. It would take a bold judge to exclude any of these from the faith
on the basis of their lack of resemblance to the most primitive manifestations
of the church. Some Christian traditions do indeed assume a particular premodern social and economic setting; others do not.

Christianity has always been a complex and multifaceted phenomenon,
so diverse that we recall C. S. Lewis's semiserious suggestion that religions,
like soups, must be either thick or clear. "By Thick, I mean those which have
orgies and ecstasies and mysteries and local attachments: Africa is full of
Thick religions. By Clear I mean those which are philosophical, ethical and
universalizing." For Lewis, thick and clear elements have always coexisted in
Christianity, and the enormous strength of the religion is its unique ability to

combine the two types—neither term is used in a pejorative sense. Christianity "takes a convert from central Africa and tells him to obey an enlightened universal ethic: it takes a twentieth-century academic prig like me and tells me to go fasting to a Mystery, to drink the blood of the Lord. The savage convert has to be Clear: I have to be Thick. That is how one knows one has come to the real religion." We can argue with Lewis's reference to the "savage," as he was writing at a time when supposedly Clear and civilized European nations were inflicting savagery on a scale unprecedented in human history; but his basic point is well taken.[11]

We can usefully apply these ideal terms to varieties of Christian belief and practice. Thick forms of Christianity work better in particular social settings, as in the charismatic or independent churches of modern Africa or Latin America; arguably, clear models might prove more suitable to prosperous postindustrial societies. Moreover, each tradition, each "consistency," reads the scriptures in a particular way. Over time, thick traditions can become clear, and vice versa. But neither need be more or less authentically Christian, or more orthodox, and indeed, each contains within itself part of the other. Assuredly, churches *can* deviate from the historic faith and fall prey to outrageous errors, usually arising from misconceived compromises with modernity—we think of the widespread seduction of Euro-American churches by eugenic doctrines in the early twentieth century.[12] But the fact that a church operates harmoniously in a modern or postmodern society does not of itself mean that it has sold out its Christian credentials.

Repeatedly, individuals who exemplify the rational and philosophical aspects of the religion also demonstrate in their lives a consciousness of the radically mysterious, the ecstatic. We think of the sober-minded second-century philosopher Justin joyously giving himself to martyrdom, or the mystical experiences that led Thomas Aquinas to dismiss all the writings of his life as being like straw. Dietrich Bonhoeffer, who spoke of humanity's coming of age, is often quoted in Death of God theology. He also conspired to assassinate the leader he saw as Antichrist, and was duly martyred.

To be thrilled by the vigor of global South Christianity today, to see in it a fervor more fitted for the second century than the twenty-first, should not necessarily lead us to write off the traditions of the North. But even without trying to draw such object lessons, a comparative view can still teach us much about the nature of Christianity. The lessons are not necessarily new, but it is one thing to read about the effects of the new religions in a textbook on medieval history and quite another to observe firsthand changes under way in the world today, or even to hear about them from neighbors on American soil.

If we live in Western cultures profoundly shaped by Christianity and Christian values over centuries, we can be startled to watch the transforming effects of the religion on a society, when so often this process is grounded in scriptural texts that have for us lost much of their power to surprise. We see the power of Christianity to overturn hierarchies and traditions. The chief beneficiaries are often the traditionally excluded groups, women and racial minorities, the poor, even those suffering under traditional stigmas or caste rules. Empowered by the Bible, they learn to speak out and claim their place in society. Living in a society in which Judeo-Christian ideas are part of the air we breathe, we can scarcely appreciate the impact of concepts of individual responsibility—the idea that people should not be held responsible for hereditary crimes, or that a woman is married to an individual man, rather than to his whole family or clan. The fact that these are dead issues for us reminds us of the overwhelming cultural debt that Western societies owe to their religious roots.

Amidst the horrors of the First World War, Karl Barth warned against attempts to find in the Bible answers to specific queries about politics, history, or culture; to seek anything grounded in the real-life experience of any society, past or present. Viewed in this light, he said, the Bible would always disappoint. The danger is always in trying to understand the Bible by human standards and expectations, and not recognizing its fundamental difference from the experience of its readers. Always, "within the Bible there is a new world, the world of God." Reading the Bible through fresh eyes constantly reminds us of the depths that still remain to be discovered there. At the least, knowing this should provide some kind of defense against the next spurious claim about the real truth of Christianity, the great secret about the authentic sources of the religion, based on documents unaccountably hidden from the world until recently. In reality, the answers in plain sight are quite amazing enough.

Appendix 1
Psalm 91
(King James Version)

1 He that dwelleth in the secret place of the most High shall abide under the shadow of the Almighty.

2 I will say of the LORD, He is my refuge and my fortress: my God; in him will I trust.

3 Surely he shall deliver thee from the snare of the fowler, and from the noisome pestilence.

4 He shall cover thee with his feathers, and under his wings shalt thou trust: his truth shall be thy shield and buckler.

5 Thou shalt not be afraid for the terror by night; nor for the arrow that flieth by day;

6 Nor for the pestilence that walketh in darkness; nor for the destruction that wasteth at noonday.

7 A thousand shall fall at thy side, and ten thousand at thy right hand; but it shall not come nigh thee.

8 Only with thine eyes shalt thou behold and see the reward of the wicked.

9 Because thou hast made the LORD, which is my refuge, even the most High, thy habitation;

10 There shall no evil befall thee, neither shall any plague come nigh thy dwelling.

11 For he shall give his angels charge over thee, to keep thee in all thy ways.

12 They shall bear thee up in their hands, lest thou dash thy foot against a stone.

13 Thou shalt tread upon the lion and adder: the young lion and the dragon shalt thou trample under feet.

14 Because he hath set his love upon me, therefore will I deliver him: I will set him on high, because he hath known my name.

15 He shall call upon me, and I will answer him: I will be with him in trouble; I will deliver him, and honour him.

16 With long life will I satisfy him, and shew him my salvation.

Appendix 2
The Epistle of James
(King James Version)

Chapter 1

1 James, a servant of God and of the Lord Jesus Christ, to the twelve tribes which are scattered abroad, greeting.

2 My brethren, count it all joy when ye fall into divers temptations;

3 Knowing this, that the trying of your faith worketh patience.

4 But let patience have her perfect work, that ye may be perfect and entire, wanting nothing.

5 If any of you lack wisdom, let him ask of God, that giveth to all men liberally, and upbraideth not; and it shall be given him.

6 But let him ask in faith, nothing wavering. For he that wavereth is like a wave of the sea driven with the wind and tossed.

7 For let not that man think that he shall receive any thing of the Lord.

8 A double minded man is unstable in all his ways.

9 Let the brother of low degree rejoice in that he is exalted:

10 But the rich, in that he is made low: because as the flower of the grass he shall pass away.

11 For the sun is no sooner risen with a burning heat, but it withereth the grass, and the flower thereof falleth, and the grace of the fashion of it perisheth: so also shall the rich man fade away in his ways.

12 Blessed is the man that endureth temptation: for when he is tried, he shall receive the crown of life, which the Lord hath promised to them that love him.

13 Let no man say when he is tempted, I am tempted of God: for God cannot be tempted with evil, neither tempteth he any man:

14 But every man is tempted, when he is drawn away of his own lust, and enticed.

15 Then when lust hath conceived, it bringeth forth sin: and sin, when it is finished, bringeth forth death.

16 Do not err, my beloved brethren.

17 Every good gift and every perfect gift is from above, and cometh down from the Father of lights, with whom is no variableness, neither shadow of turning.

18 Of his own will begat he us with the word of truth, that we should be a kind of firstfruits of his creatures.

19 Wherefore, my beloved brethren, let every man be swift to hear, slow to speak, slow to wrath:

20 For the wrath of man worketh not the righteousness of God.

21 Wherefore lay apart all filthiness and superfluity of naughtiness, and receive with meekness the engrafted word, which is able to save your souls.

22 But be ye doers of the word, and not hearers only, deceiving your own selves.

23 For if any be a hearer of the word, and not a doer, he is like unto a man beholding his natural face in a glass:

24 For he beholdeth himself, and goeth his way, and straightway forgetteth what manner of man he was.

25 But whoso looketh into the perfect law of liberty, and continueth therein, he being not a forgetful hearer, but a doer of the work, this man shall be blessed in his deed.

26 If any man among you seem to be religious, and bridleth not his tongue, but deceiveth his own heart, this man's religion is vain.

27 Pure religion and undefiled before God and the Father is this, To visit the fatherless and widows in their affliction, and to keep himself unspotted from the world.

Chapter 2

1 My brethren, have not the faith of our Lord Jesus Christ, the Lord of glory, with respect of persons.

2 For if there come unto your assembly a man with a gold ring, in goodly apparel, and there come in also a poor man in vile raiment;

3 And ye have respect to him that weareth the gay clothing, and say unto him, Sit thou here in a good place; and say to the poor, Stand thou there, or sit here under my footstool:

4 Are ye not then partial in yourselves, and are become judges of evil thoughts?

5 Hearken, my beloved brethren, Hath not God chosen the poor of this world rich in faith, and heirs of the kingdom which he hath promised to them that love him?

6 But ye have despised the poor. Do not rich men oppress you, and draw you before the judgment seats?

7 Do not they blaspheme that worthy name by the which ye are called?

8 If ye fulfil the royal law according to the scripture, Thou shalt love thy neighbour as thyself, ye do well:

9 But if ye have respect to persons, ye commit sin, and are convinced of the law as transgressors.

10 For whosoever shall keep the whole law, and yet offend in one point, he is guilty of all.

11 For he that said, Do not commit adultery, said also, Do not kill. Now if thou commit no adultery, yet if thou kill, thou art become a transgressor of the law.

12 So speak ye, and so do, as they that shall be judged by the law of liberty.

13 For he shall have judgment without mercy, that hath shewed no mercy; and mercy rejoiceth against judgment.

14 What doth it profit, my brethren, though a man say he hath faith, and have not works? can faith save him?

15 If a brother or sister be naked, and destitute of daily food,

16 And one of you say unto them, Depart in peace, be ye warmed and filled; notwithstanding ye give them not those things which are needful to the body; what doth it profit?

17 Even so faith, if it hath not works, is dead, being alone.

18 Yea, a man may say, Thou hast faith, and I have works: shew me thy faith without thy works, and I will shew thee my faith by my works.

19 Thou believest that there is one God; thou doest well: the devils also believe, and tremble.

20 But wilt thou know, O vain man, that faith without works is dead?

21 Was not Abraham our father justified by works, when he had offered Isaac his son upon the altar?

22 Seest thou how faith wrought with his works, and by works was faith made perfect?

23 And the scripture was fulfilled which saith, Abraham believed God, and it was imputed unto him for righteousness: and he was called the Friend of God.

24 Ye see then how that by works a man is justified, and not by faith only.

25 Likewise also was not Rahab the harlot justified by works, when she had received the messengers, and had sent them out another way?

26 For as the body without the spirit is dead, so faith without works is dead also.

Chapter 3

1 My brethren, be not many masters, knowing that we shall receive the greater condemnation.

2 For in many things we offend all. If any man offend not in word, the same is a perfect man, and able also to bridle the whole body.

3 Behold, we put bits in the horses' mouths, that they may obey us; and we turn about their whole body.

4 Behold also the ships, which though they be so great, and are driven of fierce winds, yet are they turned about with a very small helm, whithersoever the governor listeth.

5 Even so the tongue is a little member, and boasteth great things. Behold, how great a matter a little fire kindleth!

6 And the tongue is a fire, a world of iniquity: so is the tongue among our members, that it defileth the whole body, and setteth on fire the course of nature; and it is set on fire of hell.

7 For every kind of beasts, and of birds, and of serpents, and of things in the sea, is tamed, and hath been tamed of mankind:

8 But the tongue can no man tame; it is an unruly evil, full of deadly poison.

9 Therewith bless we God, even the Father; and therewith curse we men, which are made after the similitude of God.

10 Out of the same mouth proceedeth blessing and cursing. My brethren, these things ought not so to be.

11 Doth a fountain send forth at the same place sweet water and bitter?

12 Can the fig tree, my brethren, bear olive berries? either a vine, figs? so can no fountain both yield salt water and fresh.

13 Who is a wise man and endued with knowledge among you? let him shew out of a good conversation his works with meekness of wisdom.

14 But if ye have bitter envying and strife in your hearts, glory not, and lie not against the truth.

15 This wisdom descendeth not from above, but is earthly, sensual, devilish.

16 For where envying and strife is, there is confusion and every evil work.

17 But the wisdom that is from above is first pure, then peaceable, gentle, and easy to be intreated, full of mercy and good fruits, without partiality, and without hypocrisy.

18 And the fruit of righteousness is sown in peace of them that make peace.

Chapter 4

1 From whence come wars and fightings among you? come they not hence, even of your lusts that war in your members?

2 Ye lust, and have not: ye kill, and desire to have, and cannot obtain: ye fight and war, yet ye have not, because ye ask not.

3 Ye ask, and receive not, because ye ask amiss, that ye may consume it upon your lusts.

4 Ye adulterers and adulteresses, know ye not that the friendship of the world is enmity with God? whosoever therefore will be a friend of the world is the enemy of God.

5 Do ye think that the scripture saith in vain, The spirit that dwelleth in us lusteth to envy?

6 But he giveth more grace. Wherefore he saith, God resisteth the proud, but giveth grace unto the humble.

7 Submit yourselves therefore to God. Resist the devil, and he will flee from you.

8 Draw nigh to God, and he will draw nigh to you. Cleanse your hands, ye sinners; and purify your hearts, ye double minded.

9 Be afflicted, and mourn, and weep: let your laughter be turned to mourning, and your joy to heaviness.

10 Humble yourselves in the sight of the Lord, and he shall lift you up.

11 Speak not evil one of another, brethren. He that speaketh evil of his brother, and judgeth his brother, speaketh evil of the law, and judgeth the law: but if thou judge the law, thou art not a doer of the law, but a judge.

12 There is one lawgiver, who is able to save and to destroy: who art thou that judgest another?

13 Go to now, ye that say, To day or to morrow we will go into such a city, and continue there a year, and buy and sell, and get gain:

14 Whereas ye know not what shall be on the morrow. For what is your life? It is even a vapour, that appeareth for a little time, and then vanisheth away.

15 For that ye ought to say, If the Lord will, we shall live, and do this, or that.

16 But now ye rejoice in your boastings: all such rejoicing is evil.

17 Therefore to him that knoweth to do good, and doeth it not, to him it is sin.

Chapter 5

1 Go to now, ye rich men, weep and howl for your miseries that shall come upon you.

2 Your riches are corrupted, and your garments are motheaten.

3 Your gold and silver is cankered; and the rust of them shall be a witness against you, and shall eat your flesh as it were fire. Ye have heaped treasure together for the last days.

4 Behold, the hire of the labourers who have reaped down your fields, which is of you kept back by fraud, crieth: and the cries of them which have reaped are entered into the ears of the Lord of sabaoth.

5 Ye have lived in pleasure on the earth, and been wanton; ye have nourished your hearts, as in a day of slaughter.

6 Ye have condemned and killed the just; and he doth not resist you.

7 Be patient therefore, brethren, unto the coming of the Lord. Behold, the husbandman waiteth for the precious fruit of the earth, and hath long patience for it, until he receive the early and latter rain.

8 Be ye also patient; stablish your hearts: for the coming of the Lord draweth nigh.

9 Grudge not one against another, brethren, lest ye be condemned: behold, the judge standeth before the door.

10 Take, my brethren, the prophets, who have spoken in the name of the Lord, for an example of suffering affliction, and of patience.

11 Behold, we count them happy which endure. Ye have heard of the patience of Job, and have seen the end of the Lord; that the Lord is very pitiful, and of tender mercy.

12 But above all things, my brethren, swear not, neither by heaven, neither by the earth, neither by any other oath: but let your yea be yea; and your nay, nay; lest ye fall into condemnation.

13 Is any among you afflicted? let him pray. Is any merry? let him sing psalms.

14 Is any sick among you? let him call for the elders of the church; and let them pray over him, anointing him with oil in the name of the Lord:

15 And the prayer of faith shall save the sick, and the Lord shall raise him up; and if he have committed sins, they shall be forgiven him.

16 Confess your faults one to another, and pray one for another, that ye may be healed. The effectual fervent prayer of a righteous man availeth much.

17 Elias was a man subject to like passions as we are, and he prayed earnestly that it might not rain: and it rained not on the earth by the space of three years and six months.

18 And he prayed again, and the heaven gave rain, and the earth brought forth her fruit.

19 Brethren, if any of you do err from the truth, and one convert him;

20 Let him know, that he which converteth the sinner from the error of his way shall save a soul from death, and shall hide a multitude of sins.

Abbreviations

ACS	*African Christian Studies*
AJET	*African Journal of Evangelical Theology*
ATJ	*Africa Theological Journal*
AJPS	*Asian Journal of Pentecostal Studies*
AJT	*Asia Journal of Theology*
CLAIM	Christian Literature Association in Malawi
CPCR	*Cyberjournal for Pentecostal Charismatic Research*
ER	*Ecumenical Review*
IRM	*International Review of Missions*
JACT	*Journal of African Christian Thought*
JRA	*Journal of Religion in Africa*
JTSA	*Journal of Theology for Southern Africa*
NIV	New International Version
NYT	*New York Times*
RIBLA	*Revista de Interpretación Bíblica Latinoamericana*
SWC	*Studies in World Christianity*

Notes

Preface

1. Lamin Sanneh, *Whose Religion Is Christianity?* (Grand Rapids, Mich.: W. B. Eerdmans, 2003).

2. Birgit Meyer, "Christianity in Africa," *Annual Review of Anthropology* 33 (2004), 447–74.

Chapter 1

1. Stephen Bates, *A Church at War* (New York: I. B. Tauris, 2004); Grant LeMarquand, "The Changeless, the Changeable, and the Changing," *Anglican Theological Review* 86 (2004), 401–22; N. T. Wright, *The Last Word* (San Francisco: HarperSanFrancisco, 2005); Hugh McLeod, ed., *Cambridge History of Christianity: World Christianities 1914–2000* (New York: Cambridge University Press, 2006).

2. Philip Jenkins, *The Next Christendom* (New York: Oxford University Press, 2002). The point about labeling "Latin American perspectives" is from Robert McAfee Brown, *Gustavo Gutierrez* (Maryknoll, N.Y.: Orbis, 1990), xix. Joel Carpenter, "The Christian Scholar in an Age of Global Christianity," in Douglas V. Henry and Michael D. Beaty, eds., *Christianity and the Soul of the University* (Grand Rapids, Mich: Baker Academic, 2006).

3. Harry Emerson Fosdick, "Shall the Fundamentalists Win?" *Christian Work*, June 10, 1922, 716–22.

4. Kenneth A. Locke, "The Bible on Homosexuality," *Journal of Homosexuality* 48 (2) (2004), 125–. The Leviticus parody can be found at many sites, but see, for instance, http://jeromekahn123.tripod.com/againstreligion/id3.html.

5. The relevant Pauline references to homosexuality are Rom. 1:18–32 and 1 Cor. 6:10. For regulations about women's hair, see 1 Cor. 11. Scott Thumma, *Gay Religion* (Walnut Creek, Calif.: AltaMira Press, 2005); Andrew Linzey and Richard Kirker,

eds, *Gays and the Future of Anglicanism* (Winchester, UK: O Books, 2005). Within the Anglican tradition, Wright's *The Last Word* seeks a middle way between the extreme manifestations of biblical literalism and liberalism.

6. Rachel Zoll, "An Anglican Archbishop Says Episcopal Church Can't Be Trusted," Associated Press, appeared in *Boston Globe*, October 8, 2004. "The Church of Nigeria (Anglican Communion) and the Homosexuality Issue," online at http://www.anglican-nig.org/hobstatementaug.htm.

7. Aggrey Ouma, "Gay Unions Are Not Biblical, Says Archbishop Gitari," *East African Standard* (Nairobi), July 25, 2002, online at http://www.mask.org.za/sections/africapercountry/abc/kenya/kenya_1.htm.

8. "The Church of Nigeria (Anglican Communion) and the Homosexuality Issue."

9. Bishop Obare's letter is found at http://www.missionsprovinsen.se/the_letter_from_bishop_w_obare_to_the_archbishop_kg_hammar_(eng).htm. Immigrant churches are the subject of a rapidly growing literature, in both North America and Europe. See, for instance, R. Stephen Warner and Judith G. Wittner, eds., *Gatherings in Diaspora* (Philadelphia: Temple University Press, 1998); Fenggang Yang, *Chinese Christians in America* (University Park: Pennsylvania State University Press, 1999); Jeffrey M. Burns, Ellen Skerrett, and Joseph M. White, eds., *Keeping Faith* (Maryknoll, N.Y.: Orbis, 2000); Helen Rose Ebaugh and Janet Saltzman Chafetz, eds., *Religion and the New Immigrants* (Walnut Creek, Calif.: AltaMira Press, 2000); Tony Carnes and Anna Karpathakis, eds., *New York Glory* (New York: New York University Press, 2001); Ho Youn Kwon, Kwang Chung Kim, and R. Stephen Warner, eds., *Korean Americans and Their Religions* (University Park: Pennsylvania State University Press, 2001); Gerrie ter Haar, *African Christians in Europe* (Nairobi, Kenya: Acton, 2001); and idem, ed., *Religious Communities in the Diaspora* (Nairobi, Kenya: Acton, 2001); Jame Iwamura and Paul Spickard, eds., *Revealing the Sacred in Asian and Pacific America* (New York: Routledge, 2003); Fumitaka Matsuoka and Eleazar S. Fernandez, eds., *Realizing the America of Our Hearts* (St. Louis, Mo.: Chalice Press, 2003); Tony Carnes and Fenggang Yang, eds., *Asian American Religions* (New York: New York University Press, 2004); Russell Jeung, *Faithful Generations* (New Brunswick, N.J.: Rutgers University Press, 2004); Su Yon Pak, Unzu Lee, Jung Ha Kim, and Myungji Cho, *Singing the Lord's Song in a New Land* (Louisville, Ky.: Westminster John Knox Press, 2005).

10. Hannah W. Kinoti and John M. Waliggo, eds., *The Bible in African Christianity* (Nairobi, Kenya: Acton, 1997); Justin S. Ukpong, "Developments in Biblical Interpretation in Modern Africa," *Missionalia* 27 (3) (1999), 313–29; Grant LeMarquand, "New Testament Exegesis in (Modern) Africa," in Gerald O. West and Musa W. Dube, eds., *The Bible in Africa* (Leiden: Brill, 2000), 72–102; Allan H. Anderson, *African Reformation* (Trenton, N.J.: Africa World Press, 2001); Donald M. Lewis, ed., *Christianity Reborn* (Grand Rapids, Mich.: W. B. Eerdmans, 2004); Ogbu U. Kalu, ed., *African Christianity* (Pretoria, South Africa: University of Pretoria, 2005); David Maxwell, "Post-Colonial Christianity in Africa," in Hugh McLeod, ed., *Cambridge History of Christianity: World Christianities 1914–2000* (New York: Cambridge University Press, 2006), 401–21.

11. Carpenter, "The Christian Scholar in an Age of Global Christianity."

12. For "Southern" currents in U.S. Christianity, see James M. Ault, *Spirit and Flesh* (New York: Knopf, 2005).

13. Contemporary Bible scholarship from the global South is amply represented, for instance, in R. S. Sugirtharajah, ed., *Voices from the Margin* (Maryknoll, N.Y.:

Orbis, 1995); Kwok Pui-Lan, *Discovering the Bible in the Non-Biblical World* (Maryknoll, N.Y.: Orbis, 1995); Daniel Carro and Richard F. Wilson, eds., *Contemporary Gospel Accents* (Macon, Ga.: Mercer University Press, 1996); Susan Brooks Thistlethwaite and Mary Potter Engel, eds., *Lift Every Voice*, rev. ed. (Maryknoll, N.Y.: Orbis Books, 1998); West and Dube, eds., *The Bible in Africa*; Fernando F. Segovia, *Decolonizing Biblical Studies* (Maryknoll, N.Y.: Orbis, 2000); Justin S. Ukpong, Musa W. Dube, Gerald O. West, Alpheus Masoga, Norman K. Gottwald, Jeremy Punt, Tinyiko S. Maluleke, and Vincent L. Wimbush, eds., *Reading the Bible in the Global Village* (Atlanta, Ga.: Society of Biblical Literature, 2002); Miguel A. De La Torre, *Reading the Bible from the Margins* (Maryknoll, N.Y.: Orbis Books, 2002); John Parratt, ed., *Introduction to Third World Theologies* (New York: Cambridge University Press, 2004); J. N. K. Mugambi and Johannes A. Smit, eds., *Text and Context in New Testament Hermeneutics* (Nairobi, Kenya: Acton, 2004); Stephen D. Moore and Fernando F. Segovia, *Postcolonial Biblical Criticism* (Edinburgh: T. & T. Clark, 2005).

14. R. S. Sugirtharajah, "Introduction," in Sugirtharajah, ed., *Voices from the Margin*, 1. Sugirtharajah's other books include *The Postcolonial Bible* (Sheffield, UK: Sheffield Academic Press, 1998); *Asian Biblical Hermeneutics and Postcolonialism* (Maryknoll, N.Y.: Orbis Books, 1998); *The Bible and the Third World* (New York: Cambridge University Press, 2001); *Postcolonial Criticism and Bible Interpretation* (New York: Oxford University Press, 2002); *The Bible and Empire* (New York: Cambridge University Press, 2005); and *The Postcolonial Biblical Reader* (Oxford: Blackwell, 2005).

15. R. S. Sugirtharajah, *Post-Colonial Reconfigurations* (St. Louis, Mo.: Chalice, 2003), 164. For such "top-down" ecclesiastical liberalism, see, for instance, Peter C. Phan, ed., *The Asian Synod* (Maryknoll, N.Y.: Orbis Books, 2002).

16. For liberation theologies in the 1970s and 1980s, see, for instance, Walbert Buhlmann, *The Coming of the Third Church* (Slough, UK: St. Paul, 1976); Norman K. Gottwald, ed., *The Bible and Liberation* (Maryknoll, N.Y.: Orbis, 1983); and Robert McAfee Brown, *Unexpected News* (Philadelphia: Westminster Press, 1984). In terms of American religious publishers, I am thinking of firms such as Orbis, an outstanding press offering a magnificent range of titles and authors, but usually with an avowedly progressive theological agenda.

17. Malika Sibeko and Beverley Haddad, "Reading the Bible 'With' Women in Poor and Marginalized Communities in South Africa," *Semeia* 78 (1997), 83–92; Gerald O. West, *The Academy of the Poor* (Sheffield, UK: Sheffield Academic Press, 1999); Justin Ukpong, "Bible Reading with a Community of Ordinary Readers," in Mary Getui, Tinyiko Maluleke, and Justin Ukpong, eds., *Interpreting the New Testament in Africa* (Nairobi, Kenya: Acton, 2001), 188–212. See also the section "People as Exegetes," in Sugirtharajah, ed., *Voices from the Margin*, 407–56.

18. For studies of sermon texts, see Harold W. Turner, *Profile Through Preaching* (Geneva: World Council of Churches, Commission on World Mission and Evangelism, Edinburgh House Press, 1965); Andrew E. Kim, "Korean Religious Culture and Its Affinity to Christianity," *Sociology of Religion* 61 (2) (2000), 117–33; Hilary B. P. Mijoga, *Separate But Same Gospel* (Blantyre, Malawi: CLAIM, 2000); and idem, "Interpreting the Bible in African Sermons," in Getui, Maluleke, and Ukpong, eds., *Interpreting the New Testament in Africa*, 123–44. For comparison, see Justo L. González and Pablo A. Jiménez, eds., *Púlpito: An Introduction to Hispanic Preaching* (Nashville, Tenn.: Abingdon Press, 2005).

Throughout this book, I have drawn from journals such as (for Africa) *African Christian Studies*; *African Ecclesial Review*; *African Journal of Evangelical Theology*; *Africa Theological Journal*; *Journal of African Christian Thought*; *Journal of Theology for Southern Africa*; *Missionalia*; *Revue Africaine de Théologie*; and *Scriptura: International Journal of Bible, Religion and Theology in Southern Africa*. Important sources for Asian Christianity include *Asia Journal of Theology*, *Asian Journal of Pentecostal Studies*, *Chinese Theological Review*, *CTC Bulletin*, *Journal of Asian and Asian American Theology*, *Pacific Journal of Theology*, *Philippiniana Sacra*, and *World Mission*. Other major journals include *Ecumenical Review*, *International Bulletin of Missionary Research*, *International Review of Missions*, and *Studies in World Christianity*.

19. The religious statistics used here are drawn from *Status of Global Mission, 2005*, at http://www.globalchristianity.org/resources.htm. For future projections, see David B. Barrett, George T. Kurian, and Todd M. Johnson, *World Christian Encyclopedia*, 2nd ed. (New York: Oxford University Press, 2001), 12–15. The map described can be found in Todd M. Johnson and Sandra S. Kim, "Describing the Worldwide Christian Phenomenon," *International Bulletin of Missionary Research* 29 (2) (2005), 80–84. Lamin O. Sanneh and Joel A. Carpenter, eds., *The Changing Face of Christianity* (New York: Oxford University Press, 2005). For European secularization, see Callum G. Brown, *The Death of Christian Britain* (London: Routledge, 2001); Hugh McLeod and Werner Ustorf, eds., *The Decline of Christendom in Western Europe, 1750–2000* (New York: Cambridge University Press, 2003); and Mary Anne Perkins, *Christendom and European Identity* (Berlin: Walter de Gruyter, 2004). The notion of a Euro-American "captivity of the church" dates back at least to R. H. S. Boyd, *India and the Latin Captivity of the Church* (New York: Cambridge University Press, 1974). For the "North Atlantic Captivity," see Diane B. Stinton, *Jesus of Africa* (Maryknoll, N.Y.: Orbis, 2004), 29; also see John S. Pobee and Philomena Njeri Mwaura, "Health, Healing and Religion," *IRM* 90 (2001), 55–69, at 57.

20. Barrett et al., *World Christian Encyclopedia*; David Aikman, *Jesus in Beijing* (Chicago: Regnery, 2003).

21. Andrew Wingate, Kevin Ward, Carrie Pemberton, and Wilson Sitshebo, eds., *Anglicanism* (New York: Church Publishing, 1998). Titus Presler, "Old and New in Worship and Community," *Anglican Theological Review* (Fall, 2000). For Adventism, see, for instance, Eva Keller, *The Road to Clarity* (New York: Palgrave Macmillan, 2005).

22. Peter Gomes, *The Good Book* (New York: W. Morrow, 1996).

23. Judith Nagata, "Beyond Theology: Toward an Anthropology of Fundamentalism," *American Anthropologist* 103 (2) (2001), 481–98.

24. Martin E. Marty, *Fundamentalisms Observed* (Chicago: University of Chicago Press, 1991); Martin E. Marty and F. Scott Appleby, *The Fundamentalism Project*, 5 vols. (Chicago: University of Chicago Press, 1991–95). Gerrie Ter Haar and James J. Busuttil, eds., *The Freedom to Do God's Will* (New York: Routledge, 2003).

25. Quoted by Gerald O. West, *Biblical Hermeneutics of Liberation* (Pietermaritzburg, South Africa: Cluster, 1991), 158.

26. Quoted in David S. Lim, "Consolidating Democracy: Filipino Evangelicals in between People Power Events," paper delivered to conference on "The Bible and the Ballot: Evangelicals and Third World Democracy," Potomac, Md., June 2002.

27. The quote about Pentecostal hermeneutic is from Ogbu U. Kalu, "Historical Perspectives," *JACT* 1 (2) (1998), 3–16, at 11. Harvey Cox, *Fire from Heaven* (Reading, Mass.: Addison-Wesley, 1995); David Martin, *Pentecostalism* (Oxford, UK: Blackwell, 2002); Allan Anderson, *An Introduction to Pentecostalism* (New York: Cambridge University Press, 2004).

28. For left-wing evangelicalism, see, for example, Jim Wallis, *God's Politics* (San Francisco: HarperSanFrancisco, 2005); Charles Marsh, *The Beloved Community* (New York: Basic Books, 2005). For evangelicals and gender, see Brenda E. Brasher, *Godly Women* (New Brunswick, N.J.: Rutgers University Press, 1998).

29. Vincent L. Wimbush, *African Americans and the Bible* (New York: Continuum, 2000); idem, *The Bible and African Americans* (Minneapolis, Minn.: Fortress Press, 2003).

30. Benjamin Disraeli, *Sybil* (New York: World's Classics edition, Oxford University Press, 1999).

31. Henry Chadwick, *The Early Church* (London: Penguin, 2005).

32. See, for instance, Diarmaid MacCulloch, *The Reformation* (New York: Viking, 2004).

33. For personal attacks on Akinola, see Pat Ashworth, "Global South Won't Split Communion, Says Venables," *Church Times*, September 16, 2005; John Bryson Chane, "A Gospel of Intolerance," *Washington Post*, February 26, 2006. The reference to "monkeying around" is cited from Ethan Vesely-Flad, "For the Soul of the Church," *Colorlines* 8 (1) (2005), 11–18.

34. Lamin Sanneh, *Whose Religion Is Christianity?* (Grand Rapids, Mich.: W. B. Eerdmans, 2003).

Chapter 2

1. "The Church of Nigeria (Anglican Communion) and the Homosexuality Issue," online at http://www.anglican-nig.org/hobstatementaug.htm.

2. Tom Murphy, "Brazil Becomes Feverish Market for Bibles," Associated Press, August 19, 2004.

3. Barbara Harris is quoted by Ethan Vesely-Flad, "For the Soul of the Church," *Colorlines* 8 (1) (2005), 11–18; for Korea, see "Theologian Takes on Establishment," *Joongang Daily*, June 24, 2004, online at http://service.joins.com/asp/print_article_english.asp?aid=2432270&esectcode=e_life&title=theologian+takes+on+establishment. Young-Gwan Kim, "The Confucian-Christian Context in Korean Christianity," *British Columbia Asian Review* 13 (Spring, 2002), 70–91.

4. Kevin Ward, Brian Stanley, and Diana K. Witts, eds., *The Church Mission Society and World Christianity, 1799–1999* (Grand Rapids, Mich.: W. B. Eerdmans, 1999); Christopher Hodgkins, *Reforming Empire* (Columbia: University of Missouri Press, 2002); Andrew Porter, ed., *The Imperial Horizons of British Protestant Missions, 1880–1914* (Grand Rapids, Mich.: W. B. Eerdmans, 2003). For Derek Prince ministries, see http://www.dpmusa.org/; the website of Reinhard Bonnke ministries is http://www.cfan.org/.

5. To take one example of many, the greatest work of Brazilian literature, *The Revolt of the Backlands*, tells of a huge, apocalyptic separatist movement led by a would-be messiah of the late nineteenth century.

6. Steve Brouwer, Paul Gifford, and Susan D. Rose, *Exporting the American Gospel* (New York: Routledge, 1996); J. Kwabena Asamoah-Gyadu, *African Charismatics* (Leiden: Brill, 2005).

7. Paul Gifford, *Ghana's New Christianity* (Bloomington: Indiana University Press, 2004). Gerald O. West is quoted from "Response," in Khiok-Khng Yeo, ed., *Navigating Romans through Cultures* (Edinburgh: T. & T. Clark, 2004), 89.

8. David Kwang-Sun Suh, "Asian Theology in a Changing Asia," proceedings of the Congress of Asian Theologians (CATS), May 25–June 1, 1997, Suwon, Korea, online at http://www.cca.org.hk/resources/ctc/ctc97-cats1/ctc97-cats1f.htm.

9. Aloo Osotsi Mojola, "100 Years of the Luganda Bible," in Gerald O. West and Musa W. Dube, eds., *The Bible in Africa* (Leiden: Brill, 2000), 529.

10. Yvonne Vera, *Nehanda* (Bedminster, N.J.: Baobab Books, 1993), 104–5.

11. Jonathan A. Draper, *Orality, Literacy, and Colonialism in Southern Africa* (Pietmaritzburg, South Africa: Cluster, 2002); Vincent Wimbush, "Reading Texts through Worlds, Worlds through Texts," *Semeia* 62 (1993), 129–40.

12. Isabel Hofmeyr, *The Portable Bunyan* (Princeton, N.J.: Princeton University Press, 2003); idem, "African Christian Interpretations of *The Pilgrim's Progress*," *JRA* 32 (4) (2002), 440–56, at 445; Lionel Caplan, *Class and Culture in Urban India* (Oxford: Clarendon, 1987), 184.

13. "African Christian Interpretations of *The Pilgrim's Progress*," 449, 455. Shembe is quoted in Jonathan Draper, "The Bible as Poison Onion, Icon and Oracle," *JTSA* 112 (2002), 39–56. For Shembe's church, see Bengt Sundkler, *Bantu Prophets in South Africa*, 2nd ed. (London: Oxford University Press, 1961); Irving Hexham, ed., *The Scriptures of the AmaNazaretha of Ekuphakameni* (Calgary: University of Calgary Press, 1994). For revealed scripts, see Elizabeth Isichei, *A History of Christianity in Africa* (Grand Rapids, Mich.: W. B. Eerdmans, 1995), 9, 202–3.

14. Diarmaid MacCulloch, *The Reformation* (New York: Viking, 2004).

15. Kwame Bediako, "Epilogue," in Ype Schaaf, *On Their Way Rejoicing* (Carlisle, UK: Paternoster Press, 1994). Lamin O. Sanneh, *Translating the Message* (Maryknoll, N.Y.: Orbis, 1989); idem, *Encountering the West* (Maryknoll, N.Y.: Orbis, 1993). Phillip C. Stine and Ernst R. Wendland, eds., *Bridging the Gap* (New York: American Bible Society, 1990); Lewis S. Robinson, "The Bible in Twentieth Century Chinese Fiction," in Irene Eber, Sze-Kar Wan, Knut Walf, and Roman Malek, eds., *The Bible in Modern China* (Sankt Augustin: Institut Monumenta Serica, 1999), 237–77. Statistics for Bible translation and distribution are from the website of the United Bible Societies at http://www.biblesociety.org/index2.htm. See also Aloo Osotsi Mojola, "The Challenge of Ngugi wa Thiong'o," in Ernest R. Wendland and Jean-Claude Loba-Mkole, eds., *Biblical Texts and African Audiences* (Nairobi, Kenya: Acton, 2004), 15.

16. Peter Brown, *The Rise of Western Christendom* (Oxford: Blackwell, 2003), 14–15.

17. The reference to hearing the word does not exclude private reading, since reading aloud was the universal ancient practice. Walter J. Ong, *Orality and Literacy* (London and New York: Routledge, 1982). The Augustine reference is from Michael C. McCarthy, "An Ecclesiology of Groaning," *Theological Studies* 66 (1) (2005), 23–48. For aural religious cultures in American history, see Leigh Schmidt, *Hearing Things* (Cambridge: Harvard University Press, 2000).

18. For the Zimbabwean service, see Titus Presler, *Transfigured Night* (Pretoria, South Africa: UNISA Press, 1999), 205. Jean-Marc Ela, *My Faith as an African* (Maryknoll, N.Y.: Orbis, 1988), 45–46.

19. Kenneth R. Ross, "Preaching in Mainstream and Independent Churches in Malawi," *JRA* 25 (1) (1995), 3–24. John Wesley Zwomumondiita Kurewa, *Preaching and Culture Identity* (Nashville, Tenn.: Abingdon Press, 2000).

20. Musimbi Kanyoro, "Reading the Bible from an African Perspective," *ER* 51 (1) (1999), 18–24. The verse read was 1 Cor. 16:21–24.

21. Ernest M. Ezeogu, "Bible and Culture in African Christianity," *IRM* 87 (1998), 25–38.

22. Stephen D. Glazier, *Marchin' the Pilgrims Home* (Westport, Conn.: Greenwood Press, 1983), 27; Nahashon Ndungu, "The Bible in an African Independent Church," in Hannah W. Kinoti and John M. Waliggo, eds., *The Bible in African Christianity* (Nairobi, Kenya: Acton, 1997), 58–67.

23. Carlos Mesters, "The Use of the Bible in Christian Communities of the Common People," in Norman K. Gottwald, ed., *The Bible and Liberation* (Maryknoll, N.Y.: Orbis, 1983), 119–33, at 123; Carlos Mesters, *Defenseless Flower* (Maryknoll, N.Y.: Orbis, 1989).

24. Kwok Pui-Lan, *Discovering the Bible in the Non-Biblical World* (Maryknoll, N.Y.: Orbis, 1995), 44–56; "An Asian Feminist Perspective," in R. S. Sugirtharajah, ed., *Voices from the Margin* (Maryknoll, N.Y.: Orbis, 1995), 255–66. The Indonesian case study is from John Mansford Prior, "Inculturation of Worship and Spirituality," online at http://www.sedos.org/.

25. Gerald O. West, "On the Eve of an African Bible Studies," *JTSA* 99 (1997), 105, 107. Daniel Arichea, "Reading Romans in Southeast Asia," in Yeo, ed., *Navigating Romans through Cultures*. For the problem of cows and oxen in Indian translation, see R. S. Sugirtharajah, *Post-Colonial Reconfigurations* (St. Louis, Mo.: Chalice, 2003), 42. Stine and Wendland, eds., *Bridging the Gap*.

26. John Lonsdale, "Religion and Politics in Kenya," the Henry Martyn Lectures, 2005, at http://www.martynmission.cam.ac.uk/CJLonsdale..html. The Malawian pastor is quoted in Hilary B. P. Mijoga, *Separate But Same Gospel* (Blantyre, Malawi: CLAIM, 2000), 159–60. For the transition from oral to textual traditions in ancient Israel, see William Schniedewind, *How the Bible Became a Book* (New York: Cambridge University Press, 2004).

27. Philip Jenkins, *History of Modern Wales* (London: Longman, 1990). Christopher Boyd Brown, *Singing the Gospel* (Cambridge, Mass.: Harvard University Press, 2005); David Hempton, *Methodism: Empire of the Spirit* (New Haven, Conn.: Yale University Press, 2005). For tactics of popular evangelism in American history, see Jon Butler, *Awash in a Sea of Faith* (Cambridge: Harvard University Press, 1990); and Christine Leigh Heyrman, *Southern Cross* (New York: Knopf, 1997). For the power of hymns in American Christianity, see Richard J. Mouw and Mark Noll, eds., *Wonderful Words of Life* (Grand Rapids, Mich.: W. B. Eerdmans, 2004); and Edith L. Blumhofer and Mark A. Noll, eds., *Singing the Lord's Song in a Strange Land* (Tuscaloosa: University of Alabama Press, 2004).

28. Jonathan Chaves, *Singing of the Source* (Honolulu: University of Hawai'i Press, 1993); Nicolas Standaert, "Christianity Shaped by the Chinese," in R. Po-chia Hsia, ed., *Cambridge History of Christianity: Reform and Expansion 1500–1660* (New York: Cambridge University Press, 2006).

29. J. A. Loubser, "How Al-Mokattam Mountain Was Moved," in Gerald O. West and Musa W. Dube, eds., *The Bible in Africa* (Leiden: Brill, 2000), 107.

30. The quote about Shembe is from B. N. Mthethwa, "Shembe's Hymnody and the Ethical Standards and Worldview of the AmaNazaretha," in G. C. Oosthuizen and Irving Hexham, eds., *Empirical Studies of African Independent/Indigenous Churches* (Lewiston, N.Y.: Edwin Mellen, 1992). Thomas Lehmann, "African Ethnomusicology and Christian Liturgy," in Teresa Okure, Paul van Thiel et al., eds., *32 Articles Evaluating Inculturation of Christianity in Africa* (Eldoret, Kenya: AME-CEA Gaba Publications, 1990), 201–10; Christopher Brooks, "In Search of an Indigenous African Hymnody," *Black Sacred Music* 8 (2) (1994), 30–42; J. Nathan Corbett, *The Sound of the Harvest* (Grand Rapids, Mich.: Baker Books, 1998); C. Michael Hawn, *Gather Into One* (Grand Rapids, Mich.: W. B. Eerdmans, 2003); Gregory F. Barz, *Performing Religion* (Amsterdam: Rodopi, 2003). Compare Daniel Ramírez, "*Alabaré a mi Señor*: Hymnody as Ideology in Latino Protestantism," in Blumhofer and Noll, eds., *Singing the Lord's Song in a Strange Land*.

31. Hannah W. Kinoti, "An African Perspective on Psalm 23," in Jon R. Levison and Priscilla Pope-Levison, eds., *Return to Babel* (London: Westminster John Knox Press, 1999); Ezra Chitando, *Singing Culture* (Uppsala: Nordic Africa Institute, 2002).

32. Daniel Patte, J. Severino Croatto, Nicole Wilkinson Duran, Teresa Okure, and Archie Chi Chung Lee, eds., *Global Bible Commentary* (Nashville, Tenn.: Abingdon Press, 2004), 490.

33. Philip T. Laryea, "Ephraim Amu as a Theologian in Song," *JACT* 5 (1) (2002), 25–.

34. Mark K. Nikkel, *Dinka Christianity* (Nairobi, Kenya: Paulines Publications, 2001). Idem, "The Cross of Bor Dinka Christians," *SWC* 1 (2) (1995), 160–85.

35. Fergus J. King, "Nyimbo Za Vijana," in West and Dube, eds., *The Bible in Africa*, 365.

36. Ezra Chitando, "Theology from the Underside," *JTSA* 101 (1998), 23–34. Compare Ezra Chitando, "Christianity in a Pluralistic Context: Religious Challenges in Zimbabwe," in James L. Cox and Gerrie Ter Haar, eds., *Uniquely African?* (Trenton, N.J.: Africa World Press, 2003), 109–28.

37. For the *Jesus* video, see http://www.jesusfilm.org/progress/statistics.html. Asonzeh F-K Ukah, "Advertising God," *JRA* 33 (2) (2003), 203–31. Compare Marleen de Witte, "Alta-Media's *Living Word*: Televised Charismatic Christianity in Ghana," *JRA* 33 (2) (2003), 172–202; Rosalind I. J. Hackett, "Charismatic/Pentecostal Appropriation of Media Technologies in Nigeria and Ghana," *JRA* 28 (3) (1998), 258–77.

38. Bishop Sarpong is quoted from Peter Wasswa Mpagi, *African Christian Theology in the Contemporary Context* (Nairobi, Kenya: Marianum Publishing, 2002), 89. "For the African Christians" is from Zablon Nthamburi and Douglas Waruta, "Biblical Hermeneutics in African Instituted Churches," in Hannah W. Kinoti and John M. Waliggo, eds., *The Bible in African Christianity* (Nairobi, Kenya: Acton, 1997), 40–57, at 51.

39. "To read the bible contextually" is from Victor Zinkuratire, "Inculturating the Biblical Message," *ACS* 20 (1) (2004), 41–70, at 47; Grant LeMarquand, "New Testament Exegesis in (Modern) Africa," in West and Dube, eds., *The Bible in Africa*, 72–102, at 93.

40. Tinyiko Sam Maluleke, "The Bible among African Christians," in Teresa Okure, ed., *To Cast Fire upon the Earth* (Pietermaritzburg, South Africa: Clusters, 2000), 87–112, at 97.

41. Sathianathan Clarke, "Viewing the Bible through the Eyes and Ears of Subalterns in India," online at http://www.religion-online.org/showarticle.asp?title=2450.

42. Clarke, "Viewing the Bible through the Eyes and Ears of Subalterns in India." Lionel Caplan, *Class and Culture in Urban India* (Oxford: Clarendon, 1987), 224–43. The Kenyan congregation is reported from Nahashon Ndungu, "The Bible in an African Independent Church," 61–65. For West Papua, see Charles E. Farhadian, *Christianity, Islam and Nationalism in Indonesia* (New York: Routledge, 2005), 117. For the magical character of the Bible among some Latin American Protestants, see Jorge Pixley, "Un Llamado a Lanzar las Redes," *RIBLA* 10 (1991), 99–107.

43. Musa W. Dube, "Divining Ruth for International Relations," in A. K. M. Adam, ed., *Postmodern Interpretations of the Bible* (St. Louis, Mo.: Chalice Press, 2001), 67–79. David T. Adamo, "The Use of Psalms in African Indigenous Churches in Nigeria," in West and Dube, eds., *The Bible in Africa*, 336–49.

44. "The Bible is used to ward off evil spirits" is from Justin Ukpong, "Popular Readings of the Bible in Africa," in West and Dube, eds., *The Bible in Africa*, 582–94, at 587. Ezeogu, "Bible and Culture in African Christianity," 25. For the Wordless Bible, see Eliza F. Kent, "Redemptive Hegemony and the Ritualization of Reading," in Selva J. Raj and Corinne G. Dempsey, eds., *Popular Christianity in India* (Albany: State University of New York Press, 2002), 204–5. C. H. Spurgeon, "The Wordless Book" (1866), online at http://berean.org/bibleteacher/spurgeon.html.

45. Elizabeth Isichei, *A History of Christianity in Africa* (Grand Rapids, Mich.: W. B. Eerdmans, 1995), 295. Gerald West, "1 and 2 Samuel," in Daniel Patte, J. Severino Croatto, Nicole Wilkinson Duran, Teresa Okure, and Archie Chi Chung Lee, eds., *Global Bible Commentary* (Nashville, Tenn.: Abingdon Press, 2004), 93. R. S. Sugirtharajah, ed., *Asian Faces of Jesus* (Maryknoll, N.Y.: Orbis, 1993). For the widespread veneration of the apostle Thomas, see Roger E. Hedlund, ed., *Christianity Is Indian*, rev. ed. (New Delhi: ISPCK, 2004).

46. Chinua Achebe, *Things Fall Apart* (1959. New York: Fawcett Paperback, 1969), 137.

47. Nathan Faries, "The Narratives of Contemporary Chinese Christianity," doctoral dissertation, Pennsylvania State University, 2005, 311. Lewis S. Robinson, "The Bible in Twentieth Century Chinese Fiction," 237–77; idem, *Double-Edged Sword* (Hong Kong: Tao Fong Shan Ecumenical Centre, 1986). The passage from 1 Corinthians is from the NIV translation.

48. Zhang Sheng reads Rom. 1:18–29. Faries, "Narratives of Contemporary Chinese Christianity," 374–90. For missionary uses of the Romans passage, see Andrew Walls, *The Missionary Movement in Christian History* (Maryknoll, N.Y.: Orbis, 1996), 55–67; Alfred Muli, "The Modern Quest for an African Theology in the Light of Romans 1: 18–25," *AJET* 16 (1) (1997), 31–50.

49. Lewis R. Rambo, *Understanding Religious Conversion* (New Haven, Conn.: Yale University Press, 1993); Robert W. Hefner, ed., *Conversion to Christianity* (Berkeley: University of California Press, 1993). Bruce is quoted from Walls, *The Missionary Movement in Christian History*, 55.

50. Alan Cowell, "Church of England Advances Bid to Ordain Women as Bishops," *NYT*, July 12, 2005.

51. Presler, *Transfigured Night*, 165. Ela is quoted in Diane B. Stinton, *Jesus of Africa* (Maryknoll, N.Y.: Orbis, 2004), 73. For the Korean theologian, see Wonsuk Ma, "When the Poor Are Fired Up" *Christian Today*, May 10, 2005, at http://www.christiantoday.com/news/church/wonsuk.ma.when.the.poor.are.fired.up.the.role.of.pneumatology.in.pentecostcharismatic.mission/545.htm. The "long ending" of Mark is included in *The African Bible* (Nairobi, Kenya: Paulines Publications Africa, 1999), 1720–21.

Chapter 3

1. Akiki K. Nyabongo, *Africa Answers Back* (London: G. Routledge and Sons, 1936), 203–9. "Everywhere in" is quoted at 208; "How is it that king" is at 213.

2. Mary Getui, Knut Holter, and Victor Zinkuratire, eds., *Interpreting the Old Testament in Africa* (New York: P. Lang, 2000). Knut Holter, "Old Testament Scholarship in Sub-Saharan Africa North of the Limpopo River," in Gerald O. West and Musa W. Dube, eds., *The Bible in Africa* (Leiden: Brill, 2000), 54–71.

3. John F. A. Sawyer, *The Fifth Gospel* (New York: Cambridge University Press, 1996). For typology in the early church, see, for instance, the Epistle of Barnabas.

4. For Marcionism, see Philip Jenkins, *Hidden Gospels* (New York: Oxford University Press, 2001). Benjamin Disraeli, *Sybil* (New York: World's Classics edition, Oxford University Press, 1999).

5. Tania Oldenhage, *Parables for Our Time* (New York: Oxford University Press, 2002); Jim Wallis, *God's Politics* (San Francisco: HarperSanFrancisco, 2005).

6. Milton Shain, "Ambivalence, Antipathy, and Accommodation," in Richard Elphick and Rodney Davenport, eds., *Christianity in South Africa* (Berkeley: University of California Press, 1997). Though note John S. Mbiti, "The Role of the Jewish Bible in African Independent Churches," *IRM* 93 (2004), 219–37.

7. "The annihilation of six million" is from "Address by Njongonkulu Ndungane, Archbishop of Cape Town, at the Centenary Reunion of the Rhodes Trust" (2003), at http://www.tac.org.za/Documents/Speeches/ArchbishopSpeech-RhodesCentenary-20030201.doc. Njongonkulu Ndungane, "Sermon for Healing of Memories Service" (1999), at http://www.cpsa.org.za/about/synod99/sermon.html; idem, *A World with a Human Face* (London: SPCK, 2003). For other references to the Nazis and the Holocaust, see David Gitari, *In Season and Out of Season* (Carlisle, UK: Regnum, 1996), 142; and Desmond Tutu, "Dark Days," *JTSA* 118 (2004), 27–39. "Starting from the period" is from Wang Hsien-Chih, "The Portrayal of the Human One (Son of Man) of John," *CTC Bulletin* 13 (3) (1995), at http://www.cca.org.hk/resources/ctc/ctc95-03/1.wang.htm.

8. Rebecca Yawa Ganusah, "Pouring Libation to Spirit Powers among the Ewe-Dome of Ghana," in West and Dube, eds., *The Bible in Africa*, 278–91; Kwesi A. Dickson, *Theology in Africa* (Maryknoll, N.Y.: Orbis, 1984); Musimbi R. A. Kanyoro, "Interpreting Old Testament Polygamy through African Eyes," in Mercy Amba Oduyoye and Musimbi R. A. Kanyoro, eds., *The Will to Arise* (Maryknoll, N.Y.: Orbis Press, 1992), 87–100.

9. The quote is from M. A. Ameagodosu, "Paul's Theology of Salvation in Romans," *AJT* 23 (1) (2000), 44. Justin S. Ukpong, *Ibibio Sacrifices and Levitical Sacrifices* (doctoral dissertation, Rome: Pontifical University, 1990).

10. Sammy Githuku, "Taboos on Counting" in Getui et al., *Interpreting the Old Testament in Africa*, 113–17. Fook-Kong Wong, "1 and 2 Chronicles," in Daniel Patte, J. Severino Croatto, Nicole Wilkinson Duran, Teresa Okure, and Archie Chi Chung Lee, eds., *Global Bible Commentary* (Nashville, Tenn.: Abingdon Press, 2004), 122; Archie Chi Chung Lee, "Lamentations," in ibid., 226–30.

11. Modupe Oduyoye, *The Sons of the Gods and the Daughters of Men* (Maryknoll, N.Y.: Orbis, 1984), v, 11.

12. For Walls, see http://www.dacb.org/stories/egypt/desert_people.html. Mark McEntire, "Cain and Abel in Africa," in West and Dube, eds., *The Bible in Africa*, 248–59.

13. Gerald West, "1 and 2 Samuel," in Patte et al., eds., *Global Bible Commentary*, 94; Madipoane Masenya, "Wisdom and Wisdom Converge," in Mary Getui et al., eds., *Interpreting the Old Testament in Africa*, 133–46 at 145.

14. Philip Jenkins, *Dream Catchers* (New York: Oxford University Press, 2004), 10.

15. Wonsuk Ma, "Toward an Asian Pentecostal Theology," *CPCR*, at http://www.pctii.org/cyberj/cyberj1/wonsuk.html.

16. The Cameroonian pastor is quoted in John S. Mbiti, "The Role of the Jewish Bible in African Independent Churches," *IRM* 93 (2004), 219–37; Nahashon Ndungu, "The Bible in an African Independent Church," in Hannah W. Kinoti and John M. Waliggo, eds., *The Bible in African Christianity* (Nairobi, Kenya: Acton, 1997), 58–67.

17. Joseph Enuwosa, "The Soteriological Significance of Matthew 2:15 in his use of Hosea 11:1 from an African Perspective," *ATJ* 24 (2) (2001), 50; Zablon Nthamburi and Douglas Waruta, "Biblical Hermeneutics in African Instituted Churches," in Hannah W. Kinoti and John M. Waliggo, eds., *The Bible in African Christianity* (Nairobi, Kenya: Acton, 1997), 40–57, at 45; Knut Holter, *Yahweh in Africa* (New York: P. Lang, 2000); David Tuesday Adamo, *Africa and the Africans in the Old Testament* (Eugene, Oreg.: Wipf and Stock, 2001); Marta Høyland Lavik, "The African Texts of the Old Testament and Their African Interpretation," in Getui et al., eds., *Interpreting the Old Testament in Africa*, 43–53; Edwin M. Yamauchi, *Africa and the Bible* (Grand Rapids, Mich.: Baker Academic, 2004). Sipho Tshelane, "The Spirituality of the African Initiated Churches," in Celia Kourie and Louise Kretzschmar, eds., *Christian Spirituality in South Africa* (Pietmaritzburg, South Africa: Cluster, 2000), 138–56, at 154; Benjamin A. Ntreh, "Africa in the New Testament," in Mary Getui, Tinyiko Maluleke, and Justin Ukpong, eds., *Interpreting the New Testament in Africa* (Nairobi, Kenya: Acton, 2001), 68–82.

18. Dominic Odipo, "Doctoring the Bible and Hiding the Role of Africa," http://www.africanewsonline.com/_disc16/000001c9.htm. The Congregational minister is the Reverend Rupert Hambira, quoted in Tudutso Setsiba, "Whose God?" *Mmegi/The Reporter* (Botswana), September 16, 2005, at http://www.dehai.org/archives/dehai_archive/0168.html.

19. David Maxwell, "The Durawall of Faith," *JRA* 35 (1) (2005), 4–32, at 10; Philip Gourevitch, *We Wish to Inform You That Tomorrow We Will Be Killed with Our Families* (New York: Farrar, Straus, and Giroux, 1998).

20. Matt. 15:21–28. Musa Dube, "Readings of Semoya," *Semeia* 73 (1996), 111–30.

21. Bengt Sundkler, *Bantu Prophets in South Africa* (London: Lutterworth Press, 1948), 277. Philomena Njeri Mwaura, "The Old Testament in the Nabii Christian

Church of Kenya," in Getui et al., eds., *Interpreting the Old Testament in Africa*, 165–69.

22. Mangosuthu Buthelezi, "Unveiling of the Plaque of the Shembe House Museum," http://www.ifp.org.za/Archive/Speeches/211201sp.htm. B. N. Mthethwa, "Shembe's Hymnody and the Ethical Standards and Worldview of the AmaNazaretha," in G. C. Oosthuizen and Irving Hexham, eds., *Empirical Studies of African Independent/Indigenous Churches* (Lewiston, N.Y.: Edwin Mellen, 1992).

23. Nicholas Stebbing, "You Shall Have No Other Gods Before Me," in Greg Cuthbertson, Hennie Pretorius, and Dana Robert, eds., *Frontiers of African Christianity* (Pretoria: University of South Africa Press, 2003), 120–23.

24. Cedric Pulford, "Debate Continues on Incorporating Animal Sacrifices in Worship," *Christianity Today*, October 25, 2000, at http://www.christianitytoday.com/ct/2000/143/34.0.html.

25. Victor Zinkuratire, "Isaiah 1–39," in Patte et al., eds., *Global Bible Commentary*, 187. Mercy Amba Oduyoye, "Christian Engagement with African Culture," in James L. Cox and Gerrie Ter Haar, eds., *Uniquely African?* (Trenton, N.J.: Africa World Press, 2003), 89–108; Bregje de Kok, *Christianity and African Traditional Religion* (East Lansing: Michigan State University Press, 2005).

26. Pulford, "Debate Continues on Incorporating Animal Sacrifices in Worship"; Noel Bruyns, "Let Africans Honor Ancestors with Blood Libations in Mass, Says Bishop," April 10, 2000, http://www.christianitytoday.com/ct/2000/115/46.0.html. Jacques Hubert, *Rites Traditionnels d'Afrique: Approche pour une Théologie Liturgique Inculturée* (Paris: l'Harmattan, 2003).

27. Mbiti, "The Role of the Jewish Bible in African Independent Churches." Allan Anderson, "The Contextual Pentecostal Theology of David Yonggi Cho," *AJPS* 7 (1) (2004), 101–23.

28. Byang Kato, *Theological Pitfalls in Africa* (Kisumu, Kenya: Evangel Publishing House, 1975), 35. Bénézet Bujo and Juvénal Ilunga Muya, eds., *African Theology in the 21st Century* (Nairobi, Kenya: Paulines Publications Africa, 2003); Laurenti Magesa, *Anatomy of Inculturation* (Maryknoll, N.Y.: Orbis, 2004).

29. Harold W. Turner, *Profile through Preaching* (Geneva: World Council of Churches, Commission on World Mission and Evangelism, Edinburgh House Press, 1965); Hilary B. P. Mijoga, *Separate But Same Gospel* (Blantyre, Malawi: CLAIM, 2000); idem, "Interpreting the Bible in African Sermons," in Getui, Maluleke, and Ukpong, eds., *Interpreting the New Testament in Africa*.

30. Grant LeMarquand, "New Testament Exegesis in (Modern) Africa," in Gerald O. West and Musa W. Dube, eds., *The Bible in Africa* (Leiden: Brill, 2000), 72–102.

31. "So also should the Igbo" is quoted by Hinne Wagenaar, "Stop Harassing the Gentiles!" *JACT* 6 (1) (2003), 44–54, at 52. Ukachukwu Chris Manus, "Paul's Speech at the Areopagus," in Mary Getui, Tinyiko Maluleke, and Justin Ukpong, eds., *Interpreting the New Testament in Africa* (Nairobi, Kenya: Acton, 2001), 213–30. Dickson Kazuo Yagi, "Christ for Asia," *Review and Expositor* 88 (4) (1991), 375. Paul's speech at Lystra is found at Acts 14:16–17; his speech on the Athenian Areopagus is from Acts 17:16–34.

32. Teresa Okure, "Hebrews," in Patte et al., eds., *Global Bible Commentary*, 535–38.

33. Kwame Bediako, *Jesus and the Gospel in Africa* (Maryknoll, N.Y.: Orbis, 2004), 27–28, 33; idem, *Theology and Identity* (Oxford: Regnum Books, 1992); idem, *Christianity in Africa* (Edinburgh: Edinburgh University Press/Orbis, 1995).

34. Fidon R. Mwombeki, "The Book of Revelation in Africa," *Word and World* 15 (2) (1995), 145–50.

35. Ukpong, *Ibibio Sacrifices and Levitical Sacrifices*, 3.

36. Mijoga, *Separate But Same Gospel*, 69, 84–85.

37. Nathaniel I. Ndiokwere, *Prophecy and Revolution* (London: SPCK, 1981); Sheila S. Walker, *The Religious Revolution in the Ivory Coast* (Chapel Hill: University of North Carolina Press, 1983); Afe Adogame, "Old Wine in New Wine Bottles," in James L. Cox and Gerrie Ter Haar, eds., *Uniquely African?* (Trenton, N.J.: Africa World Press, 2003), 241–60. The hymn is from Bengt Sundkler, *Bantu Prophets in South Africa*, 2nd ed. (London: Oxford University Press, 1961), 282. For African prophets as the precursor to modern Pentecostal movements, see Jones Darkwa Amanor, "Pentecostalism in Ghana," *CPCR* 13 (2004), at http://www.pctii.org/cyberj/cyberj13/amanor.html.

38. "When I asked them" is quoted in Elizabeth Isichei, *A History of Christianity in Africa* (Grand Rapids, Mich.: W. B. Eerdmans, 1995), 5. Nelson Osamu Hayashida, *Dreams in the African Literature* (Amsterdam: Rodopi, 1999).

39. Leo G. Perdue, *Wisdom and Creation* (Nashville, Tenn.: Abingdon Press, 1994); Roland E. Murphy, *The Tree of Life*, 2nd ed. (Grand Rapids, Mich.: W. B. Eerdmans, 1996). For a liberationist approach to Wisdom, see Dianne Bergant, *Israel's Wisdom Literature* (Minneapolis, Minn.: Fortress Press, 1997).

40. Prov. 13:24.

41. Wisd. of Sol. 7:25–26; Luke 7:35; Matt. 11:19. John S. Kloppenborg, *The Formation of Q*, rev. ed. (Harrisburg, Pa.: Trinity Press International, 2000); Philip Jenkins, *Hidden Gospels* (New York: Oxford University Press, 2001); Grace Ji-Sun Kim, *The Grace of Sophia* (Cleveland, Ohio: Pilgrim Press, 2002).

42. *The African Bible* (Nairobi, Kenya: Paulines Publications Africa, 1999), 1007. Madipoane Masenya, "Wisdom and Wisdom Converge," 145; Mercy Oduyoye, "Calling the Church to Account," *ER* 47 (1995), 479; Sampson S. Ndoga, "Teaching the Old Testament from an African Perspective," *JACT* 6 (2) (2003), 22–27. Friedemann W. Golka, *The Leopard's Spots* (Edinburgh: T & T Clark, 1993); Delbert Howard Tarr, *Double Image* (Mahwah, N.J.: Paulist Press, 1994).

43. Elsa Támez, *When the Horizons Close* (Maryknoll, N.Y.: Orbis, 2000), 145–46.

44. Anne Nasimiyu-Wasike is quoted in Joseph Healey and Donald Sybertz, *Towards an African Narrative Theology* (Maryknoll, N.Y.: Orbis, 1996). *The African Bible*, 1007.

45. Mijoga, *Separate But Same Gospel*, 135; also 89–91.

46. "Many African languages" is from *The African Bible*, 2095.

47. Patrick J. Hartin, *James and the 'Q' Sayings of Jesus* (Sheffield, UK: JSOT Press, 1991); Patrick J. Hartin and Daniel J. Harrington, eds., *James* (Collegeville, Minn.: Liturgical Press, 2003); Luke Timothy Johnson, *The Letter of James* (New York: Doubleday Anchor, 1995).

48. Richard Bauckham, *James: Wisdom of James, Disciple of Jesus the Sage* (London: Routledge, 1999); Luke Timothy Johnson, *Brother of Jesus, Friend of God* (Grand Rapids, Mich.: W. B. Eerdmans, 2004).

49. Nthamburi and Waruta, "Biblical Hermeneutics in African Instituted Churches," 45; Turner, *Profile through Preaching*; "James addresses" is from *The African Bible*, 2052.

50. *The African Bible*, 2052.

51. F. Kefa Sempangi, with Barbara R. Thompson, *A Distant Grief* (Glendale, Calif.: Gl Regal Books, 1979), 38.

52. A. O. Igenoza, "The *Vaticinia Ex Eventu* Hypothesis and the Fall of Jerusalem," *ATJ* 24 (2001), 3–16, at 14–15.

53. 2 Chron. 7:14; Paul Gifford, *Ghana's New Christianity* (Bloomington: Indiana University Press, 2004), 161–62; Tokunboh Adeyemo, *Is Africa Cursed?* (Nairobi, Kenya: Christian Learning Materials Centre, 1997); A. Scott Moreau, "Gaining Perspective on Territorial Spirits," in A. Scott Moreau, Tokunboh Adeyemo, David Burnett, Bryant Myers, and Hwa Yung, eds., *Deliver Us from Evil*: (Monrovia, Calif.: Marc, 2002), 263–78.

54. Tshelane, "The Spirituality of the African Initiated Churches." Another popular text is "that there were such an heart in them, that they would fear me, and keep all my commandments always, that it might be well with them, and with their children for ever!" Deut. 5:29. For the Lord's Prayer, see John Lonsdale, "Religion and Politics in Kenya," the Henry Martyn Lectures, 2005, at http://www.martynmission.cam. ac.uk/CJLonsdale..html.

55. Andrew E. Kim, "Korean Religious Culture and Its Affinity to Christianity," *Sociology of Religion* 61 (2) (2000), 117–33; Robert E. Buswell Jr. and Timothy S. Lee, eds., *Christianity in Korea* (Honolulu: University of Hawai'i Press, 2005).

56. Quoted in Elizabeth Isichei, *A History of Christianity in Africa* (Grand Rapids, Mich.: W. B. Eerdmans, 1995), 256.

57. Geert De Clercq, "Gibson's Passion Gets Blessing of Manila Bishop," Reuters, March 29, 2004; "Frenzy and Fury as Jesus Film Hits SA," *Sunday Times* (South Africa), March 30, 2004, at http://www.suntimes.co.za/2004/03/28/news/news01.asp.

58. Arturo J. Banuelas, ed., *Mestizo Christianity* (Eugene, Oreg.: Wipf & Stock, 2004).

59. Alessandro Gallazzi, "Ezekiel 40–48," in Patte et al., eds., *Global Bible Commentary*, 246–52.

60. Amy-Jill Levine et al., "The Disease of Post-Colonial New Testament Studies and the Hermeneutics of Healing/Response," *Journal of Feminist Studies in Religion* 20 (1) (2004), 91–132. "Marked by this sacred sign" is quoted from Hannah Chen, "Circumcision by a Pagan Woman," *CTC Bulletin* 20 (2) (2004), at http://www.cca.org.hk/resources/ctc/ctc04-02/ctc04-02g.htm.

61. Quoted in Levine et al., "The Disease of Post-Colonial New Testament Studies and the Hermeneutics of Healing/Response."

62. Song is quoted from Peter C. Phan, *Being Religious Inter-Religiously* (Maryknoll, N.Y.: Orbis, 2004), 170; Levine et al., "The Disease of Post-Colonial New Testament Studies and the Hermeneutics of Healing/Response."

63. Kwok Pui-Lan, in Levine et al., "The Disease of Post-Colonial New Testament Studies and the Hermeneutics of Healing/Response."

Chapter 4

1. Leslie J. Hoppe, *There Shall Be No Poor among You* (Nashville, Tenn.: Abingdon Press, 2004).

2. Wonsuk Ma, "Toward an Asian Pentecostal Theology," *CPCR*, at http://www.pctii.org/cyberj/cyberj1/wonsuk.html.

3. Francisco Goldman, "Matthew," in Richard Holloway, ed., *Revelations* (London: Canongate, 2005), 210; Justin S. Ukpong, ed., *Gospel Parables in African Context* (Port Harcourt, Nigeria: CIWA Press, 1988). For global social trends and the continuing prevalence of poverty and corruption, see National Intelligence Council, *Mapping the Global Future* (2004), at http://www.cia.gov/nic/nic_globaltrend2020.html.

4. Hilary B. P. Mijoga, *Separate But Same Gospel* (Blantyre, Malawi: CLAIM, 2000), 21; Ma, "Toward an Asian Pentecostal Theology."

5. "Not since Europe's Renaissance" is from Richard N. Ostling, "Africa's Artistic Resurrection," *Time*, March 27, 1989; Martin Ott, *African Theology in Images* (Blantyre, Malawi: Kachere, 1999), 264–65.

6. Matt. 20:1–16.

7. Justin Ukpong, "Bible Reading with a Community of Ordinary Readers," in Mary Getui, Tinyiko Maluleke, and Justin Ukpong, eds., *Interpreting the New Testament in Africa* (Nairobi, Kenya: Acton, 2001), 188–212, at 196.

8. Justin Ukpong, "The Parable of the Shrewd Manager (Luke 16: 1–13)," *Semeia* 73 (1996), 189–210.

9. The Tamil hymn is from Zoe C. Sherinian, "Dalit Theology in Tamil Christian Folk Music," in Selva J. Raj and Corinne G. Dempsey, eds., *Popular Christianity in India* (Albany: State University of New York Press, 2002), 244. François Kabasele Lumbala, *Celebrating Jesus Christ in Africa* (Maryknoll, N.Y.: Orbis, 1998); Peter W. Mwikisa, "The Limits of Difference," in Gerald O. West and Musa W. Dube, eds., *The Bible in Africa* (Leiden: Brill, 2000), 163–83.

10. Ps. 126:5–6.

11. William M. Thomson, *The Land and the Book*, 3 vols. (original edition, 1862; popular edition, New York: Harper & Brothers, 1880–1885). Charles H. Spurgeon, "The Treasury of David," at http://www.spurgeon.org/treasury/ps126.htm.

12. Hernando de Soto, *The Mystery of Capital* (New York: Basic Books, 2000). Stephen Ellis and Gerrie ter Haar, *Worlds of Power* (New York: Oxford University Press, 2004).

13. Matt. 18:23–34.

14. Lev. 25:10. Wilson Muyinda Mande, "A Biblical Response to Africa's External Debt Crisis," in Getui et al., eds., *Interpreting the New Testament in Africa*, 231–52; Musa Dube, "To Pray the Lord's Prayer in the Global Economic Era," in West and Dube, eds., *The Bible in Africa*, 611–30; Luke Ssemakula, "The Hebrew Jubilee Year in Leviticus 25," *ACS* 18 (1) (2002), 5–33; Ross Kinsler and Gloria Kinsler, eds., *God's Economy* (Maryknoll, N.Y.: Orbis Books, 2005).

15. In 1990, *RIBLA* published a special issue (5–6) on debt and debt forgiveness, entitled "Perdónanos Nuestras Deudas." Paulo Lockmann, "Perdónanos Nuestras Deudas," 7–14; J. Severino Croatto, "La Deuda en la Reforma Social de Nehemías," 27–37; idem, "Deuda y Justicia en Textos del Antiguo Oriente," 39–43; Jung Mo Sung, "La Lucha contra la Deuda Externa," 45–54; Dagoberto Ramírez Fernández, "El Juicio de Dios a las Transnacionales," 55–74; Néstor O. Míguez, "El Imperio y los Pobres en el Tiempo Neotestamentario," 87–101.

16. Oscar S. Suarez, "That They May Have Life," *CTC Bulletin* 12 (2) (1994), at http://www.cca.org.hk/resources/ctc/ctc94-02/9.oscar.htm. Barbara Goldoftas, *The Green Tiger* (New York: Oxford University Press, 2005).

17. Marc Nikkel, "Death Has Come to Reveal the Faith," in Andrew Wingate, Kevin Ward, Carrie Pemberton, and Wilson Sitshebo, eds., *Anglicanism: A Global*

Communion (New York: Church Publishing, 1998), 74. Compare Marc Nikkel, *Why Haven't You Left?* edited by Grant LeMarquand (London: Church Publishing, 2005). Andrew Wheeler, ed., *Announcing the Light* (Nairobi, Kenya: Paulines Publications Africa, 1998); idem, ed., *Land of Promise* (Nairobi, Kenya: Paulines Publications Africa, 1997).

18. Tinyiko Sam Maluleke, "A Rediscovery of the Agency of Africans," in Peter Kanyandago, ed., *Marginalized Africa in the Context of the Jubilee* (Nairobi, Kenya: Paulines Publications Africa, 2002), 167. Teresa Okure, "Africa, a Martyred Continent," in Teresa Okure, Jon Sobrino, and Felix Wilfred, eds., *Rethinking Martyrdom* (London: SCM Press, 2003).

19. Johannes Malherbe, "Child Theology in Africa?" (2004), at http://www.petra.co.za/docs/child%20theology%20in%20africa.pdf. Tri Budiardjo, "In Search of Child Theology in Asian Context," http://www.asia.viva.org/download/asiace/2005/p2_child_theology_in_asian_context.pdf.

20. See, for instance, "Plague of Locusts Hits Africa," http://www.news24.com/News24/Africa/News/0,6119,2-11-1447_1638319,00.html.

21. Stephen Ellis, *The Mask of Anarchy* (New York: New York University Press, 1999); Roy Woodbridge, *The Next World War* (Toronto: University of Toronto Press, 2004).

22. Nikkel, "Death Has Come to Reveal the Faith," 75. Idem, " 'Children of Our Fathers' Divinities' or 'Children of Red Foreigners'?" in Andrew Wheeler, ed., *Land of Promise* (Limuru, Kenya: Paulines Publications Africa, 1997), 61–78; Roland Werner, William Anderson, and Andrew Wheeler, *Day of Devastation, Day of Contentment* (Nairobi, Kenya: Paulines Publications Africa, 2000); Sharon E. Hutchinson, "A Curse from God?" *Journal of Modern African Studies* 39 (2) (2001), 307–31.

23. Archie Chi Chung Lee, "Lamentations," in Daniel Patte, J. Severino Croatto, Nicole Wilkinson Duran, Teresa Okure, and Archie Chi Chung Lee, eds., *Global Bible Commentary* (Nashville, Tenn.: Abingdon Press, 2004), 232–33; *The African Bible* (Nairobi, Kenya: Paulines Publications Africa, 1999), 1398. Tod Linafelt, *Surviving Lamentations* (Chicago: University of Chicago Press, 2000).

24. John Lonsdale, "Religion and Politics in Kenya," the Henry Martyn Lectures, 2005, at http://www.martynmission.cam.ac.uk/CJLonsdale.html. Jean-Marc Ela, *My Faith as an African* (Maryknoll, N.Y.: Orbis, 1988), 87; Kim-Kwong Chan, "Gospel and Opium: A Case Study in China," April 2001, at http://legacywww.coventry.ac.uk/legacy/acad/isl/forgive/images/gospel.doc. Compare Masao Takenaka, *God Is Rice* (Geneva: World Council of Churches, 1986).

25. For global water issues, see, for instance, the proceedings of the third World Water Forum, http://www.world.water-forum3.com/; http://www.worldwatercouncil.org/.

26. 1 Kings 17–18. The Epistle of James (5:17) cites the story of Elijah.

27. 2 Kings 6:24–33.

28. The passage is quoted in Kwame Bediako, *Jesus and the Gospel in Africa* (Maryknoll, N.Y.: Orbis, 2004), 13.

29. For gay uses of Ruth 1:16, see, for instance, http://www.mcchurch.org/rstory2/samesex.htm; and http://www.buddybuddy.com/vows-3.html. Musimbi Kanyoro, "Reading the Bible from an African Perspective," *ER* 51 (1) (1999), 18–24; Wai Ching Angela Wong, "Building Communities," *CTC Bulletin* 20 (1) (2004), at

http://www.cca.org.hk/resources/ctc/ctc04-01/ctc04-01b.htm. Viola Raheb, "Women in Contemporary Palestinian Society," in Silvia Schroer and Sophia Bietenhard, eds., *Feminist Interpretation of the Bible and the Hermeneutics of Liberation* (New York: Continuum, 2003).

30. Musa Dube, "Mark's Healing Stories in an AIDS Context," in Patte et al., eds., *Global Bible Commentary*, 379. J. N. K. Mugambi and A. Nasimiyu-Wasike, eds., *Moral and Ethical Issues in African Christianity*, 2nd ed. (Nairobi, Kenya: Acton, 1999). Susan Hunter, *AIDS in Asia* (New York: Palgrave Macmillan, 2005); Musa W. Dube and Musimbi Kanyoro, eds., *Grant Me Justice!* (Maryknoll, N.Y.: Orbis, 2006). For the impact of AIDS, see National Intelligence Council, *Mapping the Global Future*.

31. "WHO Issues New Healthy Life Expectancy Rankings" (2000), at http://www.who.int/inf-pr-2000/en/pr2000-life.html.

32. Hilary B. P. Mijoga, *Separate But Same Gospel* (Blantyre, Malawi: CLAIM, 2000), 144–45; Gerald West, "Reading the Bible in the Light of HIV/AIDS in South Africa" *ER* 55 (4) (2003), 335–45.

33. Thaddeus Tarhembe, "Jesus and the Samaritan Woman," *East Asian Pastoral Review* 40 (1) (2003), 44–61; Robert K. Aboagye-Mensah, "Ethnicity and the Gospel," *JACT* 2 (2) (1999), 18–21.

34. Ginger Thompson, "A Saint Who Guides Migrants to a Promised Land," *NYT*, August 14, 2002.

35. F. Kefa Sempangi, with Barbara R. Thompson, *A Distant Grief* (Glendale, Calif.: Gl Regal Books, 1979), 167; Zephania Kameeta, *Why, O Lord?* (Geneva: World Council of Churches, 1986), 48; *The African Bible*, 2030. For the Amin persecution, see also Festo Kivengere, *I Love Idi Amin* (London: Marshall, Morgan and Scott, 1977).

36. Eleazar S. Fernandez and Fernando F. Segovia, eds., *A Dream Unfinished* (Maryknoll, N.Y.: Orbis, 2001).

37. Fook-Kong Wong, "1 and 2 Chronicles," in Patte et al., eds., *Global Bible Commentary*, 120, 126; Wai Ching Angela Wong, "Esther," in ibid., 135. Kah-Jin Jeffrey Kuan, "Diasporic Reading of a Diasporic Text," in Fernando F. Segovia, ed., *Interpreting Beyond Borders* (Sheffield, UK: Sheffield Academic Press, 2000), 161–74.

38. Benny Tat-Siong Liew, "Acts," in Patte et al., eds., *Global Bible Commentary*, 419–28; Katharine L. Wiegele, *Investing in Miracles* (Honolulu: University of Hawai'i Press, 2004).

39. In this section, I am drawing on several chapters in Hugh McLeod, ed., *Cambridge History of Christianity: World Christianities 1914–2000* (New York: Cambridge University Press, 2006): these include John Roxborough, "Christianity in Southeast Asia: 1914–2000"; Richard Fox Young "East Asia"; and Chandra Mallampalli, "South Asia, 1911–2003."

40. Joel Carpenter, "The Christian Scholar in an Age of Global Christianity," in Douglas V. Henry and Michael D. Beaty, eds., *Christianity and the Soul of the University* (Grand Rapids, Mich.: Baker Academic, 2006). See also Thomas C. Fox, *Pentecost in Asia* (Maryknoll, N.Y.: Orbis, 2002); Sebastian C. H. Kim, *In Search of Identity* (New Delhi and New York: Oxford University Press, 2003); Eric Reinders, *Borrowed Gods and Foreign Bodies* (Berkeley: University of California Press, 2004); Paul Crowley, *Rahner Beyond Rahner* (Lanham, Md.: Rowman & Littlefield, 2005); Daniel H. Bays and James H. Grayson, "Christianity in East Asia," in Sheridan Gilley

and Brian Stanley, eds., *Cambridge History of Christianity: World Christianities 1815–1914* (Cambridge: Cambridge University Press, 2005), 493–512; and Peter Phan, "Christianity in Indochina," in Gilley and Stanley, eds., *Cambridge History of Christianity: World Christianities 1815–1914*, 513–27; Ida Glaser, *The Bible and Other Faiths* (Downers Grive, Ill.: InterVarsity Press, 2005); Ines Zupanov and R. Po-chia Hsia, "Reception of Hinduism and Buddhism in Early Modern Christianity," in R. Po-chia Hsia, ed., *Cambridge History of Christianity: Reform and Expansion 1500–1660* (New York: Cambridge University Press, 2006); and David Cheetham, "Relations between Christians and Buddhists and Hindus," in Hugh McLeod, ed., *Cambridge History of Christianity: World Christianities 1914–2000* (New York: Cambridge University Press, 2006), 502–7.

For Christian adaptations to an overwhelmingly Hindu society, see Rowena Robinson, *Conversion, Continuity, and Change* (Walnut Creek, Calif.: AltaMira, 1998); Rowena Robinson, *Christians of India* (Thousand Oaks, Calif.: Sage Publications, 2003); Leonard Fernando, *Christian Faith Meets Other Faiths* (Delhi: Vidyajyoti Education and Welfare Society and ISPCK, 1998); Robert Eric Frykenberg and Alaine M. Low, eds., *Christians and Missionaries in India* (Grand Rapids, Mich.: W. B. Eerdmans, 2003); Leonard Fernando and George Gispert-Sauch, *Christianity in India* (Delhi: Penguin India, 2004).

41. Dickson Kazuo Yagi, "Christ for Asia," *Review and Expositor* 88 (4) (1991), 375; Daniel Arichea, "Reading Romans in Southeast Asia," in Khiok-Khng Yeo, ed., *Navigating Romans through Cultures* (Edinburgh: T. & T. Clark, 2004), 218; Choan-Seng Song, *Theology from the Womb of Asia* (Maryknoll, N.Y.: Orbis, 1985). For the interaction between Christianity and its Japanese environment, see Mark R. Mullins, *Christianity Made in Japan* (Honolulu: University of Hawai'i Press, 1998).

42. Tissa Balasuriya, *Mary and Human Liberation* (Harrisburg, Pa.: Trinity Press International, 1997); Franklyn J. Balasundaram, *Contemporary Asian Christian Theology* (Delhi: ISPCK, reprint ed., 1998); Fox, *Pentecost in Asia*; John C. England, Jose Kuttianimattathil, John Mansford Prior, Lily A. Quintos, David Suh Kwang-Sun, and Janice Wickeri, eds., *Asian Christian Theologies*, 3 vols. (Maryknoll, N.Y.: Orbis Books, 2002–2004).

43. The Japanese bishop, Kazuko Koda, is quoted in Henry Chu, "Across Globe, Joy Mixes with Regret," *Los Angeles Times*, April 20, 2005. Peter C. Phan, ed., *The Asian Synod* (Maryknoll, N.Y.: Orbis Books, 2002).

44. For one Chinese missionary movement, see http://www.backtojerusalem.com/. Paul Hattaway, *Back to Jerusalem* (Portland, Oreg.: Gabriel Publishing, 2003).

45. Chen Nan-Jou, "Jonah," in Patte et al., eds., *Global Bible Commentary*, 291–94; Paul Swarup, "Zechariah," in ibid., 318–24; Kwok Pui-Lan, *Discovering the Bible in the Non-Biblical World* (Maryknoll, N.Y.: Orbis, 1995). Grant LeMarquand, "New Testament Exegesis in (Modern) Africa," in Gerald O. West and Musa W. Dube, eds., *The Bible in Africa* (Leiden: Brill, 2000), 88. For modern African parallels to second-century Christianity, see Kwame Bediako, *Theology and Identity* (Oxford: Regnum Books, 1992).

46. R. S. Sugirtharajah, *Postcolonial Criticism and Bible Interpretation* (New York: Oxford University Press, 2002); idem, ed., *Asian Faces of Jesus* (Maryknoll, N.Y.: Orbis, 1993), 264; idem, "Matthew 5–7," in Patte et al., eds., *Global Bible Commentary*, 365. K. C. Abraham, *Third World Theologies* (Maryknoll, N.Y.: EAT-WOT/Orbis, 1993); Jacob Kavunkal and F. Hrangkhuma, eds., *Bible and Mission in*

India Today (Bandra, Bombay: St. Pauls, 1993); George Soares-Prabhu, "Two Mission Commands," in R. S. Sugirtharajah, ed., *Voices from the Margin* (Maryknoll, N.Y.: Orbis, 1995), 319–38; George Soares-Prabhu, *A Biblical Theology for India* (Pune, India: Anand, 1999); and idem, *The Dharma of Jesus* (Maryknoll, N.Y.: Orbis, 2003); K. P. Aleaz, *A Convergence of Advaita Vedanta and Eastern Christian Thought* (Delhi: ISPCK, 2000); Khiok-Khng Yeo, *What Has Jerusalem to Do with Beijing?* (Harrisburg, Pa.: Trinity Press International, 1998); Peter C. Phan, *Christianity with an Asian Face* (Maryknoll, N.Y.: Orbis, 2003); Heup Young Kim, *Christ and the Tao* (Hong Kong: Christian Conference of Asia, 2003); Roger Hedlund, "The Biblical Approach to Other Religions," *Global Missiology* (2004), at http://www.globalmissiology.net/docs_pdf/contemporary/hedlund_biblical_approa ch_to_other_religions.PDF.

47. John B. Carpenter, "Prosperity in Proverbs and Confucius" *AJT* 13 (1) (1999), 71–93; Aloysius Pieris, *An Asian Theology of Liberation* (Quezon City, Philippines: Claretian Publications, 1989).

48. Elsa Támez, *The Scandalous Message of James*, rev. ed. (New York: Crossroad, 2002).

49. Kosuke Koyama, *Water Buffalo Theology,* 25th anniversary ed. (Maryknoll, N.Y.: Orbis, 1999). Compare Aloysius Pieris, *Fire and Water* (Maryknoll, N.Y.: Orbis, 1996); Kenneth Fleming, *Asian Christian Theologians in Dialogue with Buddhism* (New York: P. Lang, 2002). One remarkable claim about James concerns the cryptic reference in 3:6 to *trochos tes geneseos,* usually translated as "cycle of nature." However, translated as "wheel of birth," the phrase sounds distinctly South Asian. Sugirtharajah remarks, "If there is any influence of Eastern ideas, it is here that it is visibly prominent." R. S. Sugirtharajah, *Post-Colonial Reconfigurations* (St. Louis, Mo.: Chalice, 2003), 108. Alternatively, the term may derive from Greek mystery religions.

50. Koyama, *Water Buffalo Theology,* 119, 121; *The African Bible,* 2052.

51. The Dalai Lama, "Introduction," in Holloway, ed., *Revelations,* 359–66. John P. Keenan, *The Wisdom of James* (New York: Newman Press, 2005).

52. Eccles. 10:20. John Mansford Prior, "Ecclesiastes," in Patte et al., eds., *Global Bible Commentary,* 176; idem, "When all the Singing Has Stopped" *IRM* 91 (2002), 7–23. Opinions vary about how troubled the author of Ecclesiastes was by the social changes he observed. For Qoheleth as an establishment voice, see R. R. S. Sugirtharajah, *Postcolonial Criticism and Bible Interpretation* (New York: Oxford University Press, 2002), 81.

53. Michael Amaladoss, "The Asian Face of the Good News," at http:// www.sedos.org/english/amaladoss_6.htm.

54. Seree Lorgunpai, "The Book of Ecclesiastes and Thai Buddhism," in R. S. Sugirtharajah, ed., *Voices from the Margin* (Maryknoll, N.Y.: Orbis, 1995), 339–48. John Roxborough, "Christianity in Southeast Asia: 1914–2000," in McLeod, ed., *Cambridge History of Christianity: World Christianities 1914–2000,* 436–49.

55. "Church of the Mighty Dollar," *Business Week,* May 23, 2005. See also "Creflo Dollar Ministries," at http://www.worldchangers.org/; Simon Coleman, *The Globalisation of Charismatic Christianity* (New York: Cambridge University Press, 2000); Milmon F. Harrison, *Righteous Riches* (New York: Oxford University Press, 2005); Shayne Lee, *T. D. Jakes: America's New Preacher* (New York: New York University Press, 2005); Michael Luo, "Preaching a Gospel of Wealth in a Glittery Market, New York," *NYT,* January 15, 2006.

56. Andrew E. Kim, "Korean Religious Culture and Its Affinity to Christianity," *Sociology of Religion* 61 (2) (2000), 117–33; Hong Young-Gi, "The Backgrounds and Characteristics of the Charismatic Mega-Churches in Korea," *AJPS* 3 (1) (2000), 99–118; Hwa Yung, "Missiological Implications of Dr. David Yonggi Cho's Theology," *CPCR* 13 (2004), http://www.pctii.org/cyberj/cyberj13/yung.html.

57. Paul Gifford, *Ghana's New Christianity* (Bloomington: Indiana University Press, 2004), 72, and 71–80 passim; J. Kwabena Asamoah-Gyadu, *African Charismatics* (Leiden: Brill, 2005).

58. Asamoah-Gyadu, *African Charismatics,* 201–32; Gifford, *Ghana's New Christianity.* Mark 10:29–30.

59. Grant LeMarquand, "New Testament Exegesis in (Modern) Africa," in Gerald O. West and Musa W. Dube, eds., *The Bible in Africa* (Leiden: Brill, 2000), 96; Compare *The African Bible,* 1783; Suarez, "That They May Have Life"; Wang Hsien-Chih, "The Portrayal of the Human One (Son of Man) of John," *CTC Bulletin* 13 (3) (1995), at http://www.cca.org.hk/resources/ctc/ctc95-03/1.wang.htm. Mary N. Getui and Matthew M. Theuri, eds., *Quests for Abundant Life in Africa* (Nairobi, Kenya: Acton, 2002).

60. Kameeta, *Why, O Lord?* 6.

61. Mal. 3:10–11. Asamoah-Gyadu, *African Charismatics*; Judy Mbugua, with Connie Kisuke, *Judy: A Second Chance* (Nairobi, Kenya: Precise Communications, 1997), 85–86; Judy Mbugua, ed., *Our Time Has Come* (Grand Rapids, Mich.: Baker Books, 1994).

62. "A blend of Corinthians and Hallmark" is from Frank Bruni, "Faith Fades Where It Once Burned Strong," *NYT*, October 13, 2003. The account of the scandal is from "How Ashimolowo Landed in Trouble" (2005), at http://www.onlinenigeria.com/links/Ashimolowoadv.asp?blurb=638.

63. Chris Ngwodo, "Dead Flies in the Ointment," *Vanguard* (Lagos), July 15, 2004; "Churches Have Failed the Nation," July 19, 2004, at http://www.dondoweb.com/headlines/churches%20failed%20the%20nation.htm. The archbishop of Lagos is quoted from Norimitsu Onishi, "Africans Fill Churches That Celebrate Wealth," *NYT*, March 13, 2002; Jonathan Luxmoore, "Africans Warn 'False Gospel of Prosperity' May Displace Churches," *Christianity Today*, June 16, 2000, at http://www.christianitytoday.com/ct/2000/124/54.0.html.

64. "Debt is like bodily sin": David Maxwell, "Delivered from the Spirit of Poverty," *JRA* 28 (3) (1998), 350–73, at 353. Elizabeth E. Brusco, *The Reformation of Machismo* (Austin: University of Texas Press, 1995).

65. "The U.S. Prosperity Controversy Travels Overseas," *Connection*, August 2002, at http://www.connectionmagazine.org/2002_08/ts_us_prosperity.htm. For contemporary Nigerian Christianity, see the essays by David Oyedepo, Sunday Adelaja, and others in C. Peter Wagner and Joseph Thompson, eds., *Out of Africa* (Ventura, Calif.: Regal Books, 2003).

66. John Vidal, "People Wake Up Angry at Being Alive in a Society Like This," *Guardian*, March 5, 2005. Karl Meier, *This House Has Fallen* (London: Allen Lane, 2001); Mike Davis, "Mega-Slums," *New Left Review* 26 (March–April 2004); AbdouMaliq Simone and Abdelghani Abouhani, eds., *Urban Africa* (London: Zed Books, 2005). "Planning is not for the poor" is from Roger Cohen, "Two Rooms with No View of a Promising Future," *NYT*, March 8, 2006.

67. Sempangi, *A Distant Grief,* 91, 96.

Chapter 5

1. Jim Wallis, *God's Politics* (San Francisco: HarperSanFrancisco, 2005); Amanda Porterfield, *Healing in the History of Christianity* (New York: Oxford University Press, 2005).

2. Peter Brown, *The Rise of Western Christendom* (Oxford: Blackwell, 2003), 19. *St. Gregory Thaumaturgus: Life and Works*, translated by Michael Slusser (Washington, D.C.: Catholic University of America Press, 1998). For the persistence of demonic theories in European Christianity during the Reformation era, see Philip C. Almond, *Demonic Possession and Exorcism in Early Modern England* (New York: Cambridge University Press, 2004); Sarah Ferber, *Demonic Possession and Exorcism in Early Modern France* (New York: Routledge, 2004); H. C. Erik Midelfort, *Exorcism and Enlightenment* (New Haven, Conn.: Yale University Press, 2005).

3. Olusegun Obasanjo, *This Animal Called Man* (Abeokuta, Nigeria: Alf Publications, 1998), 97. See also Olusegun Obasanjo's website, http://www.olusegun-obasanjo.com/. Stephen Ellis and Gerrie ter Haar, *Worlds of Power* (New York: Oxford University Press, 2004).

4. "Introduction," *African Ecclesial Review* 45 (3) (2003), 193.

5. Peter Kenny, "Christian Leaders Urge Politicians: After Tsunami, Heed Climate Change" (2004), at http://www.ecusa.anglican.org/3577_56321_eng_htm.htm; Onyinyechi Udeogu, "Tsunami, an Act of Devil—Cleric," *This Day* (Lagos, Nigeria), January 6, 2005. For a Western theological view of the catastrophe, see David Bentley Hart, *The Doors of the Sea* (Grand Rapids, Mich.: W. B. Eerdmans, 2005).

6. Mark D. Baker and J. Ross Wagner, "The Righteousness of God and Hurricane Mitch," in Khiok-Khng Yeo, ed., *Navigating Romans through Cultures* (Edinburgh: T. & T. Clark, 2004), 95–132, at 99; authors' emphasis.

7. For conversion statistics, see David B. Barrett, George T. Kurian, and Todd M. Johnson, *World Christian Encyclopedia*, 2nd ed. (New York: Oxford University Press, 2001). Birgit Meyer, *Translating the Devil* (Trenton, N.J.: Africa World Press, 1999); Emefie Ikenga Metuh, ed., *The Gods in Retreat*, new ed. (Enugu, Nigeria: Fourth Dimension Publishers, 2002). Han Malsook, *Hymn of the Spirit* (New York: Fremont Publications, 1983). The power of Korean shamanism and folk religion also emerges from a film such as *Daughter of the Flames* (1983).

8. Obed Minchakpu, "Human Sacrifice Redux," *Christianity Today*, November 22, 2004, at http://www.christianitytoday.com/ct/2004/012/16.22.html. For myths of human sacrifice and vampirism in Africa, see Luise White, "On Unpacking the Occult," at http://history.wisc.edu/bernault/magical/luise%20white%20occult.htm. For secret societies, see Ellis and ter Haar, *Worlds of Power*. Igbo Christianity is described in David Asonye Ihenacho, *African Christianity Rises*, vol. 1 (2004), at http://www.iUniverse.com.

9. Obasanjo, *This Animal Called Man*, 197.

10. For Akinola, see "Statement from the Bishops of the Anglican Church of Nigeria (21 November 2003)," http://www.anglican-mainstream.org.za/nigeria.html. Datak Yong Ping Chung is quoted from Larry B. Stammer, "Their Truths Shall Set Them Apart," *Los Angeles Times*, June 30, 2001.

11. Wonsuk Ma, "Toward an Asian Pentecostal Theology," *CPCR*, at http://www.pctii.org/cyberj/cyberj1/wonsuk.html. "The existence of evil ones and enemies"

is from David Tuesday Adamo, "Psalms," in Daniel Patte, J. Severino Croatto, Nicole Wilkinson Duran, Teresa Okure, and Archie Chi Chung Lee, eds., *Global Bible Commentary* (Nashville, Tenn.: Abingdon Press, 2004), 151. For doctrines of *han* and sin, see Andrew Sung Park, *The Wounded Heart of God* (Nashville, Tenn.: Abingdon Press, 1993). For older ideas of supernatural affliction in India, see Graham Dwyer, *The Divine and the Demonic* (New York: Routledge/Curzon, 2003).

12. Grant LeMarquand, "New Testament Exegesis in (Modern) Africa," in Gerald O. West and Musa W. Dube, eds., *The Bible in Africa* (Leiden: Brill, 2000), 72–102, at 87. Meyer, *Translating the Devil*.

13. Justin Martyr, *Second Apology*, ch. 85; Origen, *Contra Celsum*, 7:4; Tertullian, *Apology*, ch. 22–23; *The African Bible* (Nairobi, Kenya: Paulines Publications Africa, 1999), 2030. Park Jae Soon, "Cross: From Killing to Interliving," *CTC Bulletin* 13 (3) (1995); Lung-Kwong Lo, "The Nature of the Issue of Ancestral Worship among Chinese Christians," *SWC* 9 (1) (2003), 30–42.

14. "Having spoiled principalities and powers" is from Col. 2:15; "Led captivity captive" is Eph. 4:8. The Transvaal hymn is quoted in Paul-Gordon Chandler, *God's Global Mosaic* (Downers Grove, Ill.: InterVarsity Press, 2000), 102. Afua Kuma is quoted in Kwame Bediako, *Jesus and the Gospel in Africa* (Maryknoll, N.Y.: Orbis, 2004), 11.

15. Eph. 6:12. For American notions of exorcism and spiritual warfare, see Bill Ellis, *Lucifer Ascending* (Lexington: University Press of Kentucky, 2004); idem, *Raising the Devil* (Lexington: University Press of Kentucky, 2000); Michael W. Cuneo, *American Exorcism* (New York: Doubleday, 2001).

16. For the relationship between "mainstream" and independent churches, see Afe Adogame and Akin Omyajowo, "Anglicanism and the Aladura Churches in Nigeria," in Andrew Wingate, Kevin Ward, Carrie Pemberton, and Wilson Sitshebo, eds., *Anglicanism* (New York: Church Publishing, 1998), 90–97. Michael Bergunder, "Miracle Healing and Exorcism," *IRM* 90 (2001), 103–12.

17. Luke 4:18–19: The quotation is from Isa. 61:1–2.

18. John 11:44. J. Kwabena Asamoah-Gyadu, *African Charismatics* (Leiden: Brill, 2005), 165–200. J. Nathan Corbett, *The Sound of the Harvest* (Grand Rapids, Mich.: Baker Books, 1998).

19. Harold W. Turner, *Profile through Preaching* (Geneva: World Council of Churches, Commission on World Mission and Evangelism, Edinburgh House Press, 1965). "To Pentecostal believers" is from Myung Soo Park, "Korean Pentecostal Spirituality as Manifested in the Testimonies of Believers of the Yoido Full Gospel Church," *AJPS* 7 (1) (2004), 35–56; Carlos Annacondia, *Listen to Me, Satan!* (Lake Mary, Fla.: Creation House, 1998). Opoku Onyinah, "Deliverance as a Way of Confronting Witchcraft in Modern Africa," *CPCR*, at http://www.pctii.org/cyberj/cyberj10/onyinah.html; idem, "Contemporary 'Witchdemonology' in Africa," *IRM* 93 (2004), 330–45.

20. R. E. K. Mchami, "Demon Possession and Exorcism in Mark 1: 21–28," *ATJ* 24 (1) (2001), 17–38, at 31.

21. Ps. 91:10; Matt. 4:6.

22. Charles H. Spurgeon, "The Treasury of David," at http://www.spurgeon.org/treasury/ps091.htm.

23. David T. Adamo, "The Use of Psalms in African Indigenous Churches in Nigeria," in West and Dube, eds., *The Bible in Africa*, 336–49, at 336. Compare Luke

10:19: "Behold, I give unto you power to tread on serpents and scorpions, and over all the power of the enemy: and nothing shall by any means hurt you."

24. David Frankfurter, "The Binding of Antelopes," *Journal of Near Eastern Studies* 63 (2) (2004), 97–109.

25. Evangelist Ruth's devotion available at http://www.voiceofafricaradio.com/devotions8.php. "Bible Passages for Certain Life Situations," at http://www.anglican-nig.org/bible_passages.htm.

26. "I pray psalm 91" is from http://www.gfa.org/gfa/; "I assured my parents" is at http://www.newcreation.org.sg/homtestimonies.htm.

27. Mary Wiltenburg, "Rwanda's Resurrection of Faith," *Christian Science Monitor*, April 12, 2004, at http://www.csmonitor.com/2004/0412/p06s02-woaf.html.

28. "The Full Gospel faith" is quoted from Park, "Korean Pentecostal Spirituality as Manifested in the Testimonies of Believers of the Yoido Full Gospel Church." For changing concepts of darkness, see A. Roger Ekirch, *At Day's Close* (New York: W. W. Norton, 2005).

29. Ela is quoted in Diane B. Stinton, *Jesus of Africa* (Maryknoll, N.Y.: Orbis, 2004), 73. Titus Presler, *Transfigured Night* (Pretoria, South Africa: UNISA Press, 1999), 173.

30. Samuel Kunhiyop, "Witchcraft: A Philosophical and Theological Analysis," *AJET* 21 (2) (2002), 127–46, at 142. Peter Geschiere, *The Modernity of Witchcraft* (Charlottesville: University of Virginia Press, 1997); Adam Ashforth, *Madumo: A Man Bewitched* (Chicago: University of Chicago Press, 2000); Isak A. Niehaus, Eliazaar Mohlala, and Kally Shokane, *Witchcraft, Power and Politics* (London: Pluto Press, 2001); Adam Ashforth, *Witchcraft, Violence, and Democracy in South Africa* (Chicago: University of Chicago Press, 2005); Todd Vanden Berg, "Culture, Christianity and Witchcraft in a West African Context," in Lamin O. Sanneh and Joel A. Carpenter, eds., *The Changing Face of Christianity* (New York: Oxford University Press, 2005), 45–62. For the European experience, see Wolfgang Behringer, "Demonology," in R. Po-chia Hsia, ed., *Cambridge History of Christianity: Reform and Expansion 1500–1660* (New York: Cambridge University Press, 2006).

31. Peter Wasswa Mpagi, *African Christian Theology in the Contemporary Context* (Nairobi, Kenya: Marianum Publishing, 2002), 70. Robert Lavertu, "Pastoral Approach to Witchcraft," *African Ecclesial Review* 45 (3) (2003), 232–46, at 236–37. Lionel Caplan, *Class and Culture in Urban India* (Oxford: Clarendon, 1987), 198–209.

32. Bishop Peter K. Sarpong, "The Gospel as Good News for Africa Today" (1998), at http://www.sedos.org/english/sarpong.html; Bulus Y. Galadima and Yusufu Turaki, "The Church in the African State Towards the 21st Century," *JACT* 1 (1) (1998), 43–52, at 51. Maia Green, *Priests, Witches and Power* (New York: Cambridge University Press, 2003), 55–57.

33. Madame Nanan, "The Sorcerer and Pagan Practices," in Judy Mbugua, ed., *Our Time Has Come* (Grand Rapids, Mich.: Baker Book House, 1994), 81–87, at 82.

34. Kathryn Hauwa Hoomkwap, "Women in Church and Society," at http://www.afrikaworld.net/synod/hoomkwap.htm; the Cameroonian bishop is quoted from Thomas Reese, "The Synod on the Church in Africa," at http://www.americamagazine.org/reese/america/a-saf1.htm.

35. Philomena Njeri Mwaura, "The Old Testament in the Nabii Christian Church of Kenya," in Mary Getui, Knut Holter, and Victor Zinkuratire, eds., *Interpreting the Old Testament in Africa* (New York: P. Lang, 2000), 165–69.

36. 1 John 5:7–8. Ogbu U. Kalu, " 'Globecalisation' and Religion," in James L. Cox and Gerrie Ter Haar, eds., *Uniquely African?* (Trenton, N.J.: Africa World Press, 2003), 235.

37. F. Kefa Sempangi, with Barbara R. Thompson, *A Distant Grief* (Glendale, Calif.: Gl Regal Books, 1979), 73, 77–78. Onyinah, "Deliverance as a Way of Confronting Witchcraft in Modern Africa"; idem, "Contemporary 'Witchdemonology' in Africa".

38. Myung Soo Park, "Korean Pentecostal Spirituality as Manifested in the Testimonies of Believers of the Yoido Full Gospel Church."

39. Salome Jones, "Burning the Largest Haul of Witchcraft Items To-Date," at http://www.cfan.org/_includes/printerfriendly.asp?id=0000040&page=01& printversion=true&server=www.cfan.org&lang=english-intl&site=uk_site.

40. Samuel Kunhiyop, "Witchcraft: A Philosophical and Theological Analysis" *AJET* 21 (2) (2002), 127–46, at 139.

41. E. O. Omoobajesu, *My Conversion: From a Witch-Doctor to an Evangelist* (1968. Manchester, UK: O'Dine, 1987). The whole text of Emmanuel Eni's *Delivered from the Powers of Darkness* is online at http://www.threeq.com/remotesites/ delivered%20from%20the%20powers%20of%20darkness.htm.

42. 1 Cor. 12:8–10. "A strong expectation" is quoted from Luke Wesley, "Is the Chinese Church Predominantly Pentecostal?" *AJPS* 7 (2) (2004), 225–54. Philomena Njeri Mwaura, "The Use of Power in African Instituted Churches," *Wajibu* 14 (3) (1999). Compare Mathew N. Schmalz, "Charismatic Transgressions," in Selva J. Raj and Corinne G. Dempsey, eds., *Popular Christianity in India* (Albany: State University of New York Press, 2002), 163–87.

43. Andrew E. Kim, "Korean Religious Culture and Its Affinity to Christianity," *Sociology of Religion* 61 (2) (2000), 117–33.

44. "Very soon, a neighbor" is from Wonsuk Ma, "When the Poor Are Fired Up," *Christian Today*, May 10, 2005, at http://www.christiantoday.com/news/ church/wonsuk.ma.when.the.poor.are.fired.up.the.role.of.pneumatology.in. pentcostcharismatic.mission/545.htm. "I look at [Jesus] as a healer" is from Diane B. Stinton, *Jesus of Africa* (Maryknoll, N.Y.: Orbis, 2004), 65.

45. David Olugbenga Ogungbile, "Water Symbolism in African Culture and Afro-Christian Churches," *Journal of Religious Thought* 53/54 (1997), 21–38; Afe Adogame, "Doing Things with Water," *SWC* 6 (1) (2000), 59–77. For the Aladura, see also Afe Adogame, "Engaging the Rhetoric of Spiritual Warfare: The Public Face of Aladura in Diaspora," *JRA* 34 (2004), 493–522.

46. Philomena Njeri Mwaura, "The Old Testament in the Nabii Christian Church of Kenya," in Getui et al., eds., *Interpreting the Old Testament in Africa*, 165–69. The Ecclesiastes story is from Caplan, *Class and Culture in Urban India*, 224.

47. James 5:14–18; Keith Warrington, "James 5:14–18: Healing Then and Now," *IRM* 93 (2004), 346–67. "Bible Passages for Certain Life Situations."

48. For Winner's Chapel, see Paul Gifford, *Ghana's New Christianity* (Bloomington: Indiana University Press, 2004). 60. For the Mosama Disco Church, see John S. Pobee and Philomena Njeri Mwaura, "Health, Healing and Religion," 57.

49. Turner, *Profile through Preaching*. For Winners Chapel, see Gifford, *Ghana's New Christianity*, 59. For the Pauline miracles, see Acts 19:11–12.

50. David Frankfurter, *Elijah in Upper Egypt* (Minneapolis, Minn.: Fortress Press, 1993). Elijah also occupies an enormous role elsewhere in the Orthodox world, particularly in Russia, where folklore gave the prophet many characteristics of the ancient Slavic thunder god.

51. David Frankfurter, "Syncretism and the Holy Man in Late Antique Egypt," *Journal of Early Christian Studies* 11 (3) (2003), 339–85; Ramsay MacMullen, *Christianity and Paganism in the Fourth to Eighth Centuries* (New Haven, Conn.: Yale University Press, 1999).

52. Laurel Kendall, *Shamans, Housewives, and Other Restless Spirits* (Honolulu: University of Hawai'i Press, 1985); David Chung, *Syncretism: The Religious Context of Christian Beginnings in Korea* (Albany: State University of New York Press, 2001); Allan Anderson, "The Contextual Pentecostal Theology of David Yonggi Cho," *AJPS* 7 (1) (2004), 101–23, at http://www.apts.edu/ajps/04-1/04-1-anderson.pdf. Erika Bourguignon, "Suffering and Healing, Subordination and Power," *Ethos* 32 (4) (2004), 557–74.

53. David Tuesday Adamo, "Psalms," in Patte et al., eds., *Global Bible Commentary*, 151. "And when it comes to" is quoted by Stinton, *Jesus of Africa*, 86. Klaus Fiedler, Paul Gundani, and Hilary Mijoga, eds., *Theology Cooked in an African Pot* (Zomba, Malawi: Association of Theological Institutions in Southern and Central Africa, 1998); J. N. K. Mugambi and Laurenti Magesa, eds., *Jesus in African Christianity*, 2nd ed. (Nairobi, Kenya: Acton, 1998).

54. Alpheus Masoga, "Redefining Power," in Justin S. Ukpong, Musa W. Dube, Gerald O. West, Alpheus Masoga, Norman K. Gottwald, Jeremy Punt, Tinyiko S. Maluleke, and Vincent L. Wimbush, eds., *Reading the Bible in the Global Village* (Atlanta, Ga.: Society of Biblical Literature, 2002), 95–109, at 104–7.

55. John 5:14; Exod. 15:26.

56. Deut. 18:9; Isa. 8:19. Nicholas Stebbing, "You Shall Have No Other Gods Before Me," in Greg Cuthbertson, Hennie Pretorius, and Dana Robert, eds., *Frontiers of African Christianity* (Pretoria: University of South Africa Press, 2003), 120–36. The Malawian preacher is quoted from Hilary B. P. Mijoga, *Separate But Same Gospel* (Blantyre, Malawi: CLAIM, 2000), 161.

57. 2 Kings 5.

58. Kristina Cooper, "Spiritual Warfare in Africa," *Tablet* (London), September 28, 2002. Dom Frei Boaventura Kloppenburg, "Pai . . . Livrai de Mal" *Revista Eclesiástica Brasileira* 250 (2003), 373–92.

59. *Traditional Healing: A Pastoral Challenge for the Catholic Church in Zambia* (Lusaka, Zambia: Inculturation Task Force/Jesuit Centre for Theological Reflection, 2004), at http://www.jctr.org.zm/downloads/tradheal.pdf. For Catholicism in Tanzania, see Green, *Priests, Witches and Power*. African Catholicism has long faced difficulties in responding to popular demands for healing ministries: Gerrie ter Haar, *Spirit of Africa* (London: Hurst, 1992).

60. *Traditional Healing: A Pastoral Challenge for the Catholic Church in Zambia*; *The African Bible* (Nairobi, Kenya: Paulines Publications Africa, 1999), 1188.

61. "Bible Passages for Certain Life Situations."

62. Ezek.18:2–4.

63. J. Aruldoss, "Dalits and Salvation," in Andrew Wingate, Kevin Ward, Carrie Pemberton, and Wilson Sitshebo, eds., *Anglicanism* (New York: Church Publishing, 1998), 294–300. George Koonthanam, "Yahweh the Defender of the Dalits," in R. S. Sugirtharajah, ed., *Voices from the Margin* (Maryknoll, N.Y.: Orbis, 1995), 105–16; Sathianathan Clarke, *Dalits and Christianity* (New Delhi: Oxford India Paperbacks, 1999); Samuel Jayakumar, *Dalit Consciousness and Christian Conversion* (Delhi: ISPCK, 1999); Chandra Mallampalli, "South Asia, 1911–2003," in Hugh McLeod, ed., *Cambridge History of Christianity: World Christianities 1914–2000* (New York:

Cambridge University Press, 2006), 422–35; David Cheetham, "Relations between Christians and Buddhists and Hindus," in McLeod, ed., *Cambridge History of Christianity: World Christianities 1914–2000*, 502–7.

64. "How in the name of inculturation" is from the interview with Father Dr. Anthony Raj Thumma, at http://www.islaminterfaith.org/may2005/interview.htm.

65. "[S]alvation in the African context" is from J. Kwabena Asamoah-Gyadu, *African Charismatics* (Leiden: Brill, 2005), 184; idem, "Mission to Set the Captives Free," *IRM* 93 (2004), 389–406. Chinua Achebe, *Things Fall Apart* (1959. New York: Fawcett Paperback, 1969).

66. John 9:1–3.

67. Anna Borzello, "Crackdown on Nigeria TV Miracles," April 30, 2004, at http://news.bbc.co.uk/2/hi/africa/3672805.stm.

68. Daniel Chiquete, "Healing, Salvation and Mission," *IRM* 93 (2004), 474–85. Mark 5:34 and 10:46–52. John Kanyikwa in Andrew Wheeler, ed., *Voices from Africa* (London: Church House Publishing, 2002), 13; Isaiah Majok Dau, *Suffering and God* (Nairobi, Kenya: Paulines Publications Africa, 2002).

69. Rom. 8:28, cited by Chiquete, "Healing, Salvation and Mission."

70. Keith Thomas, *Religion and the Decline of Magic* (London: Weidenfeld & Nicolson, 1971).

71. Samuel Olarewaju, "The Efficacy of Prayer in the Blood of Christ in Contemporary African Christianity," *AJET* 22 (1) (2003), 31–45; Kunhiyop, "Witchcraft: A Philosophical and Theological Analysis," 139, 145; Eleuthere Kumbu, "Chrétiens D'Afrique devant la Maladie et la Souffrance," *Revue Africaine de Théologie* 23 (45–46) (1999), 209–24.

72. Juliana Senavoe, "Akan Widowhood Rites," *JACT* 4 (1) (2001), 39–46, at 43.

73. From a large literature on the Satanism scare of the 1980s, see Mary de Young, *The Day Care Ritual Abuse Moral Panic* (Jefferson, N.C.: McFarland, 2004); Philip Jenkins, *Mystics and Messiahs* (New York: Oxford University Press, 2000); idem, *Moral Panic* (New Haven, Conn.: Yale University Press, 1998); Joan Ross Acocella, *Creating Hysteria* (San Francisco: Jossey-Bass, 1999); Debbie Nathan and Michael Snedeker, *Satan's Silence* (New York: Basic, 1995).

Chapter 6

1. Paul Boyer, *When Time Shall Be No More* (Cambridge: Belknap Press of Harvard University Press, 1992); Bernard McGinn, *Antichrist* (San Francisco: HarperSanFrancisco, 1994); Robert C. Fuller, *Naming the Antichrist* (New York: Oxford University Press, 1995).

2. Sister Jong Rye Gratia Song, "Martyrdom and the Autonomy of Korean Catholic Women," *AJT* 17 (2) (2003), 364–77. For martyrs during the Korean War era, see Arch Campbell, *Christ of the Korean Heart* (Columbus, Ohio: Falco, 1954); Robert E. Buswell Jr. and Timothy S. Lee, eds., *Christianity in Korea* (Honolulu: University of Hawai'i Press, 2005). John Francis Faupel, *African Holocaust*, rev. ed. (London: G. Chapman, 1965).

3. Anna L. Peterson, *Martyrdom and the Politics of Religion* (Albany: State University of New York Press, 1997); Paul Marshall and Lela Gilbert, *Their Blood Cries Out* (Dallas: Word Books, 1997); Andrew Chandler, ed., *The Terrible Alternative*

(London: Cassell, 1998); Robert Royal, *The Catholic Martyrs of the Twentieth Century* (New York: Crossroad, 2000); Emefie Ikenga Metuh, ed., *The Gods in Retreat*, new ed. (Enugu, Nigeria: Fourth Dimension Publishers, 2002); Jon Sobrino, *Witnesses to the Kingdom* (Maryknoll, N.Y.: Orbis, 2003); Sana Hassan, *Christians versus Muslims in Modern Egypt* (New York: Oxford University Press, 2003); Teresa Okure, Jon Sobrino, and Felix Wilfred, eds., *Rethinking Martyrdom* (London: SCM Press, 2003); Richard Lloyd Parry, *In the Time of Madness* (London: Jonathan Cape, 2005); Afe Adogame, "Politicization of Religion and Religionization of Politics in Nigeria," in Chima J. Korieh and G. Ugo Nwokeji, eds., *Religion, History, and Politics in Nigeria* (Lanham, Md.: University Press of America, 2005), 128–39.

4. Quoted from *The African Bible* (Nairobi, Kenya: Paulines Publications Africa, 1999), 2176.

5. Margaret Ford, *Janani, the Making of a Martyr* (London: Marshall, Morgan and Scott, 1978), 91–93. Compare John S. Mbiti, *Bible and Theology in African Christianity* (Nairobi, Kenya: Oxford University Press, 1986), 105–6.

6. F. Kefa Sempangi, with Barbara R. Thompson, *A Distant Grief* (Glendale, Calif.: Gl Regal Books, 1979), 119. The reference to life "hidden with Christ" is to Colossians 3:3.

7. Kenneth P. Serbin, *Secret Dialogues* (Pittsburgh, Pa.: University of Pittsburgh Press, 2000); Iain S. MacLean, *Opting for Democracy?* (New York: P. Lang, 1999).

8. Stan Guthrie, with Obed Minchakpu, "A Blast of Hell," *Christianity Today*, October 7, 2002, at http://www.christianitytoday.com/ct/2002/011/15.28.html. Justus Waimiri, "Spotlight Turns to Sudan," *CAPA e-Bulletin*, at http://www. anglican.ca/partnerships/pim/africa/capa-014-04.htm; for Musiande Kasali, see Joel Carpenter, "The Christian Scholar in an Age of Global Christianity," in Douglas V. Henry and Michael D. Beaty, eds., *Christianity and the Soul of the University* (Grand Rapids, Mich.: Baker Academic, 2006).

9. Lewis S. Robinson, "The Bible in Twentieth Century Chinese Fiction," in Irene Eber, Sze-Kar Wan, Knut Walf, and Roman Malek, eds., *The Bible in Modern China* (Sankt Augustin: Institut Monumenta Serica, 1999), 237–77. In U.S. history, apocalyptic texts provided an essential intellectual framework for understanding the Civil War: James H. Moorhead, *American Apocalypse* (New Haven, Conn.: Yale University Press, 1978).

10. Elsa Támez, *The Scandalous Message of James*, rev. ed. (New York: Crossroad, 2002), 1.

11. Hilary B. P. Mijoga, "The Bible in Malawi," in Gerald O. West and Musa W. Dube, eds., *The Bible in Africa* (Leiden: Brill, 2000), 375. Julio de Santa Ana, *Good News to the Poor* (Geneva: World Council of Churches, 1977).

12. The passage about "liberating texts" is from Néstor O. Míguez, "Latin American Reading of the Bible," *Journal of Latin American Hermeneutics* 1 (2004), at http://www.isedet.edu.ar/jolah/experchallen.pdf. Rene Kruger, "Luke's God and Mammon," in Daniel Patte, J. Severino Croatto, Nicole Wilkinson Duran, Teresa Okure, and Archie Chi Chung Lee, eds., *Global Bible Commentary* (Nashville, Tenn.: Abingdon Press, 2004), 395–96; Valmor da Silva, "Nahum," in Patte et al., eds., *Global Bible Commentary*, 301–5. Gustavo Gutiérrez, *A Theology of Liberation* (Maryknoll, N.Y.: Orbis, 1973); idem, *On Job* (Maryknoll, N.Y.: Orbis, 1987); José Severino Croatto, *Biblical Hermeneutics* (Maryknoll, N.Y.: Orbis, 1987); idem,

Exodus: A Hermeneutics of Freedom (Maryknoll, N.Y.: Orbis, 1981); Leif E. Vaage, ed., *Subversive Scriptures* (Valley Forge, Pa.: Trinity Press International, 1997).

13. Míguez, "Latin American Reading of the Bible"; Matt. 11:25.

14. Ernesto Cardenal, *The Gospel in Solentiname* (Maryknoll, N.Y.: Orbis, 1976–1982).

15. Richard A. Horsley, *Hearing the Whole Story* (Louisville, Ky.: Westminster John Knox Press, 2001).

16. The "Nazareth manifesto" is found at Luke 4:16–29. Kim Young Dong, "Mission Theology of/with the Indigenous Peoples of Asia," *CTC Bulletin* 17 (2) (2001), at http://www.cca.org.hk/resources/ctc/ctc01-04/ctc0104e.htm; Ngugi Wa Thiong'o, *Petals of Blood* (New York: E. P. Dutton, 1978), quoting Matt. 25:41–43. Zephania Kameeta, *Why, O Lord?* (Geneva: World Council of Churches, 1986). The Jeremiah text is Jer. 1:10. For the "oppressive text," see Itumeleng Mosala, *Biblical Hermeneutic and Black Theology in South Africa* (Grand Rapids, Mich.: W. B. Eerdmans, 1989).

17. Park Jae Soon, "Jesus's Table Community Movement and the Church," *AJT* 7 (1) (1993), 60–83; Wi Jo Kang, *Christ and Caesar in Modern Korea* (Albany: State University of New York Press, 1997); Chung-Shin Park, *Protestantism and Politics in Korea* (Seattle: University of Washington Press, 2003). For Asian liberation theology as it developed in the Philippines, see Bishop Julio X. Labayen, *Revolution and the Church of the Poor* (Quezon City, Philippines: Claretian Publications, 1995).

18. Cyris H. S. Moon, "A Korean *Minjung* Perspective," in R. S. Sugirtharajah, ed., *Voices from the Margin* (Maryknoll, N.Y.: Orbis, 1995), 240–41. Cyris H. S. Moon, *A Korean Minjung Theology* (Maryknoll, N.Y.: Orbis, 1985). David Kwang-sun Suh, *The Korean Minjung in Christ* (Eugene, Oreg.: Wipf and Stock, 2001). In the 1980s, *minjung* theologians highlighted such prophetic verses as the bloodcurdling words of Isaiah, "I will make your oppressor eat their own flesh; they will be drunk on their own blood, as with wine. Then all mankind will know that I, the Lord, am your Savior" (Isa. 49:26). Also used is Isa. 19:20, "And it shall be for a sign and for a witness unto the lord of hosts in the land of Egypt: for they shall cry unto the lord because of the oppressors, and he shall send them a Savior, and a great one, and he shall deliver them." Andrew E. Kim, "Korean Religious Culture and Its Affinity to Christianity," *Sociology of Religion* 61 (2), 117–33. Buswell and Lee, eds., *Christianity in Korea*.

19. George Oommen, "The Emerging Dalit Theology," at http://www.religion-online.org/showarticle.asp?title=1121. Dhyanchand Carr, "Jesus' Identification with Galilee and Dalit Hermeneutic," *CTC Bulletin* 19 (3) (2003), at http://www.cca.org.hk/resources/ctc/ctc03-03/ctc03-03b.htm. V. Devasahayam, *Outside the Camp* (Madras, India: Gurukul Lutheran Theological College and Research Institute, 1994); Kirsteen Kim, "India," in John Parratt, ed., *Introduction to Third World Theologies* (New York: Cambridge University Press, 2004), 44–73; Joseph D'Souza, *Dalit Freedom Now and Forever* (Greenwood Village, Colo.: Dalit Freedom Network, 2004). Rowena Robinson, *Christians of India* (Thousand Oaks, Calif.: Sage Publications, 2003); Leonard Fernando and George Gispert-Sauch, *Christianity in India* (Delhi: Penguin India, 2004).

20. "In this capacity" is from Carr, "Jesus' Identification with Galilee and Dalit Hermeneutic." An example of Jesus' eating with the wrong people is found at Mark 2:15–16. Justin Charles, "Dalit Theology of Liberation," *CTC Bulletin* 17 (2) (2001), at http://www.cca.org.hk/resources/ctc/ctc01-04/ctc0104f.htm.

21. George Koonthanam, "Yahweh the Defender of the Dalits," in R. S. Sugirtharajah, ed., *Voices from the Margin* (Maryknoll, N.Y.: 1995), 105–16. For a characteristic biblical denunciation of the elites, see Isa. 3:12–15.

22. "The *minjung* of Korea" is from Sharon Rose Joy Ruiz-Duremdes, "Biblical Reflection," *CTC Bulletin* 17 (2) (2001), at http://www.cca.org.hk/resources/ctc/ctc01-04/ctc0104b.htm. For the "Anglican bishop of native Maori origin," see Muru Walters, "The Perceived Meanings of the Sufferings of Jesus in the Consciousness of the Suffering and Struggling People's of Asia," *CTC Bulletin* 13 (3) (1995), at http://www.cca.org.hk/resources/ctc/ctc95-03/5.maru.htm. Dhyanchand Carr, ed., *God, Christ and God's People in Asia* (Hong Kong: Christian Conference of Asia, Theological Concerns, 1995); Mark G. Brett, ed., *Ethnicity and the Bible* (Leiden: Brill, 1996); Lorraine V. Aragon, *Fields of the Lord* (Honolulu: University of Hawai'i Press, 2000); Peggy Brock, ed., *Indigenous Peoples and Religious Change* (Leiden: Brill, 2005). For the Bible and the defense of minority cultures and languages, see Samuel M. Tshehla, "Can Anything Good Come Out of Africa?" *JACT* 5 (1) (2002), 15–24.

23. Dora Mbuwayesango, "Joshua," in Patte et al., eds., *Global Bible Commentary*, 64, 72.

24. Quoted from Wang Hsien-Chih, "The Portrayal of the Human One (Son of Man) of John," *CTC Bulletin* 13 (3) (1995), at http://www.cca.org.hk/resources/ctc/ctc95-03/1.wang.htm. Naim Ateek, *Justice, and only Justice* (Maryknoll, N.Y.: Orbis, 1989).

25. Robert Allan Warrior, "A Native American Perspective," in Sugirtharajah, ed., *Voices from the Margin*, 277–87. For tribal communities in India, see Subhadra Channa, ed., *The Christian Mission* (New Delhi: Cosmo Publications, 2002).

26. Jione Havea, "Numbers," in Patte et al., eds., *Global Bible Commentary*, 49–50.

27. Ruiz-Duremdes, "Biblical Reflection," on "This land is mine . . . God gave this land to me (I Kings 21)"; Desmond Tutu, "Dark Days," *JTSA* 118 (2004), 27–39.

28. Mercedes Garcia Bachmann, "Deuteronomy," in Patte et al., eds., *Global Bible Commentary*, 58. Jong Sun Noh, "Joshua Syndrome and Emerging Threats to Life in the World," *CTC Bulletin* 20 (1) (2004), at http://www.cca.org.hk/resources/ctc/ctc04-01/ctc04-01c.htm.

29. Edward R. Norman, *Christianity in the Southern Hemisphere* (Oxford: Oxford University Press, 1981).

30. Cardenal is quoted in Reed Johnson, "The Soul of a Lost Cause," *Los Angeles Times*, April 26, 2005. Karla Poewe, ed., *Charismatic Christianity as a Global Culture* (Columbia: University of South Carolina Press, 1994); R. Andrew Chesnut, *Born Again in Brazil* (New Brunswick, N.J.: Rutgers University Press, 1997); idem, *Competitive Spirits* (New York: Oxford University Press, 2003); Rebecca Pierce Bomann, *Faith in the Barrios* (Boulder, Colo.: Lynne Rienner, 1999); Mika Vähäkangas and Andrew A. Kyomo, eds., *Charismatic Renewal in Africa* (Nairobi, Kenya: Acton, 2003). For the continuing influence of liberation ideas, see Kathleen M. Nadeau, *Liberation Theology in the Philippines* (Westport, Conn.: Praeger, 2002); John Burdick, *Legacies of Liberation* (Aldershot, UK: Ashgate, 2004); Jose Miguez Bonino, "Latin America," in Parratt, ed., *Introduction to Third World Theologies*, 16–42; Ivan Petrella, ed., *Latin American Liberation Theology* (Maryknoll, N.Y.: Orbis, 2005).

31. John Lonsdale, "Religion and Politics in Kenya," the Henry Martyn Lectures, 2005, at http://www.martynmission.cam.ac.uk/CJLonsdale..html.

32. For "contemporary technocratic culture," see Stephan de Jong, "¡Quítate de Mi Sol! Eclesiastés y la Tecnocracia Helenística," *RIBLA* 11 (1) (1992), 75–85. "Qoheleth's approach" is from Mercedes Garcia Bachmann, "A Study of Qoheleth (Ecclesiastes) 9: 1–12," *IRM* 91 (2002), 382–94. Elsa Támez, *When the Horizons Close* (Maryknoll, N.Y.: Orbis, 2000), v. "Precisely these struggling base communities" is from John Prior, "When All the Singing Has Stopped," *IRM* 91 (2002), 7–23, at 17.

33. Paul Gifford, ed., *The Christian Churches and the Democratisation of Africa* (Leiden: Brill, 1995); idem, *African Christianity: Its Public Role* (Bloomington: Indiana University Press, 1998).

34. Alfred W. McCoy, *Priests on Trial* (Ringwood, Victoria / New York: Penguin Books, 1984); Peter Walshe, *Prophetic Christianity and the Liberation Movement in South Africa* (Pietmaritzburg, South Africa: Cluster, 1995); Gifford, *African Christianity: Its Public Role*; Jean-Claude Djereke, *L'Engagement Politique du Clergé Catholique en Afrique Noire* (Paris: Karthala, 2001).

35. The Pharaoh quote is from Julius Dawu, "Courage Under Fire," at http://www.belief.net/story/168/story_16840_1.html. The Luke reference is from Sharon LaFraniere, "A Humble African Cleric Fiercely Protects His Flock," *NYT*, August 28, 2004. James Roberts, "Zimbabwe's Good Shepherd," *Tablet* (London), July 31, 2004; Mavis Makuni, "Controversy-Courting Cleric," *Financial Gazette* (Zimbabwe), September 16, 2004.

36. Galia Sabar, *Church, State and Society in Kenya* (London: Frank Cass, 2002); David Gitari, *In Season and Out of Season* (Carlisle, UK: Regnum, 1996), 19, 59.

37. Gitari, *In Season and Out of Season*, 37, 41 (quoting Esther 4:14).

38. Ibid. For a similar use of Daniel, see the interview with Matthew Ashimolowo, in Wendy Griffith, "A Harvest Sown by Generations Past," at http://www.cbn.com/spirituallife/ChurchAndMinistry/ChurchHistory/HarvestSown.asp.

39. "Kenya: Primate Predicts President Moi's Kingdom Will Crumble," http://www.anglicancommunion.org/acns/acnsarchive/acns1200/acns1296.html. He is referring to Amos 7:14.

40. Toomas Gross, "Protestantism and Modernity," *Sociology of Religion* 64 (4) (2003), 479–96. The "separatist" references are to 2 Cor. 6:14–18; 1 Pet 2:9–11; Rev. 18:4.

41. Bungishabaku Katho, "Jeremiah 22: Implications for the Exercise of Political Power in Africa," in Mary Getui, Knut Holter, and Victor Zinkuratire, eds., *Interpreting the Old Testament in Africa* (New York: P. Lang, 2000), 153–58, at 157; Niels Kastfelt, ed., *Scriptural Politics* (Trenton, N.J.: Africa World Press, 2004).

42. Zech. 10:3 and 11:4–5; Paul Swarup, "Zechariah," in Patte et al., eds., *Global Bible Commentary*, 318–24.

43. Hannah W. Kinoti, "Well Being in African Society and in the Bible," in Hannah W. Kinoti and John M. Waliggo, eds., *The Bible in African Christianity* (Nairobi, Kenya: Acton, 1997), 112–22; *The African Bible*, 1468.

44. Gitari, *In Season and Out of Season*, 111, 114.

45. Sabar, *Church, State and Society in Kenya*, 199–201. Gitari, *In Season and Out of Season*, 128–30, for the use of John 10.

46. The American novel cited is Elinor Lipman, *The Inn at Lake Devine* (New York: Vintage, 1999), 123. Dorothy B. E. A. Akoto, "The Mother of the Ewe and

Firstborn Daughter as the Good Shepherd in the Cultural Hermeneutic of the Ewe Peoples," in Gerald O. West and Musa W. Dube, eds., *The Bible in Africa* (Leiden: Brill, 2000), 260, 263. John S. Mbiti, *Bible and Theology in African Christianity* (Nairobi, Kenya: Oxford University Press, 1986).

47. Moon, "A Korean *Minjung* Perspective," 240–41.

48. Kameeta, *Why, O Lord?* 29. Timothy Wangusa, *A Pattern of Dust* (Kampala, Uganda: Fountain, 1995).

49. J. Kwabena Asamoah-Gyadu, "Faith, Healing and Mission," *IRM* 370–71 (2004), 372–78.

50. Paul Spencer Sochaczewski, "Zimbabwe's 'War of the Trees' Fights on Holy Ground," (1996), at http://www.sochaczewski.com/ARTtzirrcon.html. Samson K. Gitau, *The Environment Crisis* (Nairobi, Kenya: Acton, 2000); Marthinus L. Daneel, *African Earthkeepers* (Maryknoll, N.Y.: Orbis Books, 2001); J. N. K. Mugambi and Mika Vähäkangas, eds., *Christian Theology and Environmental Responsibility* (Nairobi, Kenya: Acton, 2001); Jacques Mutikwele, "Christianity and the Health of Our Environment," *World Mission*, February 2005, at http://www.worldmission.ph/2February05/Environmental%20call.htm.

51. Gitari, *In Season and Out of Season*, 102, citing 1 Kings 21. For the apocalyptic dimension, see Barbara R. Rossing, *The Choice between Two Cities* (Harrisburg, Pa.: Trinity Press International, 1999).

52. Jean-Pierre Ruiz, "Biblical Interpretation," in Peter Casarella and Raul Gomez, eds., *El Cuerpo de Cristo* (New York: Crossroad, 1998), 86–87. Justo L. González, *For the Healing of the Nations* (Maryknoll, N.Y.: Orbis Books, 1999). Barbara R. Rossing, *The Rapture Exposed* (Boulder, Colo.: Westview Press, 2004).

53. F. Kefa Sempangi, with Barbara R. Thompson, *A Distant Grief* (Glendale, Calif.: Gl Regal Books, 1979), 129–30; Rev. 11:7. Isaiah Majok Dau, *Suffering and God* (Nairobi, Kenya: Paulines Publications Africa, 2002). For the power of millennial belief in newly Christianized tribal communities facing rapid social change, see Joel Robbins, *Becoming Sinners* (Berkeley: University of California Press, 2004).

54. Khiok-Khng Yeo, *What Has Jerusalem to Do with Beijing?* (Harrisburg, Pa.: Trinity Press International, 1998), 233–34. Compare Ung Kyu Pak, *Millennialism in the Korean Protestant Church* (New York: P. Lang, 2006).

55. My translations: Pablo Richard, "Editorial," *RIBLA* 5–6 (1990), 5; "The church's function" is from Dagoberto Ramírez Fernández, "El Juicio de Dios a las Transnacionales," ibid., 55–74, at 74.

56. Desmond Tutu, "Dark Days," *JTSA* 118 (2004), 27–39, at 30–31. Allan A. Boesak, *Comfort and Protest* (Philadelphia: Westminster Press, 1987). Richard Elphick and Rodney Davenport, eds., *Christianity in South Africa* (Berkeley: University of California Press, 1997).

57. "The Kairos Document," http://www.bethel.edu/~letnie/africanchristianity/sakairos.html. Tristan Anne Borer, *Challenging the State* (Notre Dame, Ind.: University of Notre Dame Press, 1998).

58. "In Africa today" is from Emmanuel A. Obeng, "Use of Critical Biblical Methods," in Hannah W. Kinoti and John M. Waliggo, eds., *The Bible in African Christianity* (Nairobi, Kenya: Acton, 1997), 19.

59. Hilary B. P. Mijoga, *Separate But Same Gospel* (Blantyre, Malawi: CLAIM, 2000), 40–41. For Kenya's independent churches, see Zablon Nthamburi and Douglas Waruta, "Biblical Hermeneutics in African Instituted Churches," in Hannah

W. Kinoti and John M. Waliggo, eds., *The Bible in African Christianity* (Nairobi, Kenya: Acton, 1997), 46-47.

60. For such a Chinese sermon using Philippians, see, for instance, Rob Gifford, "An Evangelist in Central China," broadcast on NPR's *All Things Considered*, July 28, 2005.

61. Kenneth R. Ross, ed., *God, People and Power in Malawi* (Blantyre, Malawi: CLAIM, 1996); idem, *Here Comes Your King!* (Blantyre, Malawi: CLAIM, 1998); Gifford, ed., *The Christian Churches and the Democratisation of Africa*; idem, *African Christianity: Its Public Role*; Laurenti Magesa and Zablon Nthamburi, eds., *Democracy and Reconciliation* (Nairobi, Kenya: Acton, 1999); Mary N. Getui and Peter Kanyandago, eds., *From Violence to Peace* (Nairobi, Kenya: Acton, 1999); Caleb Oladipo, "Piety and Politics in African Christianity," *Journal of Church and State* 45 (2) (2003), 325-; Terence O. Ranger, ed., *Evangelical Christianity and Democracy in Africa* (New York: Oxford University Press, 2005, forthcoming); Tukumbi Lumumba-Kasongo, ed., *Liberal Democracy and Its Critics in Africa* (London: Zed Books, 2005).

62. Fidele Ugira Kwasi, "Judges," in Patte et al., eds., *Global Bible Commentary*, 84. Stephen Ellis and Gerrie ter Haar, *Worlds of Power* (New York: Oxford University Press, 2004).

63. Eph. 4:16. Kenneth R. Ross, "Church Life, Civil Society, and Democratization in Malawi, 1992-96," in James L. Cox and Gerrie ter Haar, eds., *Uniquely African?* (Trenton, N.J.: Africa World Press, 2003).

64. Desmond Tutu, *No Future without Forgiveness* (New York: Doubleday, 1999); James Cochrane, John W. De Gruchy, and Stephen Martin, eds., *Facing the Truth* (Athens: Ohio University Press, 1999).

65. Ranger is quoted in Paul Freston, *Protestant Political Parties* (Aldershot, UK: Ashgate, 2004), 92.

66. Rudolf Von Sinner, "Healing Relationships in Society," *IRM* 93 (2004), 238-54. David A. Smilde, "Letting God Govern," *Sociology of Religion* 59 (3) (1998), 287-303; Iain S. MacLean, *Opting for Democracy?* (New York: P. Lang, 1999); Paul Freston, *Evangelicals and Politics in Asia, Africa, and Latin America* (New York: Cambridge University Press, 2001); idem, *Protestant Political Parties*; idem, ed., *Evangelical Christianity and Democracy in Latin America* (New York: Oxford University Press, 2005, forthcoming).

67. Bishop Obare's letter is found at http://www.missionsprovinsen.se/the_letter_from_bishop_w_obare_to_the_archbishop_kg_hammar_(eng).htm.

Chapter 7

1. Titus Presler, *Transfigured Night* (Pretoria, South Africa: UNISA Press, 1999), 133-35.

2. Elizabeth Amoah, ed., *Divine Empowerment of Women in Africa's Complex Realities* (Accra-North, Ghana: Sam-Woode Ltd., 2001); idem, ed., *Where God Reigns* (Accra-North: Ghana Sam-Woode Ltd., 1996); Eliza F. Kent, *Converting Women* (New York: Oxford University Press, 2004); Dorothy L. Hodgson, *The Church of Women* (Bloomington: Indiana University Press, 2005). For prayer fellowships in Indian churches, see Lionel Caplan, *Class and Culture in Urban India*

(Oxford: Clarendon, 1987), 185–90. For a Western feminist encounter with Asian Christianity, see Frances S. Adeney, *Christian Women in Indonesia* (Syracuse, N.Y.: Syracuse University Press, 2003).

3. "Theologian Takes on Establishment," *Joongang Daily*, June 24, 2004, online at http://service.joins.com/asp/print_article_english.asp?aid=2432270&esectcode= e_life&title=theologian+takes+on+establishment. Hyun Kyung Chung, *Struggle to Be the Sun Again* (Maryknoll, N.Y.: Orbis, 1990).

4. Eph. 5:22; Seung-Hee Sohn, "Ecclesiology from an Asian Feminist Perspective," *CTC Bulletin* 13 (3) (1995), at http://www.cca.org.hk/resources/ctc/ctc95-03/ 9.sohn.htm.

5. 1 Tim. 2:11–15; 1 Cor. 14:34. For "sitting at Jesus' feet," see Luke 10:39. Ranjini Rebera, "Polarity or Partnership?" *Semeia* 78 (1997), 93–108, at 99.

6. Eph. 5:22–24; 1 Cor. 7:5 and 11:7–9. Mercy Amba Oduyoye, *Daughters of Anowa* (Maryknoll, N.Y.: Orbis, 1995); idem, *Introducing African Women's Theology* (Sheffield, UK: Sheffield Academic Press, 2001). Madipoane Masenya, *How Worthy Is the Woman of Worth?* (New York: P. Lang, 2004); idem, "Trapped Between Two Canons," in Isabel Apawo Phiri, Beverley Haddad, and Madipoane Masenya, eds., *African Women, HIV/AIDS, and Faith Communities* (Pietermaritzburg, South Africa: Cluster, 2003), 113–27, at 118.

7. Mercy Oduyoye. "Calling the Church to Account," *ER* 47 (1995); Anne Nasimiyu-Wasike, "Christian Feminism," (2001), at http://www.kenyaconstitution. org/docs/09bd001.htm.

8. Hilary B. P. Mijoga, *Separate But Same Gospel* (Blantyre, Malawi: CLAIM, 2000), 66, 151–52; Tokunboh Adeyemo, "A Woman of Excellence," in Judy Mbugua, ed., *Our Time Has Come* (Grand Rapids, Mich.: Baker, 1994), 17–22.

9. Prov. 31:10–31: Masenya, *How Worthy Is the Woman of Worth?*; Rosemary Mumbi, "Battered Women," in Mbugua, ed., *Our Time Has Come*; Mary Dua Ogebe, "Social Injustice," in ibid., 61.

10. Catherine S. Dolan, "The Good Wife," *Journal of Development Studies* 37 (3) (2001), 39–70.

11. Musimbi R. A. Kanyoro, *Introducing Feminist Cultural Hermeneutics* (Cleveland, Ohio: Pilgrim Press, 2002); "a major endorsement" is from Dora Rudo Mbuwayesango, "Childlessness and Woman to Woman Relationships in Genesis and in African Patriarchal Society," *Semeia* 78 (1997), 27–36.

12. Gustav Niebuhr, "Council Rejects African Church That Allows Polygamy among Clergy," *NYT*, December 14, 1998. Musimbi R. A. Kanyoro, "Interpreting Old Testament Polygamy through African Eyes," in Mercy Amba Oduyoye and Musimbi R. A. Kanyoro, eds., *The Will to Arise* (Maryknoll, N.Y.: Orbis Press, 1992), 87–100. Afe Adogame, *Celestial Church of Christ: The Politics of Cultural Identity in a West African Prophetic-Charismatic Movement* (New York: P. Lang, 1999).

13. Deidre Helen Crumbley, "Patriarchies, Prophets, and Procreation," *Africa* 73 (2003), 584–605; Mary Nyangweso, "Christ's Salvific Message and the Nandi Ritual of Female Circumcision," *Theological Studies* 63 (3) (2002), 579–81. 1 Cor. 7:19.

14. Sr. Mary John Mananzan, "The Woman Question in the Philippines," at http://www.newfilipina.com/bodyandsoul/womanQ.html. Sergio Torres and Virginia Fabella eds., *The Emergent Gospel* (Maryknoll, N.Y.: Orbis, 1978); Virginia Fabella and Mercy Amba Oduyoye, eds., *With Passion and Compassion* (Maryknoll,

N.Y.: Orbis Books, 1988); Virginia Fabella and Sun Ai Lee Park, eds., *We Dare to Dream* (Hong Kong: Asian Women's Resource Centre for Culture and Theology and the EATWOT Women's Commission in Asia, 1989); Franklyn J. Balasundaram, *EATWOT in Asia* (Bangalore, India: Asian Trading Corp., 1993).

15. Okure is a Sister of the Holy Child Jesus; Nasimiyu-Wasike is a member of the Little Sisters of St. Francis of Assisi. Martin Mutua and Alari Alare, "Ndingi Censures Nun's View on Abortion," *East African Standard* (Nairobi), March 12, 2003. Teresa Okure, ed., *To Cast Fire Upon the Earth* (Pietermaritzburg, South Africa: Cluster, 2000); Anne Nasimiyu-Wasike, "Mary the Pilgrim of Faith for African Women," in Hannah W. Kinoti and John M. Waliggo, eds., *The Bible in African Christianity* (Nairobi, Kenya: Acton, 1997), 165–78. For nuns in the Philippines, compare Heather L. Claussen, *Unconventional Sisterhood* (Ann Arbor: University of Michigan Press, 2001).

16. John S. Pobee and Bärbel Von Wartenberg-Potter, eds., *New Eyes for Reading* (Oak Park, Ill.: Meyer-Stone Books, 1987); Mercy Amba Oduyoye, ed., *Transforming Power* (Accra-North, Ghana: Sam-Woode Ltd., 1997); idem, *Hearing and Knowing* (Maryknoll, N.Y.: Orbis, 1986); idem, *Introducing African Women's Theology* (Sheffield, UK: Sheffield Academic Press, 2001); idem, *Beads and Strands* (Maryknoll, N.Y.: Orbis, 2004). Isabel Apawo Phiri, "Doing Theology in Community," *JTSA* 99 (1997), 68–76; Isabel Apawo Phiri, Devarakshanam Betty Govinden, and Sarojini Nadar, eds., *Her-Stories* (Pietermaritzburg, South Africa: Cluster, 2002). Philomena Mwaura, "Empowerment of Women," *JACT* 1 (1) (1998), 28–35. Denise Ackermann, Jonathan Draper, and Emma Mashini, *Women Hold Up Half the Sky* (Pietermaritzburg, South Africa: Cluster, 1991). Musa W. Dube, *Postcolonial Feminist Interpretation of the Bible* (St. Louis, Mo.: Chalice Press, 2000); idem, ed., *Other Ways of Reading* (Geneva: Consul Oecumenique, 2002). Carrie Pemberton, *Circle Thinking* (Leiden: Brill, 2003); Musa W. Dube, "Jumping the Fire with Judith," in Silvia Schroer and Sophia Bietenhard, eds., *Feminist Interpretation of the Bible and the Hermeneutics of Liberation* (New York: Continuum, 2003); Philomena Njeri Mwaura, "Feminist Biblical Interpretation and the Hermeneutics of Liberation," in ibid.; Adelaide Maame Akua Boadi, "Engaging Patriarchy," in Chima J. Korieh and G. Ugo Nwokeji, eds., *Religion, History, and Politics in Nigeria* (Lanham, Md.: University Press of America, 2005), 172–86; Caroline Vander Stichele and Todd Penner, eds., *Her Master's Tools? Feminist and Postcolonial Engagements of Historical-Critical Discourse* (Atlanta, Ga.: Society of Biblical Literature, 2005).

17. Madipoane Masenya, "Ruth," in Patte et al., eds., *Global Bible Commentary*, 87; Musa W. Dube, "Divining Ruth for International Relations," in A. K. M. Adam, ed., *Postmodern Interpretations of the Bible* (St. Louis, Mo.: Chalice Press, 2001), 67–79; Itumeleng Mosala, "The Implications of the Text of Esther for African Women's Struggle for Liberation in South Africa," *Semeia* 59 (1992), 129–39; Gertrud Wittenberg, "The Song of a Poor Woman," in Ackermann et al., eds., *Women Hold Up Half the Sky*, 3–20. Diane Stinton, "Africa, East and West," in John Parratt, ed., *Introduction to Third World Theologies* (New York: Cambridge University Press, 2004), 105–36; Isabel Apawo Phiri, "Southern Africa," in ibid., 137–62.

18. "Theologian Takes on Establishment"; Wonsuk Ma, "Toward an Asian Pentecostal Theology," *CPCR*, at http://www.pctii.org/cyberj/cyberj1/wonsuk.html. Kwok Pui-Lan, *Introducing Asian Feminist Theology* (Sheffield, UK: Sheffield

Academic Press, 2000); idem, *Postcolonial Imagination and Feminist Theology* (London: Westminster John Knox Press, 2005).

19. Joanne Lee and Andy Salmon, "Han Myung-sook: The Minister," American Chamber of Commerce in Korea *Journal*, April/May 2001, at http://www2.gol.com/users/coynerhm/han_myungsook__the_minister.htm. Kyung Sook Lee, "The Biblical Hermeneutics of Liberation from the Perspective of Asian Christian Women," in Schroer and Bietenhard, eds., *Feminist Interpretation of the Bible and the Hermeneutics of Liberation*.

20. Eliza F. Kent, "Redemptive Hegemony and the Ritualization of Reading," in Selva J. Raj and Corinne G. Dempsey, eds., *Popular Christianity in India* (Albany: State University of New York Press, 2002), 191–209, at 197 and 202; idem, *Converting Women*. The Sword Drill idea is derived from Eph. 6:17, "take . . . the sword of the Spirit, which is the word of God" (King James Version).

21. Presler, *Transfigured Night*, 100. Wilhelmina J. Kalu, "Soul Care in Nigeria," in Korieh and Nwokeji, eds., *Religion, History, and Politics in Nigeria*, 202–15.

22. Claudia Wahrisch-Oblau, "On Prayers for the Sick and the Interpretation of Healing Experiences in Christian Churches in China and African Immigrant Congregations in Germany," *IRM* 90 (356–57) (2001), 87–100, at 89–90.

23. Philomena Njeri Mwaura, "A Burning Stick Plucked Out of the Fire," in Phiri et al., eds., *Her-Stories*, 202–24.

24. Isabel Phiri, "African Women in Mission," *Missionalia* 28 (2–3) (2000), 267–93.

25. "Theologian Takes on Establishment."

26. Monica Melanchthon, "Christology and Women," in Fabella and Park, eds., *We Dare to Dream*, 21; Anne Nasimiyu, "Christian Feminism."

27. Nyambura Njoroge, "Women, Why Are You Weeping?" *ER* 49 (1997), 427–38; idem, "Women of the Presbyterian Church of East Africa, 1891–1991" at http://www.warc.ch/dp/rw924/02.html; Presler, *Transfigured Night*, 133.

28. Philomena Mwaura, "Women in African Instituted Churches in Kenya," *ACS* 18 (3) (2002), 57–72; R. Modupe Owanikin, "The Priesthood of Church Women in the Nigerian Context," in Mercy Amba Oduyoye and Musimbi R. A. Kanyoro, eds., *The Will to Arise* (Maryknoll, N.Y.: Orbis Press, 1992), 206–19; Isabel Apawo Phiri, *Women, Presbyterianism and Patriarchy* (Blantyre, Malawi: CLAIM, 1997); Crumbley, "Patriarchies, Prophets, and Procreation"; Phiri et al., *Her-Stories*.

29. Rebera, "Polarity or Partnership?"

30. Quoted by Nyambura J. Njoroge, *Kiama Kia Ngo* (Legon, Ghana: Legon Theological Studies Series, 2000), 67.

31. Malika Sibeko and Beverley Haddad, "Reading the Bible 'with' Women in Poor and Marginalized Communities in South Africa," *Semeia* 78 (1997), 83–92; Njoroge, *Kiama Kia Ngo*, 35; Grant LeMarquand, *An Issue of Relevance* (New York: P. Lang, 2004). For interpretations of the passage elsewhere in the world, see Ada Maria Isasi-Diaz, "The Woman with the Flow of Blood," at http://users.drew.edu/aisasidi/cd/flow.html; Hisako Kinukawa, "The Story of the Hemorrhaging Woman (Mark 5:25–34). Read from a Japanese Feminist Context," *Biblical Interpretation* 2/3 (1994), 283–93.

32. Sibeko and Haddad, "Reading the Bible 'with' Women in Poor and Marginalized Communities in South Africa."

33. Teresa Okure, "The Will to Arise," in Oduyoye and Kanyoro, eds., *The Will to Arise*, 225; Musa Dube, "Talitha Cum!" in Phiri et al., eds., *African Women,*

HIV/AIDS, and Faith Communities, 71–93; Thandeki Umlilo, *Little Girl, Arise!* (Pietmaritzburg, South Africa: Cluster, 2002); Nyambura Njoroge and Musa Dube, eds., *Talitha Cum! Theologies of African Women* (Pietmaritzburg, South Africa: Cluster, 2001); Musimbi R. A. Kanyoro and Nyambura J. Njoroge, eds., *Groaning in Faith* (Nairobi, Kenya: Acton, 1996); Musimbi R. A. Kanyoro and Mercy Amba Oduyoye, eds., *Thalitha Qumi* (Ibadan, Nigeria: Daystar University Press, 1990).

34. Dolan, "The Good Wife."

35. Mercy Oduyoye, "Calling the Church to Account," *ER* 47 (1995), 479.

36. Beverley Haddad, "Choosing to Remain Silent," in Phiri et al., eds., *African Women, HIV/AIDS, and Faith Communities,* 149–67, at 159.

37. Njoroge, *Kiama Kia Ngo,* 34–35; Derek Peterson, "Wordy Women," *Journal of African History* 42 (2001), 469–89; Lynn Thomas, *Politics of the Womb* (Berkeley: University of California Press, 2003).

38. Njoroge, *Kiama Kia Ngo;* Monica Jyotsna Melanchthon, "Song of Songs," in Patte et al., eds., *Global Bible Commentary,* 183.

39. 2 Samuel 13. Gerald West, "1 and 2 Samuel," in Patte et al., eds., *Global Bible Commentary,* 96–98. Margret Gecaga, "Rape as a Tool of Violence Against Women," in Grace Wamue and Mary Getui, eds., *Violence against Women* (Nairobi, Kenya: Acton, 1996).

40. Kanyoro, *Introducing Feminist Cultural Hermeneutics.* Phiri et al., eds., *African Women, HIV/AIDS, and Faith Communities.* Joe Mdhlela and Albert Nolan, "Taking the Lead," *World Mission,* June 2005, at http://www.worldmission.ph/5June05/HIVAIDS.htm.

41. Dube, "Talitha Cum!" 84; A. C. Van Dyk and P. J. Van Dyk, "HIV/AIDS in Africa," *Old Testament Essays* 15 (2002), 209–24. Margaret A. Farley, "Partnership in Hope," *Journal of Feminist Studies in Religion* 20 (2004), 133–48; Musa W. Dube and Musimbi Kanyoro, eds., *Grant Me Justice!* (Maryknoll, N.Y.: Orbis, 2006).

42. "Holy HIV" is from Tony Kago, "AIDS is Not a Sinners' Disease, Say Clerics," *Nation* (Nairobi), June 23, 2005. Dorothy Kweyu, "Confessions a Milestone in Anti-AIDS War," ibid., June 24, 2005. Some such clergy belong to the African Network of Religious Leaders Living with or Personally Affected by HIV/AIDS (ANERELA), which has local affiliates such as Kenya's KENERELA.

43. Haddad, "Choosing to Remain Silent," 157.

44. Dorcas Olubanke Akintunde, "The Attitude of Jesus to the Anointing Prostitute," in Phiri et al., eds., *African Women, HIV/AIDS, and Faith Communities,* 94–110. Rita Nakashima Brock and Susan Brooks Thistlethwaite, *Casting Stones* (Minneapolis, Minn.: Fortress Press, 1996); Margaret Eletta Guider, *Daughters of Rahab* (Minneapolis, Minn.: Fortress Press, 1995).

45. 1 Tim. 5:3.

46. Zampi Phiri, "Inculturating African Widowhood Rites," Jesuit Center for Theological Reflection, *Bulletin* 52, at http://www.jctr.org.zm/bulletins/incult-widows.htm; "Lutherans Urge African Women to Speak about Sex," http://www.afrol.com/articles/14736; Grace Wamue, "Gender Violence and Exploitation," in Wamue and Getui, eds., *Violence against Women;* Sharon LaFraniere, "AIDS Now Compels Africa to Challenge Widows' 'Cleansing,'" *NYT,* May 11, 2005. Udit Raj, "If Gods Become Silent the Speechless Must Speak," February 21, 2004, at http://www.countercurrents.org/dalit-uditraj210204.htm. Fazal Sheikh, *Moksha* (Göttingen: Steidl, 2005).

47. Kathryn Hauwa Hoomkwap, "Women in Church and Society," at http://www.afrikaworld.net/synod/hoomkwap.htm. Benezeri Kisembo, Laurenti Magesa, and Aylward Shorter, *African Christian Marriage,* 2nd rev. ed. (Nairobi, Kenya: Paulines Publications Africa, 1998); Andrew A. Kyomo and Sahaya G. Selvan, eds., *Marriage and Family in African Christianity* (Nairobi, Kenya: Acton, 2004).

48. Njoroge, *Kiama Kia Ngo,* 89. Daisy N. Nwachuku, "The Christian Widow in African Culture," in Oduyoye and Kanyoro, eds., *The Will to Arise,* at 70–71.

49. Luke 4:24–27.

50. Presler, *Transfigured Night,* 126. The Rahab reference could be from James 2:25 or Heb. 11:31.

51. Pope Shenouda III, "The Sinful Women in the Genealogy Sequence," at http://www.coptichymns.net/mod-pagesetter-viewpub-tid-1-pid-387.html. Jane Schaberg, *The Illegitimacy of Jesus* (Sheffield, UK: Sheffield Academic Press, 1995).

52. Ogebe, "Social Injustice," 64.

53. Udit Raj, "Cry of Christ," January 11, 2004, at http://www.counter-currents.org/dalit-uditraj110105.htm. Rekha Chennattu, "Women in the Mission of the Church," at http://www.sedos.org/english/chennattu.htm. "The Samaritan woman is remarkable" is from Rekha Chennattu, "A Woman from Samaria," *World Mission Magazine,* November 2003, at http://www.worldmission.ph/December03/DECEMBERSPECIAL.htm. Jean Kyoung Kim, "A Korean Feminist Interpretation of John 4:1–42," *Semeia* 78 (1997), 109–20.

54. Musa W. Dube, "Reading for Decolonization (John 4: 1–42)," *Semeia* 75 (1996), 37–60; Musa W. Dube and Jeffrey L. Staley, eds., *John and Postcolonialism* (Sheffield, UK: Sheffield Academic Press, 2002).

55. Kwok Pui-Lan, *Discovering the Bible in the Non-Biblical World,* 71–83; Kosuke Koyama, *Water Buffalo Theology,* 25th anniversary ed. (Maryknoll, N.Y.: Orbis, 1999), 55. Hyunju Bae, "Dancing Around Life," *ER* 56 (4) (2004), 390–403.

Chapter 8

1. Jonathan Draper, ed., *The Eye of the Storm* (Pietmaritzburg, South Africa: Cluster, 2003); R. S. Sugirtharajah, *The Bible and the Third World* (New York: Cambridge University Press, 2001), 110–39.

2. John William Colenso, *The Pentateuch and Book of Joshua Critically Examined* (London: Longsmans, Green, 1862), vii.

3. Akiki K. Nyabongo, *Africa Answers Back* (London: G. Routledge and Sons, 1936), 225.

4. Kwame Bediako, *Theology and Identity* (Oxford: Regnum Books, 1992). "An Interview with Andrew Walls," http://www.religion-online.org/showarticle.asp?title=2052.

5. Colenso is quoted in Tlou Makhura, "Missionary and African Perspectives on the Politics of Witchcraft among the Xhosa and Zulu Communities in the 19th Century Cape and Natal / Zululand," http://wiserweb.wits.ac.za/pdf%20files/wirs%20-%20makhura.pdf.

6. Tinyiko Maluleke, "What if We Are Mistaken about the Bible and Christianity in Africa?" in Justin S. Ukpong, Musa W. Dube, Gerald O. West, Alpheus Masoga, Norman K. Gottwald, Jeremy Punt, Tinyiko S. Maluleke, and Vincent L. Wimbush,

eds., *Reading the Bible in the Global Village* (Atlanta, Ga.: Society of Biblical Literature, 2002); 151–72. The "mile wide and inch deep" quote is usually attributed to Kenyan scholar Douglas Waruta.

7. Pippa Norris and Ronald Inglehart, *Sacred and Secular* (New York: Cambridge University Press, 2004); Steve Bruce, *God Is Dead* (Oxford: Blackwell, 2002). Grace Davie, *Religion in Modern Europe* (New York: Oxford University Press, 2000); idem, *Europe: The Exceptional Case* (London: Darton Longman and Todd, 2002); Grace Davie, Paul Heelas, and Linda Woodhead, eds., *Predicting Religion* (Aldershot, UK: Ashgate, 2003). Bonhoeffer is quoted from his *Letters and Papers from Prison* (New York: Macmillan, 1971), letter of July 16, 1944.

8. Roger Finke and Rodney Stark, *The Churching of America, 1776–2005*, 2nd ed. (New Brunswick, N.J.: Rutgers University Press, 2005); Donald E. Miller, *Reinventing American Protestantism* (Berkeley: University of California Press, 1997).

9. Quoted in John L. Allen, "Global South Will Shape the Future Catholic Church," *National Catholic Reporter*, October 7, 2005.

10. Barbara R. Rossing, *The Rapture Exposed* (Boulder, Colo.: Westview Press, 2004).

11. C. S. Lewis, *God in the Dock* (Grand Rapids, Mich.: W. B. Eerdmans, 1994), 102–3.

12. Christine Rosen, *Preaching Eugenics* (New York: Oxford University Press, 2004).

Scripture Index

Index